Recovering the US Ment

Decades of research show that psychosocial treatments are effective for psychosis, yet they remain unimplemented as the American healthcare system relies primarily on pharmacological solutions instead. This book reviews the history and current state of research to provide a more nuanced understanding of the evidence for and barriers to psychosocial care for psychosis. It addresses a wide range of mental health research and multi-professional practice domains from historical, personal, societal, professional, and systems perspectives. The varied perspectives presented illustrate factors that limit support for recovery in SMI and psychosis as well as real hope for recovering the US mental healthcare system. With contributions of experts by training and by experience, this book represents an essential resource for students, practitioners and researchers.

MEAGHAN STACY is an Associate Professor of Psychiatry at Yale University School of Medicine and a licensed clinical psychologist.

CHARLIE A. DAVIDSON is a licensed psychologist at the Atlanta Center for Cognitive Therapy and Adjunct Lecturer at Emory University.

Recovering the US Mental Healthcare System

The Past, Present, and Future of Psychosocial Interventions for Psychosis

Edited by

Meaghan Stacy
Yale University School of Medicine

Charlie A. Davidson
Atlanta Center for Cognitive Therapy and Emory University

CAMBRIDGE
UNIVERSITY PRESS

CAMBRIDGE
UNIVERSITY PRESS

University Printing House, Cambridge CB2 8BS, United Kingdom

One Liberty Plaza, 20th Floor, New York, NY 10006, USA

477 Williamstown Road, Port Melbourne, VIC 3207, Australia

314–321, 3rd Floor, Plot 3, Splendor Forum, Jasola District Centre,
New Delhi – 110025, India

103 Penang Road, #05–06/07, Visioncrest Commercial, Singapore 238467

Cambridge University Press is part of the University of Cambridge.

It furthers the University's mission by disseminating knowledge in the pursuit of
education, learning, and research at the highest international levels of excellence.

www.cambridge.org
Information on this title: www.cambridge.org/9781108844581
DOI: 10.1017/9781108951760

First published 2022

A catalogue record for this publication is available from the British Library.

Library of Congress Cataloging-in-Publication Data
Names: Stacy, Meaghan, 1984- author. | Davidson, Charlie A., 1983– author.
Title: Recovering the US mental health care system : the past, present, and future of
    psychosocial interventions for psychosis / Meaghan Stacy, Yale University,
    Connecticut, Charlie A. Davidson, Mercer University, Georgia.
Description: Cambridge, United Kingdom ; New York, NY : Cambridge University
    Press, 2022. | Includes bibliographical references and index.
Identifiers: LCCN 2021034139 (print) | LCCN 2021034140 (ebook) |
    ISBN 9781108844581 (hardback) | ISBN 9781108948425 (paperback) |
    ISBN 9781108951760 (epub)
Subjects: LCSH: Mental health–United States. | Mental health services–United States
Classification: LCC RA790.6 .S724 2022 (print) | LCC RA790.6 (ebook) | DDC
    362.20973–dc23
LC record available at https://lccn.loc.gov/2021034139
LC ebook record available at https://lccn.loc.gov/2021034140

ISBN 978-1-108-84458-1 Hardback
ISBN 978-1-108-94842-5 Paperback

For every person who has ever needed or been
an advocate.

Contents

Figures

Tables

Contributors

OLIVIA ALTAMIRANO University of Miami

ANDREA AVILA Oregon State Hospital

CHARLIE A. DAVIDSON Atlanta Center for Cognitive Therapy and Emory University

LISA DIXON Columbia University

ERIC EVANS Disability Rights Nebraska

MARCI L. GAITHER VA Pittsburgh Healthcare System

SUSAN GINGERICH Independent NAVIGATE Trainer

LOUISE BIRKEDAL GLENTHØJ Copenhagen Research Centre on Mental Health, University of Copenhagen

SHIRLEY M. GLYNN Semel Institute of Neuroscience and Human Behavior, University of California, Los Angeles

SAMANTHA JANKOWSKI New York State Psychiatric Institute

MARY A. JANSEN Bayview Behavioral Consulting, Inc.

MATTHEW M. KURTZ Wesleyan University

PIPER MEYER-KALOS University of Minnesota Medical School

REBECCA MILLER Yale University School of Medicine

MERETE NORDENTOFT Copenhagen Research Centre on Mental Health, University of Copenhagen

ANTHONY PAVLO Yale University School of Medicine

DELBERT G. ROBINSON Donald and Barbara Zucker School of Medicine at Hofstra/Northwell

WILL SPAULDING University of Nebraska–Lincoln

MEAGHAN STACY Yale University School of Medicine

AMY WEISMAN DE MAMANI University of Miami

HELEN J. WOOD UPMC Western Psychiatric Hospital

JEROME YOMAN Life Skills Resource, LLC

Acknowledgments

We are indebted to every person with a serious mental illness with whom we have worked, who has repeatedly taught us that recovery is not only possible but probable. We appreciate our teachers, supervisors, and colleagues who have inspired us to pursue and advocate for systems change. Thank you to our contributors for dedicating their time to this project and tolerating our many iterations of feedback. Stephen and Emily, our wonderful publishing team, took a chance on an idea pitched by two early career psychologists, and subsequently tolerated our questions, numerous updates, and (hopefully minor) delays; we cannot say thank you enough for this platform and your support. To our spouses, thank you for supporting us through the late nights, chapter revisions. . . and the indexing. Finally, thanks to Billie Rose, Graham, and Joelle for napping long enough for us to finish this book; we hope you are inspired to advocate for change in your own piece of the world when you have the opportunity.

1 Recovering the US Mental Healthcare System

The Past, Present, and Future of Psychosocial Interventions for Psychosis

Charlie A. Davidson, Olivia Altamirano, Amy Weisman de Mamani, and Meaghan Stacy

You are a person who can change the future for millions of people who experience or will experience psychosis or serious mental illness (SMI). How, precisely? We don't know – that's on you. This book will summarize how we got where we are, what's currently promising, and in what directions our history and evidence point us. Armed with this knowledge, we anticipate you will be a change agent.

This chapter provides a "frame" in which the following chapters, written by experts in SMI and psychosis, may coalesce and help clinicians assist the individuals they serve to live more fulfilling lives. This chapter also briefly introduces perspectives regarding diversity, equity, and inclusion; explanatory models of psychosis; and other topics we could not address in detail in this book.

Recovering the US Mental Healthcare System may parallel personal recovery. Recovery for people and systems requires genuine hope and empowerment, countering stigma and delegitimizing narratives, and listening to lessons from history, science, and people with lived experience. Positive change is unlikely in the absence of frankly accounting for past problems and successes, *and* learning from mistakes with current innovations in mind. This book samples the history, theory, and evidence base that suggests we *can* make our country more humane and equitable for people with SMI and psychosis.

Big Picture

We ask readers to hold two seemingly contradictory facts in mind: (1) recovery happens; and (2) SMI is serious. You already know the latter, and it is baked into our culture and systems. So, while *both* can be true along with every shade of gray between, we should amplify the *fact* of recovery so that this becomes a more automatic, hope-instilling lens, rather than the current dominant narrative that SMI is a chronic disabling illness.

Fact 1: People with psychosis and/or severe mental illness "recover," meaning they can live full, meaningful, valuable lives.

Fact 2: Psychosis and SMI can be associated with incredible challenges and burdens on individuals, families, communities, and systems.

Our culture has embraced one fact and mostly ignored the other, and we allocate as much space as possible to the nondominant narrative.

This chapter emphasizes recovery, limitations and failures in healthcare, and how approaches beyond biology are essential to supporting recovery. In so doing, we risk being perceived as invalidating people's lived experience of severe challenges associated with psychosis, or discounting the work of providers who devote their careers to respectful and effective recovery support. There is no consensus on "messaging" about recovery and psychosis. This is partially because in our society, psychosis, SMI, and all of the challenges that intersect with them are potent *barriers* to recovery and representation in themselves. More conversations that prioritize voices of people with lived experience are required to simultaneously validate struggle and hold genuine beliefs about recovery. For now, our best answer is to learn from and engage with more first-person narratives of recovery, which contain the reality of and the gray between both facts. We hope to work toward more fact-based and helpful messages about psychosis in our society, acknowledging the tension created by attempting to validate both Fact 1 and Fact 2.

Consistent with prioritizing Fact 1, we will focus on three factors (highlighted in Chapter 7) needed to improve the lives of people with psychosis and SMI:

(1) Hope;
(2) Available effective interventions; and
(3) Changing attitudes to support dignity and autonomy.

As healthcare professionals, we should support people with psychosis and SMI in a manner that increases the likelihood of them experiencing recovery instead of enduring a chronic and disabling illness course, because research shows this is possible. We will talk a lot about effective interventions, but these are impossible without hope and attitude change. Extensive evidence that psychosocial interventions are effective, and that interventions can be implemented supporting (rather than denying) dignity and autonomy supports the convergence of these three factors highlighted in this book.

Target Audience and Language

This book is primarily designed for healthcare professionals and trainees, but we hope it will be useful for other stakeholders as well. The authors are primarily clinical psychologists. The editors and authors have worked together to ensure we cover a range of perspectives (including from people with lived experience) and approaches that will be useful for all readers, but we welcome feedback and questions. We hope this book starts, not ends, a conversation, and that after reading the book you will feel better informed, outraged, hopeful, concerned, motivated, and empowered to play a part in recovering the US mental healthcare system for people with SMI and psychosis.

We acknowledge that some terms we use and stances we take will seem distasteful or even offensive to people whose expertise and opinions we value. We attempt to speak humbly and respectfully in our native academic language (of clinical psychology). Clinical psychology is as guilty of maintaining the problems in the status quo as any mental health profession, if differently guilty (Luigi et al., 2020; Mueser, Silverstein, & Farkas, 2013; Reddy et al., 2010). Medical hierarchy culture and policy often reduces the roles psychologists can play within systems, but the conceptualization and research-to-practice training that characterizes clinical psychology make psychologists particularly valuable in recovery-oriented transformations, consultation, and workforce development.

Ongoing conversation is critical; only through listening to aired grievances and equitable debate between different stakeholders can we change our field, system, and people's lives. We encourage readers to actively seek out and amplify voices that have been traditionally marginalized and to engage with them because of, rather than despite, differences in opinion. First-person accounts of lived experiences have proliferated with the Internet and social media, and we have found organizations such as ISPS-US, Hearing Voices Network USA, Safe Space Radio, and many, many others invaluable.

"Psychosis" and "SMI" are convenient terms that categorize (and marginalize) an infinite array of experiences that deviate from dominant culture. Here, "dominant" means White, Western, middle-class, heterosexual, educated, suburban, without physical limitations, neurotypical, male-dominated, individualistic, English-speaking, ... culture. Hopefully, the number of qualifications listed in the last sentence illustrates another absurdity, or perhaps "dialectic": Most of us believe that some people are not normal, but "normal" is not real. Chances are, *you* are too "abnormal" to be anywhere near the "normal American" prototype we have invented. Paradoxically, almost everyone is abnormal in some way. Ten percent of people are left-handed. At least 10% of people have significant psychosis-like characteristics or experiences. More than 40% of people at any given time meet diagnostic criteria for some mental disorder. Mental "disorders" are definitively abnormal. Doesn't 40% seem a paradoxical rate for something abnormal?

The preceding thought exercise is meant to demonstrate that humans differ dramatically, and dramatic differences are normal, if not always adaptive. This simple fact of humanity is obscured by biases, stigma, and discrimination to which we are all subject. We acknowledge that the term "SMI" is controversial, in part because it implies an illness model. We emphasize "psychosis" as a full range of human experiences, and "SMI" to highlight the severe problems that can be associated with psychosis and other aspects of mental health, mirroring Fact 1 and Fact 2. It is difficult to be "dealt the cards" of mental health in our society. We cannot make assumptions about how much the effect of mental health is due to the "cards" (personal experiences and characteristics) or due to the "game" (society and environment), and it is not always easy to change either the cards or the game.

This book will cite decades of clinical and research evidence, in addition to anecdotal evidence from millions of people's lives, that demonstrates the fact of recovery and the value of *psychosocial* approaches (not just medications). Still, most healthcare professionals, healthcare trainees, and the general population think of psychosis and SMI as inherently disabling, chronic brain disorders for which palliative medication and hospitalization are the only things that can help (which is, of course, false).

In healthcare professionals, this large "blind spot" is a classic example of institutionalized stigma maintaining itself over time. Much has changed in mental health science and practice in the past century, but the marginalization of people with psychosis or SMI has mostly shifted locations rather than practices or mindsets. Now, jails and prisons are the largest US mental healthcare providers, and community mental healthcare is primarily guided by risk management rather than prevention or rehabilitation. In this context, professionals are most likely to work with people with psychosis or SMI briefly in acute inpatient units, competency restoration services, or other brief services focused on medical goals of stabilization with forensic involvement (for more information, see: Spaulding, Sullivan, Evans, & Avila, 2021). Within, and with limited exposure outside these contexts, people with psychosis and SMI are viewed as risks, liabilities, or threats. We encourage viewing people with psychosis and SMI as what they are: *people.* The largest proportion of people with psychosis and SMI are living well in the community, not spending much or any time in hospitals and healthcare settings. Institutional settings have likely been traumatizing or been associated with traumatic moments in their lives. Most healthcare professionals in those settings literally *don't see* recovery in their training or practice, or they see brief encounters as exceptions to a rule. As described in Chapter 7, stigmatized beliefs contrary to recovery are maintained by most clinical psychology training programs, and they are certainly maintained in popular media and press.

Recovery and Other Models

We will provide evidence *that* recovery happens, but you may also ask *how* it happens. As highlighted in Chapter 9, a common definition of recovery,

"A process of change through which individuals improve their health and wellness, live a self-directed life and strive to reach their full potential," hints at an appropriate response (Ellison, Belanger, Niles, Evans, & Bauer, 2018). "How" recovery happens is surprisingly simple – a person's life situation or environment changes, and how they function in it changes (not necessarily in that order). Disability Studies and related disciplines provide a useful framework for this way of thinking: "medical model" versus "social model." Heavily oversimplified, the medical model places the "cause" of mental illness within the person, whereas the social model places the cause in external factors. In the social model, the view is that society inadequately accommodates diverse behaviors and characteristics.

Astute mental health professionals may notice a parallel to attribution theory, concerning how humans assume causality for negative or positive outcomes in characteristic and biased ways. These attributions, causal assumptions, or explanatory models operate mostly automatically. That is part of how our society's bias toward medical model explanations of mental illness is "bakedin" to our perceptions of psychosis and SMI in the face of contradictory evidence. Like with attributional styles, the most helpful ways to think about psychosis and SMI account for both internal (e.g., personality, brain) and external (e.g., discrimination, disparities, luck) attributions. In the absence of hope and changing attitudes to support dignity and autonomy, we only account for mental health challenges as internal to the person, and we are thus unlikely to provide useful support and likely to contradict the humanity of people with psychosis and SMI.

Humanity and Its Aspects: Understanding Person and Context

Humans, including readers of this book, have many aspects. Here, "aspects" is a simpler way to talk about levels of analysis. Paying attention to different levels/aspects helps to understand a person and their context, similar to biopsychosocial or biosystemic formulation. Reducing problems to one aspect of a person (e.g., "soul," brain, mind, personality, behavior, environment) risks ignoring the others and the complex relationships between them. Assuming that each aspect is separate and that their relationships are ordered or linear causes substantial problems for understanding and helping people. For example, similar to other models of human functioning (e.g., the integrated biosystemic theory from Spaulding, Sullivan, and Poland, 2003, or the simple cognitive behavioral therapy triangle), when we act as if the mind and brain, brain and behavior, or even the brain and the body are truly independent (e.g., Cartesian dualism), we ignore the inseparable connections between these aspects, and we are at risk of ignoring the *person* containing a brain or mind, as well as their life and environment. This book is not intended to help us fix broken brains, organize people's minds, or remediate problematic behavior. Our aim is for society, policy, and us to truly acknowledge, support, and respect the humanity of people experiencing psychosis or SMI, and as healthcare professionals to support such people and their loved ones to do the same for themselves. Our sociopolitical, institutional, and individual histories have shaped discrimination, stigma, and injustices in all aspects of our humanity that contradict the human dignity of people seen as "other" or "less than," such as those with SMI or psychosis. We hope this book will help to recognize the flaws we *all* have in our thoughts, reactions, and behaviors so that we can contradict the injustices that are reflexively inflicted on the people we aim to support.

The symptoms that characterize psychotic disorders are extremes of human experience. Anyone will experience psychosis if they do not sleep for long enough, and most of us have heard sounds that weren't real, misperceived objects in our environment, felt paranoid, or clung to beliefs that others think are unrealistic. Psychosis is a "continuum," but we treat the term and the diagnosis like it is "present or not," and if it is present it is something "other" and distinct from normal human experience. Many people believe that psychoses are brain disorders caused by a chemical imbalance. Of course, the brain is not a soup for which "a little salt will fix it," but the problem with the chemical imbalance argument is not in pharmacokinetics but in reductionism: reducing recovery or disability to brain chemicals (Hollon, 2020). When psychoses are troublesome enough to be called "disorders," they are defined by behaviors and reactions to perceptions, thoughts, and emotions. Perhaps then, psychoses are disorders of the brain, a "mind" that is the more voluntary aspect of the brain, and behavior. This would be a more useful conceptualization (or way of understanding a problem), but it ignores several major factors, including the person's entire history (e.g., what has happened to them); the impact of their situation and immediate context; structural barriers, inequities, or opportunities and privilege; and the ways in which their civil and human rights are treated with indignity, delegitimized, or disempowered in our society and systems. Changing dopamine in one's brain may indeed help one recover across the full range of human experience, but only to the extent that the existing problems are related to dopamine and that there are known and achievable paths to recover livelihood and dignity. A person and their life recovers, not just a neurotransmitter.

Stigma, Discrimination, and Civil Rights

We hope readers feel semblances between our arguments and civil rights. This is no coincidence. Not only is mental health a civil rights issue, but also the intersections between disparities and discrimination based on mental illness and those based on other characteristics, race, ethnicity, sexuality, etc., overlap to the extent that they cannot be understood independently. We will briefly highlight the intrinsic overlap between working for the rights of people with SMI and psychosis and working toward diversity, equity, and inclusion, but we encourage readers to pursue further training and experience beyond the scope of this book.

Corrigan, Markowitz, and Watson (2004) describe that there are both intentional and unintentional consequences of structural and institutional discrimination that often diminish the opportunities available to people with mental illness. These can occur both at a macro and at a micro level. As previously mentioned, and for a myriad of reasons, prisons and jails are one of the most common places where individuals with mental illness live. The Medicaid Inmate Exclusion Policy is one example of structural discrimination that contributes to this, through the policy of suspending or terminating access to Medicaid when an individual is incarcerated. This suspension leads to gaps in treatment following release and may subsequently lead to higher recidivism because people are unable to access behavioral healthcare (which is sometimes an essential aspect of their conditional release) in the community (Albertson, Scannell, Ashtari, & Barnert, 2020). Hence, a "revolving door" is created in which individuals reenter the "criminal justice" system because they did not have access to mental health resources for succeeding in the community.

At the micro level, self-stigma that develops as a result of "buying into" (i.e., internalization of) the public's stigma of mental illness is also associated with negative outcomes. Rüsch et al. (2009) conducted a study with individuals diagnosed with psychotic spectrum disorders and found that people who perceived discrimination as legitimate (i.e., perceived that their group's lower status based on mental illness was fair and legitimate) were less likely to seek psychotherapy services compared to those who perceived discrimination as unfair and illegitimate. On the contrary, people with high self-stigma were more likely to be hospitalized. As such, Rüsch et al. (2009) suggested that "stigma resilience," the ability to reject public stigma, was more conducive to ongoing and preventive services, whereas accepting and internalizing public stigma (i.e., self-stigma) could increase the likelihood of needing to use emergency hospitalization services. In these ways, structural and institutional discrimination lead to poorer prognosis. We encourage readers to learn more about factors and interventions that target self-stigma (e.g., Bogart, Lund, & Rottenstein, 2018; Lucksted et al., 2011).

In addition to discrimination and stigmatization based on illness, some individuals experience what Gary (2005) termed "Double Stigma," which is the overlapping membership in two or more groups that face prejudice and discrimination. This is an example of "intersectionality." Intersectionality is the examination of the ways in which living in more than one category of race, sex, and national origin, among others, might play out (Crenshaw, 1989; Delgado & Stefancic, 2017). As it relates to this discussion, that overlap might be in SMI and a racial or ethnic minority group. Such intersection would lead to discriminatory experiences based on mental illness *and* discriminatory experiences related to that person's race/ethnicity. Research based on medical and prescription claims data shows that even when accounting for insurance and socioeconomic status, Black and Hispanic individuals are less likely to receive outpatient behavioral healthcare services prior to a diagnosis of first episode psychosis (Heun-Johnson et al., 2020), making them less likely to receive timely care and more likely to suffer long-term consequences as a result of untreated psychosis. In addition, results from focus groups have found that Black individuals fear a reality of interconnected systems of oppression; having been oppressed at several institutions (e.g., medical, criminal justice), they expect the same oppression to come from mental health treatment settings (Alang, 2019). Further, Hispanic Americans are less likely to both seek care and receive adequate care when they do. Some of the barriers that have been reported include discrimination, lack of health insurance, low acculturation, endorsing self-reliant attitudes, not knowing where to seek services, and protective factors such as large supportive networks (Cabassa, Zayas, & Hansen, 2006; S. R. López, Barrio, Kopelowicz, & Vega, 2012). Overall, it could be that people who live in intersections of marginalized groups are even less likely to seek psychological help than others who experience oppression for belonging to one marginalized group.

A spotlight was shone on this intersection of mental illness and race due to national attention on several Black Americans killed by police in 2020. Police-perpetrated deaths have occurred more frequently to Black individuals (Edwards, Lee, & Esposito, 2019; Rollins Jr, 2019), to individuals with mental illness (Dempsey, Quanbeck, Bush, & Kruger, 2020; Frankham, 2018), and to individuals at those intersections (Cross et al., 2014). In fact, people with SMI account for one in four victims of police-perpetrated deaths (Fuller, Lamb, Biasotti, & Snook, 2015). At the time of this writing, Daniel Prude, a Black man with mental illness, died in the hospital following complications after a police-involved psychiatric emergency response in which the police put a bag over Mr. Prude's head and pressed it into the pavement. Understandably, Black individuals are less likely to seek police assistance after witnessing police misconduct, brutality, and police-involved deaths (Desmond, Papachristos, & Kirk, 2016). As such, Black families may be more hesitant to enlist police help even when their loved one's mental health symptoms necessitate emergency assistance. As Muhammad (2020) poignantly writes, interactions between a Black man with SMI and police are "doubly fraught with peril." Nonetheless, she describes that the alternative to not calling the police in a psychiatric emergency might result in worsening psychosis; thus, ". . . we make the call and pray."

Another timely example of the present inequity has surfaced in the context of the Coronavirus 2019 (COVID-19) pandemic. The COVID-19 pandemic has increased levels of stress, depression, anxiety (Rajkumar, 2020), and suicidality (Gunnell et al., 2020; Sher, 2020), and particularly vulnerable are people with SMI (Hamada & Fan, 2020). Nemani et al. (2021) found that among people who tested positive for the virus and had either schizophrenia spectrum, mood, or anxiety disorder, only a diagnosis in the schizophrenia spectrum was significantly associated with mortality; a schizophrenia spectrum diagnosis was the second strongest factor associated with mortality (strongest predictor was age) and individuals with this diagnosis had 2.7 times the odds of dying. Moreover, the COVID-19 pandemic is disproportionately affecting Black individuals (Millett et al., 2020), via social determinants of health (e.g., income, incarceration rate, percent of households without Internet; Dalsania et al., 2021) and structural racism (Tan, deSouza, & Raifman, 2021) which might jeopardize their mental health in particular, compared to groups that are less affected by this pandemic. To our knowledge, there are no empirical studies that examine the interaction between race and SMI as it relates to COVID-19 mortality; however, one might hypothesize that racial and ethnic minorities with SMI are at a higher risk of mortality following COVID-19 than White individuals with non-SMI diagnoses.

As such, while this book focuses broadly on SMI without distinguishing the nuances of diversity's role in its treatment, we want to highlight the need for culturally-informed practices, rather than general practices, if we are to increase mental health access to marginalized groups. For example, culturally-informed strategies have been successful in disseminating psychosis literacy among the Spanish-speaking Latinx community (López et al., 2009) and in producing culturally-informed, evidence-based treatments for people with schizophrenia (Weisman de Mamani, McLaughlin, Altamirano, Lopez, & Ahmad, 2020). However, more work in these areas is needed. In a Call to Action, Mote and Fulford (2020) urged that SMI researchers highlight and critically examine race in their studies to better address the "unique challenges of the Black SMI community" brought on by issues of racism in the US that have affected and continue to affect our clients. Moreover, at an organizational level, the American Psychiatric Association (2021) issued an apology statement in which they recognized their contribution to structural racism in practices such as racialized theories of deficit, and variations of schizophrenia-spectrum diagnoses in Black, Indigenous, and other Persons of Color compared to White individuals. They further pledged to take remedial steps by working to enact anti-racist practices. While the intention to remedy these injustices is a step in the right direction, concerted efforts to design culturally-informed treatment that is developed with and for the communities in need will likely be an integral part in building trust with marginalized communities so that they may begin to experience hope and recovery.

Diagnostic Injustice

We return to the argument that recovering the US mental healthcare system for people with SMI and psychosis depends on recognizing recovery and the role of supporting people at every level. Mid-twentieth century research showed that simply making an inpatient unit more livable – i.e., like a place modern humans would live – substantially influences the prosocial behavior of people whose diagnosis previously discounted the possibility of prosocial behavior (Zarlock, 1966). For the researchers among us, the effect sizes for this and similar studies are the envy of most clinical trials for medication or psychotherapy, for potentially obvious reasons – the way we tend to treat people with psychosis and SMI perpetuates and sustains behavior consistent with chronic, disabling mental illness, regardless of the degree to which the person's experiences or characteristics actually cause chronic, disabling illness. People hospitalized with psychosis are often functionally treated as inhuman, or at least delegitimized in their autonomy ("epistemic injustice," see Chapter 8). For the delegitimized person, the most adaptive response is often to embrace a lifetime of being a "patient." This was traditionally called "the patient role" and has been more recently elaborated in anti-stigma and empowerment literature with ideas including "identity engulfment" (Corcoran, 2016; Dubreucq, Plasse, & Franck, 2021; Link & Phelan, 2001).

In the past, and unfortunately still in some cases today, people entering the system after a first experience of psychosis are given three messages: (1) You are disabled and will never work again or finish school; (2) You will always have to take psychiatric medications; and (3) This disorder is permanent and episodic. Before discussing, we invite readers to think through the implications of these messages and their context. Consider the power differentials at play; restrictiveness, control, or visibility of hope in the settings; effects of having just experienced extremes of psychosis for the first time; and heavy impact of a psychotic disorder diagnosis. If your doctor was telling you these things in that situation, what would it mean to you?

Most of our readers *should* see these three messages as a "strawman fallacy," where we are arguing against a distorted (here, outdated) problem. The term "message" was chosen carefully – a message is perceived, not necessarily stated. Further, this book is predicated on the idea that our history can shape our assumptions and beliefs in pernicious ways. We encourage readers to think deeply about the relatively strong points made in this chapter to identify ways in which our individual and institutional practices reflect biased assumptions or purvey harmful messages. In other words, avoiding the three literal phrases above is not enough. Real change requires not only recognizing the ingrained biases in our personal and cultural psyche, but also actively challenging and contradicting them.

Discussing these three messages (i.e., you will never work, you need medications, and it is permanent) with trainees inevitably leads to debate. What if it is true? What if the alternative is glossing over the real implications of a severe diagnosis? Isn't it better for a person to hear these messages in a safe place than after they are discharged? These reactions demonstrate the power of Fact 2 (severity) over Fact 1 (recovery) in our reactions even to the thought of diagnoses like schizophrenia. They also demonstrate how genuine concern and desire to support people with psychosis can turn well-intentioned messages away from recovery and toward identity engulfment. From a motivation perspective, these statements offer nothing to elicit "change talk" toward valued activities and roles. From a cognitive therapy perspective, the use of "never," "always," and "permanent" are clear sign that these messages are in some way irrational and biased.

Even if all professionals use more recovery-oriented messaging, the stigmatized beliefs that drive those three statements remain powerful in our culture. For example, if a person was diagnosed with schizophrenia but recovers or lives their life without medications and hospitalizations, we often assume that they were "misdiagnosed." This logic would affirm that a schizophrenia diagnosis means one will never recover. Many people have been misdiagnosed in pernicious ways (Metzl, 2010), but psychotic disorder diagnoses are so dangerous because we assume they are untreatable, hopeless, and result in incompetence.

We invite readers now to imagine hearing the three phrases above, and then being told "You lack insight into your illness, meaning you are not aware of your symptoms. You cannot be safely discharged until you've developed some insight." Chapter 8 will provide more depth, but it is a thorny issue worth mentioning. Lack of awareness of symptoms (or lack of insight) is thought of as an important feature of schizophrenia that predicts poor prognosis. The idea is linked to anosognosia – for example, if a person loses an arm and wonders why that hand won't grasp their coffee, or if a person loses the ability to speak coherently and doesn't know why no one can understand them. For people with psychosis, recovery is indeed more difficult for a person who does not realize their reality and experience conflicts with that of those around them. This is also true of other psychiatric problems. For example, if a socially anxious person does not believe their social-evaluative perceptions may be biased, it is more difficult for them to overcome anxiety and avoidance, or if a depressed person is unaware of or unable to process any way to interpret the world other than in a pessimistic and self-defeating manner, their depression is self-sustaining. However, the nature of "insight" as applied to SMI is interpreted as more severe and all-encompassing. The possibility of "diagnosing" a person with psychosis as "lacking insight" wagers their legitimacy and autonomy on one check box of a psychiatric evaluation form. If a person is deemed to lack insight, their role in making decisions about their life and treatment is relinquished, and the power is entirely in the hands of others. This can create a paradox for the person – having hope or believing one is getting better can be interpreted as evidence of a lack of insight. What consumers often take away from their clinical experiences is a Catch-22 message along the lines of: *You're in psychiatric treatment because you're crazy. Being crazy means you are not rational. If you think you are better and can leave the hospital/treatment, it is a sign that you are crazy AND you do not know it. If you weren't crazy, you would not be in the hospital/treatment. If you're crazy, you will never be not crazy. Therefore: If you try to leave, it's because you're crazy. If you stay, it's because you're crazy.* On the other hand, there is little evidence to suggest that "gaining insight" facilitates recovery. Healthcare professionals thus have the power to take away a person's autonomy and hope. This is a topic of much discussion from clinical, legal, and ethical perspectives, but it cannot be denied that having the power to remove a person's autonomy bears heavy responsibility and risk.

Building Both Empathy and Hope

At this point, it may be worthwhile to emphasize the more "medical model" perspective that we have purposefully underemphasized. Placing blame on our healthcare system is warranted because it needs to change, but this is not the whole truth and risks minimizing the distress sometimes associated with psychosis. Human minds and brains are amazing and terrible things – your brain will incorporate and "make sense" of any input, or anything that happens. Psychological and behavioral distress often result when either the input is incomprehensible, or the way information is integrated causes problems. For example, imagine that your negative inner monologue became louder and eventually became a recognizable external voice, or that coincidences kept happening that all point to an unthinkable threat to you and yours. Even if you maintain the belief that hearing voices or conspiracy beliefs are "not real," you would experience them, and your experience is your reality. Your mind would make sense of the experiences, and previously incomprehensible experiences are explained by previously incomprehensible beliefs. Terms like "unshared beliefs" and "nonconsensus experiences" are particularly useful to discuss realities that may cause significant problems and distress. It is not our place to determine others' reality. Some of the harm that has been done by otherwise well-meaning clinicians has been caused by their training to discount and ignore "psychotic" realities. Empathy and understanding must be accompanied by genuine hope and respect if we are to support people whose realities are so acutely distressing.

There is a growing evidence base supporting the need for healthcare professionals to develop empathy, respect, and hope toward people with psychosis, and one of the most promising approaches is listening to and engaging with people who have experienced the bad and good of psychosis and recovery (Amsalem et al., 2020; Holttum & Hayward, 2010; Tsoi et al., 2020). Simply reading a first-person narrative or watching a YouTube video (e.g., "Beyond Possible: How the Hearing Voices Approach Changes Lives") has some effect. Research and anecdotal experience suggest in-person engagement with a person with lived experience has the most lasting impact (Bromage et al., 2019; Mabe, Ahmed, Duncan, Fenley, & Buckley, 2014). Other approaches have significant power for empathy and respect. Pat Deegan created the first, to our knowledge, audio recording meant to simulate a day of life with auditory hallucinations, and spending a day with "voice simulation" on one's headphones has had an incredible impact on students and professionals (Dearing & Steadman, 2009; Smith, Tamburrino, Naskar, Lynch, & Chen, 2014). The way in which people attribute the "cause(s)" of mental illness also has a significant impact on ability to embrace both empathy and hope. These "explanatory models" are strongly influenced by culture (Brown & Brown, 2020; Weisman & López, 1997). Historically, in the early days of the National Alliance on Mental Illness (NAMI), advocates rallied to reject the prevalent "moralistic" psychoanalytic explanatory models including "schizophrenogenic parent" theories, collaborating with biological reductionist psychiatric explanatory models, which are often called "biogenetic" models. Unfortunately, the biogenetic assumption of a permanent brain-based disorder may encourage sympathy but negates hope and respect. Accordingly, NAMI has since worked to destigmatize its approach and advocacy. The most popular alternative explanatory models are psychosocial and vulnerability-stress, and although it is clear that these ways of thinking are less stigmatizing than a purely biogenetic or moralistic model, it is unclear how much training from these perspectives changes stigmatized beliefs (Schlier, Lange, Wiese, Wirth, & Lincoln, 2016; Schlier, Schmick, & Lincoln, 2014). It seems probable that individuals' experiences of psychosis and recovery are so heterogeneous, and explanatory models are so broad and flexible, that it is easy to fall back on systemic biases based on socially-accepted biogenetic models without entirely discarding the "social" or "environmental" role in a vulnerability-stress model. Reframing how we view psychosis and SMI in a broader model that incorporates both "social" and "medical" models is likely necessary but insufficient to combat deeply ingrained stigma.

Cognitive Behavioral Therapy, Psychosocial Rehabilitation and Recovery, and Evidence-Based Practice in Context

In this book, we hope to summarize a large and longstanding evidence base to bring home the fact of recovery and the necessity of psychosocial supports. "Psychosocial" support addresses social factors and individuals' thinking and behavior, not targeting brain chemistry exclusively. The research evidence for psychosocial supports and recovery does not discount biological components of mental health but is a crucial counterbalance to purely biogenetic models of psychosis and SMI. We believe strongly in the necessity of science, practice, and bringing the two together. The most common model for bridging science and practice is Evidence-Based Practice, a model borrowed from physical medicine (Goodheart, Kazdin, & Sternberg, 2006). While this model nominally emphasizes "patient preferences and characteristics," suggesting tailoring and shared decision-making, it is inherently built on a medical model perspective. There is much debate about applying evidence to practice for psychological problems, although we are not aware of a broadly embraced and effective alternative model. Instead, professionals must be critical consumers of research and understand the ways in which accumulated research does and does not apply to a given individual (a process often addressed in clinical psychology training as bridging nomothetic and idiographic information). One significant problem is heterogeneity. The diagnoses most commonly applied to psychosis and SMI, schizophrenia or schizoaffective disorder, bipolar, depression, etc., are not singular, cohesive biological entities. As they say, "If you've met one person with schizophrenia, you've met one person with schizophrenia," and the heterogeneity of biological, cognitive, behavioral, social, and environmental challenges and processes between people with these diagnoses is so wide that it is impossible that any given treatment will "work" for everyone (Spaulding, Sullivan, & Poland, 2003). Most psychosocial treatments that are nearly risk-free and objectively "good" ideas (e.g., practicing emotion recognition and social interactions) can change some people's lives, but in aggregate (across many participants in a research study) have positive but small effects overall that are not long-lasting (Dark et al., 2020; Kurtz, Gagen, Rocha, Machado, & Penn, 2016). The National Institute of Mental Health (NIMH) has realigned its research priorities with specific processes rather than diagnoses. In addition to other problems with NIMH's Research Domain Criteria (RDoC), even when recruiting people for a specific problem rather than a diagnosis, psychosis and SMI clinical research often has relatively small, short-lived effects. Part of the problem is that recovery for many people doesn't happen in a vacuum or in the constrained time period of a clinical trial. It is not clear how much time and effort, or other services or resources would be required to make a substantial, measurable change, or for whom a specific treatment approach would be most useful. Some people with SMI have been "in the system" for decades, and substantial change would mean tearing down and attempting to rebuild their identity and lifestyle – an expectation that is unreasonable for most people. Further, as suggested by Maslow's hierarchy of needs and modern versions thereof, people are unlikely to complete thought logs, practice mindfulness, etc. when other barriers are more pressing. Issues associated with legal status, home environment, transportation, housing, substance use, and other barriers often interact with symptoms and psychosocial targets of treatment. When professionals' goals are to "treat" psychosis and "cause" recovery, we are likely not only to be unsuccessful but also to ignore important aspects of a person's full humanity. Unfortunately, it is difficult to design clinical research whose outcomes extend beyond these goals. To be clear, there is a large evidence base for empirically-supported psychosocial approaches to support people with psychosis and SMI (Mueser et al., 2013), but the evidence-based practice perspective may not perfectly serve the development, evaluation, and implementation of recovery supports.

Due to perceptions of risk, the past half-century of evidence for psychosocial approaches to psychosis and SMI has largely ignored the fact that many people prescribed antipsychotics will stop or will never take them (Mitchell & Selmes, 2007). Although research and programs are being developed to test approaches without medication (Francey et al., 2020; Morrison et al., 2020), most of the evidence is difficult to translate without knowing how antipsychotics or the lack thereof impact psychosocial treatments. Common "comorbidities" such as substance use, homelessness, medical illness, or intellectual disabilities are well-studied but further complicate translating research to practice. On the other hand, while comorbid problems are prevalent and key barriers to recovery for people with SMI (Hartz et al., 2014; Shevlin et al., 2011; Villa, Ehret, & Depp, 2019), people with psychosis or SMI are often not offered evidence-based interventions to address these problems. Despite the broad research base showing that cognitive behavioral therapy (CBT) approaches are effective when adapted to psychosis, evidence-based approaches to problems like PTSD are delayed by decades for people with psychosis (Swan, Keen, Reynolds, & Onwumere, 2017). This is partially due to the small workforce specialized in psychosis or SMI, but it is also due to "psychosis" being excluded from many clinical trials due to stigmatized perceptions of risk, dangerousness, or inappropriateness, despite clear evidence that actual predictors of these problems would mediate risk, whereas a "psychosis" diagnosis by itself is a poor predictor of risk (Elbogen, Beckham, Butterfield, Swartz, & Swanson, 2008; Swanson, McGinty, Fazel, & Mays, 2015). Psychiatric disorders are also generally excluded in medical trials, perpetuating health inequities (Humphreys, Blodgett, & Roberts, 2015). The need to simultaneously support problems related to psychosis, medical issues, trauma, and substances is clearly delineated in US policy and litigation, but a diagnosis like schizophrenia seems to "overshadow" clinicians' and researchers' decision-making (Magliano et al., 2011).

Considering all these limitations, we need a broad framework for supporting people that can incorporate evidence and empirically supported treatments (often called "Evidence-Based Psychotherapies" or "EBPs") without negating aspects of their history, life, and humanity.

CBT was initially designed as an approach and toolset for dyadic or group therapy, and several specific treatments associated with CBT (e.g., Cognitive Behavioral Therapy for Psychosis; Kopelovich et al., 2019) have strong evidence for helping people with psychosis change their approach to the internal and external world to be more consistent with their goals and values. This is supported by a large and growing evidence base, although a large portion of the evidence comes from countries with universal healthcare systems and very different government funding priorities. Recovery-oriented CBT training is an essential element for many professionals involved in supporting people with psychosis. However, CBT in itself does not offer a framework to support a person with psychosis or SMI to address the multi-systemic issues they are likely to face via mental health systems and intersectional problems. There is little debate that rehabilitating socioeconomic barriers can greatly improve mental health (Gertner, Rotter, & Shafer, 2019; Haushofer, Mudida, & Shapiro, 2020), and we need a framework that can address barriers in both the individual and the environment.

Psychosocial Rehabilitation and Recovery (PSR) and the earlier term, Psychiatric Rehabilitation, has been the most effective framework for supporting recovery for decades (as detailed in Section 1 of this book; also see: Barrett, Gill, Pratt, & Roberts, 2013; Corrigan, Mueser, Bond, Drake, & Solomon, 2012). PSR is complex and has many definitions, but we note a few key components. "Rehabilitation" is somewhat different from "treatment." The targeted outcomes concern success and satisfaction in self-determined social and occupational life goals. Symptoms or diagnosis and their biological and behavioral components are often barriers to these goals. Ideal PSR genuinely values the unique perspectives of every stakeholder in a treatment team, prioritizing above all the individual at the center of rehabilitation efforts. Individualized and collaborative plans incorporate the best evidence-based approaches to overcome identified barriers. We should be clear that no single treatment or framework can (or will) address all the many barriers that people with psychosis and SMI face, and PSR is not a panacea. However, PSR has a substantial, enduring evidence base and is flexible enough to incorporate empirically supported treatment modalities, assessment and conceptualization techniques and models, and different approaches (e.g., shared decision-making or deprescribing) as research and practice evolve. The rehabilitation goal, improving functioning and wellbeing rather than necessarily symptoms, allows flexibility and the possibility of empowering one as a human in context rather than only a "patient."

The *term* "Psychiatric Rehabilitation," which is the foundation of PSR, has all but lost its meaning in most current uses. The term was assimilated by the healthcare system in service definitions and subsequently became meaningless as programs billing under psychiatric rehabilitation codes were never held accountable. While there are countless excellent Psychiatric Rehabilitation programs, there is no way to know what services or model are provided in a given program billing under "psych rehab." The term "Psychosocial Rehabilitation and Recovery" may suffer a similar fate if history continues to repeat itself. We hope this book will provide the central tenets and purpose of PSR rather than a specific model, which is bound to change for the better and for the worse in different contexts.

Both CBT and PSR evolved primarily from intersections of cognitive science with social learning theory and other behaviorist approaches. In modern forms, behavioral formulation and goals remain paramount. People change their lives for the better by changing what they are doing or how they are doing it. Thoughts, emotions, perceptions, beliefs, and other traditional targets of talk therapy are barriers to changing *behavior* to align with a person's goals and values. The strength and risk of behavioral approaches is that social learning determines what a person will do or how they will react in the absence of "thinking about it." Most of our thoughts, emotions, reactions, and actions are automatic and reflexive because our activities and environments are much too complex to "make a decision" about everything. So, behavioral principles (i.e., operant and classical conditioning) that change animal and infant behavior are equally important to adult behavior. In restrictive and intensive treatment settings that often serve people with psychosis and SMI, environmental and interpersonal contingencies and systematic reinforcement *will happen*. They are unavoidable aspects of human coexistence. Staff can assess and utilize these contingencies to increase the likelihood that people will achieve personal goals and recovery, or they can ignore them. Unfortunately, when behavioral contingencies are ignored, what evolves is unintentional reinforcement of maladaptive behaviors and manipulation that maintains control. This circumstance creates the nightmarish milieus illustrated so poignantly in *One Flew Over the Cuckoo's Nest*, and the unfortunate but understandable aversion held by many advocates toward some of the best-researched treatment approaches, like token economy and contingency management. Legal issues like commitment and competency complicate ethics in intensive and restrictive treatment settings, which is beyond the scope of this book (see: Spaulding et al., 2021). However, professional, accountable, and ethical implementation of behavioral principles in the various settings that serve people with SMI and psychosis is needed before our healthcare system can start to heal.

"Snake pit" psychiatric wards of the mid-twentieth century and continuing abuses today warrant drastic action (Wells, 2020). We argue above that we still have much to learn from otherwise outdated research from the 1960s, and this argument also applies to systems and programs. As described in Chapter 2, *good* treatment programs that are humane and budget-friendly in the long-term are often shut down for various reasons and replaced with lower-quality programs that become inhumane. This is often a case of "throwing the baby out with the bathwater." Wholesale "reform" occurs rather than actual reform, which would involve at the least identifying and protecting what works well while changing or removing what doesn't. When good treatment programs are allowed to exist and grow, they will highlight problems to address through program evaluation and reform. This is apparent in countries with more consistent and evidence-based healthcare systems, whose problems and debates are entirely different from those in the US. When good PSR programs grow and are cut suddenly, systems fall into cycles of creating then having to address the same problems over and over rather than learning from mistakes and building past them (Sullivan, 1999; Tarasenko, Sullivan, Ritchie, & Spaulding, 2013). These cycles are so prevalent that, anecdotally, SMI Psychologists are advised to expect job changes every few years as PSR programs die, and competent professionals have to find another program to serve people. We must know and learn from our history to recover US mental healthcare, and this will require meticulous identification of "babies" amidst the substantial "bathwater," along with disruption from *within* systems in addition to advocacy from outside.

Orientation and Aspiration

We hope we have oriented you in a way to help maximize what you glean from each of the following chapters, which each take deeper dives into different perspectives on our broad goals. As previously stated, we hope to overemphasize the reality of Fact 1 (recovery is real and possible for most people with psychosis and SMI) while acknowledging but not praising the status quo and Fact 2 (psychosis and SMI are often incredibly difficult for all involved). We aim to meet these goals by highlighting three factors needed to improve the lives of people with psychosis and SMI: hope; available effective interventions; and changing attitudes to support dignity and autonomy.

Our coauthors' chapters are organized in three sections. The first section, Chapters 2–4, provides three different perspectives on the long history of research, clinical practice, and sociopolitical context that have demonstrated the fact of recovery and the value of psychosocial approaches, including the many challenges and self-defeating cycles that have limited our ability to support people with psychosis and SMI. The second section, Chapters 5 and 6, highlight successes, challenges, and lessons learned from broad systems in the US and abroad implementing new approaches to support people with recent-onset psychosis. The third section, Chapters 7–9, provides clear evidence and frameworks to believe in, hope for, and participate in recovering the US mental healthcare system for people with psychosis and SMI. Finally, Chapter 10 provides a summary of lessons learned from the preceding chapters and applies organizational change management strategies to present a path forward.

We write this book in the context of intense polarization amidst racial injustice, sociopolitical turmoil, and a pandemic. Most of us aspire to change ourselves and our country for the better, which will require "crossing the aisle" despite distancing, dehumanizing beliefs, and biases held by all sides. This requires courage and overemphasis on the others' humanity, with active and explicit openness and genuine curiosity about others' reality (i.e., intellectual humility). Only when we force ourselves to connect with and understand realities that conflict with ours might we find compromise and unity. We hope the parallels to this chapter are obvious. This book does not target injustice or polarization directly. However, your "local" actions toward hope for recovery, effective interventions, and empowerment and autonomy for people with psychosis and SMI will create a better world for traditionally dehumanized and discriminated neighbors. Your local actions are one way to use your talents and energy toward "global" progress for justice and equity.

REFERENCES

Albertson, E. M., Scannell, C., Ashtari, N., & Barnert, E. (2020). Eliminating gaps in medicaid coverage during reentry after incarceration. *American Journal of Public Health, 110*(3), 317–321.

Alang, SM. Mental health care among blacks in America: Confronting racism and constructing solutions. *BMC Health Services Research*, 2019; 54: 346–355. doi:10.1111/1475-6773.13115

Amsalem, D., Yang, L. H., Jankowski, S., Lieff, S. A., Markowitz, J. C., & Dixon, L. B. (2020). Reducing stigma toward individuals with schizophrenia using a brief video: A randomized controlled trial of young adults. *Schizophrenia Bulletin, 47*(1), 7–14. doi:10.1093/schbul/sbaa114

Barrett, N. M., Gill, K. J., Pratt, C. W., & Roberts, M. M. (2013). *Psychiatric rehabilitation:* Academic Press.

Bogart, K. R., Lund, E. M., & Rottenstein, A. (2018). Disability pride protects self-esteem through the rejection-identification model. *Rehabilitation Psychology, 63*(1), 155.

Bromage, B., Encandela, J. A., Cranford, M., Diaz, E., Williamson, B., Spell, V. T., & Rohrbaugh, R. M. (2019). Understanding health disparities through the eyes of community members: A structural competency education intervention. *Academic Psychiatry, 43*(2), 244–247. doi:10.1007/s40596-018-0937-z

Brown, M., & Brown, R. S. (2020). *Emancipatory perspectives on madness: psychological, social, and spiritual dimensions.* Routledge. Oxfordshire, England, UK.

Cabassa, L. J., Zayas, L. H., & Hansen, M. C. (2006). Latino adults' access to mental health care: A review of epidemiological studies. *Administration and Policy in Mental Health, 33*(3), 316–330. doi:10.1007/s10488-006-0040-8

Canady, V. A. (2021). APA on MLK Day apologizes for its role in structural racism in psychiatry. *Mental Health Weekly, 31*(4), 1–3.

Corcoran, C. M. (2016). Ethical and epidemiological dimensions of labeling psychosis risk. *AMA Journal of Ethics, 18*(6), 633–642. doi:10.1001/journalofethics.2016.18 .6.msoc2-1606

Corrigan, P. W., Markowitz, F. E., & Watson, A. C. (2004). Structural levels of mental illness stigma and discrimination. *Schizophrenia Bulletin, 30*(3), 481–491.

Corrigan, P. W., Mueser, K. T., Bond, G. R., Drake, R. E., & Solomon, P. (2012). *Principles and practice of psychiatric rehabilitation: An empirical approach.* Guilford Press.

Crenshaw, K. (1989). Demarginalizing the intersection of race and sex: A black feminist critique of antidiscrimination doctrine, feminist theory and antiracist politics. *University of Chicago Legal Forum*, 139.

Cross, A. B., Mulvey, E. P., Schubert, C. A., Griffin, P. A., Filone, S., Winckworth-Prejsnar, K., & Heilbrun, K. (2014). An agenda for advancing research on crisis intervention teams for mental health emergencies. *Psychiatric Services, 65*(4), 530–536.

Dalsania, A. K., Fastiggi, M. J., Kahlam, A., Shah, R., Patel, K., Shiau, S., & DallaPiazza, M. (2021). The relationship between social determinants of health and racial disparities in COVID-19 mortality. *Journal of Racial and Ethnic Health Disparities*, 1–8. doi: 10.1007/s40615-020-00952-y

Dark, F., Scott, J. G., Baker, A., Parker, S., Gordon, A., Newman, E., & Penn, D. L. (2020). Randomized controlled trial of social cognition and interaction training compared to befriending group. *British Journal of Clinical Psychology, 59*(3), 384–402. doi:10.1111/bjc.12252

Dearing, K. S., & Steadman, S. (2009). Enhancing intellectual empathy: The lived experience of voice simulation. *Perspectives in Psychiatric Care, 45*(3), 173–182. doi:10.1111/j.1744-6163.2009.00219.x

Deegan, P. E. (1996). *Hearing voices that are distressing: A training and simulated experience.* Lawrence, MA: The National Empowerment Center, Inc.

Delgado, R., & Stefancic, J. (2017). *Critical Race Theory: An Introduction* (Vol. 20). NYU Press. New York.

Dempsey, C., Quanbeck, C., Bush, C., & Kruger, K. (2020). Decriminalizing mental illness: Specialized policing responses. CNS Spectrums, 25(2), 181–195.

Desmond, M., Papachristos, A. V., & Kirk, D. S. (2016). Police violence and citizen crime reporting in the black community. *American Sociological Review, 81*(5), 857–876.

Dubreucq, J., Plasse, J., & Franck, N. (2021). Self-stigma in serious mental illness: A systematic review of frequency, correlates, and consequences. *Schizophrenia Bulletin.* doi:10.1093/schbul/sbaa181

Edwards, F., Lee, H., & Esposito, M. (2019). Risk of being killed by police use of force in the United States by age, race–ethnicity, and sex. *Proceedings of the National Academy of Sciences, 116*(34), 16793–16798.

Elbogen, E. B., Beckham, J. C., Butterfield, M. I., Swartz, M., & Swanson, J. (2008). Assessing risk of violent behavior among veterans with severe mental illness. *Journal of Traumatic Stress, 21*(1), 113–117.

Ellison, M. L., Belanger, L. K., Niles, B. L., Evans, L. C., & Bauer, M. S. (2018). Explication and definition of mental health recovery: A systematic review.

Administration and Policy in Mental Health and Mental Health Services Research,
45(1), 91–102. doi:10.1007/s10488-016-0767-9

Francey, S. M., O'Donoghue, B., Nelson, B., Graham, J., Baldwin, L., Yuen, H. P., . . .
McGorry, P. D. (2020). Psychosocial intervention with or without antipsychotic
edication for first-episode psychosis: A randomized noninferiority clinical trial.
Schizophrenia Bulletin Open, 1(1). doi:10.1093/schizbullopen/sgaa015

Frankham, E. (2018). Mental illness affects police fatal shootings. *Contexts, 17*(2), 70–72.

Fuller, D. A., Lamb, H. R., Biasotti, M., & Snook, J. (2015). *Overlooked in the*
undercounted: The role of mental illness in fatal law enforcement encounters.
Treatment Advocacy Center. https://www.treatmentadvocacycenter.org/storage/
documents/overlooked-in-the-undercounted.pdf

Gary, F. A. (2005). Stigma: Barrier to mental health care among ethnic minorities.
Issues in Mental Health Nursing, 26(10), 979–999.

Gertner, A. K., Rotter, J. S., & Shafer, P. R. (2019). Association between state
minimum wages and suicide rates in the US. *American Journal of Preventive*
Medicine, 56(5), 648–654.

Goodheart, C. D., Kazdin, A. E., & Sternberg, R. J. (2006). *Evidence-based*
psychotherapy: Where practice and research meet (pp. xi–295). Washington DC,
USA. American Psychological Association.

Gunnell, D., Appleby, L., Arensman, E., Hawton, K., John, A., Kapur, N., & Caine,
E. D. (2020). Suicide risk and prevention during the COVID-19 pandemic. *The*
Lancet Psychiatry, 7(6), 468–471.

Hamada, K., & Fan, X. (2020). The impact of COVID-19 on individuals living with
serious mental illness. *Schizophrenia Research 222*, 3.

Hartz, S. M., Pato, C. N., Medeiros, H., Cavazos-Rehg, P., Sobell, J. L., Knowles, J. A.,
& Pato, M. T. (2014). Comorbidity of severe psychotic disorders with measures
of substance use. *The Journal of the American Medical Association Psychiatry,*
71(3), 248–254.

Haushofer, J., Mudida, R., & Shapiro, J. P. (2020). *The comparative impact of*
cash transfers and a psychotherapy program on psychological and economic
well-being (No. w28106). National Bureau of Economic Research. Cambridge,
MA, USA.

Heun-Johnson, H., Menchine, M., Axeen, S., Lung, K., Claudius, I., Wright, T., &
Seabury, S. A. (2021). Association between race/ethnicity and disparities in health
care use before first-episode psychosis among privately insured young patients.
JAMA psychiatry, *78*(3), 311–319.

Hollon, S. D. (2020). Is cognitive therapy enduring or antidepressant medications
iatrogenic? Depression as an evolved adaptation. *American Psychologist, 75*(9),
1207.

Holttum, S., & Hayward, M. (2010). Perceived improvements in service user
involvement in two clinical psychology training courses. *Psychology Learning &*
Teaching, 9(1), 16–24. doi:10.2304/plat.2010.9.1.16

Humphreys, K., Blodgett, J. C., & Roberts, L. W. (2015). The exclusion of people
with psychiatric disorders from medical research. *Journal of Psychiatric Research,*
70, 28–32.

Kopelovich, S. L., Hughes, M., Monroe-DeVita, M. B., Peterson, R., Cather, C., &
Gottlieb, J. (2019). Statewide implementation of cognitive behavioral therapy for

22   Charlie A. Davidson et al.

psychosis through a learning collaborative model. *Cognitive and Behavioral Practice, 26*(3), 439–452.

Kurtz, M. M., Gagen, E., Rocha, N. B. F., Machado, S., & Penn, D. L. (2016). Comprehensive treatments for social cognitive deficits in schizophrenia: A critical review and effect-size analysis of controlled studies. *Clinical Psychology Review, 43*, 80–89. doi:10.1016/j.cpr.2015.09.003

Link, B. G., & Phelan, J. C. (2001). Conceptualizing stigma. *Annual Review of Sociology, 27*(1), 363–385.

López, S. R., Barrio, C., Kopelowicz, A., & Vega, W. A. (2012). From documenting to eliminating disparities in mental health care for Latinos. *American Psychologist, 67*(7), 511–523. doi:10.1037/a0029737

López, S. R., Lara, M., Kopelowicz, A., Solano, S., Foncerrada, H., & Aguilera, A. (2009). La CLAve to increase psychosis literacy of Spanish-speaking community residents and family caregivers. *Journal of Consulting and Clinical Psychology, 77*(4), 763.

Lucksted, A., Drapalski, A., Calmes, C., Forbes, C., DeForge, B., & Boyd, J. (2011). Ending self-stigma: Pilot evaluation of a new intervention to reduce internalized stigma among people with mental illnesses. *Psychiatric Rehabilitation Journal, 35*(1), 51.

Luigi, M., Rapisarda, F., Corbière, M., De Benedictis, L., Bouchard, A. M., Felx, A., ... Lesage, A. (2020). Determinants of mental health professionals' attitudes towards recovery: A review. *Canadian Medical Education Journal, 11*(5), e62.

Mabe, P. A., Ahmed, A. O., Duncan, G. N., Fenley, G., & Buckley, P. F. (2014). Project GREAT: Immersing physicians and doctorally-trained psychologists in recovery-oriented care. *Professional Psychology: Research and Practice, 45*(5), 347.

Magliano, L., Read, J., Rega, S., Oliviero, N., Sagliocchi, A., Patalano, M., & D'Ambrosio, A. (2011). The influence of causal explanations and diagnostic labeling on medical students' views of schizophrenia. *Academic Medicine, 86*(9), 1155–1162.

Metzl, J. M. (2010). *The protest psychosis: How schizophrenia became a black disease.* Beacon Press. Boston, MA, USA.

Millett, G. A., Jones, A. T., Benkeser, D., Baral, S., Mercer, L., Beyrer, C., ... Crowley, J. S. (2020). Assessing differential impacts of COVID-19 on black communities. *Annals of Epidemiology, 47*, 37–44.

Mitchell, A. J., & Selmes, T. (2007). Why don't patients take their medicine? Reasons and solutions in psychiatry. *Advances in Psychiatric Treatment, 13*(5), 336–346. doi:10.1192/apt.bp.106.003194

Morrison, A. P., Pyle, M., Maughan, D., Johns, L., Freeman, D., Broome, M. R., ... MacLennan, G. (2020). Antipsychotic medication versus psychological intervention versus a combination of both in adolescents with first-episode psychosis (MAPS): A multicentre, three-arm, randomised controlled pilot and feasibility study. *The Lancet Psychiatry, 7*(9), 788–800.

Mote, J., & Fulford, D. (2020). Now is the time to support black individuals in the US living with serious mental illness—A call to action. *The Journal of the American Medical Association Psychiatry, 78*(2), 129–130.

Mueser, K. T., Silverstein, S. M., & Farkas, M. D. (2013). Should the training of clinical psychologists require competence in the treatment and rehabilitation of individuals with a serious mental illness? *Psychiatric Rehabilitation Journal, 36*(1), 54.

Muhammad, S. (July 9, 2020). Opinion: Daniel Prude's death is a nightmare scenario for Black families like mine. *The Washington Post*. Retrieved from https://www .washingtonpost.com/opinions/2020/09/07/daniel-prude-death-policing-mental-illness/

Nemani, K., Li, C., Olfson, M., Blessing, E. M., Razavian, N., Chen, J., ... Goff, D. C. (2021). Association of psychiatric disorders with mortality among patients with COVID-19. *JAMA Psychiatry, 78*(4), 380–386.

Rajkumar, R. P. (2020). COVID-19 and mental health: A review of the existing literature. *Asian Journal of Psychiatry, 52*, 102066.

Reddy, F., Spaulding, W. D., Jansen, M. A., Menditto, A. A., & Pickett, S. (2010). Psychologists' roles and opportunities in rehabilitation and recovery for serious mental illness: A survey of Council of University Directors of Clinical Psychology (CUDCP) clinical psychology training and doctoral education. *Training and Education in Professional Psychology, 4*(4), 254.

Rollins Jr, A. C. (2019). Assessment of public sector service quality: Gauging experiences and perceptions of racial profiling. *Journal of Public Management & Social Policy, 26*(1), 59–72.

Rüsch, N., Corrigan, P. W., Wassel, A., Michaels, P., Larson, J. E., Olschewski, M., . . . Batia, K. (2009). Self-stigma, group identification, perceived legitimacy of discrimination and mental health service use. *The British Journal of Psychiatry, 195*(6), 551–552.

Schlier, B., Lange, P., Wiese, S., Wirth, A., & Lincoln, T. (2016). The effect of educational information about treatments for schizophrenia on stigmatizing perceptions. *Journal of Behavior Therapy and Experimental Psychiatry, 52*, 11–16.

Schlier, B., Schmick, S., & Lincoln, T. M. (2014). No matter of etiology: Biogenetic, psychosocial and vulnerability-stress causal explanations fail to improve attitudes towards schizophrenia. *Psychiatry Research, 215*(3), 753–759.

Sher, L. (2020). The impact of the COVID-19 pandemic on suicide rates. *QJM: An International Journal of Medicine, 113*(10), 707–712.

Shevlin, M., Murphy, J., Read, J., Mallett, J., Adamson, G., & Houston, J. E. (2011). Childhood adversity and hallucinations: A community-based study using the National Comorbidity Survey Replication. *Social Psychiatry and Psychiatric Epidemiology, 46*(12), 1203–1210.

Smith, M. K., Tamburrino, M. B., Naskar, I., Lynch, D. J., & Chen, Y. (2014). Hearing voices: Evaluation of a medical student training experience about psychosis. *Academic Psychiatry, 38*(4), 514–515. doi:10.1007/s40596-014-0166-z

Spaulding, W. D., Sullivan, M. E., Evans, E., & Avila, A. (2021). Inpatient settings and the people they serve. In *Comprehensive Clinical Psychology (2nd ed.)*: Elsevier. https://www.sciencedirect.com/science/article/pii/B9780128186978000789?via% 3Dihub

Spaulding, W. D., Sullivan, M. E., & Poland, J. S. (2003). *Treatment and Rehabilitation of Severe Mental Illness*. Guilford Press. New York, NY, USA.

Sullivan, M. (1999). The unique roles of state hospital programs: Keeping what works in an evolving system. *New Directions for Mental Health Services, 1999*(84), 47–55.

Swan, S., Keen, N., Reynolds, N., & Onwumere, J. (2017). Psychological interventions for post-traumatic stress symptoms in psychosis: A systematic review of outcomes. *Frontiers in Psychology, 8*, 341.

Swanson, J. W., McGinty, E. E., Fazel, S., & Mays, V. M. (2015). Mental illness and reduction of gun violence and suicide: Bringing epidemiologic research to policy. *Annals of Epidemiology, 25*(5), 366–376.

Tan, S. B., deSouza, P., & Raifman, M. (2021). Structural racism and COVID-19 in the USA: A county-level empirical analysis. *Journal of Racial and Ethnic Health Disparities*, 1–11.

Tarasenko, M., Sullivan, M., Ritchie, A. J., & Spaulding, W. D. (2013). Effects of eliminating psychiatric rehabilitation from the secure levels of a mental-health service system. *Psychological Services, 10*(4), 442–451. doi:10.1037/a0030260

Tsoi, O. Y. Y., Chan, S. K. W., Chui, A. H. C., Hui, C. L. M., Chang, W. C., Lee, E. H. M., ... Chen, E. Y. H. (2020). Effect of brief social contact video compared with expert information video in changing knowledge and attitude towards psychosis patients among medical students. *Early Intervention in Psychiatry, 15*(2), 278–285.

Villa, J., Ehret, B. C., & Depp, C. A. (2019). Systematic review of the inclusion of people with psychosis in suicide-specific clinical trials. *Crisis: The Journal of Crisis Intervention and Suicide Prevention, 41*(3), 233–236.

Weisman, A. G., & López, S. R. (1997). An attributional analysis of emotional reactions to schizophrenia in Mexican and Anglo American cultures. *Journal of Applied Social Psychology, 27*(3), 223–244.

Weisman de Mamani, A., McLaughlin, M., Altamirano, O., Lopez, D., & Ahmad, S. S. (2020). *Culturally informed therapy for Schizophrenia: A family-focused cognitive behavioral approach, clinician guide.* Oxford University Press, Oxford, UK.

Wells, T. (2020). Lessons learned from Georgia's 2010 Olmstead Settlement: The good, the bad, and the limitations of a Justice Department Olmstead Settlement. *Journal of Legal Medicine, 40*(1), 45–52. doi:10.1080/01947648.2020.1731334

Zarlock, S. P. (1966). Social expectations, language, and schizophrenia. *Journal of Humanistic Psychology, 6*(1), 68–74. doi:10.1177/002216786600600107

Part I

The Past

2 Psychosocial Treatment and the Schizophrenia Spectrum
Roots and Origins

Will Spaulding, Andrea Avila, and Eric Evans

> Customers can have a car painted any color that they want, so long as it is black.
> —Henry Ford

The evolution of psychosocial treatments for schizophrenia has tracked larger historical trends in psychology, behavioral science, and mental health policy over more than a century. At times, the communication of ideas and influences of science, practice and policy has been reciprocal and mutually beneficial. At other times, there is a lack of such reciprocity, sometimes with unfortunate consequences. This chapter will review and summarize those ideas and influences in our post-modern era, and identify key landmarks in the progression toward contemporary psychosocial treatment of schizophrenia spectrum disorders.

Setting the Stage: The Early Twentieth Century

By the time Eugen Bleuler's term "schizophrenia" came into general use in the early twentieth century, its ancestral version, "dementia praecox," coined by Emil Kraepelin in the 1880s, had stimulated at least three distinct views of its psychopathology and treatment. The first was the neurologically oriented view that emerged from Kraepelin's own work, and that of other luminaries of German academic medicine (e.g., Alois Alzheimer, Franz Nissl). The original diagnostic term, translated as "early-onset dementia," effectively encapsulates the presumed etiology and prospects for treatment in this view. With an emphasis on research into genetic and pathophysiological mechanisms, this perspective was generally dominant in academic neurology departments.

A second view was the evolving psychoanalytic formulation of schizophrenia and psychosis. Although Freud had famously dismissed the promise of psychoanalysis for psychotic disorders, neo-Freudians and others persisted in developing new theories and techniques for that purpose. Most of this work was conducted in psychiatric hospitals in the US and Great Britain. Ever since Freud himself had quipped that Bleuler's proposal for theoretical rapprochement between biological and psychoanalytic psychiatry revealed that Freud had succumbed to one of his own key diagnostic criteria for schizophrenia (ambivalence), there wasn't much mutual influence between the two communities. However, in parts of Europe, Kraepelinian and psychoanalytic psychiatrists coexisted comfortably. They introduced ideas from their respective orientations into the dominant treatment model for severe mental illness at the time, *moral therapy*, a humanitarian communal approach that had been evolving in Europe for centuries.

A third view evolved in the US in the community of physicians who were medical superintendents of psychiatric institutions, which had begun to take their modern form in the late nineteenth century. Despite high regard for the biomedical sciences, the urgent pragmatics of running institutions discouraged enthusiasm for Kraepelinian neurology, which had yet to provide useful new treatments. This community was somewhat more drawn to the social and humanitarian dimensions of psychoanalysis, and so the early twentieth century did see some application of psychoanalytic concepts and treatments in private institutions that served people with schizophrenia spectrum disorders, including such iconic hospitals as Chestnut Lodge and Sheppard Pratt in Maryland, McLean and Austen Riggs in Massachusetts, and the Menninger Clinic in Kansas. Psychiatrists with a psychoanalytic orientation could be found in public institutions as well.

In the US the superintendents initially prevented a significant presence of Kraepelinian neurologists in their institutions, but they eventually did incorporate a community of physicians who had evolved from that origin. Termed "nerve doctors" reflecting their neurological roots (Harrison, 2019, pp. 32–35), and compelled by exclusion from the institutions to treat conditions less disabling than schizophrenia and dementia, they had turned to herbalism, patent medications, hypnosis and quasi-medical treatments borrowed from the folk medicine of bygone eras. Like with psychoanalysis, these approaches had more pragmatic appeal to the institutional superintendents than actual neurology, although some were grossly misguided. This may account for some of the more bizarre procedures inflicted on institutionalized patients, such as purgatives, whirling and hydrotherapy, that persisted into the twentieth century. In 1892 the Association of Medical Superintendents of American Institutions for the Insane had changed its name to the American Medico-Psychological Association, and then in 1921 to the American Psychiatric Association. This community was, in that sense, the direct ancestor of the contemporary American psychiatric establishment.

None of the three views of the early twentieth century produced robust scientific findings on schizophrenia, either about etiology or treatment outcome, and none gained ascendency. Even within the academic neurological community there was disagreement about key features of the disorder, including Bleuler's argument that there is not an inevitable progression to death, as was believed about dementias in general. The first diagnostic manual of the American Psychiatric Association, released in 1950, was a miscellany of psychoanalytic and Kraepelinian/Bleulerian constructs. Clinical practice was comparably eclectic, sometimes without clear boundaries between "psychosocial" and "biomedical" forms of treatment.

In contrast to the pre-paradigmatic disarray in psychiatry, the early twentieth century saw some significant developments in social policy relevant to severe mental illness. A towering figure of this era was Adolf Meyer, a Swiss psychiatrist who emigrated to the US. Meyer brought a sensitivity to the social and cultural context of mental illness that distinguished Swiss psychiatry (Bleuler, also Swiss, wrote at length about relationships and the social environment, a more important contribution than inventing the term "schizophrenia." He also had a collegial and congenial relationship with Swiss psychoanalyst Carl Jung). Meyer promoted a new holistic, sociological, and pragmatic perspective on mental illness. He is credited with founding the profession of social work, among other accomplishments. Meyer benefited from a larger, multidimensional social progressive movement, at whose center was a group of University of Chicago sociologists known as "the Chicago School." Sociology resonated with public health in their mutual concern for environmental determinants of human wellbeing, including mental health.

Meyer collaborated with psychologist William James and Clifford Beers, a layman who had struggled with bipolar disorder, to found the *mental hygiene movement*, a reform project explicitly intended to promote what we today recognize as a public health model for severe mental illness. The mental hygiene movement arguably achieved what psychoanalytic and Kraepelinian views had eschewed, a conceptual synthesis of biomedical, psychological, and environmental levels of analysis to inform policy and clinical practice. The science was not yet ready to support such a synthesis, but in those progressive times the practical, common sense ideas of Beers, Meyers and others had enough a priori validity to create the foundation of post-modern mental health policy.

On the eve of World War II the social progressivism of the 1930s produced the first major American research study of the sociological dimensions of psychopathology (Faris & Dunham, 1939). Conducted in urban and suburban Chicago, the study revealed a correlation between mental illness and the geographical dimensions of social status, including a marked incidence of schizophrenia in public housing and immigrant neighborhoods.

Mid-Twentieth Century

World War II, its lead-up and aftermath, affected policy and practice in mental health as profoundly as it affected cultural evolution in general. Clinical psychology as a healthcare profession had been incubating for decades, exemplified by the work of Hugo Munsterberg, Lightner Witmer, Henry Murray, and others. America's entry to the war created an urgent demand for psychology's assessment technology, and the war's consequences created an urgent demand for psychological treatment and rehabilitation. The needs of returning disabled veterans and the GI Bill brought an infusion of new psychologists and established the foundations of modern rehabilitation psychology. The famous Boulder Conference of 1948 established the *scientist-practitioner model* for training the new profession. The growing community of clinical psychologists would energize development of psychosocial treatment for generations.

Rapid growth of the clinical psychology professional and academic communities accompanied cross-fertilization between psychoanalysis and experimental, developmental, and social psychology. "Ego psychology" is generally recognized to be the dominant paradigm of treatment during the 1940s and 1950s, although its rapid evolution makes it a moving target for further description. By the mid-1950s theories and practices ranged from some that are barely distinguishable from classical psychoanalysis, to sophisticated psychometric assessment and manipulation of distinct ego functions having considerable a priori validity. Applications to the psychopathology of schizophrenia ranged from the disastrous "schizophrenogenic mother" hypothesis (Fromm-Reichmann, 1948), to Harry Stack Sullivan's (1953) integration of sociological and psychoanalytic theory, to Sylvano Arieti's (1955) ingenious (but fundamentally flawed) psycholinguistic analysis of thought disorder. In diverse ways, psychoanalytic insights about the importance of human development were fused with the promise of functional analyses of social and psychological processes in a theory of schizophrenia and its treatment.

The 1950s also began to see the fruits of American experimental psychology's first forays into mental illness research. David Shakow, founding figure and chair of the Boulder Conference, had set up a laboratory at the Worcester (MA) state hospital in the mid-1930s. By the mid-1950s, using such fundamental psychological methods as intelligence tests and reaction time measures, Shakow was addressing key questions about the nature of schizophrenia. Does it show an inevitable deterioration in psychological function? No. Does it nevertheless involve specific impairments in cognitive and intellectual processes? Yes. Shakow's 1955 theory of cognitive impairment in schizophrenia, *segmental set*, based primarily on a simple reaction time task, foreshadows contemporary neuropsychological models that emphasize impaired executive cognition. This early experimental work would have a formative effect on etiological models of schizophrenia for the next 40 years, but it would also be 40 years before the treatment implications would begin to appear. Unfortunately, it also had too little effect on subsequent mental health policy, which remained insensitive to the nuances of cognitive functioning.

The postwar years also saw new ideas in biology that were the earliest identifiable forerunners of the biosystemic models that today are coming together as the dominant paradigm, in psychopathology in general and schizophrenia in particular. Ludwig von Bertalanffy (1950) is recognized for integrating molecular and ecological biology, and articulating the need for a range of levels of analysis to understand the behavior of organism-environment systems, at micro- and macro-levels. Judd Marmor, whose influence was reflected in his presidency of the American Psychiatric Association, is recognized as among the first to see the implications of the biosystemic view for psychopathology and psychiatry (Marmor & Pumpian-Mindlin, 1950). As the psychopathology of schizophrenia evolved for the next 70 years, it gradually became the fully integrated biosystemic paradigm that these visionaries imagined. Today that paradigm provides the conceptual foundation for integrative psychiatric rehabilitation approaches that target neurophysiological, cognitive, behavioral and environmental levels of functioning (e.g., Spaulding et al., 2003)

Throughout the mid-century, genealogical studies of schizophrenia, and studies of monozygotic twins discordant for schizophrenia, accumulated evidence for complex genetic contributions. The most important conceptual development in the early 1960s was contributed by another founding figure of clinical psychology, Paul Meehl. Starting with the genealogical data at the time, Meehl (1962) reasoned that genes produce a *vulnerability state*, which Meehl named *schizotypy*, which then interacts with other factors to produce schizophrenia. This idea converged with the older idea of diathesis and led to the *vulnerability model of schizophrenia* (Zubin & Spring, 1977), which today continues to be a central feature of biosystemic models of the schizophrenia spectrum and many other disorders. By the mid-1960s, longitudinal studies of people at statistical risk (mostly identified by the diagnosis in first-degree relatives) had begun, under the inspiration and leadership of Sarnoff Mednick (Cannon & Mednick, 1993).

The genetic factors and their mechanisms and interactions with environmental factors were gradually articulated over the rest of the century. Meehl's concept of schizotypy has taken on additional meanings, and there are other vulnerabilities not necessarily associated with the original concept's key features. Research on the genetic vulnerabilities, now understood to be *endophenotypes*, has inspired hopes for prevention strategies (Gottesman & Erlenmyer-Kimling, 2001), although the concept of vulnerability has prevention implications whether the vulnerabilities are genetic or acquired. Prevention is a central concern in public health, creating an uncommon convergence of interest across the policy, psychopathology, neuropsychiatric, and psychosocial treatment communities. Today that interface is energizing research on prevention (Gur et al., 2017) and early intervention (Kane et al., 2015). Early intervention is termed *tertiary prevention* in public health argot, meaning prevention of deterioration in a population with an identified illness; prevention of illness in an identified high risk population is *secondary prevention*. Some, not all, prevention and early intervention programs integrate pharmacological and psychosocial modalities, guided by a biosystemic model of the schizophrenia spectrum.

The Mental Hygiene Movement's momentum toward a public health perspective on mental illness continued through the war. In 1946 President Truman signed the National Mental Health Act, establishing the National Institute of Mental Health. NIMH was one of the four original subdivisions of the National Institute of Health. Within a year, the first federal mental health research grant was awarded, to a psychologist, Winfred Kellogg. Journalist Albert Deutsch published a landmark indictment of American state hospitals in 1948, re-energizing public demand for reform. In 1955 an Act of Congress initiated the largest mental health research effort to date, for "an objective, thorough, nationwide analysis and reevaluation of the human and economic problems of mental health." The act produced a Joint Commission composed of 36 organizations, and a 10-volume report, *Action for Mental Health*, over the following five years (Joint Commission on Mental Illness and Health, 1961).

While the Joint Commission was doing its work in the late 1950s, research on severe mental illness was producing findings that reinforced the public health values and objectives of national policy activities. Sociologists August Hollingshead and Frederick Redlich (1958) built on Faris and Dunham's (1939) findings in a thorough exploration of socioeconomic status. A husband-wife team of experimental social psychologists, Benjamin and Dorothea Braginsky (1961), conducted a compelling program of research revealing the degree to which the behavior of both patients and caregivers is shaped by the physical and psychological features of an institutional setting. Ervin Goffman (1961) produced a landmark critique of psychiatric institutions, *Asylums*.

Together the sociological and social psychology findings reinforced growing concern, in scientific communities and in popular culture, about the role of psychiatry and psychiatric institutions in exacerbating or even causing severe mental illness. The concerns found radical voices in the so-called antipsychiatry movement, exemplified in the writings of R.D. Laing (1960) and Thomas Szaz (1961). Short of declaring mental illness a "myth" as Szaz suggested, there was a growing consensus that the incidence and morbidity of schizophrenia could be substantially reduced by reducing society-wide risk factors like poverty and social disenfranchisement, reforming or even eliminating psychiatric institutions, and developing mental health services in community settings. There was also growing agreement that to achieve those goals would require federal government involvement. The final report of the Mental Health Commission in 1961 largely reflected that consensus, although it was subject to pointed criticism that its recommendations were vague and not well supported by research data (Pasamanick, 1962). Many of the Commission's recommendations were pursued by the progressive presidential administrations of J.F. Kennedy and L.B. Johnson. The Community Mental Health Center Act was passed in 1963, initiating the extensive direct federal involvement in community-based treatment of mental illness that continues today.

Meanwhile, a new perspective on institutional treatment appeared in the 1950s, that of clinical psychologists bringing to the new profession the instrumental learning language and principles of B.F. Skinner. Ogden Lindsley (1956) was the first to describe its application to chronic schizophrenia. Teodoro Ayllon and Jack Michael (1959) proposed that psychiatric nurses be recast as "behavioral engineers" who therapeutically manipulate reinforcement of adaptive behavior. The Braginskys' findings on interpersonal processes were recapitulated in operant learning terms by another husband-wife team, Donna and Sydney Gelfand (Gelfand, Gelfand, & Dobson, 1967). Ayllon and collaborator Nathan Azrin (1968) developed the *token economy*, a comprehensive operant learning theory-based treatment approach that showed strikingly superior outcome over the usual institutional treatment of the time.

Psychoanalytic, psychological, sociological, and public health ideas converged and interacted throughout the 1950s and 1960s, in a particular practice domain for which *therapeutic milieu* is the best, though imperfect, rubric. The idea of systematically manipulating features of the patient's milieu for therapeutic purposes arguably dates back at least to the mid-nineteenth century (Dain & Carlson, 1960), a derivation of the "moral therapy" model that dominated institutional treatment at that time. It was then a set of principles and procedures designed primarily to compassionately include patients in community life within the institution, fairly consistent with the key ideas of the later mental hygiene movement. By the late 1940s psychoanalytic treatment of children with severe disorders in psychiatric institutions had assimilated comparable ideas, but cast in terms of psychoanalytic psychopathology (Bettelheim & Sylvester, 1948). A residential treatment model for adults with severe mental illness, originally developed to treat addiction, adhered more closely to the principles of moral therapy, using "patient government," literally a parliamentary-style organization of the patients/residents, to foster effective interpersonal functioning and community involvement (Hyde & Solomon, 1950). Patient government and related milieu therapy programs for adults with severe mental illness came to be known as *therapeutic communities* (Jones, 1953). They proliferated and diversified over the next three decades, reflecting differences in setting and patient population (e.g., Croog, 1956; Gerhardt, 1968; Jones, 1953; Murray & Cohen, 1959; Redl, 1959). It was especially popular in the Veterans Administration hospitals, although even in that institutional context many variants evolved (Manasse & des Jardins 1983).

A variant of therapeutic communities, the *psychosocial clubhouse model*, developed in the late 1950s, energized by the broader interest in mental health services reform. Psychosocial clubhouses are organizations of patients and helpers who live, work and support each other in a collective arrangement whose original membership requirement was being a refugee from the psychiatric institutions (this changed in the post-deinstitutionalization era). Professional involvement is mostly eschewed. The model was pioneered by two free-standing organizations, Fountain House in New York City (Fisher & Beard, 1962), and Thresholds in Chicago (Bond et al., 1984), and by social worker George Fairweather in the VA (Fairweather et al., 1969). The conceptual basis for these models was sometimes described as *psychiatric rehabilitation*, because they focused on establishing basic functional capabilities rather than treating an illness. The idea of psychiatric rehabilitation had appeared in the early 1940s as psychiatrists focused on reintegration of war veterans with psychiatric disorders, and psychologists recognized the parallels to physical rehabilitation for the same population. The psychosocial clubhouses broadened psychiatric rehabilitation's scope, and its meanings continue to evolve today.

By the mid-1960s milieu therapy had evolved into two kinds, one broadly based on the original premises of moral therapy, adapted to post-modern views of institutions, authority, social disenfranchisement, and personal responsibility, the other based rigorously on instrumental learning, most concretely in token economy programs. Both evolved rapidly, the original model because it was applied to a diversity of settings and patient populations, and the learning version because the dominant paradigm in behavioral clinical psychology was rapidly progressing, from classical and instrumental learning to include social learning theory. Behavioral techniques to complement the original token economy were proliferating. Probably the most important of the new additions was *social skills training*, originally designed for people with developmental disabilities (Wright, 1960), but appealingly similar to *psychodrama*, a psychoanalytically inspired modality that had become popular for psychiatric populations in the 1930s (Moreno, 1969).

Both types of milieu therapy could be operationally defined with *treatment manuals*, at least for a particular application, sufficient to be independent variables in controlled experimental treatment trials, with reliable measures of practitioner fidelity to the manual. Behavior therapists were generally more interested in running competitive trials, and these were important in establishing the validity of specific techniques over the next decade (e.g., Austin et al., 1976). The climax of that era of research was Gordon Paul's monumental controlled trial, comparing a social learning program combining a token economy with social skills training and related modalities, to a humanistic therapeutic community program with patient government, and treatment-as-usual in a conventional psychiatric hospital (Paul & Lentz, 1977). Both psychosocial conditions were superior to treatment-as-usual, but the social learning condition impressively outperformed the patient government condition as well.

With multiple levels of experimental control, including randomization, blinds, time-sample behavioral observation, and a 10-year study period, the Paul and Lentz (1977) trial achieved an unprecedented level of experimental rigor. It was described at the time as the largest controlled treatment trial in the history of psychiatry. It was the largest and most elaborate of many related studies of social learning-based practices for schizophrenia spectrum disorders, all showing superiority for specific purposes. It would be logical to expect that these findings would have a definitive impact on institutional practices for schizophrenia. They did not. Residential treatment with a social learning-based therapeutic milieu continued to evolve, arguably to the present day, but almost exclusively in university research centers or settings affiliated with academic researchers. There are many reasons for this. The notorious national failure to disseminate best practices for severe mental illness is not unique to social learning-based milieu therapy. It even includes dissemination of pharmaceuticals. However, the unequivocal superiority of Paul's treatment model makes it a useful exemplar. A fuller understanding of this and the other dissemination problems can usefully begin with consideration of scientific and policy developments after the 1960s.

The Deinstitutionalization Era

By 1970 the three distinct views of schizophrenia and severe mental illness that began the century had evolved into separable but overlapping sets of ideas, no longer necessarily associated with separate scientific/professional communities, but still competing for dominance in practice and policy. One set of ideas, which for heuristic purposes will be designated "reform" in this discussion, was focused primarily on public health and social policy reform, including eliminating psychiatric institutions, providing federal funding for community mental health centers, broadening the mental health workforce to include non-medical professionals, and replacing the prevailing quasi-medical and psychoanalytic treatment models with social support, counseling to enhance coping with the stresses of life, occupational/vocational rehabilitation, social empowerment, and neutralizing stigmatization. Another set of ideas, here heuristically designated "therapy," was more focused on psychosocial treatment in the traditional sense, conceptually based on combinations of ideas, including moral treatment-derived principles from social reform movements, principles adapted from humanistic and person-centered psychotherapies, the therapeutic community models that had evolved in the preceding decades, and the newer social learning-based behavioral therapies. A third set of ideas, here designated "neo-Kraepelinian," was a revival of neurological premises for psychiatry, emphasizing a need for reliable diagnostic criteria, anticipating their use as independent variables in research on the psychiatric pharmaceuticals that had begun to appear in the 1950s, and on the genetic origins of mental illness.

The "reform" view was not much concerned with specific treatments. The appearance of psychiatric drugs changed that, because effective suppression of psychotic symptoms was presumed to be advantageous for closing the institutions. The role of the community mental health centers could extend beyond "counseling," to include dispensing the drugs. The neo-Kraepelinians, like their forebears, were mostly academic research psychiatrists, not greatly concerned with social services and related concerns of the "reform" view. However, the envisioned community system was both a market for the drugs and associated prescriptive practice, and a venue for the numbers of clinical practitioners they had been training in response to federal funding for academic psychiatry departments. Like the Kraepelinians, the neo-Kraepelinians had a reductionist view of psychopathology, consistent with the "magic bullet" pharmacological solutions they sought, and a more traditional guild-oriented view of practice than mainstream psychiatry had developed by the end of the 1950s (Klerman, 1978). The neo-Kraepelinians gained ascendency in the psychiatric establishment, including medical school psychiatry departments. Psychoanalysis and ego psychology were mostly purged from psychiatry training (behavioral models had never been represented at all), and within a generation psychiatric practitioners developed an almost exclusive focus on psychopharmacology, with little or no training related to the service system envisioned and partly developed in the 1960s. The zenith of the neo-Kraepelinian era was in 1980, with the release of the third edition of the American Psychiatric Association's diagnostic manual, which eliminated or revised most diagnoses with psychoanalytic origins and organized psychopathology into families reflecting the presumed actions of psychotropic drug families.

There was an additional convergence between the neo-Kraepelinian perspective and the "reform" perspective, in the importance of non-institutional treatment of acute psychotic episodes. Psychopathology research had illuminated the significance of the episodic course of schizophrenia spectrum disorders, and the implications for institutionalization were clear. Long-term continuous disability (sometimes termed "Kraepelinian schizophrenia") was increasingly seen as the exception to an episodic course, wherein intensive and restrictive treatment was necessary only for circumscribed periods. The new drugs appeared to be especially efficacious at resolving acute episodes. The idea of a reformed treatment system wherein acute episodes were treated pharmacologically in short-term non-institutional settings (i.e., psychiatric units in general hospitals) was especially attractive. There was not much attention, in this perspective, to the role of psychosocial treatment, except for relatively isolated objections that acute psychosis can be effectively treated without drugs (e.g., Mosher, 1999).

The neo-Kraepelineans also found common cause with a consumer advocacy movement, embodied at the time as the National Alliance for the Mentally Ill (NAMI, later renamed National Alliance on Mental Illness). NAMI was an organized community of parents who had suffered through "schizophrenogenic parent" theories and angrily resonated with the neo-Kraepelinian rejection of psychoanalysis. Their agenda emphasized de-stigmatization of themselves and their children, but unfortunately the biological reductionist view of schizophrenia as an incurable brain disease is also quite stigmatizing. Much of the initial consumer advocacy agenda would be turned on its head by the turn of the century, as the community grew to include people with mental illness as well as their families, and biological reductionism receded.

Between the "reform" and the "neo-Kraepelinian" agendas, the "therapy" agenda faded into the background, at least with respect to severe mental illness. The superiority of behavioral treatments in institutions appeared to be moot, as the "reform" agenda accelerated toward radical elimination of institutions. The community mental health centers did not replace the institutions as venues for any kind of psychosocial treatment, partly because only a fraction of the number anticipated by the "reform" agenda were actually built. The American Congress has always been more reliable in endorsing social reforms than funding them, but the late 1960s saw a distinct conservative swing, marked by the election of President Richard Nixon in 1968, that opposed the social progressivism of the 1950s and early 1960s. Demand for psychosocial services in the VA did persist, but the moral therapy-derived type was strongly preferred. Milieu-based social learning programs require flexibility in professional hierarchies, staff roles and institutional administration, which biomedical mental health models simply do not have. For the same reason, residential social learning programs never replaced traditional quasi-medical treatment in the remaining psychiatric institutions. Psychosocial treatments became limited to occupational and recreational activities, ad hoc applications of patient government and other fragments of therapeutic community, and "supportive group therapy," all considered incidental to actual medical "treatment." Further development of psychosocial treatment for schizophrenia was discouraged by the failure of Carl Rogers' attempt to help institutionalized patients with his humanistic therapy approach (Rogers, 1967), and the negative results of Philip R. A. May's controlled trials of psychodynamic psychotherapy (May & Tuma, 1965).

Deinstitutionalization proceeded. By the late 1970s the national psychiatric hospital census had shrunk by about half, on its way to an eventual 90%

reduction by the end of the century. This was driven by a multiplicity of factors, including the nationwide swing to more conservative politics, which pressured state governments to eliminate the high costs of state hospitals. Federal legislation continued to indirectly support community-based health-care, most importantly through the new Medicaid program. Medicaid subsidized state-level healthcare for indigent citizens, including those with severe and disabling mental illness. Medicaid funding would have a pervasive influence on the development of service system design, not only through access to funding, but also through the rules and regulations for using the funds. Medicaid laid the foundation for our contemporary regulatory practices for mental health services, both institutional and community-based. The regulatory canon hasn't changed sufficiently, since its beginning in the 1960s, to accommodate 50 years of evolving science and clinical practice. Nevertheless, in most venues today the regulations are at least not incompatible with provision of a reasonably complete array of psychiatric rehabilitation services in community settings. Regulations cannot be the sole explanation of why such arrays are rare. Medicaid also accelerated deinstitutionalization through *the Institutions for Mental Disease (IMD) exclusion rule*, which prohibited federal Medicaid subsidies for institutional treatment (i.e., state hospitals and nursing homes).

It was soon apparent that deinstitutionalization was not working as expected (Bachrach, 1978; Jones, 1975; Klerman, 1977; Unattributed Editorial, 1974). In addition to the sheer lack of sustained support from federal and local governments, the reasons for failure were understood to be unfulfilled expectations about the benefits of antipsychotic drugs, ineffectiveness of psychotherapy models that had been developed for non-psychotic populations, failure to appreciate individual differences, including within those diagnosed with schizophrenia, and failure to develop psychosocial services to help deinstitutionalized patients adjust to life in the community.

An early response to the problems with deinstitutionalization was *assertive community treatment* (ACT; Stein & Test, 1985), not so much a treatment approach but an organizational model for supporting deinstitutionalized people in community settings. Originally described as "a hospital without walls," ACT did not stray very far from a medical-institutional model, with emphasis on drug treatment and help with activities of daily living. Controlled research supported its effectiveness at reducing institutional recidivism, but without improving personal and social functioning. ACT nevertheless became a popular policy solution, and over time some versions evolved the flexibility to incorporate treatment modalities that do improve personal and social functioning.

What happened in the remaining state hospitals is illuminated by parallel activity in the developmental disability system. Almost a decade after the

Medicaid legislation, it was revised to allow Medicaid coverage for treatment and services provided in *Intermediate Care Facilities for the Mentally Retarded (ICFs/MR)*. This was a direct result of advocacy by parents of people with developmental disabilities and a new community of professionals, primarily psychologists with special education backgrounds. The advocacy effort was substantially enhanced by a number of lawsuits directed at improving conditions in state operated institutions for people with mental retardation (e.g., *New York State Association for Retarded Children, Inc. v. Rockefeller*, 1975; *Halderman v. Pennhurst State School & Hospital*, 1977).

Subsequent regulations for accessing Medicaid funding required that facilities adopt a widely accepted developmental model to guide services, use an "interdisciplinary model," and provide individualized "active treatment," for the express purpose of habilitation, with the intent of preparing individuals to live in community settings. These regulations fostered relatively high quality services in the remaining developmental institutions as well as community services. Because the IMD exclusion rule was never changed for psychiatric services, the state hospitals never experienced these incentives. Individuals with serious mental illness in most state operated psychiatric facilities continued to languish.

Research and development on psychosocial treatment of schizophrenia did not die in the era of deinstitutionalization, it survived in a few university and medical school settings around the country, most notably Boston University, UCLA, and the University of Pittsburgh. In Boston, William Anthony (1979) formulated psychiatric rehabilitation as a translation of rehabilitation psychology to the psychiatric context, surpassing in comprehensiveness and sophistication the early efforts after World War II and the psychosocial clubhouses of the 1960s. This version of psychiatric rehabilitation changed the most fundamental premise of traditional treatment, identifying schizophrenia and other severe mental illnesses as *disabilities to be overcome*, rather than incurable diseases. At UCLA, Robert Liberman and colleagues organized a robust research center to continue development of behavior therapy applications for schizophrenia, including training materials and related resources to facilitate dissemination. Unsurprisingly, the Boston and UCLA models merged in the 1980s (Liberman & Anthony, 1986) as psychiatric rehabilitation incorporated the specific tools that behavior therapy provided. In Pittsburgh, Gerard Hogarty (a social worker by background) and colleagues progressed from rigorous study of interactions between pharmacological and psychosocial treatments to development of dyadic therapy approaches specialized for the schizophrenia spectrum (Hogarty & Flesher 1999; Hogarty et al., 1986, 1995).

The 1970s also saw the progression of behavior therapy to become *cognitive* behavior therapy, expanding exponentially in conceptual depth and scope.

A landmark relevant to the schizophrenia spectrum was the doctoral dissertation of Donald Meichenbaum, later to become a key figure in the maturation of the cognitive behavioral paradigm. Meichenbaum (1969) demonstrated that training in a self-instructional routine to focus attention and maintain concentration improved the performance of patients with schizophrenia on a variety of laboratory tasks, including an objectively scored Rorschach. That finding was soon complemented in an experimental psychopathology laboratory, with a demonstration that cognitive training in monitoring time passage and incidental task features could eliminate the reaction time abnormalities with which David Shakow built his theory of segmental set (Kaplan, 1974). The behavioral techniques developed at UCLA began to include features to compensate for the attention and short-term memory problems found in schizophrenia, enhancing both patient engagement (often a problem in therapy with patients with psychotic disorders) and effectiveness.

Perhaps inevitably, the cognitive impairments of schizophrenia themselves became the targets of cognitive behavioral therapy (Kurtz, 2015). This rankled many in the psychiatric and mental health policy establishment because the immutability of cognitive impairment, premised in the Kraepelinian and neo-Kraepelinian view of schizophrenia as a kind of dementia, was a cornerstone of policy and practice. However, this was increasingly questioned even for actual dementia, as computer technology provided the means efficiently to isolate, exercise, and sometimes restore specific cognitive impairments (Prigatano et al., 1984). By the 1990s at least three distinct but complementary models for treating the cognitive impairments of schizophrenia had been developed (Brenner et al., 1994; Hogarty & Flesher, 1999; Medalia et al., 1998). The first rigorously controlled clinical trial showing a unique contribution of cognitively-targeted therapy to outcome in a multimodal psychiatric rehabilitation program appeared at the end of the twentieth century (Spaulding et al., 1999).

Experimentation with cognitive and cognitive behavioral therapies reflected a convergence with psychopathology and neuropsychology paradigms. By the mid-1990s schizophrenia was being characterized as a neurocognitive disorder. Therapy techniques increasingly included components that addressed multiple levels of cognitive and behavioral functioning, from the conventional targets of cognitive behavioral therapy (e.g., interpersonal problem-solving) to concept processing, memory, attention and other processes from the experimental psychopathology and neuropsychology laboratories, social perception and cognition, beliefs and attitudes, and meta-cognitive processes associated with personal history and selfhood. The cross-fertilization from this convergence is ubiquitous in the current psychiatric rehabilitation research.

Despite the wealth of research showing superiority of the psychiatric rehabilitation model, it did not become the first recourse for schizophrenia and other severe mental illness, at least in the American mental health services system. The reasons are convoluted. A crucially important feature of the new psychiatric rehabilitation model was its focus on functional impairments of schizophrenia, beyond the psychotic symptoms that constitute its diagnostic criteria. This was consistent with the vision of the mental hygiene movement and the American mental health policy establishment of the 1950s and 1960s, and should have promoted psychiatric rehabilitation more than it did. Unlike token economy, the new psychiatric rehabilitation model was not dependent on the persistence of institutions, but neither was it well-suited to the medical clinic-like settings that most community mental health centers had become, limited to drug prescribing and traditional counseling approaches designed for other patient populations. Treating the diagnostic symptoms had become the exclusive focus of the neo-Kraepelinian psychiatric establishment and the psychopharmaceutical industry, and psychosocial services were not considered "treatment" (Klein, 1980). Adolf Meyer's holistic vision may have helped inspire deinstitutionalization, but did not survive it.

Disappointment with deinstitutionalization was accompanied by the realization that conditions in the remaining institutions were as bad as ever. One response of the mental health policy community was a litigation approach that began during the mental hygiene movement era. Protective standards in three primary areas were pursued: requirements for being involuntarily institutionalized, requirements for ending involuntary institutionalization, and standards for treatment while confined to the institution.

In 1951, NIMH had issued model legislation for civil commitment that required evaluations by medical professionals and other formalizations of the process. States gradually implemented versions over the years and there was significant subsequent litigation that hammered out constitutional implications, such as equal protection claims when civil commitment statutes treated similarly situated individuals differently (e.g., people with mental illness had a different standard of evidence than similar laws for people with developmental disabilities; *Heller v. Doe by Doe*, 1993). The most consistent holding across cases is that the deprivation of liberty inherent in civil commitment triggers procedural and substantive due process protections (e.g., *Specht v. Patterson*, 1967, *Youngberg v. Romeo*, 1982). Procedurally, the US Supreme Court required access to counsel as well as an opportunity to be heard, to cross-examine witnesses, and to offer evidence (*Specht v. Patterson*, 1967), although a federal court in Wisconsin went further by requiring very specific protections, such as exclusion of hearsay evidence and privilege against self-incrimination (*Lessard v. Schmidt*, 1972). The standard of evidence for these proceedings in any state must be at least clear and convincing (*Addington v. Texas*, 1979).

Substantively, the Supreme Court held that the Constitution requires that civil commitment be based on dangerousness plus a finding, grounded in scientific evidence, that there is some limit to the individual's volitional control of the dangerousness, such as a mental illness (*Kansas v. Hendricks*, 1997). Functionally, "imminent dangerousness" is now virtually a universal requirement written into state statutes controlling involuntary treatment. It is in the consideration of dangerousness and the individual's clinical needs that a familiar principle, commonly applied in legal analyses of intrusions on constitutional rights, emerges – the "least restrictive alternative" (e.g., *Lake v. Cameron*, 1966). The least restrictive alternative has given rise to a number of outpatient involuntary treatment options, such as outpatient civil commitment, outpatient competency restoration services, and outpatient supervision of people previously adjudicated *not guilty by reason of insanity* (NGRI). The latter two have become increasingly relevant as, over the past several decades, state hospital populations have shifted from primarily people who were civilly committed to include forensic populations (Melton et al., 2017). Litigation about commitment standards was a boon to the emerging discipline of forensic clinical psychology, leading to significant improvements in risk assessment and management technology, as well as the development of treatment approaches to restore a person's competence to stand trial.

The fundamental bases of beginning and ending involuntary hospitalization are two sides of the same coin: as soon as the initial justification for involuntary hospitalization is no longer met, it is unconstitutional for it to continue (*O'Connor v. Donaldson*, 1975). However, beyond constitutional requirements, the most significant case establishing standards for ending involuntary hospitalization is unquestionably *Olmstead v. L.C. ex rel Zimring* (1999). The *Olmstead* holding turned on the Americans with Disabilities Act (ADA, 1990), and specifically, its classification of "unjustified segregation" as impermissible discrimination. Although *Olmstead* has broad applications to all people with disabilities, the case arose from the situation of two women in psychiatric hospitals and has particular implications for ending involuntary hospitalizations. Essentially, once the individual and treatment team agree that community placement is appropriate, it is impermissible discrimination for the state to continue the now unjustified segregation from the community by failing to provide appropriate services in the community. Notably, a simple lack of financial resources is not an adequate defense by the state in the face of an *Olmstead* accusation.

The final litigation focus was on the "right to treatment" – the principle that people involuntarily committed have a right to effective services. In 1972, a federal court in Alabama ruled in *Wyatt v. Stickney* that people in psychiatric institutions have a right to a humane environment, qualified providers, sufficient staffing, and individualized treatment plans that provide a genuine opportunity to return to society. Although other federal courts have similarly held that insufficient treatment is tantamount to a due process violation (e.g., *Rouse v. Cameron*, 1966; *Donaldson v. O'Connor*, 1974), the US Supreme Court has certified only that people undergoing involuntary treatment have the right to safe confinement and freedom from bodily restraints (*Youngberg v. Romeo*, 1982) and that the nature and duration of confinement must be reasonably related to the purpose of confinement (*Jackson v. Indiana*, 1972). However, in recognition of the nationwide scope of this problem, the US Congress passed the Civil Rights of Institutionalized Persons Act (CRIPA), which included a special litigation section (i.e., the current Civil Rights Division) within the US Department of Justice whose mission was to litigate against state governments that were violating the standards defined in the law. The ADA and *Olmstead* are also enforced within this division. To this day, dozens of state psychiatric institutions have been indicted under the terms of CRIPA, the Americans with Disabilities Act, and *Olmstead*, with most ending in consent decrees in which the state agrees to fund and undertake reforms.

It is unclear how the litigation and legislation of the deinstitutionalization era affected institutional practices or services for severe mental illness in general. Analyses of civil commitment processes suggest that raising or lowering commitment standards do not have much effect on who gets committed or otherwise treated involuntarily. Whether outpatient commitment is even enforceable remains under debate today. Any benefits obviously depend on appropriate outpatient services being available, and unless they are, there is demonstrably no benefit. There is no reason to believe that outpatient commitment laws have stimulated development of treatment availability, and the requirement is arbitrarily limited to drug treatment in some states. The right to treatment principles and CRIPA/ADA litigation have undoubtedly generated new expenditures, but there has never been a systematic analysis of these cases and hence no evidence as to whether court-ordered reforms have produced the desired outcomes.

If this history of litigation failed to bring about meaningful reform, it could be at least partially attributable to regulatory failure. It is more difficult to show that practices are substandard when the standards are poorly defined. Medicaid regulations were never subjected to the pressures for conceptual coherence and validated practices that accrued from Medicaid funding for the institutional developmental disability system. Regulations remained generic, focused on preservation of traditional medical-model administrative structures and professional hierarchies, and meaningless criteria for "individualized treatment plans." There is still no clear demand or incentive for selective use of validated practices in regulation of Medicaid-funded services for severe and disabling mental illness. This applies even to remaining state institutions, most of which are under Medicaid-based regulations even without access to Medicaid funding.

A more indirect benefit of legal reform activity was widespread attention to *therapeutic jurisprudence* (Winick, 1991), strategic use of legal/judicial processes for therapeutic purposes (as well as justice). Mental health courts are one application, and are increasingly replacing older models of involuntary treatment (Watson et al., 2000). To the degree that an attorney or mental health court acts like a mental health practitioner, the science of psychosocial treatment is logically pertinent. However, developments in this domain have mostly been limited to ways to coerce acceptance of other treatments, especially drug treatment.

The Turn of the Twenty-First Century

Since the turn of the century the evidence-based modalities in the psychiatric rehabilitation array have continued to proliferate. It is no longer useful to validate any modality simply by showing that it is better than "treatment as usual" (generally, medication and case management). It must add meaningfully to the outcome of individualized treatment and rehabilitation regimens. Beyond demonstrating effectiveness, findings include what happens when best practices are *removed* from service systems (Spaulding & Sullivan, 2016; Tarasenko et al., 2013). The key research questions have shifted from validation of new modalities to identification of the active ingredients and optimally combining them into clinically accessible and cost-efficient packages (e.g., Kern et al., 2014; Roder & Medalia, 2010). Specific modalities, especially those in a dyadic therapy format, address recovery in five overlapping domains (Spaulding & Sullivan, 2017): (1) recruiting the client to the rehabilitation agenda, (2) identifying and committing to recovery goals, (3) improving interpersonal functioning, (4) improving emotional and psychophysiological self-regulation, and (5) resolving family conflicts. The proportion of evidence-based practices that are widely disseminated and employed has shrunk, because there are more of them.

In the mental health policy world, the twentieth century ended with another indictment of the American mental healthcare system (US Surgeon General, 1999). Beyond the failures of deinstitutionalization, the report cited failure fundamentally to understand and respond to the problems of SMI. It identified the idea of *recovery* as key to reform. The idea of recovery was by then a fusion of the message of a consumer movement, rebelling against the dehumanizing aspects of medical model public psychiatric services, with renewed concern for the needs and rights of people with disabilities, continuing the momentum of post-deinstitutionalization advocacy and legal reform.

In 2004 another national commission, The President's New Freedom Commission on Mental Health, issued its report, defining a multidimensional concept of recovery as the keynote for transformation of the mental health system (Spaulding et al., 2016). There followed several years of debate on meanings and implications, and gradually the idea did transform services, or at least the social climate of the mental health system. Recovery principles emphasize autonomy, choice, and other consumer/patient rights. This synergized with the social momentum for civil rights of people with disabilities. The right to individualized treatment is a right especially pertinent to psychiatric rehabilitation principles and practice. The recovery movement has been in a sense the mirror image of psychiatric rehabilitation, the same thing seen from the perspective of the consumer/patient versus the practitioner. At the same time, the recovery idea blurs the boundary between traditional mental health services and a supportive, beneficent social environment, a true "therapeutic community." Psychiatric rehabilitation and other professional services are only one of many types of resources for pursuing recovery. Potentially, the recovery movement can be the integration of humanitarian values, social policy and treatment technology envisioned by Beers and Meyer and lost in the deinstitutionalization era.

Advocacy groups' critiques of deinstitutionalization have also become broader critiques of service shortages, especially for the SMI population (Fuller et al., 2016; Pinals & Fuller, 2017; Torrey et al., 2008, 2012). The mental health policy agenda has expanded to address needs for longer-term residential treatment, beyond medical model "inpatient" services, to include community-based involuntary treatment, now euphemistically termed "assisted" treatment. These would obviously be new venues for application of best rehabilitation practices. However, the potential impact of such reforms is significantly limited by the recent Trump administration policy. Prior to leaving the DOJ in 2018, Attorney General Jeff Sessions set new policy limiting further use of consent decrees, requiring they be based on allegations of serious violations rather than general unconstitutional behavior, they must contain a "sunset date" rather than being enforced until improvement is shown, and they must be approved by high level political appointees rather than long-time DOJ attorneys (Benner, 2018). These changes all make it more difficult to use consent decrees to effect meaningful reform. Once again, the course of mental health reform was affected by a changing national political climate.

Advocacy has also addressed the explosion of people with SMI in correctional settings (e.g., Kim et al., 2015) and overuse of police in community settings (e.g., Teplin, 2000). It is unclear how much this reflects deinstitutionalization and underfunding versus the general increase in incarceration and related changes in policing that began in the 1990s, but either way, the issue is not limited to rehabilitation for SMI. In both institution and community, the most urgent need is for general mental health services, including for substance abuse and personality disorders. In correctional institutions, the barriers to developing best practice psychiatric rehabilitation are comparable to those of traditional psychiatric institutions.

Conclusion

To realize the promises of psychiatric rehabilitation, the recovery movement, and progressive policy, psychosocial treatment for SMI must address multiple levels of personal and social functioning, from neurocognition to social skills to freedom from stigma and access to desirable social roles, pursuing goals that have meaning and importance to the patient. The historical gap between policy-driven public health and science-driven clinical practice must be bridged. Both policy and regulation must jointly foster use of best practices, at the administrative and clinical levels. As in other areas of public health, the best policy is informed by clinical realities, and the best clinical tools can be useless when policy renders them inaccessible. The recovery movement importantly emphasizes choice, but choice becomes meaningless when the options are largely inaccessible.

REFERENCES

Addington v. Texas, 441 U.S. 418 (1979).
Americans with Disabilities Act (ADA) of 1990, 42 U.S.C. §§ 12101-12213, Pub. L. No. 101-336, 104 Stat. 328 (1990)
Arieti, S. (1955). *Interpretation of schizophrenia*. New York: R. Brunner.
Austin, N., Liberman, R., King, L., & DeRisi, W. (1976). A comparative evaluation of two day hospitals: Goal attainment scaling in behavior therapy vs. milieu therapy. *Journal of Nervous and Mental Disease, 163*, 253–261.
Ayllon, T., & Azrin, N. H. (1968). Reinforcer sampling: A technique for increasing the behavior of mental patients. *Journal of Applied Behavior Analysis*, 1, 13–20. doi:10.1901/jaba. 1968.1–13
Ayllon, T., & Michael, J. (1959). The psychiatric nurse as a behavioral engineer 1. *Journal of the Experimental Analysis of Behavior*, 2(4), 323–334.
Bachrach, L. L. (1978). A conceptual approach to deinstitutionalization. *Hospital & Community Psychiatry, 29*(9), 573–578.
Bachrach, L. L. (1983). An overview of deinstitutionalization. *New Directions for Mental Health Services, 1983*(17), 5–14. doi:10.1002/yd.23319831703
Bellak, L., Hurvich, M., & Gediman, H. (1973). *Ego functions in schizophrenics, neurotics, and normals*. New York: Wiley.
Benner, K. (2018, November). Sessions, in last-minute act, sharply limits use of consent decrees to curb olice abuses. *The New York Times*.
Bettelheim, B., & Sylvester, E. (1948). A therapeutic milieu. *American Journal of Orthopsychiatry, 18*(2), 191–206. doi:10.1111/j.1939-0025.1948.tb05078.x
Von Bertalanffy, L. (1950). An outline of general system theory. *British Journal for the Philosophy of Science, 1*, 134–165. doi:10.1093/bjps/I.2.134
Bond, G., Dincin, J., Setze, P., & Witheridge, T. (1984). The effectiveness of psychiatric rehabilitation: A summary of research at Thresholds. *Psychosocial Rehabilitation Journal, 7*, 6–22.
Braginsky, B. M., Braginsky, D. D., & Ring, K. (1969). *Methods of madness: The mental hospital as last resort*. New York: Holt, Rhinehart & Winston.

Brenner, H., Roder, V., Hodel, B., Kienzle, N., Reed, D., & Liberman, R. (1994). *Integrated psychological therapy for schizophrenic patients.* Toronto: Hogrefe & Huber.

Cannon, T. D., & Mednick, S. A. (1993). The schizophrenia high-risk project in Copenhagen: Three decades of progress. *Acta Psychiatrica Scandinavica, 87* (370), 33–47. doi:10.1111/j.1600-0447.1993.tb05359.x. PMID 8452053

Cerreto, M. C. (2001). Olmstead: The Brown v. Board of Education for Disability Rights – Promises, limits, and issues. *Loyola Journal of Public Interest Law, 3,* 47.

Croog, S. H. (1956). Patient government—Some aspects of participation and social background on two psychiatric wards. *Psychiatry: Journal for the Study of Interpersonal Processes, 19,* 203–207.

Dain, N., & Carlson, E. T. (1960). Milieu therapy in the nineteenth century: Patient care at the Friend's Asylum, Frankford, Pennsylvania, 1817–1861. *Journal of Nervous and Mental Disease, 131,* 277–290. doi:10.1097/00005053-196010000-00001

Deutsch, A. (1948). *The shame of the states.* New York: Harcourt Brace World.

Donaldson v. O'Connor 493 F.2d 507 (1974).

Fairweather, G., Sanders, D., Maynard, H., & Cressler, D. (1969). *Community life for the mentally ill: An alternative to institutional care.* Chicago: Aldine.

Faris, R., & Dunham, H. (1939). *Mental disorders in urban areas: An ecological study of Schizophrenia and other psychoses.* Oxford, England: University of Chicago Press.

Fisher, S. H., & Beard, J. H. (1962). Fountain house: A psychiatric rehabilitation program. *Current Psychiatric Therapies, 2,* 211–218.

Fromm-Reichmann F. (1948). Notes on the development of treatment of schizophrenics by psychoanalytic psychotherapy. *Psychiatry, 11*(3), 263–273.

Fuller, D.A., Sinclair, E., Geller, J., Quanbeck, C., & Snook, J. (2016). *Going, going, gone: Trends and consequences of eliminating state psychiatric beds.* Treatment Advocacy Center: Arlington, VA.

Gelfand, D. M., Gelfand, S., & Dobson, W. R. (1967). Unprogrammed reinforcement of patients' behavior in a mental hospital. *Behaviour Research and Therapy, 5*(3), 201–207.

Gerhardt, S. (1968). The evolution of a patient government. *Hospital & Community Psychiatry, 19*(10), 329–330.

Goffman, E. (1961). *Asylums.* Garden City, NY: Doubleday, Anchor Books.

Gottesman, I. I., & Erlenmeyer-Kimling, L. (2001). Family and twin strategies as a head start in defining prodomes and endophenotypes for hypothetical early-interventions in schizophrenia. *Schizophrenia Research, 51*(1), 93–102. doi:10.1016/S0920-9964(01)00245-6

Gur, R. E., Gur, R. C., Keshavan, M. S., Kohler, C., & Walker, E. (2017). Prevention of schizophrenia. In D. L. Evans, E. B. Foa, R. E. Gur, H. Hendin, C. P. O'Brien, D. Romer, M. E. P. Seligman, & B. T. Walsh (Eds.), *Treating and preventing adolescent mental health disorders: What we know and what we don't know: A research agenda for improving the mental health of our youth.*, 2nd ed. (pp. 157–180). New York, NY: Oxford University Press.

Halderman v. Pennhurst State School & Hospital, 446 F. Supp. 1295, 1306 (E.D. Pa. 1977)

Harrison, A. (2019). *Mind fixers: Psychiatry's troubled search for the biology of mental illness.* New York: Norton.

Heller v. Doe by Doe, 509 U.S. 312 (1993)

Hogarty, G., Anderson, C., Reiss, D., Kornblith, S., Greenewald, D., Javno, C., & Madonia, M. (1986). Family psycho-education, social skills training and maintenance chemotherapy: I. One-year effects of a controlled study on relapse and expressed emotion. *Archives of General Psychiatry, 43*, 633–642.

Hogarty, G., Kornblith, S., Greenwald, D., & DiBarry, A. (1995). Personal therapy: A disorder-relevant psychotherapy for schizophrenia. *Schizophrenia Bulletin, 21*(3), 379–393.

Hogarty, G. E., & Flesher, S. (1999). Practice principles of cognitive enhancement therapy for schizophrenia. *Schizophrenia Bulletin, 25*(4), 693708.

Hollingshead, A. B., & Redlich, F. (1958). *Social class and mental illness.* New York: Wiley.

Hyde, R. W., & Solomon, H. C. (1950). Patient government: A new form of group therapy. *Digest of Neurology & Psychiatry, 18*, 207–218.

Jackson v. Indiana, 406 U.S. 715 (1972)

Joint Commission on Mental Illness and Health. (1961). *Action for mental health: Final report of the Joint Commission on Mental illness and Health.* New York: Basic Books.

Jones, M. (1953). *The therapeutic community.* New York: Basic Books.

Jones, M. (1975). Community care for chronic mental patients: The need for a reassessment. *Hospital & Community Psychiatry, 26*(2), 94–98.

Kane, J. M., Robinson, D. G., Schooler, N. R., Mueser, K. T., Penn, D. L., Rosenheck, R. A., . . . & Heinssen, R. K. (2016). Comprehensive versus usual community care for first-episode psychosis: 2-year outcomes from the NIMH RAISE early treatment program. *American Journal of Psychiatry, 173*(4), 362–372.

Kaplan, R. (1974). *The cross-over phenomenon: Three studies of the effect of training and information on process schizophrenic reaction time.* (Unpublished doctoral dissertation), University of Waterloo, Ontario, Canada.

Kansas v. Hendricks, 521 U.S. 346 (1997)

Kern, R., Horan, W., Glynn, S., Reddy, L., Holden, J., Granholm, E., . . . & Spaulding, W. (2014). Psychosocial rehabilitation and psychotherapy approaches. In P. Janicak, S. Marder, R. Tandon and M. Goldman (eds.) *Schizophrenia: Recent advances in diagnosis and treatment* (Chapter 14). New York: Springer.

Kim, K., Becker-Cohen, M., & Serakos, M. (2015). *The Processing and treatment of mentally ill persons in the criminal justice system: A scan of practice and background analysis.* Washington, DC: Urban Institute Research Report.

Klein, D. (1980). Psychosocial treatment of schizophrenia, or psychosocial help for people with schizophrenia? *Schizophrenia Bulletin, 6*(1), 122–130.

Klerman, G. (1977). Better but not well: Social and ethical issues in the deinstitutionalization of the mentall ill. *Schizophrenia Bulletin, 3*, 617–631.

Klerman, G. (1978). The evolution of a scientific nosology. In J. Shershow (Ed.), *Schizophrenia: Research and practice* (pp. 99–121). Cambridge, MA: Harvard University Press.

Kurtz, M. M. (2015). *Schizophrenia and its treatment: Where is the progress?* Oxford University Press, Oxford, UK.

Lake v. Cameron, 364 F.2d 657 (1966)

Laing, R. (1960). *The divided self.* New York: Pantheon.

Lessard v. Schmidt, 349 F.Supp. 1078 (1972)

Lindsley, O. R. (1956). Operant conditioning methods applied to research in chronic schizophrenia. *Psychiatric Research Reports, 5*, 118–139.

Manasse, G. O., & des Jardins, L. (1983). Highlights of a survey of patient governments and councils in VA medical centers. *Hospital & Community Psychiatry, 34*(2), 168–169.

Marmor, J., & Pumpian-Mindlin, E. (1950). Toward an integrative conception of mental disorder. *Journal of Nervous and Mental Disease, 111*, 19–29. doi:10 .1097/00005053-195011110-00002

May, P. R. A., & Tuma, A. H. (1965). Treatment of schizophrenia: An experimental study of five treatment methods. *The British Journal of Psychiatry, 111*(475), 503–510. doi:10.1192/bjp.111.475.503

Medalia, A., Aluma, M., Tryon, W., & Merriam, A. E. (1998). Effectiveness of attention training in schizophrenia. *Schizophrenia Bulletin, 24*(1), 147–152. doi:10 .1093/oxfordjournals.schbul.a033306

Meehl, P. E. (1962). Schizotaxia, schizotypy and schizophrenia. *American Psychologist, 17*, 827–838.

Meichenbaum, D. (1969). The effects of instructions and reinforcement on thinking and language behavior of schizophrenics. *Behavior Research and Therapy, 7*, 101–114.

Melton, G. B., Petrila, J., Poythress, N. G., Slobogin, C., Otto, R. K., Mossman, D., & Condie, L. O. (2017). *Psychological evaluations for the courts: A handbook for mental health professionals and lawyers.* Guilford Press, New York, NY, USA: Guilford Publications.

Moreno, J. L. (1969). *Psychodrama volume 3: Action therapy and principles of practice.* New York: Beacon House.

Mosher, L. (1999). Soteria and other alternatives to acute psychiatric hospitalization: A personal and professional review. *Journal of Nervous and Mental Disease, 187*, 142–149.

Murray, E. J., & Cohen, M. (1959). Mental illness, milieu therapy, and social organization in ward groups. *The Journal of Abnormal and Social Psychology, 58*(1), 48–54. doi:10.1037/h0049173

New York State Ass'n for Retarded Children, Inc. v. Rockefeller, 357 F. Supp. 752, 764 (1975)

O'Connor v. Donaldson, 422 U.S. 563 (1975)

Olmstead v. L.C. ex rel Zimring, 527 U.S. 581 (1999)

Pasamanick, B. (1962). Review of Action for mental health: Final report of the Joint Commission on Mental Illness and Health. *American Journal of Orthopsychiatry, 32*(3), 539–550. doi:10.1111/j.1939-0025.1962.tb00305.x

Paul, G. L., & Lentz, R. J. (1977). *Psychosocial treatment of chronic mental patients: Milieu vs. social learning programs.* Cambridge: Harvard University Press.

Pinals, D.A., & Fuller, D. (2017). *Beyond beds: The vital role of a full continuum of psychiatric care.* Arlington, VA: Treatment Advocacy Center:

Prigatano, G. P., Fordyce, D. J., Zeiner, H. K., Roueche, J. R., Pepping, M., & Wood, B. C. (1984). Neuropsychological rehabilitation after closed head injury in young adults. *Journal of Neurology, Neurosurgery & Psychiatry, 47*(5), 505–513. doi:10 .1136/jnnp.47.5.505

Redl, F. (1959). The concept of a 'therapeutic milieu'. *American Journal of Orthopsychiatry, 29*(4), 721–736. doi:10.1111/j.1939-0025.1959.tb00243.

Roder, V., & Medalia, A. (Eds.). (2010). *Neurocognition and social cognition in schizophrenia patients: Basic concepts and treatment.* Basel: Karger.

Rogers, C. (Ed.). (1967). *The therapeutic relationship and its impact: A study of psychotherapy with schizophrenics.* Madison, WI: University of Wisconsin Press.

Rouse v. Cameron, 373 F.2d 451 (1966)

Smith, D. S., & Hawthorne, M. E. (1949). Psychiatric rehabilitation: A follow-up study of 200 cases. *Naval Medical Bulletin, 49,* 655–669.

Spaulding, W., Montague, E., Avila, A., & Sullivan, M. (2016). The idea of recovery. In N. Singh, J. Barber & S. Van Sant (Eds.), *Handbook of recovery in inpatient psychiatry* (pp. 3–38). New York: Springer.

Spaulding, W., Reed, D., Sullivan, M., Richardson, C., & Weiler, M. (1999). Effects of cognitive treatment in psychiatric rehabilitation. *Schizophrenia Bulletin, 25*(4), 657–676.

Spaulding, W., & Sullivan, M. (2016). Treatment of cognition in the schizophenia spectrum: The context of psychiatric rehabilitation. *Schizophrenia Bulletin, 42*(suppl.1), s53–s61.

Spaulding, W., & Sullivan, M. (2017). Psychotherapy and the schizophrenia spectrum. In A. Consoli, L. Beutler & B. Bongar (Eds.), *Comprehensive textbook of psychotherapy: Theory and Practice* (2nd edition) (Chapter 25). New York: Oxford University Press.

Spaulding, W., Sullivan, M., & Poland, J. (2003). *Treatment and rehabilitation of severe mental illness.* New York: Guilford.

Specht v. Patterson, 386 U.S. 604 (1967)

Stein, L. I., & Test, M. A. (1985). The evolution of the Training in Community Living model. *New Directions for Mental Health Services, 26,* 7–16. doi:10.1002/yd .23319852603

Sullivan, H. S. (1953). *The interpersonal theory of psychiatry.* W W Norton & Co.

Szaz, T. (1961). *The myth of mental illness.* New York, NY, USA: Harper & Row.

Tarasenko, M., Sullivan, M., Ritchie, A. J., & Spaulding, W. D. (2013). Effects of eliminating psychiatric rehabilitation from the secure levels of a mental-health service system. *Psychological Services, 10,* 442–451.

Teplin, L. A. (2000). Keeping the peace: Police discretion and mentally ill persons. *National Institute of Justice Journal, 244,* 8–15.

Torrey, E. F., Entsminger, K., Geller, J., Stanley, J., & Jaffe, D. J. (2015). The shortage of public hospital beds for mentally ill persons. Montana, 303(20.9), 6–9.

Torrey, E., Fuller, D., Geller, J., Jacobs, C., & Ragosta, K. (2012). *No Room at the inn: Trends and consequences of closing public psychiatric hospitals 2005–2010.* Arlington, VA: Treatment Advocacy Center:

Unattributed Editorial. (1974). Community treatment—A broken promise? *Schizophrenia Bulletin, 1*(10), 4–5. doi:10.1093/schbul/1.10.4

U.S. Surgeon General. (1999). *Mental health: A report of the Surgeon General.* Rockville MD: National Institutes of Health, DHHS. Retrieved from http://profiles .nlm.nih.gov/ps/retrieve/ResourceMetadata/NNBBHS

Watson, A., Luchins, D., Hanrahan, P., Heyman, M., & Lurigio, A. (2000). Mental health court: Promises and limitations. *Journal of the American Academy of Psychiatry and the Law, 28,* 476–482.

Winick, D. (Ed.) (1991). *Essays in therapeutic jurisprudence*, Durham, NC: Carolina Academic Press.

Wright, B. A. (1960). *Physical disability—A psychological approach* (Training in social skills, pp. 274–287). New York, NY: Harper & Row.

Wyatt v. Stickney, 344 F.Supp. 387 (1972)

Youngberg v. Romeo, 457 U.S. 307 (1982)

Zubin, J., & Spring, B. (1977). Vulnerability: A new view of schizophrenia. *Journal of Abnormal Psychology, 86*, 103–126.

3 The Rehabilitation Model for Persons with Psychosis

History, Challenges, Controversies, and Future Prospects

Jerome Yoman

A discussion of the history of the rehabilitation model in mental health best begins by defining it. This is a formidable task as the model has been shaped by a dialectic between conceptual models, research, and sociopolitical factors. Spaulding, Sullivan, and Poland's (2003) observation of "confusion and disagreement about what constitutes rehabilitation" (p. 3) still applies, notwithstanding the comprehensive model they proposed. This chapter begins by trying to capture aspects unique and essential to rehabilitation in mental health, which also tend to be areas of agreement among various conceptions of it. These include rehabilitation's target population, a focus on disabilities or disadvantages, the primacy of the client's goals, the role of functional assessment, and a set of components in the rehabilitation plan. This effort will also attempt to explicate details that heretofore have remained implicit. With this as grounding, an overview will ensue of the history of the rehabilitation model and its usefulness going forward.

Defining Psychiatric Rehabilitation

Target Population

Researchers on rehabilitation (e.g., Anthony, Cohen, & Farkas, 1990; Anthony & Liberman, 1986; Spaulding et al., 2003) for persons with mental health problems have adopted the term "psychiatric rehabilitation" for their work. Psychiatric rehabilitation's understanding of its target population, the human beings it endeavors to help, has shaped, and continues to shape its definition. In the United States, a group of people with difficulties living in the community (i.e., disabilities or disadvantages – see below) came into public view after well-intended, but ill-conceived deinstitutionalization in the 1960s. These disabilities may have been the reason they were institutionalized in the first place, or a result of the iatrogenic, and often neglectful and abusive, institutional environment. The community mental health services of that era struggled to serve these individuals if they tried at all. The earliest roots of psychiatric rehabilitation in this country lie in the efforts of researchers, clinicians, and advocates to serve these people who were "falling through the cracks." The population served by rehabilitation has evolved as people have responded to improved services, and with rehabilitation's successes and failures in disseminating and implementing such services and engaging those who might benefit.

Although rehabilitation has primarily focused on people with psychosis and those who fall somewhere on the DSM-5 (American Psychiatric Association, 2013) schizophrenia spectrum (Anthony et al., 1990 – the focus of this book), diagnosis has been an imperfect way to define the target population. Rehabilitation programs have also served individuals without psychosis who carry diagnoses of severe depression, obsessive-compulsive disorder, and bipolar disorder.

One might broadly define the population as people with mental health disabilities, who, due to a mental health problem or condition, have difficulties with functional and coping skills, or lack needed supports, instrumental in achieving life satisfaction or quality of life (cf., Anthony et al., 1990; Anthony & Liberman, 1986). Of course, what constitute "difficulties" and "quality of life" can be heavily influenced by expectations in American culture for employment, independence, and community integration. This highlights the importance of cultural humility and client-direction in formulating rehabilitation goals.[1]

Impairments, Disabilities, and Disadvantages

The distinction between impairments, disabilities, and disadvantages (WHO, 1980; the latter traditionally called "handicaps") is helpful in delineating the target population and goals of psychiatric rehabilitation, and has been important in its definition and development (Anthony & Liberman, 1986; Spaulding et al., 2003; Yoman & Edelstein, 1994; WHO, 1988). These serve as levels of assessment for mental health problems. *Impairments*, defined as "any loss or abnormality of psychological, physiological, or anatomical structure or function" (Anthony & Liberman, 1986, p. 545; cf. WHO, 1980), correspond most closely to diagnostic signs and symptoms of DSM-5 mental disorders. *Disabilities* are "any restriction or lack ... of ability to perform an activity in the manner or within the range considered normal for a human being"

---

[1] "*Client*" is used here to denote the intended beneficiary of professional rehabilitation services. This term has precedent in law, finance, etc., to best denote a collaborative and consultative relationship between one or more professionals and those they serve. The writer acknowledges that this is a label some persons with lived experience of mental health problems reject. It is meant only to denote the intended relationship in rehabilitation settings and not as a term to be used outside those settings. Part of productive collaboration is respect for the chosen identities of individual participants.

(Anthony & Liberman, 1986, p. 545; cf. WHO, 1980). An example of a disability might be that someone does not know how to deliver an effective apology.

Yoman and Edelstein (1994) defined the *disadvantage* level of assessment as the gap between clients' performance and the demands of key environments (working, educational, living, leisure) where the client wishes to succeed (see Figure 3.1). This definition rejects the reliance on the slippery concept "normal" (see Maddux, Gosselin, & Winstead, 2008) in WHO's (1980) definition, potentially promoting more culturally responsive assessment in rehabilitation. It also directs assessment toward the fundamental focus of rehabilitation on both client skills and community supports (Anthony et al., 1990; Anthony & Liberman, 1986; Corrigan, 2016). Examples of disadvantages include a client's dating skills falling short of important expectations of potential romantic partners in his/her community, or the work environment offered by an employer failing to adequately accommodate for a client's concentration difficulties in his/her workplace. This definition of disadvantage addresses concerns of disability advocates (e.g., Crow, 1996) about the omission of social constraints such as discrimination from the definition, and better reflects the biopsychosocial model of disability adopted in WHO's more recent International Classification of Functioning, Disability and Health (WHO, 2002; see also Spaulding et al., 2003).

Most mental health problems can be assessed at any of these three levels. For example, one could neuropsychologically measure mild to major *impairments* in a client's attentional function (and through brain imaging implicate *impairments* in brain structure), but only some of these would result in *disabilities* to perform activities such as conversation or studying for school (by a standard of "normality" such as difference from the mean), and only some disabilities would create *disadvantages* in any particular environment (e.g., a construction job) in which the client wished to succeed (and may create *no* disadvantage in any key environment for the client). These levels of assessment exemplify the biopsychosocial model (see Chapter 2) with their inclusion of biological (e.g., brain structure), psychological (e.g., concentration abilities), and social (key environment) elements of mental health problems. Hopefully the reader can see that as one moves from the impairment to the disadvantage level, the focus and rehabilitation relevance of assessment increases. Assessment at the disadvantage level can help tailor rehabilitation to the client's goals, as well as incorporating systemic barriers and reasonable accommodations.

The Client's Goals

As Corrigan (2016) puts it, the client's goals are "the defining center of rehabilitation" (p. 50). This also places the client at the center of rehabilitation,

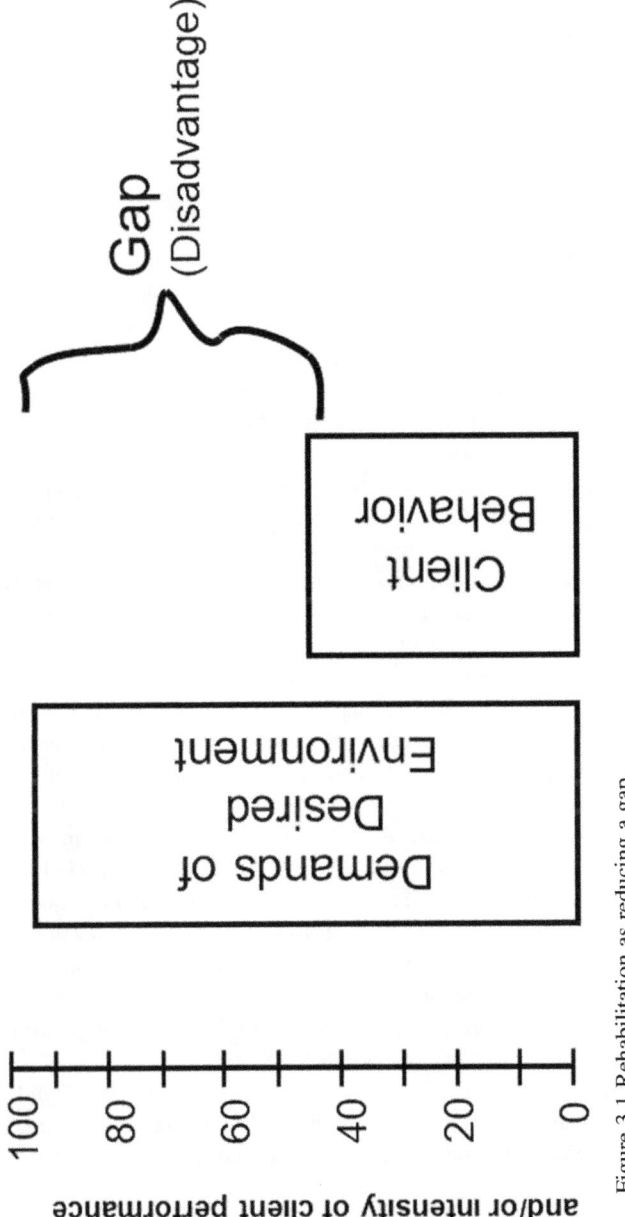

Figure 3.1 Rehabilitation as reducing a gap.

with his/her choices guiding that process (Spaulding et al., 2003). Clients may state the goals of rehabilitation in various ways: overcoming disabilities and barriers, improving independent functioning, success and satisfaction in environments of his/her choice, and enhanced quality of life (Anthony, Cohen, & Farkas, 1990; Anthony & Liberman, 1986; Corrigan 2016; Spaulding et al., 2003; Yoman & Edelstein, 1994).

Functional Assessment

Assessment in psychiatric rehabilitation is called "functional assessment" (Spaulding et al., 2003; Yoman & Edelstein, 1994). It begins with operationally defining (i.e., describing specific observable actions involved in) the client's goals. Functional assessment then measures a client's community living skills, and environmental demands and supports, vis-à-vis his/her goals to establish targets for individualized rehabilitation plans.[2] Functional assessment thus yields a formulation of smaller objectives relevant to the client's goals. Several parameters outline the scope of assessment.

The first parameter is *key environments*. These are the environments in which the client wishes to succeed. They are summarized in the acronym, "WELL": *W*ork, *E*ducation, *L*iving, and *L*eisure (cf. Anthony et al., 1990; Corrigan, 2016). Understanding an individual client's key environments is an important part of culturally competent rehabilitation.

The second parameter is *quality of life* (Pratt, Gill, Barrett, & Roberts, 1999). Two facets of quality of life appear in research. *"Objective quality of life"* (McCall, 1975) refers to external or material success in such areas as income, employment, relationships, health, and safety. This can be operationalized by progress toward, or accomplishment of, individual measurable (usually long-term) goals. *"Subjective quality of life"* is "the sense of well-being and satisfaction experienced by people under their current life conditions" (Lehman, 1983, p. 143, italics added). This has been operationalized by validated questionnaires such as the Quality of Life Inventory (Frisch, 1994) and Satisfaction With Life Scale (Stein & Test, 1980). Smaller goals and objectives are usually necessary to enhance quality of life. Setting quality of life goals may require exploration, reflection, and values clarification with the client. These are long-term goals and the client may prefer to work on shorter-term ones.

The third parameter is *collaboration* centered on identifying and defining the client's goals (Anthony et al., 1990). The client's values and desires provide the direction and focus of functional assessment. Rehabilitation

---

[2] Functional assessment should be distinguished from functional analysis, a fundamental tool of operant conditioning, which identifies antecedents and consequences as part of a behavior change effort (see Yoman, 2008; Yoman & Edelstein, 1994).

professionals listen and draw him/her out on these topics. See Greenwood et al. (2010) and Treichler and Spaulding (2017) for examples.

Rehabilitation Plan Components

Functional assessment sets the stage for an individualized operational definition of psychiatric rehabilitation known as the rehabilitation plan. Rehabilitation participants can then use this operational definition to measure progress and hold each other accountable for implementing rehabilitation. Below is a list of components of a rehabilitation plan that help the client accomplish his/her goals:

1. Client Strengths: What the client is already able to do (e.g., start a conversation)
2. Client Resources:
   a. Available help from friends and family (e.g., help in finding housing from a realtor parent)
   b. Material possessions that might be useful (e.g., a car)
3. Client objectives: shorter-term changes in client behavior (steps) toward the overall goal (e.g., identifying recreational activities of interest)
4. Support person objectives:
   a. Secure new help and support from family and friends (e.g., assistance in writing a resume from a brother who just took a class on this)
   b. Develop relationships and mobilize support from new support persons (e.g., a potential employer willing to offer accommodations for client's distractibility)
5. Services:
   a. Incorporate strengths and resources, (e.g., helping client problem-solve how:
      i. initiating conversations might help identify people willing to join him/her in a recreational activity
      ii. he/she might use his/her car to explore housing options in his/her neighborhood)
   b. Promote accomplishment of client objectives (e.g., engaging the client in behavioral rehearsal of how to ask for registration information at the community college.)
   c. Promote accomplishment of support person objectives (e.g., job developer discussing client's strengths and needs for accommodation with a potential employer)
6. Outcome Assessment Plan: (cf. Spaulding et al., 2003)
   a. How the rehabilitation team will assess progress and success on goals and objectives
   b. Schedule for periodic assessment and review

Hopefully the reader can see from the examples above, how common rehabilitation services such as skills training, family therapy, and supported education, employment, and housing might be employed in such a plan.

In summary, then, *psychiatric rehabilitation* is an approach to serving persons with mental health-related disabilities and disadvantages that promotes accomplishment of their goals. Rehabilitation begins with a functional assessment that clarifies client goals, strengths, and resources, and identifies client and support person objectives toward those goals. Assessment generates a rehabilitation plan that details services to be provided and further assessments to track progress.

The History of Psychiatric Rehabilitation

As noted in the introduction, the history of psychiatric rehabilitation in the United States mental healthcare system has involved the development of conceptual models, advances in research, and the contemporaneous emergence of sociopolitical factors[3] (see Table 3.1 for an overview). Since relevant sociopolitical factors were in motion long before rehabilitation models and research appeared, this overview will begin with the former.

Sociopolitical Factors

The 1943 Amendments to the Vocational Rehabilitation Act were likely prompted by the wounded from World War II (see Spaulding et al., this volume). Important to psychiatric rehabilitation, these amendments made people with mental health disabilities eligible for financial support and vocational rehabilitation, establishing employment-oriented roots for psychiatric rehabilitation (Anthony et al., 1990; Anthony & Liberman, 1986).

Similarly, the Social Security Amendments of 1956 included people over 50 years old with mental health disabilities among those eligible for Social Security Disability Insurance (SSDI). Eligibility required a judgment that these individuals were unemployable. The age restriction was dropped in 1960, along with the requirement for a judgment of permanent unemployability (see Drake, Skinner, Bond, & Goldman, 2009).

As Grob (1992) describes in detail, during these decades, over a half-million people remained confined in "asylums." Policymakers in the nineteenth century had considered asylums as an enlightened and progressive improvement over past abuse and neglect. Grob (1992) goes on to detail how, by the start of

---

[3] In line with the scope and page limits of this volume, this chapter will focus on modern era history in the United States. The reader is referred to Spaulding, Avila, and Evans (this volume), Spaulding et al. (2003), and Anthony and Liberman (1986) for links to history in other countries.

Table 3.1. *A timeline of the history of psychiatric rehabilitation*

Era	Sociopolitical	Research and Conceptual
Pre-1960	1943 Amendments to VRA 1956 SSDI Amendments	1948 Fountain House opened
1960s	Goffman's (1961) *Asylums* Deinstitutionalization began 1963 CMHC Act	Allyon & Azrin's token economy
1970s	CSX Movement grows SS Amendments of 1972 Rehabilitation Act of 1973 1977 CSP created Chamberlain's *On Our Own*	Anthony adapts rehabilitation Paul, Liberman behavioral and social learning work begins Center for Psychiatric Rehab and UCLA sites established
1980s	CSX self-help programs grow	Liberman's work continues to today
	First "Alternatives Conference"	Psych Rehab Journal established
1990s	ADA passed 1990 More self-help expansion More CSX groups First peer support specialists	SIG at ABCT established Further development of rehabilitation methods continues to today
2000 on	National MH Coalition formed Highlander Statement issued New Freedom Commission 2003	

the twentieth century, these state hospitals were characterized by long-term stays, though they had previously regularly discharged large numbers of patients. Local governments hospitalized many people with dementia due to policy changes that eliminated fiscal incentives for continuing to care for them in municipal almshouses. The hospitals, in turn, had little to offer these patients, and a custodial model of care soon extended to patients of all diagnoses. To compound matters these institutions were neglected financially during the Great Depression and World War II. The decline of state hospitals was further accelerated by the exodus of psychiatrists. They preferred to practice emerging psychodynamic therapies in community and private clinics that emerged after World War II. They suggested that people discharged from the state hospitals could be treated in those clinics, but this never came to fruition.

Not surprisingly, the custodial care in institutions had profoundly detrimental and inhumane effects (e.g., Goffman, 1961). This gave rise in the 1960s to a deinstitutionalization movement advocating for the civil rights and humane care of people with mental health problems in the least restrictive setting. In 1955, 77.4% of mental health care episodes were in inpatient facilities, but by 1968 only 47.3% were (Grob, 1992). Unfortunately, necessary community care for people with mental health disabilities, especially in such quality of life areas as housing and employment, did not follow.

Beginning in 1948, with Fountain House (Propst, 1997), the Clubhouse Model (also sometimes known as "psychosocial rehabilitation centers") emerged. Similar programs, Thresholds and Fairweather Lodge, were established in 1959 (Thresholds, n.d.) and 1963 (Fairweather, Sanders, & Tornatzky, 1974), respectively. Depending primarily on self-help and mutual support among people with mental health disabilities, these programs helped members cope with stress and addressed areas the mental healthcare system neglected: housing and employment (Anthony & Liberman, 1986; Spaulding et al., 2003). These programs continue to this day.

The Community Mental Health Centers Act of 1963 was another attempt to redress the neglect of people with mental health disabilities (Anthony & Liberman, 1986; Grob, 1992). Unfortunately, it failed to hire and train staff to provide intensive services necessary to serve such people, echoing the failures of previous decades.

Ball (1973) describes the implications of the Social Security Amendments of 1972 for people with mental health disabilities. These amendments established Supplemental Security Income (SSI), for which people with mental health disabilities and limited income were eligible (effective in 1974). It also extended Medicare coverage to people with disabilities, which subsequently became the means by which many individuals purchase mental healthcare services. The amendments required acceptance of referral to vocational services to maintain eligibility.

The next year, the Rehabilitation Act of 1973 arrived (Anthony & Liberman, 1986). This established affirmative action for people with disabilities, and the government as a model employer. It mandated interventions with the client, but also recognized the value of intervention with society. It took until 1977, after a 25-day demonstration by persons with disabilities, for its anti-discrimination provisions to be implemented (Grim, 2015).

The Community Support Program (CSP; Department of Health and Human Services, 1994) was created in 1977 by the National Institute of Mental Health (NIMH). CSP provided grants to assist states, communities, and technical resource centers in improving opportunities and services for adults with mental health disabilities. It was an overdue first step toward fulfillment of deinstitutionalization ideals and extended into communities work that had begun in hospitals (see below). Unfortunately, its impact and reach were limited.

The movement today called the Consumer/Survivor/Ex-Patient, or CSX, is often traced to the publication of Clifford Beers' (1953) book, "A Mind That Found Itself," originally published in 1908 after Beers was discharged from a psychiatric hospital (Bluebird, n.d.). Less often acknowledged are the early self-help programs of The Clubhouse Model that emerged in the late 1940s. (The information below relies on the history provided by Bluebird, n.d., unless otherwise noted.) This CSX movement increased its numbers and coalesced in the 1970s during the deinstitutionalization movement (Bluebird, n.d.; Davidson, 2016). Its early members tended to identify themselves as "survivors" of the abuses of institutions (e.g., indiscriminate use of electroconvulsive therapy, psychosurgery, seclusion, and restraint – e.g., Chamberlin, 1978) and identified with other civil rights movements of the time (e.g., for African-Americans, women, and LGBTQ people). In 1973, the International Conference on Human Rights and Against Psychiatric Oppression was held (MindFreedom, n.d.a). Judi Chamberlin's (1978) landmark book "On Our Own: Patient Controlled Alternatives to the Mental Health System" codified the grievances and agenda of the movement.

By the 1980s the movement had shifted from an emphasis on demonstrations to the establishment of self-help programs (MindFreedom, n.d.a). The Community Support Program at the NIMH began to provide funding for these alternative programs, including the first annual Alternatives Conference in 1985. Attendees at this conference decided on the term "consumer" to signify mental health care recipients' choice in services. The Substance Abuse and Mental Health Services Administration (SAMHSA) also provided funding for self-help programs.

The 1990s saw a continued expansion of these self-help programs, and a proliferation of consumer groups. Consumer input began to be integrated into systems of care, for example in offices of consumer affairs at state mental health departments. Peer support specialists (CSX persons offering assistance to other CSX persons) began to be hired in paid positions at mental health programs (Davidson, 2016).

In 1990, the Americans with Disabilities Act was passed (see Office of Technology Assessment, 1994). This prohibited discrimination in employment or public services toward people with disabilities. It established serious mental illnesses as among the conditions that might result in disabilities (Davidson, 2016). It also required reasonable accommodations in employment and access to private businesses. It prohibited requiring medical exams or making medical inquiries prior to a job offer.

According to Bluebird (n.d.) and Davidson (2016), the start of the twenty-first century has seen increasing numbers of peer specialists (CSX persons) being trained across the country to work with consumers in a variety of mental healthcare settings. The National Mental Health Coalition has formed to bring together CSX groups. CSX leaders continue to advocate for civil rights, empowerment, and self-determination in actions such as the "Highlander Statement of Concern and Call to Action" (Mind Freedom, n.d. b). The movement has affected rehabilitation by increasing the degree to which consumers can direct their own care and receive it from their peers. The federal government has endorsed the concept of recovery (e.g., President's New Freedom Commission on Mental Health, 2003).

Research and Conceptual Factors

Research on serious mental illnesses and mental health disability began in parallel to the sociopolitical developments detailed above (see Table 3.1). However, the influence of the sociopolitical on research and conceptualization of these problems has become more explicit in recent decades.

Operant and Social Learning Interventions

Psychologists Ayllon and Azrin (1965, 1968) were pioneers in applying operant conditioning to motivate improved functioning in persons hospitalized for mental health disabilities in the mid-to-late 1960s. Their research used a token economy to positively reinforce such behaviors as completion of work assignments, exercise, and grooming. This was a directive approach to making the institutional environment more helpful in preparing patients for discharge, and to counteract some of the iatrogenic aspects of the institution. Patients earned tokens for improved behavior, which they could exchange for special privileges and commissary items.

Psychologist Gordon Paul (Paul & Lentz, 1977) implemented token economies with people with mental health disabilities in similar fashion, using operant techniques such as shaping, and adding social learning techniques (Bandura, 1977), such as modeling, to teach new skills. Among these skills were problem solving, communication, and self-care skills. The program also sought to reduce behaviors likely to cause rehospitalization and/or problems in the community. It used ambitious and careful assessment, staff feedback, and outcome evaluation to attain and demonstrate its effectiveness. Long-term community placement occurred in 97% of the individuals who received the experimental treatment.

Psychiatrist Robert Paul Liberman, an admirer of Paul and Lentz's work (Liberman, 1980), had begun his own operant work in the 1970s with people who had mental health disabilities at the Research Unit at Camarillo State Hospital, and the Clinical Research Center for Schizophrenia and Psychiatric Rehabilitation at the University of California at Los Angeles (see Glynn, 2014, for an overview). His work evolved to emphasize social learning techniques in outpatient settings. In perhaps their greatest contribution, Liberman and colleagues developed, standardized, tested, and disseminated skills training manuals for interpersonal behaviors, problem-solving skills, and symptom and medication management (e.g., Psychiatric Rehabilitation Consultants,

1990). Glynn (2014) suggests his addition of coping (e.g., managing stress and symptoms) and competence (e.g., successes in independent living) to the vulnerability-stress model (Liberman, Mueser, & Wallace, 1986) and his career-long emphasis on clients' valued goals (e.g., Liberman, King, DeRisi, & McCann, 1975), were precursors of the emphasis on strengths and self-determination in the recovery model (see below). Liberman was a pioneer in developing and testing interventions (see Falloon & Liberman, 1983) for families affected by mental health disabilities (Kopelowicz & Zarate, 2014). He trained clinical psychologists and psychiatrists in these techniques, and research methods for demonstrating their efficacy. He began conceptualizing his work as rehabilitation in the early 1980s (Anthony & Liberman, 1986; Liberman & Foy, 1983).

While the use of social learning models continues in current skills training approaches to psychiatric rehabilitation, the use of strongly evidence-based (see Dickerson, Tenhula, & Green-Paden, 2005; Glynn, 1990) operant or contingency management methods such as the token economy has faded in recent decades. Corrigan (1995) made similar observations. Some of the reasons for the decline of token economies are reviewed below.

In the 1960s and 1970s, token economies developed and proliferated in institutional settings. As deinstitutionalization continued in the 1980s and 1990s, hospital stays also became shorter. The fact that token economies are more challenging to implement in community settings (Corrigan, 1991; Corrigan & McCracken, 1995; Glynn, 1990) may be one reason for their decline. Yet institutions have not disappeared. According to the National Mental Health Services Survey (https://www.samhsa.gov/data/sites/default/files/reports/rpt29388/2019_NMHSS/2019-NMHSS-R.pdf), over 1600 inpatient and residential mental health treatment facilities existed in 2019. There is evidence that token economies make such facilities safer and more humane (Corrigan, 1995), and they have been widely implemented to reduce medication use (Paul & Lentz, 1977) and restrictive measures such as seclusion and restraint (Dickerson, Ringel, Parente, & Boronow, 1994; LePage, 1999). Related to this is their reduction in clients' assaultive behavior (e.g., LePage, 1999), an important change to promote clients' discharge from residential treatment, retention in less restrictive settings, and avoidance of the correctional system. The worst abuses in institutional settings result from punitive practices. An important principle of token economies is maximizing positive reinforcement and minimizing punishment (Dickerson et al., 2005; LePage, 1999). For all these reasons, token economies may reduce the traumatic nature of inpatient and residential admissions.

While such issues as buy-in from the client's support system and the availability of competing reinforcers can be obstacles, token economies can be successfully implemented in community outpatient settings (Dickerson

64   Jerome Yoman

et al., 2005; Glynn, 1990). Corrigan (1991; Corrigan & McCracken, 1995) made recommendations for addressing some of the associated challenges. These include enlisting family and the whole treatment team to support and extend the benefits of the program (Corrigan, 1991)

A second reason for the decline in the use of token economies may be the challenges of implementing them in any setting. Such challenges may include staff and administrative attitudes and motivations (Dickerson et al., 2005; Glynn, 1990) and the need for intensive training and management of staff (Dickerson et al., 2005). The creation and effectiveness of such programs requires a great deal of organizational support, influence, and accountability for faithful implementation and the benefits to clients. In contrast to token economies, more widely available services such as supported employment or skills training can be offered by consultants or freestanding dedicated organizations with hand-picked staff, independent of large hospitals or multi-site clinics.

As mental health law and ethics have evolved, some of the institutional controls incorporated in early token economy programs (e.g., contingent personal amenities such as room furnishings) have come to be judged unethical or illegal (Dickerson et al., 2005; Glynn, 1990; Kazdin, 1982). This was a source of criticisms that such programs were coercive, controlling, and disempowering (e.g., Biklen, 1976). It has become recommended practice that token economies introduce new reinforcers into the environment rather than making existing ones contingent (cf. Kazdin, 1982). Moreover, Corrigan (1997) argues that, when used carefully and ethically, contingency management can empower clients by clarifying their daily choices, highlighting related decisions, serving as a bridge to self-management, and motivating practice of skills that contribute to successful independent living.[4] Participation in LePage's (1999) token economy was voluntary, yet 98% of clients chose to participate, demonstrating that such programs can succeed while respecting informed consent. Similarly, Corrigan (1995) points out that client satisfaction with token economies has been similar to satisfaction with other psychotherapeutic approaches.

Some have objected to the contingent use of positive reinforcement in token economies. However, as Corrigan (1995) points out, reinforcement occurs "in all interpersonal engagements" (p. 1260) such as employees receiving pay, students receiving grades, and friends exchanging social invitations. Dickerson et al. (2005) put it more succinctly: "reinforcement contingencies are ubiquitous." In mental health programs the reinforcers of staff time, attention, effort,

---

[4] In light of advocating for token economies, and implementing 50 of them (Corrigan, 1995), it is notable that Corrigan has also been a leader in fighting the stigma of mental illnesses (Corrigan, Roe, & Tsang, 2011).

favors, care, etc. can often be delivered in arbitrary or even discriminatory fashion, which may well impede clients' progress. Contingency management programs teach staff to be aware that they can't *not* reinforce behavior. Thus, they need to be aware that potential reinforcers would best be delivered in a planful fashion according to explicit guidelines about which clients are well-informed.

Individualization of token economies can address criticisms of token economies (e.g., that they are infantilizing, Zeldow, 1976) and maximize their effectiveness. From its earliest origin, the token economy sought to target behaviors which were "necessary or useful" to clients (Ayllon & Azrin, 1965, p. 357) to counter the effects of institutionalization. Positive reinforcement should always be used to help motivate progress on the client's individualized treatment goals, especially in the face of self-management difficulties (LePage, 1999). Similarly, backup reinforcers, for which tokens are exchanged, can be individualized, for example using level systems (Corrigan, 1995; Glynn, 1990; LePage, 1999). Tokens are also a handy reinforcer which can also be used in personal contingency management programs for individuals within a token economy program.

As Corrigan (1995) points out, the criticisms above are far more likely to be true of poorly designed or managed token economies. Similarly, if not done in the context of a strongly collaborative relationship, contingency management can result in disempowerment and discrimination (Corrigan, 1997).

Rehabilitation Concepts

Rehabilitation psychologist William Anthony (1972, 1977) adapted ideas from physical and vocational rehabilitation to people with mental health disabilities, building on early roots in industrial therapy previously practiced and studied in hospital settings (Anthony & Liberman, 1986). The humanistic, non-directive, person-centered psychology of Carl Rogers (1956) was an influence on Anthony's work, for example, in its emphasis on strengths and consumer choice in mental health services (see Farkas, Anthony, Montenegro, & Gayvoronskaya, 2016). Anthony established the Center for Psychiatric Rehabilitation at Boston University in 1979 (Center for Psychiatric Rehabilitation, n.d.). There, Anthony and colleagues conduct research, provide training, and deliver services to people with mental health disabilities. Their work has focused on supported education (e.g., Unger, Anthony, Sciarappa, & Rogers, 1991), the "choose-get-keep" model of supported employment (e.g., Danley, Sciarappa, & MacDonald-Wilson, 1992), and family involvement in rehabilitation (e.g., Zipple, Spaniol, & Rogers, 1990). They played an important role in the rising prominence of the rehabilitation model in the 1980s (Anthony et al., 1990). The Center and the International Association of

Psychosocial Rehabilitation Services began co-publishing the Psychiatric Rehabilitation Journal in 1982 (Psychiatric Rehabilitation Association, n.d.). Anthony (1993) was an early advocate for the concept of recovery (see below).

Research Findings

Early pharmacological (Sharif, Bradford, Stroup, & Lieberman, 2007) and psychological (e.g., Liberman, Mueser, & Wallace, 1986) treatments focused on preventing symptom relapse and rehospitalization. However, the limitations of medicine in reducing negative symptoms (Glynn, 2014) and the frequent persistence of symptoms in general, irrespective of intervention, helped shift services to a rehabilitative focus (Anthony & Liberman, 1986). The accumulation of research in the 1970s and 1980s revealed that such symptoms (cf. impairments above) were not correlated with functioning or quality of life (Anthony & Liberman, 1986; Anthony et al., 1990). Related to this, findings such as those of the Vermont Longitudinal Study (Harding, Brooks, Ashikaga, Strauss, & Breier, 1987) provided empirical evidence that sustained improvements in symptoms and functioning were possible (see also Kurtz, this volume).

Early skills training programs discovered the difficulties people with mental health disabilities often have generalizing skills they have learned to new environments (Anthony et al., 1990). This had been an early concern of behavior therapy (see Stokes & Baer, 1977). This has led to "train-in-place" (e.g., Carling, 1995) and In Vivo Amplified Skills Training (IVAST; Liberman et al., 2002) approaches to compensate for this disability.

In 1990, researchers and practitioners interested in cognitive-behavioral approaches to psychiatric rehabilitation founded the Schizophrenia and Other Chronic Mental Disorders Special Interest Group within the Association for the Advancement of Behavioral Therapies (AABT) (M.E. Sullivan, personal communication, July 21, 2020). This group meets annually to share their research and participate in trainings at the larger association's convention. They also present a Trailblazer Award (PASS-SIG, n.d.) to accomplished colleagues, whose work is often reflected in the citations of this chapter. Both the group and the larger association have changed their names since their founding to Psychosis and Schizophrenia Spectrum Special Interest Group (PASS-SIG) and the Association for Behavioral and Cognitive Therapies (ABCT), respectively.

The twenty-first century has seen continued developments in psychiatric rehabilitation, represented by ongoing research. Among these advancements affecting research and practice in the United States are: supported employment (Bond, Drake, & Becker, 2008), cognitive therapy for psychosis (Kingdon & Turkington, 2008), illness management and recovery (Mueser et al., 2006), and cognitive remediation (Kurtz, this volume; Medalia & Choi, 2009).

The Recovery Movement

The seeds of the recovery movement lay dispersed among the origins of The Clubhouse Model, the CSX movement, and the rehabilitation model. At the core of this movement, spearheaded by CSX persons, is an aspirational definition of "recovery."

Similar to defining rehabilitation, diverse, and sometimes contentious opinions emerged (see Bellack, 2006; Fisher, 2010; Liberman, 2012). One of the main contentions has been whether recovery is a process or an outcome. The discussion below suggests how these views might be reconciled.

Recovery as Process

Conceived as a process, Davidson et al.'s (2001) notion of "inclusion" may best capture the process perspective on recovery. They advocated for inclusion in naturalistic social support networks and meaningful activities, and through affirmation of the hopes, worth, and competence of people with mental health disabilities, ". . . not so much [as] the rewards of recovery as the prerequisites for recovery" (p. 379). This resembles Corrigan's (2016) conception of the process of recovery as founded in "hope," "opportunity," and "success" (p. 49). In rehabilitation, a recovery orientation encourages a hopeful, validating relationship with clients (cf. Davidson, 2016) that has many similarities to that recommended in psychotherapy (see Kanfer & Schefft, 1988).

There is a substantial role for disassembling discrimination and prejudice in this definition of recovery (Davidson, 2016), and its origins in the civil rights struggles of CSX persons (e.g., Chamberlin, 1978) are apparent (Bellack, 2006; Cohen, 2005). Thus, in forming relationships with rehabilitation clients, providers are encouraged not to exclude, or form expectations of, clients based on stereotypical assumptions about their capabilities or readiness.

Empowerment is an important element in the process definition of recovery, and its definitions overlap greatly with definitions of recovery process (Cohen, 2005; Hogan, 2003). The implications for rehabilitation are to maximize self-determination, self-direction, and individualization. SAMHSA's heavily CSX-influenced consensus conceptualization of recovery (SAMHSA, 2012) acknowledges that some clients may struggle with this (see also Frese, Stanley, Kress, & Vogel-Scibilia, 2001). Rehabilitation providers can approach this as "supported empowerment." As in supported employment, the rehabilitation team places the client in the role of plan leader and, as needed, helps him/her identify/develop the skills and supports needed for success (see Greenwood et al., 2010; Treichler & Spaulding, 2017). The process definition of recovery also emphasizes the use and effectiveness of peer and naturalistic community supports and advocacy, empowering CSX persons in general and highlighting resources that a person in recovery may possess or develop.

Recovery as Outcome

Defined as an outcome, recovery may include overcoming disabilities (Corrigan, 2016; Spaulding et al., 2003), reduction or elimination of illness symptoms (Bellack, 2006; Corrigan, 2016); attaining or restoring functioning in the community (e.g., independent living, work, social relationships, engagement in peer or community organizations – Bellack, 2006; SAMHSA, 2012), maintained over an extended period (e.g., two years). The reader will note the substantial overlap with objective quality of life as defined above.

Some elements of the process definition of recovery might also be understood as subjective quality of life outcomes. Examples from SAMHSA's (2012) "10 Guiding Principles of Recovery" include: increased hopefulness, sense of belonging, and feelings of self-efficacy or confidence. Liberman (2012) argues against these as sole indicators of recovery, but it also seems that, without them, the definition of recovery would be incomplete and exclude important perspectives of the person in recovery. Each of these subjective outcomes can be measured in validated ways (e.g., Beck, 1988; Leary, Kelly, Cottrell, & Schreindorfer, 2013; Scherbaum, Cohen-Charash, & Kern, 2006; Snyder et al., 1996), and their role in recovery and rehabilitation studied.

The above areas for reconciliation of the rehabilitation and recovery models arise from the intertwined roots of the models and the great and growing influence of the CSX and recovery movements on rehabilitation. Remaining differences in the models are mostly those of emphasis, with the recovery model prioritizing peer-directed services, recovery as a process, advocacy against discrimination and prejudice (systemic disadvantage), and empowerment and potential power differentials in the recovery process.

Values in Recovery and Rehabilitation

One can understand these differences in terms of values, those things regarded as holding enduring importance or worth in life. What one values represents perhaps the most fundamental set of choices in life: the person one strives to become or the world he/she works to create. Values often conflict and call for prioritization.

The CSX and recovery movements prioritize advocacy and empowerment, which largely concern the distribution of power and resources. In this sense they are political movements. Their most explicit focus is on empowerment in the environments of mental health services and the mental health community (i.e., the *process* of recovery). Yet some clients may not value more than minimal involvement with these environments and the political aspects of the movements.

Rehabilitation, true to its origins, prioritizes restoring the independent community functioning of people with disabilities (see *"Recovery as Outcome"* above). Client empowerment during the rehabilitation process serves this. But more important is building skills and supports to empower the client in the broader worlds of work, education, living, and leisure according to his/her values. The need for such empowerment is present in every human being at one or more points in his/her life, but is greater among CSX individuals, in the presence of disability and discrimination. It is greater still in those whose mental health disabilities are complicated by racism, homophobia, addiction, intellectual disabilities, poverty, trauma, and fraught encounters with the law enforcement and correctional systems.

One might also understand recovery in terms of the philosophical concepts of negative and positive liberty (or "freedom from" and "freedom to", respectively). According to Carter (2019), "Negative liberty is the absence of obstacles, barriers or constraints." Negative liberty might be the goal of an anti-stigma campaign, for example. Carter states that, "Positive liberty is the possibility of acting – or the fact of acting – in such a way as to take control of one's life and realize one's fundamental purposes." Both are present in recovery and rehabilitation, but positive liberty is likely to represent the client's values more profoundly. Its greatest overlap is with objective quality of life and recovery as an outcome.

The Future of Psychiatric Rehabilitation: Competition, Choice, or Consensus?

As discussed above, proponents of both the rehabilitation and the recovery models have had difficulty reaching consensus on their definitions, and the two models can conflict over priorities. As Spaulding et al. (2003) note, "social values by themselves do not necessarily lead to technical solutions, and the biobehavioral sciences do not necessarily lead to social values" (p. 5). Enduring change in the lives of CSX persons will benefit from finding and moving forward on established areas of agreement.

Collaborative decision making (Drake, Deegan, & Rapp, 2010; Treichler & Spaulding, 2017) is an example of this. Another avenue might be training in evidence-based services for providers with lived experience. The supported employment model would be very helpful in making this a success.

While emphasized in the recovery model, both the recovery and rehabilitation models need to consider mental health politics if they are to serve CSX persons' values most effectively. This is especially so regarding entities that pay for mental health services (Royse, Thyer, & Padgett, 2016). Public programs are funded according to the priorities of politicians and voters. Nonprofit programs are funded according to the priorities of foundations and other donors. Private for-profit programs are funded according to insurers' priorities and demand from premium and out-of-pocket payers. The default agenda, which may be unrealistic for underserved CSX persons and typically underfunded programs, is cost savings.

Those who wish to help CSX persons must (often repeatedly) convince payers that they are delivering something of value for the money. This involves demonstrating meaningful outcomes and cost-benefit ratios (see Rogers, 1997; Royse et al., 2016, for a discussion of the latter). Objective quality of life outcomes appear to be the best grounds for consensus among payers, providers, clients, and other stakeholders in this process, and are often included in cost-benefit analyses. Such analyses show that psychiatric rehabilitation programs such as supported employment, skills training, and family psychoeducation reduce symptoms and hospitalizations, and improve community functioning and employment, while quite consistently demonstrating favorable cost-benefit ratios (e.g., Barton, 1999; Chandler, Spicer, Wagner, & Hargreaves, 1999; Rogers, 1997).

Nonetheless, further advocacy with payers may be required to align their priorities with research and consumers' valued outcomes. For example, transparency about outcomes is risky for new programs. Staff training and other organizational changes take time and money. These efforts must be effective before an evidence-based service can be implemented. Negative early program evaluation findings may result in loss of funding when payers feel pressure to tighten budgets. If the program was on a realistic trajectory to ultimate effectiveness, such budget cuts actually represent a loss of time, money, and consumer benefits. This, in turn, suppresses outcomes in the system of care, and can become a rationalization for system-wide underfunding or budget cuts, reducing service options available to consumers.

If we are serious about consumer choice it is important to find transparent and comprehensible ways to communicate outcome research findings to them. A lay person's version of the American Psychological Association, Division 12's listing of Research-Supported Psychological Treatments (https://div12.org/psychological-treatments/) could be helpful in conveying the relative strength of empirical support for the wide array of programs and services which now claim evidence for their efficacy. Collaborative decision making (Drake et al., 2010; Treichler & Spaulding, 2017) might then be enlisted to help consumers and their advocates compare the benefits of their service options.

Moreover, determined efforts at dissemination where research has identified effective services (e.g., Lehman, Steinwachs, & PORT Co-investigators, 1998) will increase meaningful choice for consumers. The promise of Surgeon

General David Satcher's Report (Davidson, 2016; U.S. Department of Health and Human Services, 1999) and the Presidential New Freedom Commission on Mental Health, (2003) in this regard remains largely unfulfilled. For example, Davidson (2016) notes, "Although firm conceptual and empirical foundations have been established for such programs as supported employment ... current estimates of its penetration rate within statewide systems of care hover around 2 percent" (p. 1094). A dissemination challenge is that many otherwise competent health, and even mental health, providers outside of psychiatric rehabilitation are unaware of the existence of evidence-based services for persons with schizophrenia or other psychosis, beyond medication. Adoption of such services depends largely on the availability of funding as described above. Once adopted, the heart of successful implementation of evidence-based programs is effective staff training and follow-up consultation and supervision. Yet this rarely occurs.

The commitment to recovery does not end with the implementation of evidence-based programs. Ongoing program evaluation (Cook & Shadish, 1987; Royse et al., 2016) can ensure that a specific program in a specific community retains fidelity to evidence-based techniques (i.e., matches them sufficiently to retain their "active ingredients") and attains outcomes valued by consumers and other mental health stakeholders. Without program evaluation the benefits of psychiatric rehabilitation at the local level cannot be persuasively documented. Those wishing to promote psychiatric rehabilitation and program evaluation would do well to familiarize themselves with the trend toward evidence-based policy reflected in the Foundations for Evidence-Based Policymaking Act of 2018. Were this applied to government funded mental health programs, it could prove a very useful tool.

The current diversity of programs should not mean abandoning research on identifying active ingredients and what works for whom when (Paul, 1967). This will lead to more meaningful fidelity measures (i.e., those that assess the match between interventions implemented in community settings and those demonstrated as effective in research). Toward this end, program models advance the availability of effective services if they move toward the specifiable, reproducible, and trainable. Similarly, we must not be complacent about our limited understanding of the causes of success, barriers, and disabilities among CSX persons. Philosophical or theoretical assumptions about the best model must be validated both for their consistency with basic research findings and their contribution to engagement and outcomes as demonstrated in research. In other words, such assumptions must not by themselves inflexibly limit or expand the model. The ultimate goal is a comprehensive and more consensual model (e.g., Spaulding et al., 2003), but this may long be a work in progress. Component analyses and service comparison studies are vital in building such a model. Sociopolitical forces will complicate this process.

Research is needed to identify where cultural adaptation of evidence-based programs is necessary (e.g., Kopelowicz et al., 2012).

The current eclectic pragmatic (Anthony et al., 1990; Corrigan, 2016) rehabilitation model is a starting point, not the finish line. Intuitive eclecticism does not have a good track record in the provision of mental health services (Beutler & Harwood, 2000). Psychiatric rehabilitation services such as illness management and recovery and behavioral family therapy do. The way forward involves further refining such services and integrating them with each other and helpful ideas from the recovery movement.

As outlined above, the history of mental health services is too often one of poorly conceived sweeping trends reflected in labor-intensive system realignments and/or staff training, and resulting in no improvement, or even worsening, of the lives of CSX persons. This is history we do not want to repeat. The tools of psychiatric rehabilitation have already changed the course of history and will continue to do so in the decades ahead.

REFERENCES

American Psychiatric Association. (2013). *Diagnostic and statistical manual of mental disorders* (5th ed.). Arlington, VA: Author.

American Psychological Association, Division 12. (n.d.). *Research-supported psychological treatments.* American Psychological Association, Division 12. https://div12.org/psychological-treatments/.

Anthony, W. A. (1972). Societal rehabilitation: Changing society's attitudes toward the physically and mentally disabled. *Rehabilitation Psychology, 19*(3), 117–126.

Anthony, W. A. (1977). Psychological rehabilitation: A concept in need of a method. *American Psychologist, 32*(8), 658–662.

Anthony, W. A. (1993). Recovery from mental illness: The guiding vision of the mental health service system in the 1990s. *Psychosocial Rehabilitation Journal, 16*, 11, 13.

Anthony, W., Cohen, M., & Farkas, M. (1990). *Psychiatric rehabilitation.* Boston, MA: Center For Psychiatric Rehabilitation.

Anthony, W. A., & Liberman R. P. (1986). The practice of psychiatric rehabilitation: Historical, conceptual, and research base. *Schizophrenia Bulletin, 12*, 542–559.

Ayllon, T., & Azrin, N. H. (1965). The measurement and reinforcement of behavior of psychotics. *Journal of the Experimental Analysis of Behavior, 8*, 357–383.

Ayllon, T., & Azrin, N. H. (1968). *The token economy: A motivational system for therapy and rehabilitation.* New York: Appleton-Century-Crofts.

Ball, R. M. (1973). *Social Security amendments of 1972: Summary and legislative history.* Social Security. https://www.ssa.gov/history/1972amend.html#:~:text=On%20February%2023%2C%201972%2C%20Chairman,the%20contribution%20and%20benefit%20base.

Bandura, A. (1977). *Social learning theory.* Englewood Cliffs, NJ: Prentice Hall.

Barton, R. (1999). Community support systems: A review of outcomes and policy recommendations. *Psychiatric Services, 50*, 525–534.

Beck, A. T. (1988). *Beck Hopelessness Scale.* New York: The Psychological Corporation.

Beers, C. W. (1953). *A mind that found itself: An autobiography.* Garden City, NY: Doubleday.

Bellack, A. S. (2006). Scientific and consumer models of recovery in schizophrenia: Concordance, contrasts, and implications. *Schizophrenia Bulletin, 32*(3), 432–442.

Beutler, L. E., & Harwood, T. M. (2000). *Prescriptive psychotherapy: A practical guide to systematic treatment selection.* Oxford University Press.

Biklen, D. P. (1976). Behavior modification in a state mental hospital: A participant-observer's critique. *American Journal of Orthopsychiatry, 46*, 53–61.

Bluebird, G. (n.d.). *History of the consumer/survivor movement.* National Empowerment Center, Inc. *https://power2u.org/wp-content/uploads/2017/01/History-of-the-Consumer-Survivor-Movement-by-Gayle-Bluebird.pdf.*

Carling, P. J. (1995). *Return to community: Building support systems for people with psychiatric disabilities.* New York: Guilford Press.

Carter, I. (2019). Positive and negative liberty. In Edward N. Zalta (Ed.), *The Stanford Encyclopedia of Philosophy* (Winter Edition), https://plato.stanford.edu/archives/win2019/entries/liberty-positive-negative/.

Center for Psychiatric Rehabilitation (n.d.). About our founder. https://cpr.bu.edu/about/history/about- our-founder/.

Chamberlin, J. (1978). *On our own: Patient-controlled alternatives to the mental health system.* New York, NY, USA: McGraw-Hill.

Chandler, D., Spicer, G., Wagner, M., & Hargreaves, W. (1999). Cost-effectiveness of a capitated assertive community treatment program. *Psychiatric Rehabilitation Journal, 22*(4), 327–336.

Cohen, O. (2005). How do we recover? An analysis of psychiatric survivor oral histories. *Journal of Humanistic Psychology, 45*(3), 333–354.

Cook, T. D., & Shadish, Jr., W. R. (1987). Program evaluation: The worldly science (pp. 31–70). In W. R. Shadish, Jr.,& Reichardt (Eds.), *Evaluation studies review annual* (Vol. 12). Newbury Park, CA: Sage Publications.

Corrigan, P. W. (1991). Strategies that overcome barriers to token economies in community programs for severe mentally ill adults. *Community Mental Health Journal, 27*(1), 17–30.

Corrigan, P. W. (1995). Use of a token economy with seriously mentally ill patients: Criticisms and misconceptions. *Psychiatric Services, 46*(12), 1258–1263.

Corrigan, P. W. (1997). Behavior therapy empowers persons with severe mental illness. *Behavior Modification, 21*(1), 45–61.

Corrigan, P. W. (2016). *Principles and practice of psychiatric rehabilitation: An empirical approach* (2nd ed.). New York: Guilford Press.

Corrigan, P. W., & McCracken, S. G. (1995). Refocusing the training of psychiatric rehabilitation staff. *Psychiatric Services, 46*, 1172–1177.

Crow, L. (1996). Including all of our lives: Renewing the social model of disability. In C. Barnes & G. Mercer (Eds.), *Disability and Illness: Exploring the Divide* (pp. 55–72). Leeds, UK: The Disability Press.

Danley, K. S., Sciarappa, K., & MacDonald-Wilson, K. (1992). Choose-get-keep: A psychiatric rehabilitation approach to supported employment. *New Directions for Mental Health Services, 53*, 87–96.

Davidson, L. (2016). The recovery movement: Implications for mental health care and enabling people to participate fully in life. *Health Affairs, 35*, 1091–1097.

Davidson, L., Stayner, D. A., Nickou, C., Styron, T. H., Rowe, M., & Chinman, M. L. (2001). "Simply to be let in": Inclusion as a basis for recovery. *Psychiatric Rehabilitation Journal, 24*(4), 375–388

Department of Health and Human Services. (1994). *Revitalizing the Community Support Program.* Washington, DC: Office of Inspector General, Department of Health and Human Services.

Dickerson, F., Ringel, N., Parente, F., & Boronow, J. (1994). Seclusion and restraint, assaultiveness, and patient performance in a token economy. *Hospital and Community Psychiatry, 45*(2), 168–170.

Dickerson, F. D., Tenhula, W. N., & Green-Paden, L. (2005). The token economy for schizophrenia: Review of the literature and recommendations for future research. *Schizophrenia Research, 75*, 405–416.

Drake, R. E., Deegan, P. E., & Rapp, C. (2010). The promise of shared decision making in mental health [Editorial]. *Psychiatric Rehabilitation Journal, 34*(1), 7–13.

Drake, R. E., Skinner, J. S., Bond, G. R., & Goldman, H. H. (2009). Social Security and mental illness: Reducing disability with supported employment. *Health Affairs, 28*(3), 761–770.

Fairweather, G. W., Sanders, D. H., & Tornatzky, L. G. (1974). *Creating change in mental health organizations.* New York: Pergamon.

Falloon, I. R. H., & Liberman, R. P. (1983). Behavioral family interventions in the management of chronic schizophrenia. In W. R. McFarlane (Ed.), *Family therapy in schizophrenia* (pp. 117–140). New York: Guilford.

Farkas, M., Anthony, W., Montenegro, R., & Gayvoronskaya, E. (2016). Person-centered psychiatric rehabilitation. In J. E. Mezzich, M. Botbol, G. N. Christodoulou, C. R. Cloninger, & I. M. Salloum (Eds.), *Person Centered Psychiatry* (pp. 277–289). Springer International Publishing.

Fisher, D. (2010). The evolution of the concept of recovery. *E-News*, Issue 2, Recovery to Practice Resource Center for Mental Health Professionals, U.S. Department of Health and Human Service, Substance Abuse and Mental Health Services Administration.

Foundations for Evidence-Based Policymaking Act of 2018. 5 USC 101 (2019). Retrieved July 16, 2020 from https://www.congress.gov/bill/115th-congress/house-bill/4174.

Frese, F. J., Stanley, J., Kress, K., & Vogel-Scribilia, S. (2001). Integrating evidence-based practices and the recovery model. *Psychiatric Services, 52*, 1462–1468.

Frisch, M. B. (1994). *Quality of life inventory.* Minneapolis, MN: National Computer Systems.

Glynn, S. M. (1990). Token economy approaches for psychiatric patients: Progress and pitfalls over 25 years. *Behavior Modification, 14*(4), 383–407.

Glynn, S. M. (2014). Bridging psychiatric rehabilitation and recovery in schizophrenia: A life's work. *American Journal of Psychiatric Rehabilitation, 17*(3), 214–224.

Goffman, E. (1961). *Asylums: Essays on the social situation of mental patient and other inmates.* New York: Anchor Books.

Greenwood, K. E., Sweeney, A., Williams, S., Garety, P., Kuipers, E., Scott, J., & Peters, E. (2010). Choice of outcome in CBT for psychoses (CHOICE): The development of a new service user-led outcome measure of CBT for psychosis. *Schizophrenia Bulletin, 36*(1), 126–135.

Grim, A. (July 8, 2015). *Sitting-in for disability rights: The Section 504 protests of the 1970s.* National Museum of American History. https://americanhistory.si.edu/ blog/sitting-disability-rights-section-504-protests-1970s.

Grob, G. N. (1992). Mental health policy in America: Myths and realities. *Health Affairs, 11*(3), 7–22.

Harding, C., Brooks, G., Ashikaga T., Strauss, J., & Breier, A. (1987). The Vermont longitudinal study of persons with severe mental illness: Methodology, study sample, and overall status 32 years later. *American Journal of Psychiatry, 144*, 718–726.

Hogan, M. F. (2003). New Freedom Commission report: The President's New Freedom Commission recommendations to transform mental health are in America. *Psychiatric Services, 54*, 1467–1474.

Kanfer, F. H., & Schefft, B. K. (1988). *Guiding the process of therapeutic change.* Research Press.

Kazdin A. E. (1982). The token economy: A decade later. *Journal of Applied Behavior Analysis, 15*(3), 431–445.

Kopelowicz, A., & Zarate, R. (2014). The role of Robert Liberman in the development of family psychoeducation. *American Journal of Psychiatric Rehabilitation, 17*(3), 197–213.

Kopelowicz, A., Zarate, R., Wallace, C. J., Liberman, R. P., Lopez, S. R., & Mintz, J. (2012). The impact of multifamily groups to improve treatment adherence in Mexican Americans with schizophrenia. *Archives of General Psychiatry, 69*, 265–273.

Leary, M. R., Kelly, K. M., Cottrell, C. A., Schreindorfer, L. S. (2013). Construct validity of the need to belong scale: Mapping the nomological network. *Journal of Personality Assessment, 95*(6), 610–624.

Lehman, A. F. (1983). The effects of psychiatric symptoms on quality of life assessments among the chronically mentally ill. *Evaluation and Programme Planning, 6*, 143–151.

Lehman, A. F., Steinwachs, D., & PORT Co-investigators (1998). The Schizophrenia Patient Outcomes Research Team (PORT) treatment recommendations. *Schizophrenia Bulletin, 24*, 1–10.

LePage, J. P. (1999). The impact of a token economy on injuries and negative events on an acute psychiatric unit. *Psychiatric Services, 50*(7), 941–944.

Liberman, R. P. (1980). A review of Paul and Lentz's psychological treatment for chronic mental patients: Milieu versus social-learning programs. *Journal of Applied Behavior Analysis, 13*, 367–371.

Liberman, R. P. (2012). Recovery from schizophrenia: Form follows functioning. *World Psychiatry, 11*, 161–162.

Liberman, R. P., & Foy, D. W. (1983). Psychiatric rehabilitation for chronic mental patients. *Psychiatric Annals, 13*(7), 539–545.

Liberman, R. P., Glynn, S., Blair, K. E., Ross, D., & Marder, S. R. (2002). In Vivo Amplified Skills Training: Promoting generalization of independent living skills for clients with schizophrenia. *Psychiatry: Interpersonal and Biological Processes, 65*(2), 137–155.

Liberman, R. P., King, L. W., DeRisi, W. J., & McCann, M. (1975). *Personal effectiveness: Guiding people to assert themselves and improve their social skills.* Champaign, IL: Research Press.

Liberman, R. P., Mueser, K. T., & Wallace, C. J. (1986). Social skills training for schizophrenic individuals at risk for relapse. *American Journal of Psychiatry, 143*(4), 523–526.

Liberman, R. P., Mueser, K. T., Wallace, C. J., Jacobs, H. E., Eckman, T., & Massel, H. K. (1986). Training skills in the psychiatrically disabled: Learning coping and competence. *Schizophrenia Bulletin, 12*, 631–647.

Maddux, J. E., Gosselin, J. T., & Winstead, B. A. (2008). Conceptions of psychopathology: A social constructionist perspective. In J. E. Maddux & B. A. Winstead, (Eds.) *Psychopathology: Foundations for a contemporary understanding* (2nd ed.) (pp. 3–18). New York, NY: Routledge/Taylor & Francis.

McCall, S. (1975). Quality of life. *Social Indicator Research, 2*, 229–248.

Medalia, A., & Choi, J. (2009). Cognitive remediation in schizophrenia. *Neuropsychology Review, 19*(3), 353–364.

MindFreedom (n.d.a). *Origins of the C/S/X movement.* https://mindfreedom.org/kb/voices-for-choices/origins-of-the-c-s-x-movement-voices-for-choices/.

MindFreedom (n.d.b). *The Highlander Statement of Concern and Call to Action March 25, 2000.* https://mindfreedom.org/kb/highlander-2000/.

Mueser, K. T., & Glynn, S. M. (1999). *Behavioral family therapy for psychiatric disorders* (2nd ed.). Oakland, CA: New Harbinger.

Mueser, K. T., Meyer, P. S., Penn, D. L., Clancy, R., Clancy, D. M., & Salyers, M. P. (2006). The Illness Management and Recovery program: Rationale, development, and preliminary findings. *Schizophrenia Bulletin, 32*(Suppl 1), S32–43.

National Mental Health Services Survey (https://www.samhsa.gov/data/sites/default/files/reports/rpt29388/2019_NMHSS/2019-NMHSS-R.pdf)

Office of Technology Assessment. (1994). *Psychiatric disabilities, employment, and the Americans with Disabilities Act.* Washington, DC: U.S. Government Printing Office.

PASS-SIG (n.d.). Trailblazer Award. https://schizpsychosis.org/trailblazer-award/

Paul, G. L. (1967). Strategy of outcome research in psychotherapy. *Journal of Consulting Psychology, 31*, 109–118.

Paul, G. L., & Lentz, R. J. (1977). *Psychosocial treatment of chronic mental patients: Milieu versus social learning programs.* Cambridge, MA: Harvard University Press.

Pratt, C. W., Gill, K. J., Barrett, N. M., & Roberts, M. M. (1999). *Psychiatric rehabilitation.* San Diego, CA: Academic Press.

Propst, R. N. (1997). Stages in realizing the international diffusion of a single way of working: The clubhouse model. *New Directions in Mental Health Services, 74*, 53–66.

Psychiatric Rehabilitation Consultants (1990). *Social and independent living skills: Basic conversation skills module.* Camarillo, CA: Psychiatric Rehabilitation Consultants.

Rogers, C. R. (1956). Client-centered theory. *Journal of Counseling Psychology 3*, 115–120.

Rogers, E. S. (1997). Cost-benefit studies in vocational services. *Psychiatric Rehabilitation Journal, 20*(3), 25–33.

Royse, D., Thyer, B. A., & Padgett, D. K. (2015). *Program evaluation: An introduction to an evidence-based approach.* Boston, MA: Cengage Learning, Inc.

SAMHSA. (2012). *SAMHSA's working definition of recovery: 10 guiding principles of recovery.* Rockville, MD: Substance Abuse and Mental Health Services Administration. https://store.samhsa.gov/sites/default/files/d7/priv/pep12-recdef.pdf.

Scherbaum, C. A., Cohen-Charash, Y., & Kern, M. J. (2006). Measuring general self-efficacy: A comparison of three measures using item response theory. *Educational and Psychological Measurement, 66,* 1047–1063.

Sharif, Z., Bradford, D., Stroup, S., & Lieberman, J. (2007). Pharmacological treatment of schizophrenia. In P. E. Nathan & J. M. Gorman (Eds.), *A Guide to Treatments that Work* (pp. 203–242). New York: Oxford University Press.

Snyder, C. R., Sympson, S. C., Ybasco, F. C., Borders, T. F., Babyak, M. A., & Higgins, R. L. (1996). Development and validation of the State Hope Scale. *Journal of Personality and Social Psychology, 70*(2), 321–335.

Spaulding, W. D., Sullivan, M. E., & Poland, J. S. (2003). *Treatment and rehabilitation of severe mental illness.* New York, NY, USA: The Guilford Press.

Stein, L. I., & Test, M. A. (1980). Alternative to mental hospital treatment, I: Conceptual model, treatment, program and clinical evaluation. *Archives of General Psychiatry, 37,* 392–397.

Stokes, T. F., & Baer, D. M. (1977). An implicit technology of generalization. *Journal of Applied Behavior Analysis, 10,* 349–367.

Thresholds (n.d.). About. https://www.thresholds.org/about/.

Treichler, E. B. H., & Spaulding, W. D. (2017). Beyond shared decision-making: Collaboration in the age of recovery from serious mental illness. *American Journal of Orthopsychiatry, 87*(5), 567–574.

Unger, K. V., Anthony, W. A., Sciarappa, K., & Rogers, E. S. (1991). A supported education program for young adults with long-term mental illness. *Psychiatric Services, 42*(8), 838–842.

World Health Organization (1980). *International classification of impairments, disabilities, and handicaps: A manual of classification relating to the consequences of disease.* Geneva, Switzerland: World Health Organization.

World Health Organization. (2002). *Towards a common language for functioning, disability and health: The International Classification of Functioning, Disability and Health.* Geneva: World Health Organization.

Yoman, J. (2008). A primer on functional analysis. *Cognitive and Behavioral Practice, 15,* 325–340.

Yoman, J., & Edelstein, B. A. (1994). Functional assessment in psychiatric disability. In J. R. Bedell (Ed.), *Psychological assessment and treatment of persons with severe mental disorders* (pp. 31–56). Washington, DC: Taylor and Francis.

Zeldow, P. B. (1976). Some antitherapeutic effects of the token economy: A case in point. *Psychiatry, 39*(4), 318–24.

Zipple, A., Spaniol, L., & Rogers, E. S. (1990). Training mental health practitioners to assist families of persons who have a psychiatric disability. *Rehabilitation Psychology, 35*(2), 121–129.

4 Outcome and Cognitive Treatments in Schizophrenia-Spectrum Illness, Past and Present: An Overview

Matthew M. Kurtz

The goals of this chapter are fourfold: (1) to provide a brief historical overview of clinical and academic opinion in Western societies around outcome in schizophrenia, beginning with the emergence of the concept of *dementia praecox* as formulated by Emil Kraepelin in psychiatric textbooks in the 1890s; (2) to complement this historical view with a critical review of a select group of empirical studies focused on descriptive evaluations of long-term outcome in people with diagnoses of schizophrenia beginning in the 1970s; (3) to briefly discuss the emergence of the recovery movement in the US and its role in instigating the development and evaluation of novel psychosocial interventions for people diagnosed with schizophrenia; and (4) to describe the emergence and empirical status of a new class of psychosocial interventions focused on cognitive and social cognitive deficits and biases that have been increasingly linked to long-term outcome and recovery.

Client Outcome Serves as Key Feature of Early Diagnostic Formulations of Schizophrenia

Emil Kraepelin and Dementia Praecox

From a historical perspective, the significance of clinical outcome as a key feature of schizophrenia is emphasized by its central role in shaping earliest conceptualizations of the disorder. Emil Kraepelin (1856–1926), a nineteenth century German academic psychiatrist, is widely regarded as having formulated the first diagnostic category that most closely approximates contemporary DSM-5 (APA, 2013) conceptualizations of schizophrenia: a category Kraepelin labeled *dementia praecox*, or literally a mental decline with onset in youth. Kraepelin was the first to group what had been several different disorders categorized according to different patterns of symptoms, into a larger category of *dementia praecox* defined by the illnesses' common deleterious clinical progression and outcome (Shorter, 1997).

In a series of widely hailed (and sometimes criticized) academic textbooks, Kraepelin was among the first psychiatrists to begin to create a systematized approach to delineating distinct psychiatric disorders with unique clinical trajectories. Kraepelin's conclusions emerged from the study of hundreds of patients admitted to the psychiatric clinics at the University of Heidelberg where he and his residents carefully documented symptoms on each new client admission on note cards, and then followed each client's clinical course longitudinally often over many years. Kraepelin distinguished been the current expression of symptoms or phenomenology of a psychiatric disorder (that he hypothesized was often not predictive of future outcome), from the subsequent outcome (good versus deteriorating) for groups of clients. Kraepelin hypothesized outcome had only a tenuous relationship with presenting clinical symptoms (Berrios & Hauser, 1988; Kendler & Jablensky, 2011; Kraepelin, 1919). In the 1893 edition of his textbook entitled *The Compendium of Psychiatry*, Kraepelin differentiated psychosis into what has been since labeled the "Kraepelinian dichotomy": (1) "circular insanity" and other forms of psychiatric illness characterized by disruptions in affect and mood, with typically good subsequent outcome, on the one hand, and (2) "dementia praecox" characterized by disruptions in thought, characterized by a downward clinical course, and expected to typically culminate in poorer long-term outcomes, on the other (Shorter, 1997). This conceptualization of schizophrenia as defined as a disorder with a downward progression was to influence the field for a hundred years to come, and was one factor in stymieing the robust development of rehabilitative interventions early in the history of schizophrenia research, as well as the incorporation of client experiences into the formation and assessment of client-valued psychosocial treatments.

Eugen Bleuler Coins the Diagnostic Label Schizophrenia and Shifts Conceptions of Outcome

The Swiss psychiatrist Eugen Bleuler (1857–1939), who first coined the term schizophrenia, was influenced by the ideas of Kraepelin as well as those of Pierre Janet and Sigmund Freud. An asylum, rather than an academic, psychiatrist, Bleuler served as Director of the Burgholzli Hospital in Zurich and in influential textbooks placed greater emphasis on the psychological state of the person with schizophrenia than had Kraepelin. Known as an outstanding observational clinician, always keeping a notepad nearby to record the thoughts of clients, Bleuler drew a line between what he considered fundamental symptoms: these included the splitting of mental associations from one another, the splitting of mental associations from related emotional functions, persistent ambivalence and a reduction in goal-related behavior, disruptions in mood and a disconnection from reality. Bleuler distinguished these fundamental symptoms, from what he called accessory symptoms, which were more directly observable. According to Bleuler's model observable symptoms, such as delusions and hallucinations, were viewed as a product of these more primary symptoms (Harrington, 2019; Kaplan, 2008).

While Bleuler's broader conception of the disorder has been criticized by some as one of the sources of inconsistencies in diagnosis of schizophrenia that emerged in psychiatry in the 1960s and 1970s (e.g., Stephens, 1978), Bleuler's approach has also been lauded as viewing schizophrenia as consisting of a diversity of etiologies, symptoms and outcomes that can be placed on a continuum with healthy psychiatric functioning. In this sense Bleuler's work has been interpreted as "de-othering" the client with schizophrenia (Kaplan, 2008) as well as expanding our understanding of the range of possible outcomes for people with the illness. The broader conceptions around clinical presentation and greater bandwidth of outcomes delineated by Bleuler, as compared to the downward progression of the illness which emerged from Kraepelin's model, served to set the stage for detailed, long-term follow-up studies in the US in the late twentieth century. Indeed, as detailed below, clinical research in the second half of the twentieth century demonstrated substantial heterogeneity in outcomes for people with schizophrenia and questioned the idea that a diagnosis based on observable symptoms of schizophrenia in itself predicts deteriorating outcome.

Critical Review of Key Long-Term Outcome Studies of People with a Diagnosis of Schizophrenia-Spectrum Illnesses

While an exhaustive review of all longer-term follow-up studies of people with schizophrenia is beyond the scope of this chapter, several naturalistic follow-up studies were selected for their influence on the field, methodological rigor and illustrative findings and are described below (see Kurtz, 2015, for a broader analysis of extant longitudinal outcome studies in schizophrenia).

Iowa 500 Retrospective Study

In one of the landmark studies of its time, Ming Tsuang and colleagues (1979) at the University of Iowa created a database of 525 people with a psychiatric illness and measured their outcome 30–40 years after an index hospital admission; 200 had a diagnosis of schizophrenia, 100 had a diagnosis of mania and 225 had depression. They were compared to a group of surgical outpatients without history of mental illness. Participants were identified through consecutive hospital admissions to the University of Iowa clinics between the years 1934 and 1944. Participants were from rural areas, and almost universally from lower socioeconomic status with limited educational opportunities. Making use of detailed University hospital records, as well as records from four state psychiatric clinics and conducting careful tracing, participants and first-degree family members were identified as part of the study and then contacted and interviewed (along with a family member if possible) with a systematic interview tool, typically 30–40 years after the index admission. The study was retrospective, and diagnoses were formulated based on evidence presented in the chart at the time of admission. The study applied criteria similar to those of the current DSM-5.

Several interesting findings emerged. First, people diagnosed with schizophrenia did generally show poorest outcome relative to people with mania, depression or surgical, psychiatrically healthy controls. This was true when rated according to employment status, living status (independent or with relatives, in a board-and-care facility, or in a hospital), marital status (married, divorced, never married), and psychiatric status (the degree to which the client was currently showing psychiatric symptoms at the 30+ year follow-up). While the range of ratings for each domain was limited (good, fair or poor), the range of dimensions of outcome measured was a strength of the study. Mortality rates were also evaluated, and here too people with schizophrenia were the most likely to die at an earlier age, life expectancy in the schizophrenia group was 52 years compared to 62 years for the control group. On the one hand these findings provided some support for the "Kraepelinian dichotomy" between mood and thought disorders and outcome. At the same time, the chronic, deteriorating course described by Kraepelin was not supported by the study. Indeed, over a third of the participants in their sample diagnosed with schizophrenia were rated as having "good" residential status and work status at the 30–40 year follow-up. More specifically, 35% were employed, retired or an active homemaker, or a student, 35% lived at home or in another residential setting with relatives, 21% were married and 20% had no symptoms. These findings demonstrating the possibility of improvement and/or recovery were particularly remarkable given the types and availability of treatments during this historical epoch. Treatment would have been markedly different from current practices; widespread treatment with antipsychotic medications did not emerge until the 1950s and 1960s, and somatic treatments administered during the 1940s and 1950s would have seemed barbaric by current standards, likely including insulin shock therapy, chemical induction of seizures, and frontal lobotomy for at least a subgroup of these clients (Harrington, 2019).

WHO Prospective Longitudinal Studies

In an attempt to construct a common language for understanding schizophrenia and other mental disorders, and to assess universality versus specificity of mental illnesses across cultures, the World Health Organization (WHO) conducted a series of longitudinal studies of people with a diagnosis of schizophrenia at a variety of sites around the world. The first of these efforts, The

International Pilot Study of Schizophrenia (IPSS, WHO, 1973; Sartorius, Jablensky, & Shapiro, 1978), was conducted in nine countries selected for diversity of cultural norms and practices: Taiwan (Taipei), Columbia (Cali), Czechoslovakia (Prague), Denmark (Aarhus), India (Agra), Nigeria (Ibadan), the Soviet Socialist Republics (Moscow), the United Kingdom (London), and the United States of America (Washington, DC). The questions investigated included the degree to which schizophrenia was evident in different parts of the world, the degree to which the disorder manifested differently in different parts of the world, and the degree to which long-term outcome was different in these different cultures. In the initial sample of over 800 people with schizophrenia it was concluded that clients with very similar symptom profiles could be identified in all nine country clusters by trained symptom raters across sites; indeed, these findings were confirmed with mathematical and computer modeling of symptoms. Furthermore, these clients could be distinguished symptomatically from clients with an affective disorder diagnosis or other functional mental disorder at all study sites.

With respect to follow-up data, 97.1% of clients were successfully traced two years after initial assessment in the study and over 80% were formally assessed. Information collected using standardized and more open-ended narrative histories were used to assess outcome. Across centers 26% fell into the best outcome group (i.e., psychotic during less than 15% of the two-year follow-up period, not socially impaired and with full disease remission), while 18% fell into the worst outcome group (i.e., continuously psychotic and impaired socially). With regard to course, 27% of all clients had a single, relatively short psychotic period followed by full symptom recovery without relapse and social impairment. Another 26% never had a full remission during the two-year period.

Surprisingly, when compared across cultures a greater proportion of people with schizophrenia in study sites in India, Columbia, and Nigeria had a favorable course and outcome than was the case in the UK, USSR, Czechoslovakia, and the US. When centers were compared, sites in Nigeria and India had the best course and outcome among people with schizophrenia in all centers: 58% of clients in Ibadan, Nigeria and 47% of clients in Agra, India were free of symptoms at a two-year follow-up. A potential confound in these studies is that clients were diagnosed with schizophrenia without the six-month duration required by DSM-III, -IV, and -5. However, among those clients who had onset more than six months before entry into the study, course and outcome remained better for clients in developing countries. Also of interest, factors that explained some of the variance in outcome in sites in developed countries failed to produce prediction in sites in the developing world. Similar findings were borne out at the five-year follow-up of these same clients in the related International Study of Schizophrenia (Leff et al., 1992).

In summary, these findings suggested that a substantial minority of people with schizophrenia around the world had a mild course of illness with complete symptom remission and limited long-term disability and a majority of clients did not have continuous symptoms illness during multi-year follow-up. Differences in symptom and functional outcome across cultures argued for a substantial cultural influence on the nature of disorder progression.

Chicago Prospective Longitudinal Studies

Martin Harrow and colleagues in the Chicago longitudinal study investigated 200 people with psychosis at an index psychiatric hospitalization (43 with schizophrenia and 10 with schizophreniform disorder), all early in the development of their illness (mean age 23 years), over six follow-up assessments over a 20-year period (follow-ups at 2 years, 4.5 years, 7.5, 10, 15, and 20 years). The work is of particular significance as it is the only study of its kind to follow people with schizophrenia prospectively over such an extended period of time, and there was little attrition, ensuring that results did not simply reflect clients with particularly good or poor outcome who might be more easily located for follow-up. Similar to the Iowa and IPSS studies, there was substantial heterogeneity of outcome with little evidence of a consistent and unremitting downward progression resulting in worsening symptoms and more impaired psychosocial function for people with a diagnosis of schizophrenia.

With respect to outcome, these investigators created a category of "recovered" which was defined as consisting of four dimensions: (1) at least a year of no schizophrenia-related symptoms (psychosis and negative symptoms), (2) at least half-time employment, (3) no psychiatric rehospitalization, and (4) regular social activity. Remarkably, during the first 15 years of the study nearly half of the sample (41% of participants with a diagnosis of schizophrenia) had experienced at least a year of recovery (Harrow et al., 2005). Furthermore, at each follow-up interval, 19–29% of individuals with schizophrenia were working full-time. The recovery data from this study may have underestimated positive outcomes in this group of clients by requiring improvement in symptoms, work function and socialization to meet the threshold of "recovery." Clients, for example, who were successfully working but remained symptomatic would not have met the study criteria for "recovery," although this may have reflected significant improvement or was personally viewed as "recovery" by the client. Also of note, 39% of the schizophrenia sample was not on antipsychotic medication at the 15-year follow-up in this study, and a majority of those classified as recovered in this study were not on antipsychotics at the time of their assessment (Harrow & Jobe, 2007).

Vermont Retrospective Studiesand the Role of Rehabilitation in Promoting Positive Outcomes

Courtenay Harding and her colleagues (Harding et al., 1987), in a retrospective, longitudinal study at an average of 32 years after hospital admission, evaluated a cohort of chronically hospitalized people with schizophrenia in a series of seminal papers published in the 1980s. Harding evaluated outcomes in this sample using the narrow DSM-III criteria to re-diagnose clients with schizophrenia hospitalized in the Vermont state hospital system from detailed chart records collected during an index hospitalization in the 1950s. This group of clients had been hospitalized for extended periods of time and were selected for a federally funded rehabilitation program based on their illness chronicity (16 years on average), long period of disability and resistance to treatment. All clients had been disabled for at least one year (as defined as an inability to function in day-to-day role capacities). Most study participants had been administered neuroleptic medications for at least 2.5 years without enough improvement to merit discharge.

These clients were released to the community in the 1950s with a careful plan in place for intensive rehabilitation. Rehabilitation services were provided through an integration of state hospital resources and Vermont state vocational rehabilitation programs. Vocational rehabilitation provided new community residences, work options, and case management for clients in the study. Continuity of care across settings was ensured as teams of hospital and vocational workers established halfway houses, found job openings, made job placements and linked client to supports in the community.

Of 118 people with schizophrenia, 70% were alive and assessed (n = 82), 24% were deceased, 3% refused to participate and 3% were lost to follow-up. Of these 82 participants, nearly half had been hospitalized for more than six years at their index hospitalization. Of these clients (mean age 61 years at follow-up), well over half (68%) showed no positive or negative signs or symptoms of schizophrenia at all at follow-up. Fifty percent were not using psychotropic medications. Sixty percent were rated in the "good" category on the Global Assessment Scale (GAS; Harding et al., 1987). There was a marked diversity of outcomes; in the middle-range there were many participants successfully working with good personal and family relationships who still had persistent delusions and hallucinations. In many cases clients learned to control or not discuss these symptoms. Other clients had minimal symptoms, continued to work, but had restricted social contacts. Yet others had strong social networks and minimal symptom expression, but did not work. The diversity of outcomes in this study emphasized the need for personalized care in the treatment of people with schizophrenia.

In a fascinating add-on to the Vermont study, Harding and her colleague Michael DiSisto (DeSisto et al., 1995) compared findings from the Vermont

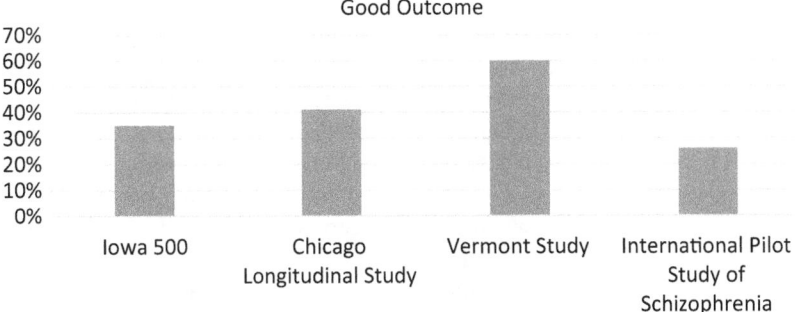

Figure 4.1 Proportion of people diagnosed with schizophrenia with good subsequent outcome in at least one domain.

cohort to those of a separate cohort matched to Vermont clients by age, gender, diagnosis and length of hospitalization from the state hospital system in Maine. This careful matching of individuals in each sample permitted conclusions to be drawn regarding the effects of psychiatric rehabilitation on function without confusing these effects with effects associated with age, gender and other key individual differences. The Maine cohort received more traditional care (pharmacotherapy) beginning 1955–1956 and aftercare with little or no vocational rehabilitation involvement and little coordination between hospital and vocational services. Development of halfway houses in Maine came 16 years after that in Vermont. The samples were similar with respect to sociocultural background, which was almost exclusively rural in both groups. Results revealed that the Maine clients spent significantly more time in the hospital over the follow-up period (50% versus 13% of the 32-year follow-up period) and a substantially greater number of Vermont subjects were employed between 1960 and 1975 (30.9% versus 12.7%). Courtenay Harding and her colleagues surmised that the close relationship between hospital and vocational services, coupled with job placement and help with housing afforded by the federal grant rehabilitation program in Vermont, may have explained the marked differences in outcomes between the two groups.

Figure 4.1 presents a summary of results from this section of the chapter. While the nature of the study samples, assessment intervals and the measurement of outcome differed markedly between studies, it is clear from the graph that whether outcome was measured by persistence of symptoms, number and persistence of hospitalizations, successful work and social function, and/or independence in living situation, outcomes in all samples described in this section were remarkably diverse both across individuals, and also across different clinical psychosocial features within individuals. These findings are not at all consistent with schizophrenia defined as progressing in a largely unitary downward clinical trajectory as hypothesized by Kraepelin and others at the turn of the nineteenth century. These findings also provide only mixed evidence for long-term antipsychotic medication as crucial for successful long-term recovery, and support the use of community rehabilitation as important for improving long-term outcomes. In concert with findings from the 1960s onward supporting the efficacy of a range of environmental modifications and psychosocial interventions for promoting recovery (see Chapter 2), long-term outcome studies conducted from the 1970s to the current time suggest that recovery in people with schizophrenia is achievable and not at all uncommon.

Emergence of the Recovery Model and Psychosocial Treatment in Schizophrenia

Several factors have led to the emergence of the "recovery model" as a set of guiding values in the formation of systems of care as well as direct treatment of people with severe mental illness. First, follow-up studies reviewed in the previous section revealed that despite Kraepelin's view of a deteriorating trajectory, estimates ranged from 20% to 60% of people with schizophrenia "recovered" as measured by absence of symptoms, lack of need for rehospitalizations and/or medications, successful work and independent living, and a variety of other indices of successful outcome. Furthermore, programs of psychiatric rehabilitation clearly revealed improved rates of recovery with behavioral treatments responsive to clients' goals. Second, deinstitutionalization in the 1960s coupled with stronger laws around reducing involuntary commitment to treatment created larger communities of people with severe mental illnesses who met to describe their experiences of psychiatric treatment and began to advocate publicly for a more consumer-centered approach to treatment (Mueser et al., 2013).

Many consumers in the 1960s viewed psychiatric treatment as predicated on a model valuing short-term clinical stabilization and symptom reduction at the expense of consumer-centered values, which included empowerment and the creation of meanings in the face of persistent disability. Treatment goals focused on "normalization" were viewed as demeaning and disrespectful of clients' individuality. Rather than pushing people with psychiatric illness to conform to a normative value, by this view psychiatric treatment should accept the person with psychiatric symptoms on their own terms, and in so doing expand the sense of "normal" (Deegan, 1988, 1996). Indeed, psychiatric treatment was viewed by some consumers at this time as deeply antithetical to their needs and experiences as humans (Deegan, 1996). Thus, the process of diagnosis and treatment itself was often deemed as coercive, and "soul-crushing" with respect to prognosis, and also leading to social discrimination, stigma, and a loss of self-esteem. Indeed, from the perspective of this model, a crucial element of any plan of person-centered recovery from psychiatric illness includes addressing the trauma associated with traditional psychiatric treatment in addition to the confrontation of problems in living posed by the illness itself (Anthony, 1993; Farkas, 2007).

In contrast to the traditional, hierarchical and medicalized treatment model, the goal of the recovery model is to place the client perspective at the center of treatment and emphasize "process" rather than a specific "target" in recovery. Recovery emphasizes the role of ongoing identity change, in which the sense of self expands beyond the narrow role of consumer of mental health services and in which the initial catastrophe of mental illness is integrated into a sense of self that includes socially- and individually-valued role functions (e.g., Anthony, 1993). Embracing notions of hope, destigmatization of mental illness, and empowerment of the individual, the outcome of treatment is at least partially predicated on the desires of the person affected and should involve choice. These ideas have been supported by analyses of common themes in the narratives of people in recovery from mental illness, which research has suggested usually include four key tenets: (1) the importance of work as a way to increase self-esteem, provide material support and help one interpersonally through the camaraderie of other workers; (2) creating a sense of control over one's symptoms; (3) developing relationships as a way of increasing connectedness with the world; and (4) removing barriers to relationships with others including internalized stigma, and negative attitudes and shame around symptoms and low perceptions of self-worth (see Roe, 2001).

The recovery approach to treatment has influenced the emergence of a new generation of psychosocial interventions targeted at outcomes of central importance to consumers that go well beyond short-term clinical stabilization and symptom reduction, and instead target improved personal relationships, return to competitive work, and improved quality of life as key treatment endpoints. Indeed, assessment of these psychosocial interventions is increasingly focused not only on objective or clinician-rated improvement on consumer-valued treatment outcomes, but on the consumers' own experience of treatment and treatment outcomes, through the increased use of subjective scales of well-being and attitudes in studies of psychosocial intervention. In the next section we discuss the recent emergence of one class of psychosocial interventions: *cognitive and social cognitive treatments*, as examples of the broader field of psychosocial interventions which are all targeted at improving functioning of people diagnosed with schizophrenia and other severe mental illnesses in a sustained manner.

As carefully detailed in Chapter 2, psychosocial rehabilitation has a long history extending well prior to the era of deinstitutionalization in the 1960s. As already described, the emergence of empirically-based, highly effective integrated social learning and behavioral therapies in inpatient settings pointed to the potential of rehabilitation for meeting recovery and treatment goals (e.g., Paul & Lentz, 1977). More recently, related behavioral therapies, including social skills training (Bellack et al., 2004), family (Falloon et al., 1984), and group-based interventions (e.g., McFarlane, 2002), supported vocational services (Bond, 2004), culturally-tailored interventions (Weisman de Mamani et al., 2016) and cognitive-behavioral therapy (Beck et al., 2011) have all been shown to be effective at meeting client-centered goals. In this section of the chapter we focus on the emergence and empirical support for one of the newest waves of behavioral treatment tailored to meet the recovery goals of people with schizophrenia: cognitive and social cognitive training.

Emergence of Cognitive and Social Cognitive Treatments for Schizophrenia

Cognition and Cognitive Remediation for People With Schizophrenia

While difficulties in thinking and remembering had been noted in the writings of Kraepelin and Bleuler as a core feature of their understanding of psychosis, and the seminal work of David Shakow in the early 1960s placed emphasis on attentional deficits as measured by reaction time in schizophrenia (Shakow, 1963), there remained limited scholarly and clinical attention toward measurement and treatment of these disorder manifestations through the 1980s. This changed when a growing scholarly and clinical knowledge base began to emerge and effloresce by the 1990s that cognitive deficits were common in schizophrenia across a broad array of cognitive skills, of a substantial magnitude and intimately tied to a variety of aspects of functional outcome. A series of experimental studies revealed that in addition to symptoms of delusions, hallucinations, social withdrawal, blunted affect, symptoms that all played a crucial role in diagnosis, there were less obvious but in many cases more functionally disabling symptoms of disruptions in concentration, attention, verbal and visual memory, problem solving, working memory and processing speed.

In one of the key studies of this era, Saykin et al (1991) investigated performance on a battery of cognitive tests used to assess cognitive domains of abstraction, verbal intelligence, spatial organization, semantic memory, visual memory, verbal learning, language, visuo-motor processing, auditory processing and motor tests, in a sample of 36 people with DSM-III schizophrenia and 36 matched healthy controls. Two strengths of the design included: (1) matching according to parental education and parental estimated IQ. Given that the illness interferes with the development of cognitive skills assessed by test of IQ, as well as attainment of educational goals, matching according to parental IQ avoided matching people with a diagnosis to an under-performing healthy control sample. And (2) using standardized residual scores as a means of addressing task differences in difficulty level and psychometric differences between tests. Results revealed generalized neuro-cognitive impairment in schizophrenia across all domains of cognition in the range of 1–2 standard deviations below healthy control test performance. Furthermore, deficits in learning and memory appeared to be selectively more impaired than other areas of cognition, and this impairment was beyond that accounted for by disruptions in attention. Follow-up studies revealed this pattern of deficits were evident in people in a first episode of schizophrenia without exposure to neuroleptics, arguing against the notion of these deficits as an epiphenomenon of pharmacological treatment (Saykin et al., 1994).

Findings from this era were summarized in a meta-analysis published in 1999 consisting of 204 studies of cognition in schizophrenia (Heinrichs & Zakzanis, 1998). Their results revealed substantial deficits in cognition evident in every area of cognition investigated, including global verbal memory, motor skill, attention, executive function non-verbal memory, verbal fluency and other areas. The magnitude of impairment was largest for measures of verbal memory, motor skill, performance IQ and sustained vigilance with more modest impairments on measures of vocabulary, and visuospatial skill (line orientation and Block Design from the WAIS-III). While there was evidence that deficits in global verbal memory were largest, deficits were evident across a wide variety of measures without clear evidence of a selective deficit, as evidenced by magnitude of impairment, in any one specific area. The authors noted the barriers to establishment of selective deficits in light of differences in psychometric characteristics of tests studied in their analysis such as reliability and task difficulty.

Subsequent meta-analyses have confirmed these findings. Schaefer et al. (2013) investigated studies of cognition in schizophrenia between the years 2006 and 2011 to compare with results from previous meta-analyses. A set of 100 non-overlapping studies were identified during this period and analyzed by cognitive domain and region of the world in which the study was conducted. Results were remarkably consistent with those from previous meta-analyses with test performance that was on average a standard deviation less than that for healthy controls. The magnitude of these impairments was largely consistent regardless of the region of the world in which the study was conducted (North America, Europe, or Asia).

Links Between Cognition and Function

In a group of highly influential theoretical reviews and one meta-analysis, Michael Green and colleagues (Green, 1997; Green et al., 2000, 2004, 2015) investigated links between cognition and functioning in people with a diagnosis of schizophrenia. Green grouped outcome into three major domains: (1) progress in skills training programs: These programs included social skills training, life skills training, or any formalized program designed to enhance life skills. These were approaches where acquisition of skills content could be measured on an ongoing basis during training, providing a discrete outcome to correlate with baseline cognitive performance. (2) Performance on instrumental tasks: These measures included demonstrations of social skills, such as appropriateness of eye contact or vocal tone, as well as relevance of orally expressed content, during a simulated social encounter with a clinician in a lab setting. These measures also included demonstrations of everyday life skills such as rescheduling an appointment with a health care provider or creating a shopping list based on items missing from a simulated pantry, and are similarly demonstrated in the lab and (3) measures of community function. In this last category, outcome is assessed usually through an interview with the client, often with the provision of collateral information from family members or treaters. These scales usually touch on work function, social function, independence in living kills and living status, reflect the success of the client in their local environment, and are the most comprehensive indices of outcome.

Results from these reviews revealed moderate to large links between cognition and function, with 20–60% of the variability in progress in skills training programs, instrumental skills, and interview-based assessments of community function explained by composite measures of neurocognitive function. While correlational, these links, evident both in cross-sectional and longitudinal studies, suggested that improving cognitive skills might in turn improve benefit from programs of rehabilitation, performance-based indices of function and community function.

Cognitive Remediation for Psychosis-Spectrum Illness

Cognitive remediation (CR) is a behavioral intervention consisting of extensive task practice and/or the acquisition of cognitive strategies with the aim of producing sustained changes in cognitive skills that generalize to functioning (Cognitive Remediation Experts Workshop; Florence, Italy, April 2010). Development of therapies for cognitive deficits were neglected until the 1990s for at least three key reasons: (1) it was unclear whether cognitive deficits were a primary feature of the illness, or secondary to distractions linked to positive symptoms such as delusions and hallucinations; (2) as schizophrenia became linked to neurological deficits as part of the first (mid-late 1800s) and second (1980s on) waves of biological psychiatry, a view emerged that cognitive deficits were linked to static neurological lesions and thus unmalleable; and (3) it remained unclear until emerging data from the 1990s whether these deficits played a role in outcome of central interests to clients such as work and social function.

First, as mentioned in the last chapter section, a growing literature in the 1990s revealed links between a variety of aspects of cognition and different domains of function. Second, numerous studies have shown the independence of positive symptoms from cognitive difficulties (e.g., Saykin et al., 1991), with some limited overlap between cognitive deficits and negative symptoms. Further, studies designed to test for the immutability of cognitive deficits, by training people with schizophrenia on a measure of problem-solving thought to be linked to frontal lobe function, showed that a variety of strategies, including step-by-step corrective feedback on these tasks, led to large and in some cases durable improvements on these cognitive measures. These proof-of-concept studies argued persuasively that cognitive deficits were not immutable in schizophrenia and could in fact be improved through a variety of behavioral approaches (e.g., Choi & Kurtz, 2009).

As a result, over the past 25 years there has been marked growth in the number of controlled trials investigating the efficacy of extended forms of CR in schizophrenia-spectrum disorders. The CR literature has been marked by diversity in both approach (e.g., having a client practice remembering word lists in a rote manner as a way to improve verbal memory versus teaching a client semantic grouping strategies to enhance recall), treatment targets (e.g., number of cognitive areas trained, merging of CR with other rehabilitation interventions) and administration (e.g., with a coach, by a computer). Despite this conceptual and methodological diversity, Wykes et al. (2011) in a meta-analysis of cognitive remediation across 40 studies and 2,104 participants showed CR was moderately beneficial in the improvement of cognitive ability. The quality of study design, as well as a variety of client factors, such as duration of illness, severity of symptoms, educational level, and dose of antipsychotic medication, did not serve as a barrier to clients' ability to benefit from these treatments. Importantly, results revealed that these CR effects generalized to measures of function, particularly when CR was administered with other psychosocial interventions, suggesting that improvements in cognitive function may translate into aspects of work function, social relationships and independence in living.

Two more recent meta-analyses, focused on computerized programs of CR only, have supported these initial results. Prikken et al. (2019) in a survey of studies investigating computerized, drill-and-practice programs of CR revealed small to moderate effects from 24 studies consisting of 1262 people with schizophrenia. Significant small to moderate effects were evident in attention and working memory, with unexpected effects on positive symptoms and depression. Significant effects were also evident in other domains of cognition. Kambietz-Ilankovic et al. (2019) investigated the role of supplementary human guidance (SHG) on computerized CR approaches. In this larger meta-analysis the authors coded studies as to whether treatment was conducted alone or in combination with a coach providing some type of encouragement and/or strategy. Results here also revealed significant effects of CR on a variety of cognitive domains including attention, working memory, verbal memory, and problem-solving. Effects were also evident on psychosocial function and SHG did bolster treatment effects on several cognitive outcomes: verbal memory, working memory, and real-world cognitive skill.

Deficits in Social Cognition

In somewhat later but parallel work increasing research interest was focused on the characteristic ways in which people with schizophrenia constructed beliefs around themselves and even more importantly the world around them (e.g., Penn et al., 1997). These skills, labeled *social cognition*, are formally defined as the internal processes involved in understanding, thinking about and acting on information from the social world. These skills are hypothesized to be consequential for the emergence of symptoms, psychosocial impairment, as well as each person's journey of recovery.

Measures of social cognition are different from elementary cognition in several key respects. First, cognitive measures typically use stimuli that are words, numbers and other symbols that are typically affectless and static over time. In contrast, measures of social cognition use social stimuli (faces, descriptions of social situations, other bodily displays of affect and social signaling) that may change over time. Further, these measures may be reflexive; there is a person observing the social stimuli and in turn there may be another participant watching the observer. Third, performance on measures of cognition is typically measured as a deficit. While certainly some measures of social cognition involve the measurement of deficits, some focus on biases in attention and interpretation of the social world instead. For example, a participant in a study may tend to blame others for negative social interactions. Such a bias would not be considered a deficit per se, but might play an important role in the emergence of specific psychiatric symptoms. Lastly, the way in which participants make sense of stimuli in social cognitive paradigms is of the utmost importance. Inferences based on bodily posture, vocal tone, facial affect, the back-and-forth between different actors in a social scene are what are measured by social cognitive indices. For cognitive measures task performance is typically observable (Penn et al., 1997).

Social cognitive skills have typically been grouped into four major categories: social perception, affect perception, mentalizing or theory-of-mind (ToM), and attributional style. ToM involves the ability to make accurate attributions about the dispositions and intentions of others. Social perception involves the understanding of social roles, social rules and context. It includes relationship perception and relies on non-verbal, verbal and paraverbal cues. Affect perception involves the analysis of facial expression, vocal tone and other bodily and verbal cues that suggest a specific affect. Attributional style is the tendency to make attributions about the source of negative events. The source may be situational, the source may be actions of the self, or the source may be the actions of others. (Penn, Sanna, & Roberts, 2008).

The presence of deficits was established in a key meta-analysis consisting of 112 studies with close to 4,000 people with schizophrenia (Savla et al., 2013). Results revealed large impairments on measures of social perception, ToM, emotion perception and processing, with greater deficits in social and emotional perception associated with inpatient status and greater deficits in emotion processing associated with longer illness duration.

Links Between Social Cognition and Functional Outcome

Given the prevalence and magnitude of these deficits in social cognition, questions were raised as to what degree these deficits and biases might play a role in functional outcome similar to that of cognition. Models of links between deficits in social cognition and consequent disruptions in psychosocial function were formulated in which deficits in elementary social cognition such as facial affect perception, biases in attributions and disruptions in ToM could produce downstream effects in functioning across a variety of functional domains. In these models deficits in affect perception could produce wrong conclusions about another person's mental state ("my coworker is angry at me" when in fact the coworker is distressed). In turn, biased attributions that tend toward blaming others may lead the individual with social cognitive deficits to assume the worker is angry with them for no good reason leading to further anger and distress. Deficits in mentalizing serve as a barrier to the person placing themselves in the shoes of someone else and recognizing that negative affect might reflect the results of other pressures at work, rather than anger targeted at the person with deficits. Lastly, feelings of frustration and anger generated by poor affect recognition, biased attribution and limited ToM skills could: (1) impede the expression of appropriate social skills with the coworker, and might lead the person with deficits to act in ineffective ways (trying to disrupt or sabotage the worker), (2) cause sufficient emotional distress to influence successful performance of their job, and (3) motivate the person with social cognitive deficits to socially withdraw as a means of avoiding interactions with the coworker (see Penn, Sanna & Roberts, 2008).

To test these hypotheses, in a synthetic analysis of the extant literature, Couture et al. (2006) collected data from 23 studies investigating at least one measure of social cognition and one aspect of function. Function was grouped into four major categories: (1) milieu measures of function that typically consisted of the assessment of client behavior in an institutionalized setting such as an inpatient unit; (2) measures of community function that assessed aspects of work, interpersonal skills and independent living typically through interview for clients living in the community; (3) social skills; directly observed aspects of social skill (vocal tone, eye contact, etc.); and (4) social problem-solving in which clients are asked to generate solutions to social problems encountered in everyday life. Their results revealed that social perception was repeatedly linked to a variety of outcomes including community function, behavior in the milieu and social problem-solving. Emotion perception had a consistent, yet modest, relationship with community function, social skills and social behavior in the milieu, while ToM was linked to community behavior and behavior within the milieu. Taken together these findings suggested a link between social cognition and functioning in people with schizophrenia.

A subsequent question remains as to the incremental validity of social cognitive deficits and biases in explaining outcomes in schizophrenia relative to elementary cognitive deficits. This question was addressed in a recent meta-analysis comparing social cognitive and cognitive predictors of a variety of aspects of psychosocial function (Halverson et al., 2019). Consisting of 166 studies, correlations between cognition, social cognition and functional outcome suggested small but significant links between these illness domains. Social cognition explained more unique variation than neurocognition (7.3% versus 4.4%) in studies that measured both cognitive and social cognitive skills in the same sample, and there was evidence that social cognition served as a partial mediator of neurocognition and function relationships. The authors concluded that interventions optimized to target both cognitive and social cognitive impairments in schizophrenia may be most likely to produce improvements in outcome.

Social Cognitive Treatments

Over the past decade a growing number of investigators and clinicians have focused on developing new treatment strategies tailored to the types of social cognitive skills outlined in the last section. One example of a prominent approach has been Social Cognitive and Interaction Training (SCIT), developed by David Penn, David Roberts and their colleagues (e.g., Penn et al., 2007; Wolwer et al., 2010). This is a broad-based approach designed to address deficits and biases in several different domains of social cognitive processing including emotion recognition, ToM and attributional style. Comprised of three phases and lasting 20–24 weeks SCIT is a comprehensive "stand-alone" manualized treatment approach. The first phase of treatment provides information about emotions and their relationships to thoughts and situations, defines basic emotions, improves emotion perception skills with computerized facial expression training tools and ends with a section teaching clients to distinguish between justified and unjustified suspiciousness. The second phase is focused on the pitfalls of jumping to conclusions. Exercises are designed to enhance cognitive flexibility in social situations, distinguish between personal and situational attributions, and differentiate social "facts" (e.g., the color of someone's hair) from social "guesses" (she threw the ball at the wall because she is angry). The last phase of training teaches clients to assess the certainty of facts and guesses around them in their personal lives, help them recognize that sometimes they must be good detectives and get additional information to assess guesses made about their social environment, and teach social skills for effectively obtaining additional information about social guesses from others. Both targeted and broad-based approaches to treating social cognitive deficits and biases have yielded promising results to date with effects sizes in the medium to large range for emotion perception, social perception, and ToM in controlled studies (Kurtz & Richardson, 2012; Nijman et al., in press).

The Concept of Recovery and Measuring Outcome in Studies of Cognitive and Social Cognitive Training and Other Psychosocial Interventions

A major issue confronting studies of psychosocial interventions, including the types of cognitive interventions discussed in this chapter, is the degree to which the concept of "recovery" can be captured by the types of clinician-administered measures of psychosocial function commonly used in psychosocial intervention studies. In these scales, clinicians or research assistants typically ask questions regarding clients' frequency of social contacts, whether they are employed and if so, the nature and amount of work, and questions around a client's living situation and the degree to which the client is independent in carrying out day-to-day activities. However, over the past 20 years, as viewpoints around mental health outcomes have expanded and increasingly incorporated consumer views, there has been a corresponding increase in emphasis placed on the concept of subjective "life satisfaction" or "quality of life" and "self-esteem" as key endpoints in investigation of interventions.

However, at the same time, as these scales have been increasingly incorporated into studies of rehabilitation intervention, concerns that improvements in objective psychosocial function may not correspond to equivalent improvements in client life satisfaction have taken on particular importance as a growing number of studies have failed to document expected associations. Indeed, perceptions of life satisfaction may be affected by appraisal processes that shift regarding key expectations as functioning improves. Other factors, such as depression, psychotic symptoms, cognitive and social cognitive skills, and personality traits may all play a role in mediating the relationships between objective improvements in psychosocial function and anticipated changes in subjective experience around these central life domains. For example, in a study of 40 people with schizophrenia Brekke et al. (2001) evaluated the role of executive function, as measured by the Wisconsin Card Sorting Test, as a moderator of the relationship between life satisfaction and measured psychosocial function during community-based rehabilitation. While clients with poor executive function showed moderate improvements in subjective life satisfaction as objective functioning improved during community rehabilitation, clients with intact executive function showed modest *negative* relationships between improvements in function and subjective life satisfaction. Based on these results the authors speculated that clients with intact executive function were likely better able to mentally represent and compare current functioning with stronger premorbid function, and other, higher-functioning, reference groups leading to more negative attitudes toward the self. Clients with less cognitive skill in representing and comparing premorbid skills, and life skills in other reference groups, saw no disruption in the relationship of life satisfaction to improvements in psychosocial function.

Further research has emphasized that different domains of psychosocial function (work life, social relationships, living situation) may track differently with attitudes around satisfaction with life and the self. Edmondson et al. (2012) in a longitudinal study of 145 people with schizophrenia evaluated both role functioning and satisfaction with life across three separate domains of psychosocial function: work, social function, and living situation during 12 months of community treatment. Interestingly, while global indices of function and life satisfaction mirrored one another over the 12-month study period, only perceptions of quality of living situation were directly tied to improvements in clients' living situations, while neither satisfaction around work life, nor around social relationships tracked with objective improvements in these domains. These findings suggest that other aspects of social and work function that are not attended to in traditional psychosocial outcome scales may be influencing subjective experiences of life satisfaction and thus this behooves researchers and clinicians to tailor interventions to address these unmet needs.

Conclusion

In conclusion, early initial diagnostic formulations of schizophrenia as a disorder characterized by clinical decline and profound functional impairment have not been supported by carefully designed, descriptive longitudinal research. Research has instead supported the notion of a diversity of potential outcomes, both between individuals and within different functional life domains in the same individual. These findings, coupled with a rich array of complex social forces, have led to a growing psychiatric consumer recovery movement that has appropriately demanded a greater participatory role in the development and evaluation of new treatments. The recovery movement has advocated for treatments that go well beyond short-term clinical stabilization, that include choice and empowerment of the client, and that promote positive psychosocial outcomes that are sustained and meaningful to individuals diagnosed with schizophrenia. Two examples of novel treatment approaches of this type, cognitive and social cognitive training, are particularly promising with respect to improving quality of life and social and role functioning in people with a diagnosis of schizophrenia. Further research should be aimed at: (1) determining which key elements of these psychosocial treatments produce the largest change in client-preferred outcomes so that that a new generation of treatments may be formulated to build on small to moderate effects evident from current research, (2) attending more carefully to client-centered outcomes such as life satisfaction and self-esteem, to ensure that novel psychosocial interventions address the needs of the whole person diagnosed with schizophrenia, and (3) tailoring behavioral treatment technologies to flexibly address those disabilities that are unique and personally meaningful to each client.

REFERENCES

American Psychiatric Association. (1994). *DSM-IV: Diagnostic and statistical manual of mental disorders* (4th edition). American Psychiatric Association.
American Psychiatric Association. (2013). *DSM-5: Diagnostic and statistical manual of mental disorders* (5th edition). American Psychiatric Association.
Anthony, W. A. (1993). Recovery from mental illness: The guiding vision of the mental health service system of the 1990s. *Psychosocial Rehabilitation Journal, 16,* 11–23.
Beck, A. T., Rector, N. A., Stolar, N., Grant, P. (2011). *Schizophrenia. Cognitive Theory, Research and Therapy.* Guilford Press.
Bellack, A. S., Mueser, K. T., Gingerich, S., & Agresta, J. (2004). *Social Skills Training for Schizophrenia: A Step-by-Step Guide.* Guilford Press.
Berrios, G., & Hauser, R. (1988). The early development of Kraepelin's ideas on classification: A conceptual history. *Psychological Medicine, 18,* 813–821.
Bleuler, E. (1950). *Dementia Praecox or The Groups of Schizophrenias* (J. Zinkin, trans.). International Universities Press.

Bond, G. (2004). Supported employment: Evidence for an evidence-based practice. *Psychiatric Rehabilitation Journal, 27,* 345–359.

Brekke, J. S., Kohrt, B., & Green, M. F. (2001). Neuropsychological functioning as a moderator of the relationship between psychosocial functioning and the subjective experience of self and life in schizophrenia. *Schizophrenia Bulletin, 27,* 697–708.

Choi, J., & Kurtz, M. M. (2009). A comparison of remediation techniques on the Wisconsin Card Sorting Test in schizophrenia. *Schizophrenia Research, 107,* 76–82.

Couture, S. M., Penn, D. L., & Roberts D. L. (2006). The functional significance of social cognition in schizophrenia: A review. *Schizophrenia Bulletin, 32,* S44–S63

Deegan, P. E. (1988). Recovery: The lived experience of rehabilitation. *Psychosocial Rehabilitation Journal 11,* 11–19.

Deegan, P. E. (1996). Recovery as a journey of the heart. *Psychosocial Rehabilitation Journal, 19,* 91–97.

DeSisto, M., Harding, C. M., McCormick, R. V., Asikaga, T., & Brooks, G. W. (1995). The Maine and Vermont three decade studies of serious mental illness II. Longitudinal course comparisons. British Journal of Psychiatry, *167,* 338–342.

Edmondson, M. Pahwa, R. Lee, K. K., Hoe, M., & Brekke, J. S. (2012). A dual change model of life satisfaction and functioning in individuals with schizophrenia. *Schizophrenia Research, 139,* 110–115.

Experts in cognitive remediation workshop. 2010, Florence, Italy.

Falloon, I., Boyd, J., & McGill, C. (1984). *Family Care of Schizophrenia.* Guilford

Farkas M. (2007). The vision of recovery today: What it is and what it means for services. *World Psychiatry 6,* 4–10.

Green, M. F. (1997). What are the functional consequences of neurocognitive deficits in schizophrenia? *American Journal of Psychiatry, 153,* 321–330.

Green, M. F., Kern, R. S., Braff, D. L., & Mintz, J., (2000). Neurocognitive deficits and functional outcome in schizophrenia: Are we measuring the "right stuff"? *Schizophrenia Bulletin, 26*(1), 119–136.

Green, M. F., Kern, R. S., & Heaton, R. K., (2004). Longitudinal studies of cognition and functional outcome in schizophrenia: Implications for MATRICS. *Schizophrenia Research, 72,* 41–51.

Green, M. F., Llerena, K., & Kern, R. S. (2015). The "Right Stuff" revisited: What have we learned about the determinants of daily function in schizophrenia? *Schizophrenia Bulletin, 41,* 781–785.

Halverson, T. F., Orleans-Pobee, M., Merritt, C., Sheeran, P., Fett, A. K., & Penn, D. L. (2019). Pathways to functional outcomes in schizophrenia spectrum disorders: A meta-analysis of social cognitive and neurocognitive predictors. *Neuroscience and Biobehavioral Reviews, 105,* 212–219.

Harding, C. M., Brooks, G. W., Ashikaga, T., Strauss, J., & Breier, A. (1987). The Vermont longitudinal study of persons with severe mental illness; II. Long-term outcome of subjects who retrospectively met DSM-III criteria for schizophrenia. *American Journal of Psychiatry, 144,* 727–735.

Harrington, A. (2019). *Mind Fixers. Psychiatry's Troubled Search for the Biology of Mental Illness.* W.W. Norton.

Harrow, M., Grossman, L. S., Jobe, T. H., & Herbener, E. S. (2005). Do patients with schizophrenia ever show periods of recovery? A 15-year multi-follow-up study. *Schizophrenia Bulletin, 144,* 727–735.

Harrow, M., & Jobe, T. H. (2007). Factors involved in outcome and recovery in schizophrenia patients not on antipsychotic medications: A 15-year follow-up study. *Journal of Nervous and Mental Disease, 195,* 406–415.

Heinrichs, R. W., & Zakzanis, K. K. (1998). Neurocognitive deficit in schizophrenia: A quantitative review of the evidence. *Neuropsychology, 12,* 426–445.

Kambeitz-Ilankovic, L, Betz, LT, Dominike, C, Haas, S, Subramaniam, K, Fisher, M, Kambeitz, J. (2019). Multi-outcome meta-analysis (MOMA) of cognitive remediation in schizophrenia: Revisiting the relevance of human coaching and elucidating interplay between multiple outcomes. *Neuroscience and Biobehavioral Reviews, 107,* 826–845.

Kaplan, R. M. (2008). Being Bleuler: The second century of schizophrenia. *Australasian Psychiatry, 16,* 305–311.

Kendler, K. S., & Jablensky, A. (2011). Kraepelin's concept of psychiatric illness. *Psychological Medicine, 41,* 1119–1126.

Kraepelin, E. (1919). *Dementia Praecox.* Translated by R. M. Barclay. E. S. Livingstone, Ltd.

Kurtz, M. (2015). *Schizophrenia and its treatment: Where is the progress?* Oxford University Press.

Kurtz, M. M., & Richardson, C. L. (2012). Social cognitive training for schizophrenia: A meta-analytic investigation of controlled research. *Schizophrenia Bulletin, 38,* 1092–1104.

Leff, J., Sartorius, N., Jablensky, A. Korten, A., & Ernberg, G. (1992). The International Pilot Study of Schizophrenia. Five-year follow-up. *Psychological Medicine, 22,* 131–145.

McFarlane, W. R. (2002). *Multifamily groups in the treatment of severe psychiatric disorders.* Guilford Press.

Mueser, K. T., Deavers, F., Penn, D. L., & Cassisi, J. E. (2013). Psychosocial treatment for schizophrenia. *Annual Review of Clinical Psychology, 9,* 465–497.

Nijman, S. A., Veling, W., van der Stouwe, E. C., & Pijnenborg, G. H. (2020). Social cognition training for people with a psychotic disorder: a network meta-analysis. *Schizophrenia bulletin, 46*(5), 1086–1103.

Paul, G. L. & Lentz, R. J. (1977). *Psychosocial Treatment of Chronic Mental Patients.* Harvard University Press.

Penn, D. L., Corrigan, P. W., Bentall, R. P., Racenstein, J. M., & Neman, L. (1997). Social cognition in schizophrenia. *Psychological Bulletin, 121,* 114–132.

Penn, D. L., Roberts, D. L., Combs, D., & Sterne, A. (2007). Best practices; the development of the social cognition and interaction training program for schizophrenia spectrum disorders. *Psychiatric Services, 58,* 449–451.

Penn, D. L., Sanna, L. J., & Roberts, D. L. (2008). Social cognition in schizophrenia: An overview. *Schizophrenia Bulletin, 34,* 408–411.

Prikken, M., Konings, M. J., Lei, W. U., Begemann, M. J. H., & Sommer, I. E. C. (2019). The efficacy of computerized drill-and-practice training for patients with a schizophrenia –Spectrum disorder: A meta-analysis. *Schizophrenia Research, 204,* 368–374.

Roe, D. (2001). Progressing from patienthood to personhood across the multidimensional outcomes in schizophrenia and related disorders. *Journal of Nervous and Mental Disease, 189,* 691–699.

100   Matthew M. Kurtz

Sartorius, N., Jablensky, A., & Shapiro, R. (1978). Cross-cultural differences in the short-term prognosis of schizophrenic psychoses. *Schizophrenia Bulletin, 4*, 102–113.

Savla, G., Vella, L., Armstrong, C., Penn, D. L., & Twamley, E. W. (2013). *Schizophrenia Bulletin, 39*, 979–992.

Saykin, A. J., Gur, R. C., Gur, R. E., Mozley, D., Mozley, L. H., Resnick, S. M., Kester, D. B., & Stafiniak, P. (1991). Neuropsychological function in schizophrenia: Selective impairment in learning and memory. *Archives of General Psychiatry, 48*, 618–624.

Saykin, A. J., Shtasel, D. L., Gur, R. E., Kester, D. B., Mozley, L. H., Stafiniak, P., & Gur, R. C. (1994). Neuropsychological deficits in neuroleptic naive patients with first-episode schizophrenia. *Archives of General Psychiatry, 51*(2), 124–131.

Schaefer, J., Giangrande, E., Weinberger, D. R., & Dickinson, D. (2013). The global cognitive impairment in schizophrenia: Consistent over decades and around the world. *Schizophrenia Research, 150*, 42–50.

Shakow, D. (1963). Psychological deficit in schizophrenia. *Behavioral Science, 8*, 275–305.

Shorter, E. (1997). *A History of Psychiatry*. Wiley.

Stephens, J. H. (1978). Long-term prognosis and follow-up in schizophrenia. *Schizophrenia Bulletin, 4*, 25–47.

Tsuang, M. T., Woolson, R. F., & Fleming, J. A. (1979). Long-term outcome of major psychoses. I. Schizophrenia and affective disorders compared with psychiatrically symptom free surgical conditions. *Archives of General Psychiatry, 36*, 1295–1301.

Weisman de Mamani, A., & Suro, G. (2016). The effect of a culturally-informed therapy on self-conscious emotions and burden in caregivers of patients with schizophrenia. *A randomized clinical trial. Psychotherapy, 53*, 57–67. DOI: 10.1037/pst0000038

Wolwer, W., Combs, D., Fromann, N., & Penn, D. L. (2010). Treatment approaches with a special focus on social cognition: Overview and empirical results. In V. Roder, A. Medalia (Eds) *Neurocognition and social cognition in schizophrenia patients. Basic concepts and treatments. Key issues in mental health*. Karger 177, 61–78.

World Health Organization. (1973). *International pilot study of schizophrenia*. New York: Author.

Wykes, T., Huddy, V., Cellard, C., McGurk, S. R., & Czobor, P. (2011). A meta-analysis of cognitive remediation for schizophrenia: Methodology and effect-sizes. *American Journal of Psychiatry, 168*, 472–485.

Part II

The Present

5 Training US Community Mental Health Centers in Evidence-Based Coordinated Specialty Care for First Episode Psychosis

Observations from the NAVIGATE Program Trainers

Shirley M. Glynn, Susan Gingerich, Piper Meyer-Kalos, and Delbert G. Robinson

As detailed in a recent article by Kendler (2020), while Kraepelin's original ideas about the long-term nature of schizophrenia evolved over time, he envisioned many of those diagnosed with the disorders as having a life-long, deteriorating course. However, in the 1950s and 1960s, as antipsychotic and mood stabilizing medications were serendipitously found to reduce some schizophrenia and affective symptoms, an inchoate sense of optimism about the course of schizophrenia spectrum disorders began to grow. Concurrently, psychological conceptualizations and behaviorally-based interventions for serious psychiatric illness began to be proposed, such as in Ayllon and Azrin's (1968) landmark text: *"The token economy: A motivational system for therapy and rehabilitation."*

With the deinstitutionalization movement, treatment in the community for serious mental illness (SMI) became the norm. Studies on SMI psychological interventions in the 1970s and 80s were primarily behavioral and often trans-diagnostic, and included positive trials on token economies (Paul & Lentz, 1977) and social skills training (Bellack et al.,1976). Concurrently, there was increasing recognition that environmental stress could increase vulnerability to schizophrenia symptoms (Zubin & Spring, 1977). This "vulnerability-stress" heuristic prompted efforts to reduce ambient stress for those living with schizophrenia by intervening with their loved ones (Falloon et al., 1982; Hogarty, 1986; Hogarty, 1991), and by offering comprehensive team-based services in the community to reduce hospitalizations (Assertive Community Treatment; Test & Stein, 1976). By the 1990s, especially in the United Kingdom, targeted interventions such as cognitive behavioral therapy or cognitive therapy for psychosis became more prevalent (e.g., Garety et al., 1994; Kingdon et al., 1994). These interventions utilized many of the strategies, including collaborative empiricism and gentle challenging, which had been proposed almost 50 years earlier by Beck (1952), and had been used successfully in the treatment of depression (see Dobson, 1989 for a review).

The Initiation of First Episode of Psychosis Interventions

As individuals living with schizophrenia spectrum disorders accrued benefits from these psychosocial interventions, and as better tolerated medications became available, researchers began to consider the possibility that, if offered when an individual was experiencing early symptoms, treatment might actually improve the trajectory of the illness course. Perhaps these interventions might even result in the recovery of many individuals recently diagnosed with the illness; schizophrenia may lead less often to lifetime disability. Clinical researchers embedded in national health care systems in Europe, Canada, and Australia were among the first to test the benefits of early intervention programs for schizophrenia in rigorously designed trials. National healthcare systems could support large-scale surveillance and referral initiatives, which were thought essential to mounting successful first episode psychosis (FEP) programs. These comprehensive interventions typically included tailored antipsychotic medication, family education, and individual therapy, with most also including supported employment and education. Randomized trials in Italy (Ruggeri et al., 2015), Denmark (Peterson et al., 2005), the United Kingdom (Grawe et al., 2006), and Australia (Gleeson et al., 2009) all confirmed the benefits of such comprehensive programs in improving outcomes in FEP; a large comprehensive meta-analysis mirrored these findings (Correl et al., 2018).

There is now an international movement to provide intensive coordinated specialty care (CSC; the term typically used in the USA) or early intervention in psychosis services (EIP; the term often used in other countries) to young people (typically with ages from 15 to 40) experiencing an FEP. US programs target primarily individuals experiencing a non-affective psychosis, which is understood to be a likely precursor to the development of a disorder on the schizophrenia spectrum. EIP programs are more likely to use broader diagnostic inclusion criteria. CSC and EIP programs typically include illness education, family support, individual cognitive behaviorally oriented psychotherapy, supported employment and education, and low-dose medication regimens (Azrin et al., 2015).

FEP Programs in the USA

The USA has only recently begun to offer CSC programs widely on a systematic level. Srihari et al. (2015) compared a CSC program called *Specialized Treatment Early in Psychosis* (STEP) to customary care in Connecticut. STEP includes comprehensive clinical evaluation and regular outcome assessment, medication management, and individual and group therapy. Treatment targets include school and/or work goals, problem-solving and communication skills, stress management, health and wellness, symptom reduction and personal goals. Symptom status, social functioning, and hospitalization data were collected every six months on 117 randomized participants through the one-year follow-up in their trial. STEP care resulted in significantly fewer total hospitalizations and a significantly lower likelihood of hospitalization. STEP participants were also more likely to be engaged in productive vocational activity and remain engaged in mental health treatment than those in usual treatment.

The STEP trial was conducted in a US academic setting, and the question remained – could CSC be effective even in a fragmented, multi-payer mental health system such as that found in US community care? To address this question, Kane et al. (2016) conducted a 34-site cluster randomized controlled trial funded by the National Institute of Mental Health (NIMH) comparing CSC to customary care at community mental health centers throughout the country. Four hundred and four individuals were randomized and offered a minimum of two years of CSC or customary care; the CSC was labeled "NAVIGATE." NAVIGATE included tailored manualized medication, family education and support, individual illness resiliency training, and supported employment and education. Outcome data were collected every six months on symptom and employment/educational status, quality of life, treatment retention, and rate of hospitalization; services were offered for a minimum of two years. The two-year outcomes revealed the 223 recipients of NAVIGATE remained in treatment longer, experienced greater improvement in quality of life and reductions in overall psychopathology (including depression and schizophrenia symptoms), and participated more in work and school compared to the 181 participants in community care; there were no differences in hospitalization rates, which were low for both groups.

Based on these findings, U.S. H.R 3547, the "Consolidated Appropriations Act, 2014" was passed; the legislation provided funds to the Substance Abuse and Mental Health Services Administration (SAMHSA) to provide targeted funds for the development of early psychosis treatment programs across the United States through the SAMHSA Mental Health Block Grant program to the states. Mandated by Congress, SAMHSA's block grants are noncompetitive annual funds that support substance abuse and mental health services throughout the country. A 5% set-aside (approximately $25M) was allocated to SAMHSA's Mental Health Block Grant program to support the work (Heinssen et al., 2014); it has subsequently been increased to 10%. This FEP initiative is one of the largest to be instituted in the US mental healthcare system.

The NAVIGATE Program: A Prototypic Evidence-Based FEP Program

The NAVIGATE program has been one of the CSC programs disseminated broadly throughout the USA in this initiative. NAVIGATE training has been provided to a total of 63 teams spread out over 28 states throughout the country since 2008. The teams are located in a wide variety of settings, including urban, suburban, rural, and frontier. NAVIGATE training has been provided internationally in Israel, Canada, and China.

Successful implementation of evidence-based interventions is the Achilles heel of health care (Balas & Boren, 2000; Grant et al., 2003; Morris et al, 2011). The barriers and facilitators to successful implementation have been well-documented over decades (Addis et al., 2006), with the importance of ongoing consultation after initial training being viewed as especially critical (Foa et al., 2020; Oliver & Lang, 2018). The national directive to implement FEP programs in the USA provided an opportunity to utilize a planful, comprehensive implementation strategy to promote optimal care. Of course, depending on local resources and priorities, implementation at the local level varied.

Here we describe the provision of readiness assessment, staff training and case consultation, as well as technical assistance to agency leadership, to support wide-scale implementation of the NAVIGATE program. We then detail challenges encountered and lessons learned in implementing a multifaceted intervention program in typical US community mental health care. Our goal is to acquaint readers with the NAVIGATE program as an exemplar of an evidence-based intervention for FEP and to help them consider the various elements required in any training program they might mount to support recovery from serious mental illness in the USA.

An Overview of NAVIGATE

The core principles of the NAVIGATE program can be seen in Table 5.1. Both the guiding principles and the core NAVIGATE components (described below) are comparable to many of the other prominent CSC programs in the US, such as OnTrackNY (https://www.ontrackny.org/), the Early Assessment and Support Alliance Program (http://www.easacommunity.org/) in Oregon, and the EPICENTER programs in Arizona and Ohio (Breitborde et al., 2020). NAVIGATE calls for weekly meetings among all the staff. A program director (typically a licensed mental health clinician with a minimum of a master's degree) is responsible for leading the project, engaging new participants into the program, coordinating team efforts, assuring financing, and designing and overseeing data collection for program evaluation purposes. Service users are

Table 5.1. *Core NAVIGATE principles*

* Use shared decision-making as a framework
* Keep a strength and resiliency focus
* Take a psychoeducational approach
* Use motivational enhancement when teaching skills
* Collaborate with natural supports
* Utilize evidence-based treatments
* Provide team-based collaborative care

generally offered access to the program for a minimum of two years. A fuller description of the NAVIGATE psychosocial components can be found in Mueser et al. (2015); the NAVIGATE manuals are available at navigateconsultants.org.

Essential Intervention Components of NAVIGATE

* Access to Tailored Medication – Medication in NAVIGATE follows evidence-based prescribing guidelines for FEP, while also attending to tailoring medication to address participants undesirable side effects (Robinson et al., 2018). Participants are queried prior to each prescriber visit about side effects and perceived benefits of medication. There is also close monitoring of vitals and lab values that might presage early signs of health problems such as diabetes, obesity, or hypertension.
* Individual Resiliency Training (IRT) – IRT is an individual psychotherapy which involves specialized strategies to address unique challenges associated with FEP including experiencing ongoing symptoms and engaging in mental health treatment for the first time. While IRT includes some features of cognitive behavioral therapy for psychosis, the material is expanded to include goal setting, coping skills and topics such as identifying and building on strengths and processing the psychotic episode.
* Family Education – Family members are provided with education and tools to support a loved one's recovery from an FEP, as well as access to the treatment team. The material provided to relatives parallels the information and skills taught in IRT. Individuals experiencing the psychosis may attend conjoint sessions, or they may agree to their relatives attending without them.
* Supported Employment and Education (SEE) – All NAVIGATE participants are offered SEE services at entry, and then again as they progress throughout the program if they initially decline the service. SEE focuses on helping individuals in NAVIGATE develop and pursue educational or

vocational goals; the intervention is grounded in the principles of Individual Placement and Support (Becker and Drake, 2003). Participants engage in an initial orientation and assessment to identify strengths and work or school preferences, and then are offered support (typically with "hands-on" work in the community) to find suitable opportunities to pursue these preferences. Further support is provided to help participants retain desired work and school placements.

Elements Not Part of the Original NAVIGATE Model

US CSC models like NAVIGATE were first developed almost 15 years ago. Experience with their implementation since that time has highlighted the importance of including additional intervention elements that were not included in the original model to support recovery from an FEP. These include:

- Peer Support – When the original NAVIGATE program was being developed in 2008–2009, funding was limited for peer support services, and the peer support specialist certification program was not widely available. Over time, the peer mental health workforce has been widely expanded, and it is clear that the benefits of service user access to peers are substantial. Subjective benefits of FEP service users' access to peer support include modeling, encouragement and hope (Chinman et al., 2014). There also appear to be tangible benefits to including peer support in FEP programs. For example, Ojeda et al. (2020) recently reported that the availability of peer support in FEP programs in Los Angeles and San Diego was associated with increased service use and reduced disparities due to ethnic minority status.
- Case management – Access to case management was not included in the original NAVIGATE because the program developers assumed this was a foundational component of service at mental health agencies treating individuals living with psychosis. FEP service users often have many social service needs, as they may wish to apply for social security disability or other financial support, need help with housing and transportation, need help with concurrent substance abuse treatment, and require health insurance. The availability of case management support for FEP service users is essential.

Meeting Service Users' Other Needs

It is important to note that, while a comprehensive suite of services is offered in NAVIGATE, these can be supplemented by other treatments to meet specific service user's circumstances. While the needs of most NAVIGATE service users can be met by the core set of interventions provided, sometimes other work is called for. For example, some service users may need access to supported housing, while others may need detoxification treatment. As long as these adjunctive services have a recovery focus and work in collaboration with the NAVIGATE treatment team, they can be extremely useful in improving outcomes in FEP.

NAVIGATE Training Model

While many community mental health centers are very enthusiastic about offering FEP programs, their staff backgrounds and skills, as well as organizational structure, are typically more aligned with the needs of longer-term service users. For example, many FEP service users are under 18, and adult clinics may have little familiarity with interacting with high schools and the needs and preferences of 15 or 16-year olds who have just experienced a psychotic episode. Assertively advocating to involve family members in care is often another challenge for FEP clinicians who are used to working with service users in their 30s, 40s, and 50s who may not consent to family meetings or may be estranged from their relatives. Similarly, individuals in FEP programs need much more frequent and longer prescriber appointments than the 15 minutes every one or two months that are typically offered to more stable, long-term service users, so schedules often need to be revamped.

Successful implementation of NAVIGATE involves both individual clinicians learning and implementing new skills as well as galvanizing all members of the treatment team to engage and meet the needs of individuals with a recent diagnosis of non-affective psychosis. In addition, optimal implementation requires the support of strong leadership and the team's home agency. In light of the challenges in reforming a service system targeted to long-term service users to support the recoveries of young individuals experiencing an FEP, it is perhaps not surprising that the NAVIGATE training model is comprehensive, multifaceted, and intensive.

NAVIGATE Training

NAVIGATE Training occurs in four phases, as described below. While the particulars of NAVIGATE are outlined here, many of the elements would apply to any US CSC program.

Phase 1: Readiness Assessment and Preparation of the Agency. Many mental health agencies are eager to include new innovative evidence-based treatments in their settings, and yet they often have limited awareness of what is required to mount a specific novel intervention. This mismatch between setting characteristics, available resources, and the needs of the program can lead to implementation failures. For example, if a clinical intervention is designed to be conducted by licensed mental health providers, but an agency is staffed primarily by college graduate-level case managers, the uptake of the new intervention will be problematic in spite of the best efforts of all participants.

To address this concern about agency readiness, the NAVIGATE training coordinator first schedules 1–2 phone consultations with interested parties who contact the training team. The calls are attended by facility administrative and clinical leadership, and the NAVIGATE Readiness Checklist (see Table 5.2) is useful in focusing the discussion.

Critical tasks in readiness assessment include:

- Obtaining details about the facility, including any current early psychosis offerings, characteristics of current population served at the facility, potential referral sources, etc.
- Calculating the number of first episode service users with a schizophrenia spectrum diagnosis that they can expect based on the population of their area to determine whether a targeted CSC program can be made financially feasible. Here, the calculation tool provided by Humensky et al. (2013) can be helpful.
- Based on anticipated case size, determining the staffing needs.
- Identifying potential NAVIGATE team members currently on the staff, with special attention to the requirements of the specified NAVIGATE roles (e.g., master's level clinician for Director, Family clinician, and IRT clinician; BA degree for Supported Employment and Education Specialist; MD or nurse practitioner for the prescriber).
- Reviewing local reimbursement policies for delivering NAVIGATE services and any additional funding available.
- Clarifying the activities of the team prescriber, as successful CSC services typically require longer and more frequent client meetings with the prescriber than are the norm at most community clinics. Participation of the prescriber is also needed in weekly team meetings.
- Reviewing the typical training schedule and resources needed to host the training.
- Identifying any potential impediments, including staff motivation.
- Responding to any questions administrative and clinical leadership have about the program.

The NAVIGATE training coordinator follows up the readiness call(s) with 1–2 additional hours of phone consultation focusing on program development to prepare for solid NAVIGATE implementation. This consultation includes planning for staffing the team, establishing clear patient enrollment criteria,

Table 5.2. *Preparation checklist for implementing a FEP team*

☐ Assure that there is a need for a first episode program in your community (calculate the number of first episode clients expected in your catchment area, using tools such as the OnTrack program calculator in the Humensky, Dixon, and Essock (2013) article)

☐ Based on number of first episode clients expected, determine if a team is needed, and if so, the size of the team needed (e.g., if the team is expecting to serve 25–30 clients, you may need a full team; if fewer clients, may need less than a full team)

☐ Decide on enrollment criteria (age, diagnosis, "rule-outs") and outcomes you want to measure (such as hospitalizations, days in work and school, and time retained in treatment)

☐ Meet with leadership and administrators and get their support at all levels; consider forming an advisory group that meets regularly

☐ Determine the model of FEP treatment that the team will follow, and the necessary components and staffing requirements for that model

☐ Explore funding streams to pay for the program (including Medicaid waivers, rehabilitation services, private health insurance, set-aside funding)

☐ Assure that team members will have access to the resources they need to do their work (e.g., cell phones, computers, cars, photocopying, brochures)

☐ Assure that team members have flexible hours to meet client and family needs, and have the ability to make home visits when needed

☐ Locate experienced trainers in the treatment model that has been selected and schedule training for the team (allow at least three months of lead time for trainers)

☐ Secure one year of follow-up consultation and support for the team as they work with clients and family members and other supporters using the chosen FEP model

☐ Consider long-term sustainability in all decisions made regarding funding streams, resource access, and staffing decisions

guiding work with private and public insurance to assure funding, developing a referral network, assuring protected time for team meetings and follow-up consultation calls, identifying outcome measures, developing publicity materials, preparing for outreach to local referral sources (such as inpatient facilities, emergency rooms, crisis teams, and outpatient mental health programs). In addition, the training plans are finalized, including the location, dates, who should attend each part of the training, and supplies needed (e.g., copies of the NAVIGATE manuals to be used during the training and afterwards).

Phase 2: Intensive Practical Training for the Team Members. NAVIGATE training consists of intensive work with the team, provided over the course of three days if provided in-person at the agency or spread out over the course of 3–4 weeks if provided online. The training includes a combination of didactic presentation, interactive discussions, case examples, videos, role-play demonstrations, and role-play practice.

Initial Team Building and Education. Typically, the training begins with the trainers and the local NAVIGATE team meeting together for approximately two hours, with the trainers providing basic information about FEP and the recommendations for its treatment. The trainers include CSC research and descriptions of how individuals experiencing a first episode of schizophrenia differ from those who have had multiple episodes over many years. The trainers outline the core principles underlying the NAVIGATE program and the specific interventions provided by the NAVIGATE team members. The trainers emphasize the importance of team collaboration and demonstrate an example of a team meeting in a role-play with the training participants.

This introduction is followed by a 90-minute presentation by the Prescriber Trainer about medication issues for FEP individuals. Because treatment engagement and reluctance to take medication are such significant issues in this population (Bowtell et al., 2018; Doyle et al., 2014), the trainers decided that all members of the clinical team could benefit from receiving basic information on treatment strategies and medication issues in NAVIGATE, with the objective that even non-medical professionals could support treatment adherence and program participation in their interactions with individuals in the NAVIGATE program. A key issue in this presentation and the subsequent meeting with the prescribers discussed immediately below is addressing issues of premature mortality in young people with schizophrenia (Schoenbaum et al., 2017) with a focus on the team acting proactively through an emphasis on health promotion and careful medical monitoring to address cardiovascular risk.

Following the whole team training, the trainers divide into separate groups to address in detail the roles of the Director, Prescriber, Family Education Clinician, IRT Clinician, SEE specialist, and Peer Specialist (if part of the team being trained). The specific intervention training focuses on hands-on learning, including becoming familiar with the manuals, watching videos and live demonstrations of the roles, participating in role-plays of common activities of the roles, and doing home practice assignments related to the roles.

Targeted Component Training

Director Training. The NAVIGATE Director training consists of a half day of in-person training addressing the three main stages of the Director role: (1)

forming the team and getting started, (2) leading the team and providing supervision, and (3) monitoring and maintaining NAVIGATE services. The emphasis of the training for Stage 1, *forming the team and getting started*, is on identifying and engaging suitable NAVIGATE participants. Directors are also provided with a list of common sources of NAVIGATE participant referrals, such as inpatient psychiatric facilities, emergency rooms, crisis teams, and outpatient psychiatric clinics. In addition, Directors are encouraged to explore additional referral sources such as chapters of the National Alliance on Mental Illness (NAMI), religious leaders, primary care doctors, high school counselors, police departments, and college or university counseling centers.

In the training for Stage 2, *leading the team and providing supervision*, the trainer provides an example of an agenda for the weekly NAVIGATE team meeting and reviews the role-play of a team meeting that was provided during the initial whole team training. The trainer leads a discussion of how to trouble-shoot problems that might arise in holding a weekly team meeting and provides specific strategies for conducting weekly intervention-specific supervision meetings with team members. In addition, the Directors are guided through the process of developing treatment plans and conducting collaborative treatment planning meetings that include the service user and the family (with permission of the service user).

In Stage 3, *monitoring and maintaining NAVIGATE services*, the trainer first reviews the importance of measuring service user outcomes. The nature of recommended outcome measures varies because different states have different requirements, but usually includes keeping track of hospitalizations, emergency room visits, homelessness, employment, school enrollment, and frequency of sessions attended by the service users. It is also important to monitor NAVIGATE activities, such as the number of outreach and education visits and phone calls completed, number of service users referred from each referral source, percentage of referrals who are ultimately enrolled in the program, total number of service users and families who have been engaged in services, and the length of time service users are involved in NAVIGATE services.

Prescriber Training. After the team receives information about basic medication management and health promotion, the local prescribers meet alone with the Prescriber Trainer for 90–120 mins to learn more about evidence-based prescribing practices for FEP, specific NAVIGATE-suggested treatment strategies and the necessity and strategy of gathering detailed information at each visit about the individual's symptoms and experience of side effects. The essential role of frequent lab work and following up abnormal results in the context of the population's greater cardiovascular risk is emphasized.

IRT Training. During the two intensive in-person training days for IRT, clinicians learn how to deliver the intervention and feel more confident and knowledgeable about specialized strategies to address unique challenges associated with first episode psychosis, including experiencing ongoing symptoms and being engaged in mental health treatment for the first time. IRT clinicians learn about the standard IRT modules offered to all participants (e.g., *Assessment and Goal Setting, Education about Psychosis*) as well as when and how to deliver the individualized modules to meet specific service user needs and goals (e.g., *Dealing with Negative Feelings, Having Fun and Developing Relationships*).

After an introduction to the goals of IRT and how to use the manual on the first day of training, clinicians review the first three standardized IRT modules to learn how to introduce IRT to a new service user. During the review of a module, clinicians complete some service user handouts using their own experiences and information such as completing the Brief Strengths Test (Peterson & Seligman, 2004), having trainees develop their own definition of wellness, and having trainees identify their own wellness goal(s). Clinicians also view recorded demonstration of IRT sessions and role-play with a partner to practice how to use handouts and teach skills. Lastly, during the discussion of the modules, strategies to address common challenges are reviewed, such as providing education about psychosis to individuals who do not believe they have an illness.

In day two of the in-person IRT training, clinicians learn symptom coping skills using a cognitive behavioral framework. Clinicians learn and practice the steps of skills training as an essential component of coping skills work. The remainder of the IRT training introduces the five steps of cognitive restructuring and provides an overview of the IRT *Processing the Episode* module. By the end of the IRT training, clinicians have typically learned the basics of starting a new person in IRT; have practiced key engagement and educational strategies (providing psychoeducation and setting goals); and learned the basics of cognitive behavioral approaches in IRT (helping individuals process the experience of having an episode of psychosis and delivering the five steps of cognitive restructuring).

SEE Training. The training engages SEE specialists by first providing a rationale for SEE treatment and the importance of work and school in FEP recovery and well-being. SEE specialists are provided with a manual overview and training in when and how to use key components of the manual such as addressing cognitive difficulties and completing assessments of career and education backgrounds and achievements. SEE specialists learn the SEE principles along with critical concepts specific to FEP persons such as viewing all behavior in the appropriate developmental context and encouraging participants to think about career options and opportunities, rather than limiting their vision to seeking simple entry-level job placements. During the training, SEE specialists discuss the SEE role on the NAVIGATE team and how to integrate SEE with the other NAVIGATE treatments.

SEE training includes opportunities for participants to see videos demonstrating skills, practice role-plays, and receive information and strategies to address common challenges such as disability disclosure to employers, managing cognitive deficits, and overcoming challenges when NAVIGATE participants have a history of criminal justice involvement. At the end of the SEE training, participants typically go into the local community and the trainer demonstrates job development with local businesses. SEE specialists then have an opportunity to practice job development themselves (with support from the SEE trainer).

Family Clinician Training. The 1.5 days of in-person Family Clinician training begins with a review of the research showing that family involvement improves service user outcomes and an overview of the NAVIGATE Family Education program, before diving into the Family Education manual. Trainees read some of the family handouts and clinician guidelines from the manual. This is followed by role-play demonstrations and practice of key family sessions. Additional time is spent on how to engage family members and encourage their participation in the family program, as well as how to work with service users who initially do not want their family to be involved in their treatment.

Throughout the training, strategies are provided for how to use the handouts flexibly and interactively while tailoring them to the needs of each individual family. Family Education Clinicians are encouraged to include the service user in family sessions whenever possible, especially when doing the module on *Developing A Plan for Staying Well*, which benefits from getting input from both the service user and relatives about planning for preventing the recurrence of symptoms, identifying early warning signs of relapse, and creating a plan for responding quickly if early warning signs are present.

Peer Training. If the team has a peer specialist, while the Prescriber Trainer is meeting with the prescribers, the training coordinator meets with the peer specialists to provide information about the variety of activities that they may provide on NAVIGATE teams. Peers have played many roles on NAVIGATE teams including working on engaging service users in treatment, sustaining service member participation in the program, leading recovery or support groups, cooperating on publicity efforts with the Team Leader, providing ongoing motivation, counseling and modeling for NAVIGATE service users, and acting as SEE specialists (if they have the requisite professional background and education).

Phase 3: Follow-up Consultation. There is now an ample literature showing short-term training alone rarely changes provider behavior (Beidas & Kendall, 2010; Herschell et al., 2010). Thus, a year of follow-up consultation was built into the original NAVIGATE training. Follow-up consultation, typically conducted by phone or online, begins about one month after the intensive training for the Directors, Family Clinicians, the IRT Clinicians, the SEE Specialists, and the Prescribers. The Director, Family, IRT, and SEE consultation calls are each scheduled twice a month for six months and once a month for another six months, while the prescriber calls occur once a month for 12 months.

During the follow-up consultation calls, team members can ask questions about challenges they experience using the manuals, skills, and strategies in NAVIGATE. The sessions typically begin by asking participants for items for the agenda, and each team member reports on the status of their work with service users and their families. The trainers then help NAVIGATE staff problem solve difficulties they encounter with program implementation and offer guidance to enhance engagement in treatment. The trainers also provide team members with ongoing instruction on additional skills and strategies that were unable to be covered during the intensive training days. Common teaching strategies that trainers utilize during the follow-up consultation calls include practicing skills using role-plays, reviewing key parts of the manuals and related NAVIGATE principles, and encouraging opportunities to connect with other NAVIGATE staff to increase treatment engagement and support continuity of care. Special attention is paid to improving recruitment and screening procedures to assure team viability.

Although labeled "consultation" it is important to distinguish the NAVIGATE consultation process from medical consultation or clinical supervision. In the latter, specific recommendations are made for an identified individual and there is an expectation that these recommendations will be followed. In contrast, NAVIGATE consultations are solely designed to help sites understand and implement, when appropriate, the NAVIGATE treatment model. Sites maintain their responsibility to decide if a NAVIGATE strategy or another treatment strategy is most appropriate for an individual in their care. An analogy for the role of the NAVIGATE consultant is the speaker role in question and answer periods at conferences. Attendees sometimes tell speakers that they have a particular clinical problem and ask what are the strategies to address the problem. No identifying information is presented. The trainer will then discuss the literature about evidence-based solutions for the posed problem.

Phase 4: Trained teams join the larger FEP learning community. In the later part of their consultation year, the NAVIGATE trainers begin to work toward planful termination of the consultation phase. Local teams are offered opportunities to join the larger group of mental health professionals working with FEP service users through organizations such as the International Early Intervention in Mental Health (iepa.org.au) as well as the PEPPNET Early Psychosis Consortium at Stanford (med.stanford.edu/peppnet.html) and the SAMHSA SMI Adviser program (smiadviser.org). In addition, some sites have opted to work with the NAVIGATE training teams in an intensive training so they can become local trainers in a "Train the Trainers" model.

Lessons Learned by the NAVIGATE Trainers

Over the past 13 years, the NAVIGATE trainers have been supporting the use of a complex specialized intervention model in community facilities throughout the USA. The training team has benefited from continual efforts to monitor and improve its processes and procedures to increase implementation success. Below, some of the key lessons the team has learned are offered. These may be helpful for any individual or group working to enhance the implementation of evidence-based practices at behavioral health facilities.

Advance Work is Critical

Agencies are often eager to implement novel practices. Their staff have frequently read the scientific literature and convey their enthusiasm about new interventions to their leadership, who may share their interest. However, implementation of new interventions (and larger programs) is challenging. Agency staff naturally still have a lot of questions, which if left unanswered, would result in a rocky start to training and implementation. In the case of NAVIGATE, for example, it is important for the agency to understand the educational and professional requirements of each role on the team (i.e., the IRT Clinician and Family Clinician need to have a clinical master's degree, the SEE Specialist needs a BA, and the Prescriber can be an MD or nurse practitioner) and to be staffed appropriately *before the training*. In addition, it is important for leadership to understand the enrollment (inclusion and exclusion) criteria for NAVIGATE and to be able to estimate the number of individuals they can expect in their geographical area to meet those criteria. In turn, knowing the number of individuals with FEP to expect allows them to plan for the appropriate number of service users, which in turn helps them determine the size of their team and to plan for the necessary hours of each team member. The agencies also need to think about how the time of each team member will be protected from the tasks they already have. For example, if a team is small initially, and the IRT clinician is only half-time on the team, what will prevent the non-NAVIGATE part of their job from taking away NAVIGATE time? Obtaining adequate prescriber effort is often a difficult issue as their schedules are usually fully booked at many agencies and agency administration will need to make accommodations. It has become clear that intensive preliminary work with an agency to determine their readiness and resources for change months before the actual clinician training is conducted is essential.

Training Needs to be Lively, Interactive, and "Hands-On"

NAVIGATE training follows the evidence-based behavioral skills training (BST) model, which consists of instructions, modeling, rehearsal, and feedback (Miltenberger, 2011). For example, rather than just hearing about how a weekly team meeting is conducted, it is more valuable to participate in a role-play of a team meeting, using the suggested meeting agenda. The trainer is not only teaching, but also modeling an active, hands-on approach which can then be used with colleagues and service users. As another example, rather than just hearing about strategies for engaging potential service users, it is more beneficial for trainees to see a demonstration of how the trainer would use such strategies, to have an opportunity to discuss what they observed, and then practice it themselves in role-plays. Case examples, group work, and video demonstrations can be invaluable in making the training "alive."

Integrating personal experience can also strengthen learning. For some of the components of NAVIGATE, it can be helpful for the training participants to try them out on themselves. For example, clinicians learning IRT may learnaa great deal about the value of administering the Brief Strengths Assessment with their service users by completing the assessment for themselves. Further, the clinicians may best learn the value of home practice for service users by having short home practice assignments to do on their own during the training.

Trainers Must Recognize and Build on the Unique Strengths of Each Agency, Team, and Team Member

People come to the training with a wide range of academic and clinical experience. With regard to NAVIGATE, some training participants may have a great deal of experience working with adolescents and young adults, others may have only worked with longer-term adult service users, still others may be new to the profession. Therefore, NAVIGATE trainers have found it helpful to start with providing very basic information about the model and progress to offering more nuanced information, all the while encouraging discussion. A collaborative approach is also of great importance, where the input of trainers and trainees is equally valued. The trainers need to be open to questions, to other ideas, to hearing people's clinical experiences and to recognizing staff strengths as they are evidenced. For example, at one site the staff seemed almost parental and over-involved with the NAVIGATE service users, which could be understood as in conflict with recovery values such as self-determination and autonomy. However, over multiple visits to the site, three points became clear that made this style of interaction more understandable, and not counter to recovery. First, many of the NAVIGATE service users at this site either had no family contact or had relatives who were so preoccupied by their day-to-day concerns that they had little energy to support their loved one with FEP. These NAVIGATE participants appeared to appreciate the focused attention from staff. Second, in this geographic area, elders were accorded specific respect, and thus the NAVIGATE service users actually seemed to resonate to the staff attention, which might be considered intrusive in another setting. Third, this program was located in an economically deprived area, and the staff often could help service users access resources that would be impossible for them to obtain on their own. This example highlights the importance of trainers attending to diversity issues and cultural norms when mounting a training in a geographical area of which they may be unfamiliar.

Follow-Up Consultation is Critical

The initial three-day in-person training is a good foundation for the team to start implementing NAVIGATE. However, short-term training alone rarely changes provider behavior (Beidas & Kendall, 2010; Herschell et al., 2010). The real learning occurs "on the ground," when the team members are trying to work with individuals and their families in a new way. The trainers have found it most effective to encourage the team members to start working with service users and relatives as quickly as possible after the training, and also to begin consultation calls with the trainers quickly. Without follow-up and attention, the team members often have unanswered questions and shaky new skills, and naturally drift from the model. When they drift from the model, they usually see less success, and become discouraged, inadvertently undermining the whole goal of the training. Follow-along support from trainers and local supervisors is essential.

Supporting Medication Decisions and Health Promotion is a Team Responsibility

Some individuals with FEP have family members with psychotic illnesses and these individuals and their families can have background knowledge of psychotic illnesses and their treatment. However, the majority of individuals with FEP do not have affected family members and lack this background. Individuals and their families usually look to prescribers for information about diagnosis, treatment options, health promotion and coordination with medical care, and indeed these are prime responsibilities of prescribers in the NAVIGATE model. However, prescriber time is usually limited, and the educational needs of individuals and families are large. Formally, IRT and the Family Education interventions provide materials that complement the prescribers' efforts on these issues. However, it is crucial for all team members to be able to support making these decisions that are crucial to promoting recovery. For example, the SEE specialist may observe that a particular symptom is interfering with an individual achieving a school goal. The specialist can be instrumental in helping the individual and his/her relatives understand the connection between the symptom and the individual's ability to succeed at school, and help them explore options within the NAVIGATE model for decreasing this impediment to school performance. This might include, for example, working with the IRT specialist to get on a better schedule or working with the prescriber to see if a medication adjustment might be helpful. The information that individuals and families need about symptoms/diagnosis, treatment options and health is extensive and often complex, so all team members should be prepared to provide information as appropriate for their scope of practice.

CSC models such as NAVIGATE attempt to treat individuals with the lowest effective dose of medication. A corollary to this is that if an individual is non-adherent or only partially adherent with the pharmacological agent, the medication intake can quickly change from effective to ineffective, with an associated heightened risk of relapse. Many studies report that around half of individuals across all of medicine have difficulty taking medications as prescribed (Osterberg & Blaschke, 2005). Young people with FEP have additional nonadherence risk factors such as substance misuse (Schoeler et al., 2017). Young adults often do not see themselves as having an illness, and therefore do not see the need for medications. After they improve on the medications, they may think no longer need them. In addition, despite being provided with the lowest effective doses, individuals with FEP often experience side effects. Prescribers, of course, assess individuals for adherence, relapse and side effects, but problems in these areas can be first noticed by other team members given that they are often in more frequent contact with individuals than are the prescribers.

Although the NAVIGATE psychiatrist or nurse practitioner is responsible for prescribing and managing medication and health, it is extremely important for the whole team to be knowledgeable about medication and health promotion, to be able to answer basic questions about medication (within their scope of practice) and to constantly monitor for reports of symptoms and side effects. This information then needs to be brought to the prescriber, typically in a team meeting unless the situation is urgent. Without effective team communication, early signs of relapse often are not recognized or properly treated, and early inclinations to become non-adherent, or even to quit the entire NAVIGATE program, are missed. The trainers have therefore found that it is very important to provide instruction about medication and health promotion to the whole team in the initial training.

Staff Turnover is the Norm

From the initial planning, NAVIGATE trainers needed to be very attentive to cultivating ongoing program sustainability in all their decisions and activities. The staff of many mental health agencies are often in their "starter" jobs – they may be accruing their licensing hours or seeking to gain a broad level of experience with consumers before selecting a specialty or going into private practice. Especially with more junior staff, turnover is a fact of life. Obviously, staff attrition can interfere with the provision of evidence-based care if the replacement staff are not trained, and many individuals leave positions after only giving a two weeks' notice, reducing the likelihood that the experienced staff can train a new provider.

Trainers need to plan for staff turnover from their initial contact with any agency considering implementing NAVIGATE. Strategies to address staff turnover include developing tools (checklists, refresher reviews) that can support subsequent training of new staff and assuring that NAVIGATE Directors understand all the interventions. Many Directors find it helpful to sit in on at least part of all the initial component trainings. For some teams, cross-training of staff can be useful, particularly if the staff member is trained and gets experience in one role before learning the other role. However, training in a complicated multifaceted intervention such as NAVIGATE requires resources and a broad range of knowledge (both of a specific component and the overall model) and time, which may tax many programs. While a "train the trainer" model prevails in many mental health settings, this can be a difficult model to sustain when providers are the third or fourth generation removed from the original training and/or do not envision themselves as trainers. Fidelity to the model can atrophy. One strategy the NAVIGATE trainer team has used to address this challenge is to encourage sites planning a training to invite newly hired staff from other sites that had already hosted a training to the intensive training workshops. This co-mingling of staff from multiple sites has the added benefit of contributing to the development of a NAVIGATE learning community.

Not All Staff Are Initially Enthused About Learning New Interventions

Many treatment developers offer trainings where individuals self-select to learn a new skill and often pay out-of-pocket for the opportunity to do so. Large-scale agency trainings differ. Staff members may be required to attend the trainings, and perhaps even have been assigned to implement a new program, even though they may have only modest (or no) interest in doing so. While many NAVIGATE training site providers are clearly enthusiastic about the introduction of a new FEP program at their facilities, there are occasionally providers who express skepticism about the endeavor. Perhaps they have been doing their jobs for decades and are satisfied with the status quo, or are comfortable with the current lines of authority at their facility, and do not relish the establishment of a new program and new manager.

While training can often be conceptualized as a transfer of knowledge and skills, it is increasingly clear that trainers must also motivate learners. Inspiration is important. Trainer motivational strategies include identifying motivational concerns during the initial planning meetings with the agency and revising the training materials to address them in the initial presentations, frequent use of engaging "real-world" case examples, TED talks and videos during the training, praise for any attempts at skill development, and identifying reluctant learners individually during the training to address their concerns.

Evidence-Based Treatments Evolve and Strategies to Update Skills Must be Planned in Advance

Knowledge is rapidly advancing in mental health, with estimates of knowledge half-life ranging from 10 to 12 years in clinical and rehabilitation psychology (Neimeyer et al., 2014). After initial training, maintenance of ongoing competency and refinement of skills to reflect updated information is key to providing optimal evidence-based treatment. A decade after the original creation of the NAVIGATE programs, the availability of new data, evolving public policies, and the accrual of clinical wisdom from years of implementation all contributed to a need to update the approach. While updating the NAVIGATE manuals was not difficult, it is a bigger challenge to push these advancements into the field. It is critical for evidence-based treatment program developers to generate effective strategies to ensure new information and findings can be made available to prior trainees. In the case of NAVIGATE, we have made our updated manuals available on our website and to our prior trainees, and we have offered webinars on the revisions to many past trainees. We have also presented at national conferences such as the Association of Behavioral and Cognitive Therapy (ABCT) and associated low- or no-cost continuing education offerings for professionals who may not attend conventions like ABCT. As mentioned in our description of Phase 4 of the training process above, creating a collaborative learning community has become a critical aspect of large-scale training initiatives of a new evidence-based treatment. Treatment developers not only need to think about current training efforts, but about the needs of trainees a decade down the road, and keep abreast of the technology to do so.

Conclusion

It is a time of hope in the treatment of young people experiencing a first episode of psychosis. FEP recovery is a complex process, and treatment systems are complicated (Moe et al., 2018). While the NAVIGATE model has proven efficacy in improving FEP outcomes, efforts to enhance a national mental healthcare system to make it more amenable to supporting recovery from FEP has required patience, skill, and fortitude. The NAVIGATE training model continues to evolve, and its growth mirrors the increase in FEP programs throughout the country. These new programs and the multidisciplinary approach of CSC, including NAVIGATE, have also led to more innovation in the field and the development of new models of treatment. Nevertheless, there are new challenges on the horizon for those involved in training recovery-oriented models for FEP. How can we make online training as engaging and interactive as in-person training? What is the best way to engage in collaborative development (i.e., co-production) of newer research protocols and clinical services with service users? How can these models be made even more culturally informed? There is much work to be done.

REFERENCES

Addis, M. E., Wade, W. A., & Hatgis, C. (2006). Barriers to dissemination of evidence-based practices: Addressing practitioners' concerns about manual-based psychotherapies. *Clinical Psychology: Science and Practice*, 6(4), 430–441. https://doi.org/10.1093/clipsy.6.4.430

Ayllon, T., & Azrin, N. (1968). *The token economy: A motivational system for therapy and rehabilitation*. Appleton Century Crofts. *Behaviour Research and Therapy*, 7(3), 348. https://doi.org/10.1016/0005-7967(69)90022-9

Azrin, S. T., Goldstein, A. B., & Heinssen, R. K. (2015). Early intervention for psychosis: The recovery after an initial schizophrenia episode project. *Psychiatric Annals*, 45(11), 548–553. https://doi.org/10.3928/00485713-20151103-05

Balas, E. A., & Boren, S. A. (2000). Managing clinical knowledge for health care improvement. *Yearbook of Medical Informatics*, 09(01), 65–70. https://doi.org/10.1055/s-0038-1637943

Beck, A. T. (1952). Successful outpatient psychotherapy of a chronic schizophrenic with a delusion based on borrowed guilt. *Psychiatry*, 15(3), 305–312. https://doi.org/10.1080/00332747.1952.11022883

Becker, D. R., & Drake, R. E. (2003). *A Working Life for People with Severe Mental Illness*. Oxford University Press.

Beidas, R. S., & Kendall, P. C. (2010). Training therapists in evidence-based practice: A critical review of studies from a systems-contextual perspective. *Clinical Psychology: Science and Practice*, 17(1), 1–30. https://doi.org/10.1111/j.1468-2850.2009.01187.x

Bellack, A. S., Hersen, M., & Turner, S. M. (1976). Generalization effects of social skills training in chronic schizophrenics: An experimental analysis. *Behaviour Research and Therapy*, 14(6), 391–398. https://doi.org/10.1016/0005-7967(76)90085-1

Bowtell, M., Eaton, S., Thien, K., Bardell-Williams, M., Downey, L., Ratheesh, A., Killackey, E., McGorry, P., & O'Donoghue, B. (2018). Rates and predictors of relapse following discontinuation of antipsychotic medication after a first episode of psychosis. *Schizophrenia Research, 195,* 231–236. https://doi.org/10.1016/j.schres.2017.10.030

Breitborde, N. J., Guirgis, H., Stearns, W., Carpenter, K. M., Lteif, G., Pine, J. G., ... Moe, A. M. (2020). The Ohio State University Early Psychosis Intervention Center (EPICENTER) step-based care programme for individuals at clinical high risk for psychosis: Study protocol for an observational study. *British Medical Journal Open, 10*(1), 1–8.

Chinman, M., George, P., Dougherty, R. H., Daniels, A. S., Ghose, S. S., Swift, A., & Delphin-Rittmon, M. E. (2014). Peer support services for individuals with serious mental illnesses: Assessing the evidence. *Psychiatric Services, 65*(4), 429–441. https://doi.org/10.1176/appi.ps.201300244

Correll, C. U., Galling, B., Pawar, A., Krivko, A., Bonetto, C., Ruggeri, M., ... Kane, J. M. (2018). Comparison of early intervention services vs treatment as usual for early-phase psychosis: A systematic review, meta-analysis, and meta-regression. *The Journal of the American Medical Association Psychiatry, 75*(6), 555–565. https://10.1001/jamapsychiatry.2018.0623

Dobson, K. S. (1989). A meta-analysis of the efficacy of cognitive therapy for depression. *Journal of Consulting and Clinical Psychology, 57*(3), 414–419. https://doi.org/10.1037/0022-006x.57.3.414

Doyle, R., Turner, N., Fanning, F., Brennan, D., Renwick, L., Lawlor, E., & Clarke, M. (2014). First-episode psychosis and disengagement from treatment: A systematic review. *Psychiatric Services, 65*(5), 603–611. https://doi.org/10.1176/appi.ps.201200570

Falloon, I. R. H., Boyd, J. L., McGill, C. W., Razani, J., Moss, H. B., & Gilderman, A. M. (1982). Family management in the prevention of exacerbations of schizophrenia. *New England Journal of Medicine, 306*(24), 1437–1440. https://doi.org/10.1056/nejm198206173062 40

Foa, E. B., McLean, C. P., Brown, L. A., Zang, Y., Rosenfield, D., Zandberg, L. J., ... Peterson, A. L. (2020). The effects of a prolonged exposure workshop with and without consultation on provider and patient outcomes: A randomized implementation trial. *Implementation Science, 15*(1), 59. https://doi.org/10.1186/s13012-020-01014-x

Garety, P. A., Kuipers, L., Fowler, D., Chamberlain, F., & Dunn, G. (1994). Cognitive behavioural therapy for drug-resistant psychosis. *British Journal of Medical Psychology, 67*(3), 259–271. https://doi.org/10.1111/j.2044-8341.1994.tb01795.x

Gleeson, J. F. M., Cotton, S. M., Alvarez-Jimenez, M., Wade, D., Gee, D., Crisp, K., ... McGorry, P. D. (2009). A randomized controlled trial of relapse prevention therapy for first-episode psychosis patients. *The Journal of Clinical Psychiatry, 70*(4), 477–486. https://doi.org/10.4088/jcp.08m04407

Grant, J., Green, L., & Mason, B. (2003). Basic research and health: A reassessment of the scientific basis for the support of biomedical science. *Research Evaluation, 12*(3), 217–224. https://doi.org/10.3152/147154403781776618

Grawe, R. W., Falloon, I. R. H., Widen, J. H., & Skogvoll, E. (2006). Two years of continued early treatment for recent-onset schizophrenia: A randomised controlled

study. *Acta Psychiatrica Scandinavica, 114*(5), 328–336. https://doi.org/10.1111/j
.1600-0447.2006.00799.x

Heinssen, R. K., Goldstein, A. B., & Azrin, S. T. (April 14, 2014). *Evidence-based treatments for first episode psychosis: Components of coordinated specialty care.* Https://Www.Nimh.Nih.Gov/Health/Topics/Schizophrenia/Raise/Nimh-White-Paper-Csc-for-Fep_147096.Pdf. https://www.nasmhpd.org/sites/default/files/Summary%20of%20Evidence-BasedTreament%20Components%20for%20FEP_14APR_2014_Final.pdf

Herschell, A. D., Kolko, D. J., Baumann, B. L., & Davis, A. C. (2010). The role of therapist training in the implementation of psychosocial treatments: A review and critique with recommendations. *Clinical Psychology Review, 30*(4), 448–466. https://doi.org/10.1016/j.cpr.2010.02.005

Hogarty, G. E. (1986). Family psychoeducation, social skills training, and maintenance chemotherapy in the aftercare treatment of schizophrenia. *Archives of General Psychiatry, 43*(7), 633. https://doi.org/10.1001/archpsyc.1986.01800070019003

Hogarty, G. E. (1991). Family psychoeducation, social skills training, and maintenance chemotherapy in the aftercare treatment of schizophrenia. *Archives of General Psychiatry, 48*(4), 340. https://doi.org/10.1001/archpsyc.1991.01810280056008

Humensky, J. L., Dixon, L. B., & Essock, S. M. (2013). State mental health policy: An interactive tool to estimate costs and resources for a first-episode psychosis initiative in New York State. *Psychiatric Services, 64*(9), 832–834. https://doi.org/10.1176/appi.ps.201300186

Kane, J. M., Robinson, D. G., Schooler, N. R., Mueser, K. T., Penn, D. L., Rosenheck, R. A., ... Heinssen, R. K. (2016). Comprehensive versus usual community care for first-episode psychosis: 2-Year outcomes from the NIMH RAISE early treatment program. *American Journal of Psychiatry, 173*(4), 362–372. https://doi.org/10.1176/appi.ajp.2015.15050632

Kendler, K. S. (2020). Eugen Bleuler's views on the genetics of schizophrenia in 1917. *Schizophrenia Bulletin, 46*(4), 758–764. https://doi.org/10.1093/schbul/sbz131

Kingdon, D., Turkington, D., & John, C. (1994). Cognitive behaviour therapy of schizophrenia: The amenability of delusions and hallucinations to reasoning. *The British Journal of Psychiatry, 164*(5), 581–587. https://doi.org/10.1192/bjp.164.5.581

Miltenberger, R. G. (2011). *Behavior Modification: Principles and Procedures.* Cengage Learning.

Moe, A. M., Rubinstein, E. B., Gallagher, C. J., Weiss, D. M., Stewart, A., & Breitborde, N. J. K. (2018b). Improving access to specialized care for first-episode psychosis: An ecological model. *Risk Management and Healthcare Policy, Volume 11*, 127–138. https://doi.org/10.2147/rmhp.s131833

Morris, Z. S., Wooding, S., & Grant, J. (2011). The answer is 17 years, what is the question: Understanding time lags in translational research. *Journal of the Royal Society of Medicine, 104*(12), 510–520. https://doi.org/10.1258/jrsm.2011.110180

Mueser, K. T., Penn, D. L., Addington, J., Brunette, M. F., Gingerich, S., Glynn, S. M., ... Kane, J. M. (2015). The NAVIGATE program for first-episode psychosis:

Rationale, overview, and description of psychosocial components. *Psychiatric Services, 66*(7), 680–690. https://doi.org/10.1176/appi.ps.201400413

Neimeyer, G. J., Taylor, J. M., Rozensky, R. H., & Cox, D. R. (2014). The diminishing durability of knowledge in professional psychology: A second look at specializations. *Professional Psychology: Research and Practice, 45*(2), 92–98. https://doi.org/10.1037/a0036176

Ojeda, V. D., Munson, M. R., Jones, N., Berliant, E., & Gilmer, T. P. (2020). The availability of peer support and disparities in outpatient mental health service use among minority youth with serious mental illness. *Administration and Policy in Mental Health and Mental Health Services Research*, 1–9. https://doi.org/10.1007/s10488-020-01073-8

Oliver, J. A., & Lang, J. M. (2018). Barriers and consultation needs regarding implementation of evidence-based treatment in community agencies. *Children and Youth Services Review, 94*, 368–377. https://doi.org/10.1016/j.childyouth.2018.10.004

Osterberg, L., & Blaschke, T. (2005). Adherence to medication. *New England Journal of Medicine, 353*(5), 487–497. https://doi.org/10.1056/nejmra050100

Paul, G. L., & Lentz, R. J. (1977). *Psychosocial Treatment of Chronic Mental Patients: Milieu Versus Social-Learning Programs*. Harvard University Press.

Petersen, L., Jeppesen, P., Thorup, A., Abel, M.-B., Øhlenschlæger, J., Christensen, T. Ø., . . . Nordentoft, M. (2005). A randomised multicentre trial of integrated versus standard treatment for patients with a first episode of psychotic illness. *British Medical Journal, 331*(7517), 602. https://doi.org/10.1136/bmj.38565.415000.e01

Peterson, C., & Seligman, M. (2004). *Character strengths and virtues: A handbook and classification* (1st ed.). American Psychological Association/Oxford University Press.

Robinson, D. G., Schooler, N. R., Correll, C. U., John, M., Kurian, B. T., Marcy, P., . . . Kane, J. M. (2018). Psychopharmacological treatment in the RAISE-ETP study: Outcomes of a manual and computer decision support system based intervention. *American Journal of Psychiatry, 175*(2), 169–179. https://doi.org/10.1176/appi.ajp.2017.16080919

Ruggeri, M., Bonetto, C., Lasalvia, A., Fioritti, A., de Girolamo, G., Santonastaso, P., . . . Meneghelli, A. (2015). Feasibility and effectiveness of a multi-element psychosocial intervention for first-episode psychosis: Results from the cluster-randomized controlled get up piano trial in a catchment area of 10 million inhabitants. *Schizophrenia Bulletin, 41*(5), 1192–1203. https://doi.org/10.1093/schbul/sbv058

Schoeler, T., Petros, N., Di Forti, M., Klamerus, E., Foglia, E., Murray, R., & Bhattacharyya, S. (2017). Poor medication adherence and risk of relapse associated with continued cannabis use in patients with first-episode psychosis: A prospective analysis. *The Lancet Psychiatry, 4*(8), 627–633. https://doi.org/10.1016/s2215-0366(17)30233-x

Schoenbaum, M., Sutherland, J. M., Chappel, A., Azrin, S., Goldstein, A. B., Rupp, A., & Heinssen, R. K. (2017). Twelve-month health care use and mortality in commercially insured young people with incident psychosis in the United States. *Schizophrenia Bulletin, 43*(6), 1262–1272. https://doi.org/10.1093/schbul/sbx009

Srihari, V. H., Tek, C., Kucukgoncu, S., Phutane, V. H., Breitborde, N. J. K., Pollard, J.,
 . . . Woods, S. W. (2015). First-episode services for psychotic disorders in the
 U.S. Public Sector: A pragmatic randomized controlled trial. *Psychiatric Services*,
 66(7), 705–712. https://doi.org/10.1176/appi.ps.201400236

Test, M. A., & Stein, L. I. (1976). Practical guidelines for the community treatment
 of markedly impaired patients. *Community Mental Health Journal*, *12*(1), 72–82.
 https://doi.org/10.1007/bf01435740

Zubin, J., & Spring, B. (1977). Vulnerability: A new view of schizophrenia. *Journal of
 Abnormal Psychology*, *86*(2), 103–126. https://doi.org/10.1037/0021-843x.86.2.103

6 Implementing Evidence-Based Psychosocial Interventions for Psychosis

Lessons Learned from the Danish Mental Healthcare System

Louise Birkedal Glenthøj, Samantha Jankowski, Lisa Dixon, and Merete Nordentoft

This chapter highlights how the Danish healthcare and sociopolitical contingencies have supported a different approach to psychosis compared to the USA. The evidence base and characteristics of best practices are quite similar, but implementation, access, and outcomes are quite different in Denmark and many other developed nations. Nonetheless, some US systems have adapted evidence-based approaches to early psychosis with some success, as illustrated by the second half of this chapter. By illustrating the Danish approach to psychosis treatment and its successes and pitfalls, this chapter will highlight the feasibility of effective support and recovery for people with psychosis, as well as the necessity of long-term investments in citizens' health and learning from local and global successes and mistakes. This comparative systems case study will highlight ways in which the USA may learn from its own experience as well as others', and will illustrate real hope to recover the US mental healthcare system. Effective, intensive treatment of first episode psychosis is a key focus in Danish psychosis treatment as well as recent progress in the USA. Thus, the chapter has a primary emphasis on describing the success of instituting treatment in the early phases of psychosis.

An Urgent Need for High Quality Treatment of First Episode Psychosis

People with first episode psychosis constitute a very vulnerable group at high risk of suicidal behavior and social decline (Madsen et al., 2016; Melle et al., 2006; Nordentoft et al., 2002). Studies of duration of untreated psychosis (DUP) indicate that there is often a long treatment delay (Addington et al., 2015; Jeppesen et al., 2008; Marshall et al., 2005; McGlashan & Johannessen, 1996), and it is likely that stigma, lack of mental health literacy and insight, and barriers in the healthcare system can explain why many young people have difficulties in accessing treatment soon after the first onset of psychosis

(Birchwood et al., 2013). It has been hypothesized, but never proven, that untreated psychosis has a biological toxic effect, so that people with a longer DUP have a poorer outcome of illness due to deterioration of brain function (Loebel et al., 1992). Indeed, long DUP is associated with poor prognosis and poor treatment response (Albert et al., 2017; Kane et al., 2016; Marshall et al., 2005; Penttilä, Jääskeläinen, Hirvonen, Isohanni, & Miettunen, 2014). Experiencing psychosis for a longer time clearly disrupts the social and interpersonal developmental processes in young individuals, thus creating a social toxic effect of untreated psychosis. There is no doubt that harmful social processes are at play if young people with psychosis lose affiliation with the educational system and labor market, lose contacts with families and friends, display changed interests and habits, and even become homeless.

Experiencing a first episode of psychosis can be a frightening experience both for the person and their relatives. The young person and their family may not understand the impact and consequences of the illness, and may have little knowledge of helpful and necessary resources for recovery or crisis management. Easily accessible, appealing treatment with family involvement will undoubtedly reduce the burden of disease.

Evidence for Effectiveness of Early Intervention Services

Psychosis early intervention services are provided by a multidisciplinary team, commonly consisting of psychiatrists, nurses, psychologists, social workers, occupational therapists, other vocational professions, and peer workers. The teams offer assertive clinical case management, family involvement, and recovery-oriented group therapy.

The first randomized clinical trial comparing the effect of early intervention services to standard treatment was carried out in the United Kingdom, and it showed positive effects of the specialized early psychosis intervention on risk of readmission and days hospitalized after 18 months of intensive treatment (Craig et al., 2004). Soon after, the first results of the Danish OPUS trial were published (Petersen et al., 2005), showing positive effects of early intervention services on psychotic and negative symptoms, days hospitalized, risk of readmission and drop out of service (attrition), user satisfaction and stress, and satisfaction among relatives (Jeppesen et al., 2005). These initial positive findings of specialized, early psychosis treatment were later confirmed by a large meta-analysis summarizing the findings on 13 outcomes from 10 different trials. The meta-analytical findings showed a beneficial effect of the specialized treatment on all 13 outcomes, including service use, relapse, psychotic and negative symptoms, depression and quality of life (Correll et al., 2018).

The value of early intervention services has, however, been questioned as five- and ten-year follow-up studies have not been able to demonstrate long-term clinical effects (Bertelsen et al., 2008; Chang et al., 2017; Gafoor et al., 2010; Secher et al., 2015). The Danish OPUS trial has, though, found a positive long-term effect on use of supported housing facilities, indicating an effect of the OPUS treatment on independent living (Hastrup et al., 2013; Secher et al., 2015). Furthermore, receiving treatment in early intervention services in Hong Kong was associated with a long-term reduced risk of suicide (Chan et al., 2018). Three studies have investigated whether prolonged specialized psychosis intervention can maintain the positive post-treatment findings: the Canadian PEPP study (Malla et al., 2017) and the EASY trial from Hong Kong (Chang et al., 2015) clearly demonstrated that longer duration of early intervention services is superior to shorter duration. The Danish OPUS II trial compared five years of OPUS treatment to two years of OPUS treatment followed by three years of standard treatment, including intensive assertive community treatment for the most vulnerable 20% of people with psychosis (Albert et al., 2017). The OPUS II trial showed that the positive treatment effects could be maintained in both treatment arms, but people receiving the five years of OPUS treatment were more satisfied with treatment and had a better treatment alliance.

Thus, there is strong evidence that early intervention services are effective, and that positive results can be maintained either by prolonging the treatment or by providing a stepped care model where the most vulnerable people are offered intensive treatment.

Early Intervention Services

Early Intervention Services implemented in different countries have many similarities (Csillag et al., 2018; Ruggeri et al., 2017; Ruggeri et al., 2012). Multidisciplinary teams have the capacity to provide assertive outreach, and most teams have programs for family involvement, treatment of co-occurring substance abuse, and individual placement and support. Many teams offer cognitive behavioral therapy (CBT) and cognitive remediation. There is an international network collaborating about common standards for program fidelity (Addington et al., 2018). "Fidelity" here means a system's adherence to aspects of one or more models of treatment. Across different locally developed fidelity scales, there is a substantial overlap, suggesting that key elements of early intervention services are translatable and feasible in many international contexts.

Health Economic Analyses of Early Intervention Services

The cost effectiveness of the Danish OPUS I trial was analyzed. In brief, OPUS treatment was associated with lower costs for hospitalizations and other institutions such as supported housing facilities. The OPUS treatment was associated with higher costs for outpatient treatment, which is expected as the outpatient treatment was much more intensive and the caseload remarkably lower than in standard treatment. Taken together, compared to standard treatment, the OPUS treatment was associated with lower cost of treatment, when accounting for the full spectrum of services and other costs such as medications, supported housing, and hospitalizations. Individual and community health, wellbeing, and autonomy cannot be assigned a price tag, but when cost of treatment was compared to development of psychosocial functioning, it was clear that the OPUS treatment was cheaper and better than standard treatment (Hastrup et al., 2013). There are still ongoing analyses of cost effectiveness of the OPUS II trial and other trials investigating the effect of extended treatment.

The Danish OPUS Treatment: Implementation, Funding, National Guidelines

The following section highlights some of the key elements imperative to the effectiveness and success of the Danish OPUS early psychosis treatment.

In Denmark, there is universal tax-based healthcare coverage. Regional health authorities provide mental health services, which are regulated by recommendations from the Danish Health Authority and regional and national policymakers. All services in secondary health care, hospitals and outpatient clinics are free of charge.

When the first positive results of the OPUS trial were available from two Danish regions, regional health authorities decided to fund these two teams. Soon after, state funding for further dissemination became available and such funding was repeated several years later. Thereby it was possible to implement OPUS treatment in all Danish regions. National guidelines were developed in Danish regions in 2003, recommending OPUS treatment for all people with first episode psychosis. The National Board of Health issued National Clinical Guidelines in 2015 (Baandrup et al., 2016) also recommending assertive treatment.

Quality Indicator Projects

Since 2000, a national quality improvement project (Baandrup, Voldsgaard, Cerqueira, Riis, & Nordentoft, 2012; Baandrup et al., 2016) monitored quality of treatment for people treated for schizophrenia. The quality indicators included diagnostic interview, consultation with a psychiatrist, assessment of cognitive functioning, consultation with a social worker, involvement of families, medication management, and assessment of different adverse events.

These data have been collected and published by each hospital since 2000, and the results are discussed among leaders of regional health services and clinics. This process sustains continuous program evolution and accountability. The fact that the quality improvement project included an indicator measuring whether families have been involved in treatment supported the continuous process of steadily increasing the proportion of families involved in the treatment.

Fidelity Measures

To ensure the quality of and adherence to the treatment of early psychosis treatment, fidelity assessments were carried out in the OPUS teams. After having conducted a Delphi process, a fidelity measure was developed, including structural and functional items (Melau, Albert, & Nordentoft, 2018). All OPUS teams, except one, assessed fidelity to the OPUS treatment elements. The assessment involved questionnaires, interviews, and participation in team meetings. Two-thirds of all teams had a good or excellent fidelity score. The items most often not meeting quality threshold were access to training and supervision, too high a caseload, and offices being located together with other mental health services (Melau et al., 2018). In essence, these findings indicate that it is possible to maintain a high quality treatment of early psychosis in multiple teams in different geographical regions.

Treatment Packages – Right to Treatment

In 2015, the Danish Regions decided that people with first episode schizophrenia should be offered a treatment package including assessment by a psychiatrist, assertive approach in critical situations, CBT, family involvement, recovery-oriented group treatment, medication and evaluation of physical health and adverse events. This decision implied that all people with first episode schizophrenia had the right to treatment with the elements listed above. In almost all regions, this was implemented by ensuring access to treatment in OPUS teams, but in some clinics the treatment was offered in community mental health centers. The treatment packages also implied that local health authorities had to offer training for staff members.

Manuals, Training, and Supervision

A prerequisite for maintaining a uniform, high quality treatment of psychotic disorders is the provision of treatment manuals, training, and ongoing supervision for staff. A Danish book describing the different treatment modalities of the OPUS treatment was published in 2002 (Nordentoft, Jørgensen, Gall,

Krarup, & Martinussen, 2002) and a revised edition was published in 2009 (Nordentoft, Melau, Iversen, Kjær, 2009). Currently an English version is being prepared. The book *Multifamily-groups in the Treatment of Severe Psychiatric Disorders* (McFarlane, 2002) was used as the manual for family treatment in OPUS, and it also served as teaching material in the training and supervision of staff members. OPUS teams were offered training and supervision with external supervisors for family treatment and social skills training. Ongoing supervision on clinical treatment was carried out within each OPUS team.

Individual Placement and Support

A recently published large Danish trial showed that for people with severe mental disorders in Denmark, Individual Placement and Support (IPS) was clearly superior to service as usual (Christensen et al., 2019). IPS is a Supported Employment and Education model with a strong international evidence base. The Danish trial showed that IPS can increase the duration of time in employment or education and the proportion of people in employment or education at any time during an 18-month follow-up period. It has been questioned whether IPS would be effective in countries like Denmark with a good welfare system, but the trial showed that the IPS approach was effective and cost effective. IPS is now recommended as standard service all over Denmark.

Danish Healthcare Services after First Episode Psychosis

After having treatment in OPUS teams for two or three years, people with first episode psychosis in Denmark are transferred to Community Mental Health Centers (CMHC), Assertive Community Treatment (ACT) or Flexible - Assertive Community Treatment (FACT; Nielsen, Hjorthøj, Killaspy, & Nordentoft, 2021). There are variations in organization of the outpatient treatment across different regions in Denmark, reflecting differences in population density and political decisions. However, in all five Danish regions, people with long-lasting problems related to psychosis can, free of charge, be connected with a team responsible for outpatient treatment in the secondary health service. In CMHC and FACT the caseload is higher and the treatment is not specialized, while ACT teams almost exclusively include people diagnosed with schizophrenia with a low level of functioning (Thoegersen, Morthorst, & Nordentoft, 2019). In ACT and FACT, people with severe psychotic illness will be offered frequent contact (approximately weekly contact) with a case manager and home visits if needed. For a large proportion of people who do experience that level of psychotic symptoms, the severity and negative impact are reduced during the first years after first episode (Austin et al., 2015), and some will be transferred to primary care where a private psychiatrist or a general practitioner can take over the responsibility for the treatment. In case of deterioration, people can be admitted or referred to outpatient services in the secondary health sector.

People with psychosis who have severe difficulties in daily life functioning (approximately 10%) are offered a stays in supported housing facilities. Some of these facilities are small group homes with staff present during daytime, and some are larger institutions with 24-hour staff coverage (Nordentoft, Pedersen, Pedersen, Blinkenberg, & Mortensen, 2012). Moreover, in the Capital Region of Denmark (Copenhagen) and other large cities, specialized teams are formed to serve homeless people with mental illness.

In the Capital Region, the Acute Psychiatric Emergency Service has been functioning since 1997. The service operates during evenings, nighttime and weekends. A psychiatrist is on duty and receives referrals from police, social services, and telephone services like "1813" or "112" (equivalent to 911). The people with psychosis, their relatives, social service staff, and neighbors can call "1813" and be referred to the Acute Psychiatric Emergency Service. The psychiatrist decides whether the referral should be handled with telephone consultation or outreach. In the case of outreach, the psychiatrist, together with an ambulance driver, will go to the person's home, institution or other relevant facility (can also be on the street or in a police station). The person can be admitted voluntarily and go together with the psychiatrist to the hospital in the ambulance, but involuntary admission is also possible. Often the clinical service is involved in cases in which the person's condition has worsened dramatically. Notably, the USA has recently taken initial steps toward more specific emergency and support phone numbers (Canady, 2020; Hogan & Goldman, 2020).

Tax Financed, Universal Access to Health Care

Only the Scandinavian countries have organized mental healthcare in a way where services are available in secondary healthcare, free of charge for the individual. For people with mental illnesses it is a huge advantage that access to healthcare is financed via taxes and not healthcare insurance, which might be too expensive or only have limited coverage. Of course, even in tax-based healthcare, resources are limited, and access to care is not infinite. However, it is possible to ensure nationwide provision and quality control in a tax-based system, in which different health authorities are obliged to provide evidence-based services recommended at a national level. This is the case for OPUS treatment and for long-term treatment of people with psychotic disorders, although the latter is more difficult to regulate.

Limitations to the Danish Approach to Psychosocial Treatment of Psychosis

While the Danish approach to psychosocial treatment of psychosis has obvious organizational and economic advantages, there are, however, shortcomings. Currently, the Danish psychosis treatment facilities have inadequate or restricted psychotherapeutic treatment offerings. Compelling evidence exists indicating efficacy of specific psychotherapeutic treatments on different outcomes of psychosis such as positive/negative symptoms, cognition, and functional deficits (National Institue for Health and Care Excellence (NICE), 2014; Turner, van der Gaag, Karyotaki, & Cuijpers, 2014). CBT has proven more efficacious than other therapies in reducing positive symptoms (Turner et al., 2014). Additionally, advances in delivering targeted, psychotherapeutic interventions have developed in European countries such as the United Kingdom and the Netherlands. In some instances, the technical advances have enabled the development of innovative, short-term psychological treatments that have shown highly promising results in alleviating psychotic symptoms such as auditory hallucinations and paranoid ideations (Birchwood et al., 2014; Craig et al., 2018; Pot-Kolder et al., 2018). Despite the evidence for the efficacy of psychological treatments, people with psychosis still have limited access to specialized psychological interventions in Denmark due to factors such as inadequate training of staff and time constraints in daily clinical practice. Currently, there are no uniform, manualized psychotherapeutic treatment offers for people with psychosis, except for social skills training being an integrated part of the OPUS treatment. Additionally, case managers in OPUS adopt a Cognitive Behavioral Case Management (CBCM) approach, but this does not resemble a targeted CBT intervention delivered by a specialized provider.

Given the lack of unified psychological interventions employed in Danish psychosis treatment facilities, psychotherapeutic interventions are not offered to all those that might benefit, but rather to a relatively small, selected group and of a limited duration (normally ten sessions). Furthermore, the psychotherapeutic approach is not standardized but based on the skills of the specific therapist. Implementing targeted psychotherapeutic approaches as an integrated part of the intervention programs for psychosis in Denmark therefore constitutes a substantial future area of improvement. Another treatment area that needs reinforcement in Danish psychosis treatment settings is the employment of cognitive remediation programs. Cognitive deficits are prominent in psychotic disorders and may constitute a barrier to functional recovery (Fett et al., 2011; Green, 1996). So, cognitive remediation interventions, with replicated evidence in alleviating cognitive deficits (Wykes, Huddy, Cellard, McGurk, & Czobor, 2011), should be part of the available treatment offers in

Danish psychosis settings (see also Chapter 4 in this book). These shortcomings are, however, recognized by Danish researchers and health professionals, and initial research steps have been taken in the direction of evaluating targeted psychological approaches within CBT and cognitive remediation. These research studies are funded by private funding agencies and public institutions. Furthermore, the research units and clinical settings in Denmark are closely intertwined, and research studies are therefore considerably supported by the mental health institutions having an obvious interest in advancing treatments for psychosis. This encompasses practical and logistical support along with patient referrals. The Danish funding agencies have a substantial focus on implementing research in clinical practice, and implementation plans are therefore often outlined as part of the funding application. This means that if the interventions tested are found effective, they are planned to be implemented broadly in the psychiatric treatment facilities in Denmark. Initially, selected mental health institutions will act as a test bed for the therapies, but the long-term strategy is to scale the interventions to all the Danish mental health facilities. Implementation is also facilitated by several clinicians being employed as therapists in the research studies. Hence, they will act as key personnel and supervisors when aiming to implement the new therapies in clinical settings. Furthermore, the close link between research and clinical settings in Denmark results in clinicians being very engaged in and enthusiastic about implementing new interventions.

The last decades have witnessed a movement toward instituting intervention early in the phase of psychosis to improve clinical and functional outcome (Birchwood, McGorry, & Jackson, 1997; McGorry, 2015). New research suggests that people with incipient psychosis symptoms can benefit from early intervention for primary or secondary prevention of illness progression (Phillips et al., 2002). This novel research focus on the population of individuals at Clinical High Risk (CHR) for psychosis has resulted in CHR treatment units or CHR research programs being established in countries such as Australia, the United Kingdom, and North America (Addington et al., 2007; Fusar-Poli, Byrne, Badger, Valmaggia, & McGuire, 2013; Yung et al., 2007). While CHR identification and treatment is indeed important, Denmark has no established CHR units. Although people with schizotypal personality disorder are eligible for treatment in the OPUS facilities in parts of Denmark and may resemble the CHR population (Albert et al., 2016), this population does not capture the entire CHR population. Hence, the wider population of individuals assumed to be in a pre-psychotic state constitutes a group with an unmet treatment need in Denmark. Launching CHR identification and treatment initiatives in Denmark therefore will be an important strategic focus in the next decades, building on the pivotal work done by other countries within this clinical field.

Lastly, initiating early psychosocial treatment for psychosis in Denmark has been challenged by an assumed underdiagnosing of psychotic disorders in especially child and adolescent psychiatry. Progression in psychiatric services during the last 20 years has, however, been accompanied by an increase in the incidence of schizophrenia, notably in the age group of 5–18 years old (Kühl, Laursen, Thorup, & Nordentoft, 2016). Some potential factors explaining this increased incidence may be national outreach campaigns aiming at de-stigmatizing psychiatric illnesses, enhanced clinical knowledge on, and better implementation of, diagnostic criteria for schizophrenia, and increases in treatment capacity and launching of specialized early psychosis teams. While the optimized detection and treatment of especially children and adolescents with psychosis in Denmark does indeed indicate positive progress, there may still be regional differences and inadequate awareness of schizophrenia symptomatology among clinicians. Establishing a unified national strategy on enhancing clinicians' ability to diagnose schizophrenia spectrum disorders and differentiate it from other disorders with some shared characteristics (e.g., autism spectrum disorders, attention deficit disorder, and borderline personality disorder) is a key area to pursue in the Danish psychiatric treatment organizations.

A US Perspective on Psychosocial Treatment of Psychosis

The initiation of psychosocial treatment for early psychosis in the United States was prompted by international studies on the effectiveness of early intervention services, such as OPUS, and English Lambeth Early Onset (LEO) studies (Craig et al., 2004; Petersen et al., 2005). In LEO, 144 individuals with psychosis were randomized to receive standard treatment or multi-component treatment comprised of CBT, low dose antipsychotic medications, family therapy, and vocational services. At 18-month follow-up, the intervention group had better occupational functioning and quality of life, fewer hospital readmissions, and better mediation adherence. The successes of these pioneering research studies were replicated in the United States such as Connecticut's Specialized Treatment Early in Psychosis (STEP) randomized control trial (Srihari, Shah, & Keshavan, 2012), and the Recovery After an Initial Schizophrenia Episode (RAISE) studies (Dixon, Goldman, Srihari, & Kane, 2018). Although these studies were modeled on international studies, special considerations had to be made for America's unique public health landscape. The following section will describe America's public health landscape, the STEP program and RAISE initiatives, challenges in implementation of coordinated specialty care (CSC) programs, and lessons that can be learned from Danish approaches. Other notable early psychosis programs include: Oregon's EASA program (established in 2001; http://www.easacommunity.org/),

Massachusetts's PREP, 2003 (Caplan et al., 2013), North Carolina's OASIS 2005 (Uzenoff et al., 2012), and San Francisco's PREP (2006; http://felton.org/social-services/early-psychosisschizophrenia-prep/). Promising results from early intervention services research in conjunction with policy changes, such as the Affordable Care Act in 2009 that facilitated access to mental health services for individuals with early psychosis and federal funding specific to early intervention services, created a landscape that allowed for the development of CSC programs across the United States (Goldman & Karakus, 2014).

The Public Health Landscape Prior to the RAISE Initiative

Prior to the RAISE studies, individuals with early psychosis had difficulty accessing services in both the public and private sector due to insurance limitations. Public mental health services prioritized individuals with mental illness who were already disabled, such as those with chronic schizophrenia, and relied heavily on Medicaid for funding (Frank, Goldman, & Hogan, 2003; Grob, 1994, 2006; Tessler & Goldman, 1982). Individuals with first episode psychosis (FEP) could only have access to Medicaid if they were disabled already, had dependent children, or were impoverished (Goldman, Karakus, Frey, & Beronio, 2013). They encountered similar difficulties accessing private mental health services due to insurance limitations. Individuals lost their insurance if they left their jobs or had to pay high Consolidated Omnibus Budget Reconciliation Act (COBRA) premiums to stay on their parents' health insurance network (Dixon et al., 2018). If they attempted to buy their own insurance, classification of mental illness as a pre-existing condition placed them into a high-risk insurance pool that was associated with premium inflation or exclusion from coverage. The Affordable Care Act (ACA), passed in 2009, allowed more individuals to remain on their parents' health insurance for a longer amount of time, purchase private sector insurance, or access Medicaid in states that accepted federal support to offer Medicaid to low income individuals (Dixon et al., 2018). Another factor hindering CSC dissemination included the separation of adolescent and young adult services, which contributed to inconsistent care at the critical period of psychosis onset (Srihari et al., 2012).

STEP and RAISE Implementation and Funding in the United States

The STEP and RAISE studies were implemented as a result of the success of the OPUS and LEO studies; however, they had to be adapted with the limitations of the US healthcare system in mind. Both OPUS and LEO used home-based outreach programs with small clinician to patient ratios (1:1), while the STEP study was implemented in an office setting with clinician to patient ratios of 1:30 (Srihari et al., 2012). STEP was a randomized controlled trial (RCT) of 120 FEP individuals comparing treatment as usual and an early psychosis specific treatment package of CBT, antipsychotic medications, family psychoeducation, and education and employment support (Srihari et al., 2015). After one year, the intervention group had fewer hospital admissions, fewer hospitalization days, and a higher likelihood of being employed or in school.

The two RAISE studies, the RAISE Early Treatment Program (RAISE-ETP) and the RAISE Implementation and Evaluation Study (RAISE-IES), were funded by the National Institute of Mental Health (NIMH) in 2009 (Dixon et al., 2018). These studies were intended to test the feasibility and effectiveness of what in the USA is now called coordinated specialty care (CSC), a multi-element treatment for individuals with early psychosis, in community based mental health centers. Services offered in RAISE could be viewed as derived from the accumulated work identifying evidence-based practices for individuals with schizophrenia discussed in recommendations from the Schizophrenia Patient Outcomes Research Team (PORT) (Buchanan et al., 2010; Kreyenbuhl, Buchanan, Dickerson, & Dixon, 2010; Lehman et al., 2004; Lehman & Steinwachs, 1998). The preponderance of evidence regarding the effectiveness of early intervention combined with the momentum from the RAISE studies eventually led to an increased allocation of federal funds in the mental health block grant for early psychosis care. The notion of CSC was created in this context. CSC was defined in an effort to synthesize the common elements of effective early psychosis care (Heinssen, Goldstein, & Azrin, 2014). Accordingly, the RAISE-ETP tested what we would now call a CSC, known as NAVIGATE, consisting of medication treatment utilizing a prescriber decision support system called COMPASS (Robinson et al., 2018; Chapter 5 in this book), individual therapy, supportive employment/education, and family psychotherapy and education.

The RAISE-ETP study was a cluster randomized trial involving 34 community mental health centers (n = 404 individuals with FEP) in 21 states, of which 17 were randomized to deliver NAVIGATE and 17 usual care (Kane et al., 2015). At two-year follow-up, individuals receiving NAVIGATE had lower positive and negative symptoms levels, better quality of life, and more improvements in work and school engagement (Kane et al., 2016). Notably, symptoms and quality of life improvements were moderated by DUP shorter than 74 weeks, where individuals with shorter DUP had higher improvements (Addington et al., 2015). NAVIGATE participants also had more medication visits, fewer side effects, and were more likely to be prescribed an antipsychotic and less likely to be prescribed an antidepressant (Robinson et al., 2018).

Cost-benefit analyses indicated that NAVIGATE benefits exceeded costs compared to care as usual when effectiveness was measured as a 1 standard deviation (SD) change on the Quality of Life Scale (QLS-SD) (Rosenheck et al., 2016). There was a 94% probability that NAVIGATE ($12,081/QLS-SD) was more cost effective than community care ($40,000/QLS-SD). Again, there was a difference among low and high-DUP, where costs of NAVIGATE averaged $1,368 less per person per six months in low-DUP people (DUP < 74 weeks) and $3,839 more per person per six months in high-DUP people compared to usual care.

The second study, RAISE-IES, originally began as a randomized control trial comparing the RAISE connection model (CSC) with case management plus usual care, but was redirected by the NIMH to the establishment of OnTrackNY, a statewide FEP program, in 2013 (Bello et al., 2017; Dixon et al., 2015). The RAISE-IES study was conducted at two sites (Maryland and New York) with 65 individuals with FEP. At two-year follow-up, participants had decreased symptoms and improved social and occupational functioning (Dixon et al., 2015) and fewer hospitalizations (Nossel et al., 2018). Additional qualitative studies on client and family engagement found that major factors contributing to client engagement were individually tailored care, family member involvement, and services such as supported employment and education (Lucksted et al., 2015, 2018). For families, communication and support from teams, individualized treatment, and program flexibility were major contributors. In addition to portraying the successful implementation of a CSC program, the RAISE-IES study contributed to the development of tools to help clinics to start their own CSC programs (https://www.nimh.nih.gov/health/topics/schizophrenia/raise/coordinated-specialty-care-for-first epi sode-psychosis-manual-i-outreach-and-recruitment.shtml and https://www.nimh.nih.gov/health/topics/schizophrenia/raise/csc-for-fep-manual-ii-imple mentation-manual_147093.pdf).

As the RAISE studies were being completed, the United States Congress allocated $25 million to community mental health block grants in 2014, in order to support evidence-based programs for individuals with early psychosis (Dixon et al., 2018). This amount was doubled in 2016 (Dixon, 2017). These efforts have been widely successful, with the presence of CSC increasing from programs in two states in 2008 to almost all states in 2020 (Smith & Dixon, 2020).

Limitations to the United States Approach

Although the results of RAISE and initiatives such as OnTrackNY are promising, challenges remain on how to identify individuals with FEP and get them into treatment as soon as possible, determine the optimal length of CSC, sustain benefits after discharge, determine services that should be included in CSC programs, and create a sustainable funding system for these programs (Dixon et al., 2018; Smith & Dixon 2020).

Regarding identification of individuals with FEP, there are questions about who should receive such services and when. CSC programs may need to collaborate with primary care providers, schools, and prison systems (as US correctional facilities are, unfortunately, the largest mental health institutions), in addition to mental health providers, in order to decrease DUP and engage individuals in treatment earlier (Smith & Dixon, 2020). Community education and stigma reduction programs are also necessary to educate individuals and family members about available services. Public health surveillance systems may also be useful. One such intervention has been implemented in New York City Hospitals (New York City Department of Health and Mental Hygiene, n.d.). When a person is admitted with FEP, the hospital must report the admission to a mental health oversight agency, and staff from New York City Supportive Transition and Recovery Team (NYC START) offer social worker and peer specialist services during the individual's hospitalization and for three months after discharge. Although helpful, these types of surveillance programs are also associated with privacy concerns due to data breaches and concerns about labeling individuals who may not have a mental health condition (Smith & Dixon, 2020).

Identifying Essential Components of CSC and Measuring Program Fidelity

Another area that is relevant to address is identifying essential components of CSC. Currently, the CSC model requires programs to have a recovery-oriented approach and offer medication management, therapy, case management, family education and support, and work/school support (Smith & Dixon 2020). Peer support is encouraged, although not formally required. Although these treatment components are intended to affect occupational functioning, social functioning, quality of life and independent living skills, there are currently no standardized outcome measures for these domains (Smith, Myers, Sederer, & Berezin, 2016). Regular, standardized outcomes measurements that minimize provider and client burden need to be incorporated into CSC programs in order to measure the effectiveness of services that are being provided. The PhenX Toolkit has been developed to address this concern (PhenX Toolkit, Version 22.1. (2018, n.d.). Some measures included in this toolkit have been utilized in a recent fidelity and outcome monitoring study of Pennsylvania CSC programs (Westfall et al., 2020).

Another useful measuring tool is the Early Psychosis Intervention Network (EPINET) Core Assessment Battery (CAB) available on the EPINET website (https://nationalepinet.org/). EPINET is a national learning healthcare system initiated in 2019 and involving 101 CSC programs in 15 states that aims to link early psychosis clinics through standardized measures and data sharing agreements (see https://nationalepinet.org/wp-content/uploads/2020/10/EPINET-CAB-Users-Guide-10-27-2020.pdf). The CAB includes 17 standardized baseline and follow-up measures across 21 domains, some of which include cognition, suicidality, DUP and pathways to care, and education/employment. An area that goes hand in hand with outcome measures is fidelity assessment. Policy makers should consider implementing a plan to establish baseline standards for program implementation that are not too flexible or strict (Smith & Dixon, 2020). Several states already have these program expectations, including New York OnTrack programs, nine CSC programs in Pennsylvania (Westfall et al., 2020), and the Early Assessment and Support Alliance (EASA) in Oregon (Essock & Addington, 2018; see https://www.oregon.gov/oha/HSD/AMH/Reporting%20Reqs/Practice%20guidelines%20for%20Oregon%20EASA.pdf).

Additionally, the Mental Health Block Grant (MHBG) 10% Set-Aside Early Intervention study conducted between 2016 and 2019, assessed fidelity and outcomes of 36 CSC programs across the USA using the First Episode Psychosis Fidelity Scale-Revised (Addington et al., 2020). This fidelity review included administrative admission, discharge, and staffing data, random health record reviews, and staff interviews. Sites took about 10.5 hours to prepare materials and participate. Upon review, two sites had excellent fidelity, twenty-five good, and nine fair. Five scale items received low fidelity ratings: less than 70% of families received evidence-based psychoeducation; supported employment and education services lacked evidence-based elements; more than 40% of individuals had been hospitalized before admission; most participants were in the programs for 2 years or less; and less than 60% of incident cases were admitted to programs. There were no differences in fidelity between programs based on the training model followed (EASA, OnTrackNY, etc.) or location (rural, urban, suburban). This study highlights that although many programs are able to maintain a good level of fidelity, more needs to be done to address the areas of weakness noted above.

Another fidelity study of nine CSC programs in Pennsylvania found that although most programs maintained high fidelity, there were some barriers with incorporating standardized clinical measures, including variation in staffing models, varying comfort level with data collection programs such as REDCap, and staff turnover (Westfall et al., 2020). Most of the Pennsylvania sites found data helpful for convincing funding sources and managed care organizations of CSC program necessity (Westfall et al., 2020). Similarly, there is also a lack of licensing and certification standards for providers of educational, peer, and employment services. States, such as New York, are addressing this barrier by developing specific training standards for peers whose services will be reimbursed by Medicaid (Smith & Dixon 2020).

Funding Sustainability

A final area of concern is the sustainability of funding for CSC programs. CSC poses a unique financial challenge due to it being a hybrid of medical, public health, and disability services (Smith & Dixon, 2020). Services such as supported employment/education and peer services do not fall under the category of medical services and are therefore not generally covered by Medicaid or commercial insurance programs (Smith & Dixon, 2020). This leads to sizable budget deficits. For example, Smith et al. (2019) reviewed average cost and reimbursement of activities provided to 75 Medicaid clients in 13 CSC programs. The average cost of care was $1375 per client per month, while average reimbursement was $662 per client per month.

Additionally, although the Affordable Care Act has expanded access to Medicaid for individuals with low income, not all states have expanded Medicaid, and even individuals who qualify for the program may not be able to access some benefits due to not having an established duration of mental illness (Dixon et al., 2018; Smith & Dixon 2020). According to the Kaiser Family Foundation (KFF), 39 states have expanded Medicaid as of November 2020 (see https://www.kff.org/health-reform/state-indicator/state-activity-around-expanding-medicaid-under-the-afford able-care-act/?currentTimeframe=0&sortModel=%7B%22colId%22:%22Loc ation%22,%22sort%22:%22asc%22%7D). This results in individuals having to demonstrate deficits prior to being able to enroll in a CSC program that is designed to avoid these deficits in the first place (Smith & Dixon, 2020). Since federal regulations allow states to request waivers to add new services to their Medicaid program, it may be possible for states to request waivers for non-traditional services like peer services and supported education/ employment (Smith & Dixon, 2020); Centers for Medicare & Medicaid Services, n.d.).

Some state funded programs, such as the Enhanced Program for Early Psychosis (ePEP) in North Texas (a state that has not yet expanded Medicaid according to KFF statistics), may have program requirements that require them to discharge patients who have Medicaid, private insurance, or exceed income limits, as was the case for 35% of program participants in a 2019 study conducted by North et al. These restrictive requirements only allowed about 1 of 100 patients who would have been eligible to participate and sometimes was a result of the program's success in helping these

144 Louise Birkedal Glenthøj et al.

individuals. Although this is hopefully unique to only a handful of programs, it poses a major challenge for all programs. A major challenge is determining the types of CSC services that are reimbursable and those that must be subsidized through federal grants, state funding, or other means (Smith & Dixon, 2020). Modeling tools such as those developed by Humensky, Dixon, & Essock (2013) may help policymakers estimate how many services will be needed in a specific area and how much they might cost.

Data from the MHBG 10% Set-Aside Early Intervention study described above indicates that five out of the 36 programs assessed rely completely on MHBG funding (see http://nri-inc.org/media/1621/3-financing-for-csc-programs.pdf). Medicaid was a predominant non-MHBG funding source, particularly in states with expanded Medicaid coverage, and private insurance was a funding source for 14 sites during initial evaluations and for 15 sites during subsequent evaluations. However, these private insurances did not reimburse for all components of CSC, as described above. Most programs indicated that they cannot be sustained at fidelity without block grant funding, with small programs being most susceptible. Funding problems also played a role in staff turnaround rates, with SEES and clinicians most likely to leave due to low salaries or position instability (see http://nri-inc.org/media/1622/4-staff-teams-in-csc-programs.pdf). In the MHBG study, 7 out of 36 sites experienced 50% or more staff turnover between the first and second evaluation, and 4 had no turnover. Impacts of these turnovers include increased stress for remaining staff, reduced client enrollment and trust, and lost cost due to training (as much as $70,000). To address funding issues, many sites reported a need for cost-based case rate reimbursement for billing Medicaid and private insurance (see http://nri-inc.org/media/1621/3-financing-for-csc-programs.pdf). Of note, several states including Maine and Illinois are in discussion with Medicaid and commercial insurances about the possibility of case rate payment. Additionally, the local organization of Medicaid behavioral benefits already provides Philadelphia CSC programs with case rate payment, and the Medicaid Accountable Care Organization of Marion County, Oregon created a per client, per month bundled case rate (Bao et al., 2020).

Over the last year, the NIMH funded six grants as part of an "Early Psychosis Intervention Network" (EPINET) to develop a learning healthcare system focusing on the treatment of early psychosis (see https://www.nih.gov/news-events/news-releases/nih-announces-funding-awards-national-early-psychosis-learning-community). These grants fund five networks and a coordinating center focused on early psychosis care. Several more nodes are expected to be funded over the next several months. Hopefully, this network will provide some answers to key questions facing early psychosis care in the US.

Conclusion

For many decades, the USA has spent substantially more per capita on healthcare than other industrialized countries, including Denmark (e.g., in 2009, US 17.5% of GDP healthcare spending versus Denmark 11.5%; Squires, 2012). Our healthcare system is not saving us money, even before accounting for costs of incarceration, emergency services, and other non-healthcare costs. The healthcare we support with our taxes is reactive, mostly serving demonstrable needs such as disability, aging, or dangerousness. Many other industrialized nations' systems attempt to be proactive, supporting goals like prevention, and support their citizens at lower overall cost to taxpayers.

US policies and court decisions *do* support the role of mental healthcare in preventing civil rights abuses. However, they stop substantially short of treating healthcare as a right. Denmark's healthcare policies and recommendations appear to attempt to follow the best evidence, and regions are held accountable for demonstrating fidelity and outcomes. On the other hand, US federal and even state policies and recommendations often have no "teeth" or require political whim or lawsuits for enforcement.

Nonetheless, quality dissemination and implementation research and infrastructures to facilitate sustainable systems exist and thrive in certain places in the USA (e.g., EPINET). Unfortunately, sometimes these programs only exist for as long as the politicians of the moment continue to support the investment, or as long as exceptional "champions" sustain the program through pure willpower. For example, multiple federal settlements in the state of Georgia have highlighted a dire need for community-based supports for people with disabilities, psychiatric and otherwise. Most components of CSC are required services under these federal settlements. Only 7 of Georgia's 159 counties offer CSC, and outside of these counties, even the "required" services are still inconsistently available and highly variable in quality.

Perhaps most importantly, the on-the-ground experience in the USA is strikingly different from other industrialized nations. A Dane experiencing their first psychotic symptoms and/or their family can receive medical or psychosocial care without significant barriers, namely costs due to the tax-based organization of mental health care in Denmark and other Scandinavian countries. Additionally, Denmark, in contrast to the United States, offers a lifelong treatment of psychosis which is of varying intensity and targets based on the need of the person. People with psychosis in Denmark can be confident that available services are at least *based on* evidence for best practices, regardless of their location or financial situation. After completing early intervention services, further support is available and based on individual needs. The contrast to the USA is obvious to anyone who has worked in community health. However, programs like OnTrackNY have demonstrated that effective evidence-based programs *can* be implemented in the US.A with fidelity and sustainability. Finally, several national initiatives have optimized the diagnosis and treatment of Danish children and adolescents with psychosis. As a result, early identification and intervention are the norm. Children with psychosis and their families have easy access to treatment in child and adolescent psychiatry programs and generally smooth transitions to adult psychiatry; a system where the essential ingredients of early intervention and continuity of care are ensured.

In closing, both the USA and Denmark have rolled out policies and funds to support very similar early intervention services, but the national results are starkly different. These differences illustrate the pitfalls that repeatedly hinder sustainable, accessible, and evidence-based progress in US mental healthcare despite the best of intentions. We have described two systems that are working relatively well and will continue to grow and develop if supported. As illustrated by OnTrackNY and other thriving systems, early intervention is a hopeful bright spot in the US mental healthcare landscape that has continuing momentum. Deinstitutionalization and Olmstead rights were also bright spots, but they faltered over time, as explained in Section 1 of this book. We must critically review and engage in radical change at this moment, and capitalize on existing momentum and evidence.

If history is the best predictor, early intervention services will gradually become degraded and siloed to the point that they are as inaccessible, unaccountable, unsustainable, and poorly-funded as other recovery-oriented services that are few and far between in the United States. Instead we must grasp the opportunity to learn from countries with established early intervention services and successful US programs. We can examine and address the ways in which national, state, and local policies and practices foster or prohibit such programs. We must act to spread and bolster our current momentum and embrace sustainable approaches rather than repeating our mistakes.

REFERENCES

Addington, D., Birchwood, M., Jones, P., Killackey, E., McDaid, D., Melau, M., ... Nordentoft, M. (2018). Fidelity scales and performance measures to support implementation and quality assurance for first-episode psychosis services. *Early Intervention in Psychiatry*, *12*(6), 1235–1242. https://doi.org/10.1111/eip.12684

Addington, J., Cadenhead, K. S., Cannon, T. D., Cornblatt, B., McGlashan, T. H., Perkins, D. O., ... Heinssen, R. (2007). North American prodrome longitudinal study: A collaborative multisite approach to prodromal schizophrenia research. *Schizophrenia Bulletin*, *33*(3), 665–672. https://doi.org/10.1093/schbul/sbl075

Addington, J., Cornblatt, B. A., Cadenhead, K. S., Cannon, T. D., McGlashan, T. H., Perkins, D. O., ... Heinssen, R. (2011). At clinical high risk for psychosis: Outcome for nonconverters. *The American Journal of Psychiatry*, *168*(8), 800–805. https://doi.org/10.1176/appi.ajp.2011.10081191

Addington, J., Heinssen, R. K., Robinson, D. G., Schooler, N. R., Marcy, P., Brunette, M. F., . . . Kane, J. M. (2015). Duration of untreated psychosis in community treatment settings in the United States. *Psychiatric Services*, *66*(7), 753–756. https://doi.org/10.1176/appi.ps.201400124

Addington, D., Noel, V., Landers, M., & Bond, G. R. (2020). Reliability and Feasibility of the First-Episode Psychosis Services Fidelity Scale–Revised for Remote Assessment. *Psychiatric Services*, *71*(12), 1245–1251.

Addington, J., Penn, D., Woods, S. W., Addington, D., & Perkins, D. O. (2008). Social functioning in individuals at clinical high risk for psychosis. *Schizophrenia Research*, *99*(1–3), 119–124. https://doi.org/10.1016/j.schres.2007.10.001

Addington, J., Stowkowy, J., Liu, L., Cadenhead, K. S., Cannon, T. D., Cornblatt, B. A., . . . & Woods, S. W. (2019). Clinical and functional characteristics of youth at clinical high-risk for psychosis who do not transition to psychosis. Psychological medicine, *49*(10), 1670–1677.

Albert, N., Glenthøj, L., Melau, M., Jensen, H., Hjorthøj, C., & Nordentoft, M. (2016). Course of illness in a sample of patients diagnosed with a schizotypal disorder and treated in a specialized early intervention setting. Findings from the 3.5year follow-up of the OPUS II study. *Schizophrenia Research*, *182*. https://doi.org/10.1016/j.schres.2016.10.013

Albert, N., Melau, M., Jensen, H., Emborg, C., Jepsen, J. R. M., Fagerlund, B., . . . Nordentoft, M. (2017). Five years of specialised early intervention versus two years of specialised early intervention followed by three years of standard treatment for patients with a first-episode psychosis: randomised, superiority, parallel group trial in Denmark (OPUS II). *BMJ (Clinical Research Ed.)*, *356*, i6681. Retrieved from http://www.ncbi.nlm.nih.gov/pubmed/28082379

Austin, S. F., Mors, O., Budtz-Jørgensen, E., Secher, R. G., Hjorthøj, C. R., Bertelsen, M., . . . Nordentoft, M. (2015). Long-term trajectories of positive and negative symptoms in first-episode psychosis: A 10 year follow-up study in the OPUS cohort. *Schizophrenia Research*, *168*(1–2), 84–91. https://doi.org/10.1016/j.schres.2015.07.021

Baandrup, L., Voldsgaard, I., Cerqueira, C., Riis, J. L., Nordentoft, M. (2012). The National Schizophrenia Database. *Ugeskrift for Laeger*, *174*, 2548.

Baandrup, L., Cerqueira, C., Haller, L., Korshøj, L., Voldsgaard, I., & Nordentoft, M. (2016). The Danish schizophrenia registry. *Clinical Epidemiology*, *8*, 691–695. https://doi.org/10.2147/CLEP.S99488

Baandrup, L., Østrup Rasmussen, J., Klokker, L., Austin, S., Bjørnshave, T., Fuglsang Bliksted, V., . . . Nordentoft, M. (2016). Treatment of adult patients with schizophrenia and complex mental health needs – A national clinical guideline. *Nordic Journal of Psychiatry*, *70*(3), 231–240. https://doi.org/10.3109/08039488.2015.1074285

Bao, Y., Li, Y., Jeng, P. J., Scodes, J., Papp, M. A., Humensky, J. L., . . . & Dixon, L. B. (2021). Design of a Payment Decision–Support Tool for Coordinated Specialty Care for Early Psychosis. *Psychiatric Services*, *72*(2), 180–185.

Beck, K., Andreou, C., Studerus, E., Heitz, U., Ittig, S., Leanza, L., & Riecher-Rössler, A. (2019). Clinical and functional long-term outcome of patients at clinical high risk (CHR) for psychosis without transition to psychosis: A systematic review. *Schizophrenia Research*, *210*, 39–47. https://doi.org/10.1016/j.schres.2018.12.047

Bello, I., Lee, R., Malinovsky, I., Watkins, L., Nossel, I., Smith, T., ... Dixon, L. B. (2017). OnTrackNY: The development of a coordinated specialty care program for individuals experiencing early psychosis. *Psychiatric Services*, *68*(4), 318–320. https://doi.org/10.1176/appi.ps.201600512

Bertelsen, M., Jeppesen, P., Petersen, L., Thorup, A., Øhlenschlæger, J., le Quach, P., ... Nordentoft, M. (2008). Five-year follow-up of a randomized multicenter trial of intensive early intervention vs standard treatment for patients with a first-episode of psychotic illness. *Archives of General Psychiatry*, *65*(7), 762. https://doi.org/10.1001/archpsyc.65.7.762

Birchwood, M., Connor, C., Lester, H., Patterson, P., Freemantle, N., Marshall, M., ... Singh, S. P. (2013). Reducing duration of untreated psychosis: Care pathways to early intervention in psychosis services. *British Journal of Psychiatry*, *203*(1), 58–64. https://doi.org/10.1192/bjp.bp.112.125500

Birchwood, M., McGorry, P., & Jackson, H. (1997). Early intervention in schizophrenia [editorial]. *British Journal of Psychiatry*, *170*(2), 2–5. https://doi .org/10.1192/bjp.170.1.2

Birchwood, M., Michail, M., Meaden, A., Tarrier, N., Lewis, S., Wykes, T., ... Peters, E. (2014). Cognitive behaviour therapy to prevent harmful compliance with command hallucinations (COMMAND): A randomised controlled trial. *The Lancet. Psychiatry*, *1*(1), 23–33. https://doi.org/10.1016/S2215-0366(14) 70247-0

Buchanan, R. W., Kreyenbuhl, J., Kelly, D. L., Noel, J. M., Boggs, D. L., Fischer, B. A., ... Keller, W. (2010). The 2009 schizophrenia PORT psychopharmacological treatment recommendations and summary statements. *Schizophrenia Bulletin*, *36*(1), 71–93. https://doi.org/10.1093/schbul/sbp116

Canady, V. A. (2020). Advocates praise new National Suicide Prevention Lifeline law. *Mental Health Weekly, 30*(41), 6–6.

Caplan, B., Zimmet, S. V., Meyer, E. C., Friedman-Yakoobian, M., Monteleone, T., Jude Leung, Y., ... Seidman, L. J. (2013). Prevention and Recovery in Early Psychosis (PREP®): Building a public-academic partnership program in Massachusetts, United States. *Asian Journal of Psychiatry*, *6*(2), 171–177. https://doi.org/10.1016/j.ajp.2012.10.009

Carrión, R. E., Auther, A. M., McLaughlin, D., Olsen, R., Addington, J., Bearden, C. E., ... Cornblatt, B. A. (2019). The global functioning: social and role scales-further validation in a large sample of adolescents and young adults at clinical high risk for psychosis. *Schizophrenia Bulletin*, *45*(4), 763–772. https://doi.org/10.1093/schbul/sby126

Chan, S. K., Chan, S. W. Y., Pang, H. H., Yan, K. K., Hui, C. L. M., Chang, W. C., ... Chen, E. Y. H. (2018). Association of an early intervention service for psychosis with suicide rate among patients with first-episode schizophrenia-spectrum disorders. *The Journal of the American Medical Association Psychiatry*, *75*(5), 458–464. https://doi.org/10.1001/jamapsychiatry.2018.0185

Chang, W. C., Chan, G. H. K., Jim, O. T. T., Lau, E. S. K., Hui, C. L. M., Chan, S. K. W., ... Chen, E. Y. H. (2015). Optimal duration of an early intervention programme for first-episode psychosis: Randomised controlled trial. *British Journal of Psychiatry*, *206*(6), 492–500. https://doi.org/10.1192/bjp.bp.114 .150144

Chang, W. C., Kit Wa Chan, S., Yu Hai Chen, E., Wing Yan Kwong, V., Sin Kei Lau, E., Sau Man Wong, C., . . . Chan, S. K. W. (2017). Sustainability of treatment effect of a 3-year early intervention programme for first-episode psychosis. *British Journal of Psychiatry, 211*(1), 37–44. Retrieved from http://10.0.4.168/bjp.bp.117 .198929%0Ahttp://ezproxy.usherbrooke.ca/login?url=https://search.ebscohost.com/ login.aspx?direct=true&db=pbh&AN=124325612&site=ehost-live

Christensen, T. N., Wallstrøm, I. G., Stenager, E., Bojesen, A. B., Gluud, C., Nordentoft, M., & Eplov, L. F. (2019). Effects of individual placement and support supplemented with cognitive remediation and work-focused social skills training for people with severe mental illness. *The Journal of the American Medical Association Psychiatry*, 1–9. https://doi.org/10.1001/jamapsychiatry.2019.2291

Correll, C. U., Galling, B., Pawar, A., Krivko, A., Bonetto, C., Ruggeri, M., . . . Kane, J. M. (2018). Comparison of early intervention services vs treatment as usual for early-phase psychosis: A systematic review, meta-analysis, and meta-regression. *The Journal of the American Medical Association Psychiatry, 75*(6), 555–565. https://doi.org/10.1001/jamapsychiatry.2018.0623

Cotter, J., Lin, A., Drake, R. J., Thompson, A., Nelson, B., McGorry, P., . . . Yung, A. R. (2017). Long-term employment among people at ultra-high risk for psychosis. *Schizophrenia Research, 184*(2017), 26–31. https://doi.org/10.1016/j.schres.2016.11.033

Craig, T. K. J., Garety, P., Power, P., Rahaman, N., Colbert, S., Fornells-Ambrojo, M., & Dunn, G. (2004). The Lambeth Early Onset (LEO) Team: Randomised controlled trial of the effectiveness of specialised care for early psychosis. *British Medical Journal, 329*(7474), 1067–1070. https://doi.org/10.1136/bmj .38246.594873.7C

Craig, T. K., Rus-Calafell, M., Ward, T., Leff, J. P., Huckvale, M., Howarth, E., . . . Garety, P. A. (2018). AVATAR therapy for auditory verbal hallucinations in people with psychosis: A single-blind, randomised controlled trial. *The Lancet Psychiatry, 5*(1), 31–40. https://doi.org/10.1016/S2215-0366(17)30427-3

Csillag, C., Nordentoft, M., Mizuno, M., McDaid, D., Arango, C., Smith, J., . . . Jones, P. B. (2018). Early intervention in psychosis: From clinical intervention to health system implementation. *Early Intervention in Psychiatry, 12*(4), 757–764. https://doi.org/10.1111/eip.12514

De Wit, S., Schothorst, P. F., Oranje, B., Ziermans, T. B., Durston, S., & Kahn, R. S. (2014). Adolescents at ultra-high risk for psychosis: Long-term outcome of individuals who recover from their at-risk state. *European Neuropsychopharmacology, 24*(6), 865–873. https://doi.org/10.1016/j.euroneuro.2014.02.008

Dixon, L. (2017). What it will take to make coordinated specialty care available to anyone experiencing early schizophrenia. *The Journal of the American Medical Association Psychiatry, 74*(1), 7. https://doi.org/10.1001/jamapsychiatry.2016.2665

Dixon, L. B., Goldman, H. H., Bennett, M. E., Wang, Y., McNamara, K. A., Mendon, S. J., . . . Essock, S. M. (2015). Implementing coordinated specialty care for early psychosis: The RAISE connection program. *Psychiatric Services, 66*(7), 691–698. https://doi.org/10.1176/appi.ps.201400281

Dixon, L. B., Goldman, H. H., Srihari, V. H., & Kane, J. M. (2018). Transforming the treatment of schizophrenia in the United States: The RAISE Initiative. *Annual Review of Clinical Psychology, 14*, 237–258. https://doi.org/10.1146/annurev-clinpsy-050817-084934

150   Louise Birkedal Glenthøj et al.

Fett, A.-K. J. K. J., Viechtbauer, W., Dominguez, M.-G. de G., Penn, D. L., van Os, J., & Krabbendam, L. (2011). The relationship between neurocognition and social cognition with functional outcomes in schizophrenia: A meta-analysis. *Neuroscience and Biobehavioral Reviews, 35*(3), 573–588. https://doi.org/10.1016/j.neubiorev.2010.07.001

Frank, R. G., Goldman, H. H., & Hogan, M. (2003). Medicaid And mental health: Be careful what you ask for. *Health Affairs, 22*(1), 101–113. https://doi.org/10.1377/hlthaff.22.1.101

Fusar-Poli, P., Byrne, M., Badger, S., Valmaggia, L. R., & McGuire, P. K. (2013). Outreach and support in South London (OASIS), 2001–2011: Ten years of early diagnosis and treatment for young individuals at high clinical risk for psychosis. *European Psychiatry, 28*(5), 315–326. https://doi.org/10.1016/j.eurpsy.2012.08.002

Gafoor, R., Nitsch, D., McCrone, P., Craig, T. K. J., Garety, P. A., Power, P., & McGuire, P. (2010). Effect of early intervention on 5-year outcome in non-affective psychosis. *British Journal of Psychiatry, 196*(5), 372–376. https://doi.org/10.1192/bjp.bp.109.066050

Goldman, H. H., & Karakus, M. C. (2014). Do not turn out the lights on the public mental health system when the ACA is fully implemented. *Journal of Behavioral Health Services and Research, 41*(4), 429–433. https://doi.org/10.1007/s11414-014-9394-y

Goldman, H. H., Karakus, M., Frey, W., & Beronio, K. (2013). Financing first-episode psychosis services in the United States. *Psychiatric Services, 64*(6), 506–508. https://doi.org/10.1176/appi.ps.201300106

Green, M. F. (1996). What are the functional consequences of neurocognitive deficits in schizophrenia? *The American Journal of Psychiatry, 153*(3), 321–330. https://doi.org/10.1176/ajp.153.3.321

Grob, G. N. (1994). *The mad among us: A history of the care of America's mentally ill.* New York: Free Press.

Grob, G. N. (2006). *The dilemma of federal mental health policy: radical reform or incremental change?* Piscataway, NJ: Rutgers Univ. Press.

Hastrup, L. H., Kronborg, C., Bertelsen, M., Jeppesen, P., Jorgensen, P., Petersen, L., ... Nordentoft, M. (2013). Cost-effectiveness of early intervention in first-episode psychosis: Economic evaluation of a randomised controlled trial (the OPUS study). *British Journal of Psychiatry, 202*(1), 35–41. https://doi.org/10.1192/bjp.bp.112.112300

Heinssen, R.K., Goldstein, A.B., & Azrin, S. T. (2014). *Evidence-based treatment for first-episode psychosis:* Components of coordinated specialty care.

Hogan, M. F., & Goldman, M. L. (2020). New Opportunities to Improve Mental Health Crisis Systems. *Psychiatric Services,* https://doi.org/10.1176/appi.ps.202000114.

Humensky, J. L., Dixon, L. B., & Essock, S. M. (2013). State mental health policy: an interactive tool to estimate costs and resources for a first-episode psychosis initiative in New York State. *Hospital & Community Psychiatry, 64*(9), 832–834. Retrieved from http://ovidsp.ovid.com/ovidweb.cgi?T=JS&CSC=Y&NEWS=N&PAGE=fulltext&D=psyc10&AN=2013-32461-014%0Ahttp://twuniversal.twu.edu/openurl/TXWU/twu_services_page?sid=OVID:psycdb&id=pmid:&id=doi:10.1176%2Fappi.ps.201300186&issn=1075-2730&isbn=&volume=64&issue=9&sp

Jeppesen, P., Petersen, L., Thorup, A., Abel, M.-B., Øhlenschlæger, J., Christensen, T. Ø., ... Nordentoft, M. (2005). Integrated treatment of first-episode psychosis: Effect of treatment on family burden. *British Journal of Psychiatry, 187*(S48), s85–s90. https://doi.org/10.1192/bjp.187.48.s85

Jeppesen, P., Petersen, L., Thorup, A., Abel, M.-B., Øhlenschlæger, J., Christensen, T. Ø., ... Nordentoft, M. (2008). The association between pre-morbid adjustment, duration of untreated psychosis and outcome in first-episode psychosis. *Psychological Medicine, 38*(8), 1157–1166. https://doi.org/10.1017/S0033291708003449

Kane, J. M., Robinson, D. G., Schooler, N. R., Mueser, K. T., Penn, D. L., Rosenheck, R. A., ... & Heinssen, R. K. (2016). Comprehensive versus usual community care for first-episode psychosis: 2-year outcomes from the NIMH RAISE early treatment program. American Journal of Psychiatry, *173*(4), 362–372.

Kane, J. M., Schooler, N. R., Marcy, P., Correll, C. U., Brunette, M. F., Mueser, K. T., ... Robinson, D. G. (2015). The RAISE early treatment program for first-episode psychosis. *The Journal of Clinical Psychiatry, 76*(3), 240–246. https://doi.org/10.4088/jcp.14m09289

Kreyenbuhl, J., Buchanan, R. W., Dickerson, F. B., & Dixon, L. B. (2010). The schizophrenia Patient Outcomes Research Team (PORT): Updated treatment recommendations 2009. *Schizophrenia Bulletin, 36*(1), 94–103. https://doi.org/10.1093/schbul/sbp130

Kühl, J. O. G., Laursen, T. M., Thorup, A., & Nordentoft, M. (2016). The incidence of schizophrenia and schizophrenia spectrum disorders in Denmark in the period 2000–2012. A register-based study. *Schizophrenia Research, 176*(2–3), 533–539. https://doi.org/10.1016/j.schres.2016.06.023

Lehman, A. F., Kreyenbuhl, J., Buchanan, R. W., Dickerson, F. B., Dixon, L. B., Goldberg, R., ... Steinwachs, D. M. (2004). The schizophrenia Patient Outcomes Research Team (PORT): Updated treatment recommendations 2003. *Schizophrenia Bulletin, 30*(2), 193–217. https://doi.org/10.1093/oxfordjournals.schbul.a007071

Lehman, A. F., & Steinwachs, D. M. (1998). Translating research into practice: the schizophrenia Patient Outcomes Research Team (PORT) treatment recommendations. *Schizophrenia Bulletin, 24*(1), 1–10. https://doi.org/10.1093/oxfordjournals.schbul.a033302

Lin, A., Wood, S. J., Nelson, B., Beavan, A., McGorry, P., & Yung, A. R. (2015). Outcomes of nontransitioned cases in a sample at ultra-high risk for psychosis. *American Journal of Psychiatry, 172*(3), 249–258. https://doi.org/10.1176/appi.ajp.2014.13030418

Loebel, A. D., Lieberman, J. A., Alvir, J. M. J., Mayerhoff, D. I., Geisler, S. H., & Szymanski, S. R. (1992). Duration of psychosis and outcome in first-episode schizophrenia. *American Journal of Psychiatry, 149*(9), 1183–1188. https://doi.org/10.1176/ajp.149.9.1183

Lucksted, A., Essock, S. M., Stevenson, J., Mendon, S. J., Nossel, I. R., Goldman, H. H., ... Dixon, L. B. (2015). Client views of engagement in the RAISE connection program for early psychosis recovery. *Psychiatric Services, 66*(7), 699–704. https://doi.org/10.1176/appi.ps.201400475

Lucksted, A., Stevenson, J., Nossel, I., Drapalski, A., Piscitelli, S., & Dixon, L. B. (2018). Family member engagement with early psychosis specialty care. *Early Intervention in Psychiatry, 12*(5), 922–927. https://doi.org/10.1111/eip .12403

Madsen, T., Karstoft, K.-I., Secher, R. G., Austin, S. F., & Nordentoft, M. (2016). Trajectories of suicidal ideation in patients with first-episode psychosis: Secondary analysis of data from the OPUS trial. *The Lancet Psychiatry, 3*(5), 443–450. https://doi.org/10.1016/S2215–0366(15)00518-0

Malla, A., Joober, R., Iyer, S., Norman, R., Schmitz, N., Brown, T., . . . Abadi, S. (2017). Comparing three-year extension of early intervention service to regular care following two years of early intervention service in first-episode psychosis: A randomized single blind clinical trial. *World Psychiatry, 16*(3), 278–286. https://doi.org/10.1002/wps.20456

Marshall, M., Lewis, S., Lockwood, A., Drake, R., Jones, P., & Croudace, T. (2005). Association between duration of untreated psychosis and outcome in cohorts of first-episode patients. *Archives of General Psychiatry, 62*(9), 975–983. https://doi .org/10.1001/archpsyc.62.9.975

McFarlane, W. R. (2002). *Multifamilygroups in the treatment of severe psychiatric disorders*. New York/London: Guilford Press.

McGlashan, T. H., & Johannessen, J. O. (1996). Early detection and intervention with schizophrenia: Rationale. *Schizophrenia Bulletin, 22*(2), 201–222. Retrieved from http://www.ncbi.nlm.nih.gov/pubmed/8782282

McGorry, P. D. (2015). Early intervention in psychosis: Obvious, effective, overdue. *Journal of Nervous and Mental Disease, 203*(5), 310–318. https://doi.org/10.1097/ NMD.0000000000000284

Melau, M., Albert, N., & Nordentoft, M. (2018). Programme fidelity of specialized early intervention in Denmark. *Early Intervention in Psychiatry, 13*(3), 627–632.

Melle, I., Johannesen, J. O., Friis, S., Haahr, U., Joa, I., Larsen, T. K., . . . McGlashan, T. (2006). Early detection of the first-episode of schizophrenia and suicidal behavior. *American Journal of Psychiatry, 163*(5), 800–804. https://doi.org/10 .1176/ajp.2006.163.5.800

National Institue for Health and Care Excellence (NICE). (2014). *Psychosis and schizophrenia in adults:Pprevention and management*.

Nielsen, C. M., Hjorthøj, C., Killaspy, H., & Nordentoft, M. (2021). The effect of flexible assertive community treatment in Denmark: A quasi-experimental controlled study. *The Lancet Psychiatry, 8*(1), 27–35.

Nordentoft, M., Jørgensen, P., Gall, E. M., Krarup, G., & Martinussen, M. (2002). *Integreret Indsats for Unge Med Psykose. Erfaringer fra OPUS Projektet, Copenhagen*. Hans Reitzel.

Nordentoft, M., Melau, M., Iversen, T., & Kjær, S. (2009). *Psykose hos Unge – Symptomer, Behandling og Fremtid. Erfaringer fra OPUS, København*. Psykiatrifondens Forlag.

Nordentoft, M., Jeppesen, P., Abel, M., Kassow, P., Petersen, L., Thorup, A., . . . Jørgensen, P. (2002). OPUS study: Suicidal behaviour, suicidal ideation and hopelessness among patients with first-episode psychosis. *British Journal of Psychiatry, 181*(S43), s98–s106. https://doi.org/10.1192/bjp.181.43.s98

Nordentoft, M., Pedersen, M. G., Pedersen, C. B., Blinkenberg, S., & Mortensen, P. B. (2012). The new asylums in the community: Severely ill psychiatric patients living in psychiatric supported housing facilities. A Danish register-based study of prognostic factors, use of psychiatric services, and mortality. *Social Psychiatry and Psychiatric Epidemiology, 47*(8), 1251–1261. https://doi.org/10.1007/s00127-011-0432-2

North, C. S., Simic, Z., & Burruss, J. (2019). Design, implementation, and assessment of a public comprehensive specialty care program for early psychosis. *Journal of Psychiatric Practice®, 25*(2), 91–102.

Nossel, I., Wall, M. M., Scodes, J., Marino, L. A., Zilkha, S., Bello, I., . . . Dixon, L. (2018). Results of a coordinated specialty care program for early psychosis and predictors of outcomes. *Psychiatric Services, 69*(8), 863–870. https://doi.org/10.1176/appi.ps.201700436

Penttilä, M., Jääskeläinen, E., Hirvonen, N., Isohanni, M., & Miettunen, J. (2014). Duration of untreated psychosis as predictor of long-term outcome in schizophrenia: Systematic review and meta-analysis. *British Journal of Psychiatry, 205*(2), 88–94. https://doi.org/10.1192/bjp.bp.113.127753

Petersen, L., Jeppesen, P., Thorup, A., Abel, M.-B., Øhlenschlaeger, J., Christensen, T. Ø., . . . Nordentoft, M. (2005). A randomised multicentre trial of integrated versus standard treatment for patients with a first episode of psychotic illness. *BMJ (Clinical Research Ed.), 331*(7517), 602. https://doi.org/10.1136/bmj.38565.415000.E01

PhenX Toolkit, Version 22.1. (2018, J. 18). (n.d.). *Early Psychosis Translational Research Specialty Collection.*

Phillips, L. J., Leicester, S. B., O'Dwyer, L. E., Francey, S. M., Koutsogiannis, J., Abdel-Baki, A., . . . McGorry, P. D. (2002). The PACE Clinic: Identification and management of young people at "ultra" high risk of psychosis. *Journal of Psychiatric Practice, 8*(5), 255–269. Retrieved from http://www.ncbi.nlm.nih.gov/pubmed/15985888

Pot-kolder, R. M., Geraets, C. N., Veling, W., van Beilen, M., Staring, A. B., Gijsman, H. J., . . . & van der Gaag, M. (2018). Virtual-reality-based cognitive behavioural therapy versus waiting list control for paranoid ideation and social avoidance in patients with psychotic disorders: a single-blind randomised controlled trial. *The Lancet Psychiatry, 5*(3), 217–226.

Robinson, D. G., Schooler, N. R., Correll, C. U., John, M., Kurian, B. T., Marcy, P., . . . Kane, J. M. (2018). Psychopharmacological treatment in the RAISE-ETP study: Outcomes of a manual and computer decision support system based intervention. *American Journal of Psychiatry, 175*(2), 169–179. https://doi.org/10.1176/appi.ajp.2017.16080919

Rosenheck, R., Leslie, D., Sint, K., Lin, H., Robinson, D. G., Schooler, N. R., . . . Kane, J. M. (2016). Cost-effectiveness of comprehensive, integrated care for first-episode psychosis in the NIMH RAISE Early Treatment Program. *Schizophrenia Bulletin, 42*(4), 896–906. https://doi.org/10.1093/schbul/sbv224

Ruggeri, M., Bonetto, C., Lasalvia, A., De Girolamo, G., Fioritti, A., Rucci, P., . . . & Tansella, M. (2012). A multi-element psychosocial intervention for early psychosis (GET UP PIANO TRIAL) conducted in a catchment area of 10 million inhabitants: study protocol for a pragmatic cluster randomized controlled trial. *Trials, 13*(1), 1–16.

Ruggeri, M., Lasalvia, A., Santonastaso, P., Pileggi, F., Leuci, E., Miceli, M., ...
Bonetto, C. (2017). Family burden, emotional distress and service satisfaction in
first-episode psychosis. Data from the GET UP trial. *Frontiers in Psychology*,
8(MAY). https://doi.org/10.3389/fpsyg.2017.00721

Secher, R. G., Hjorthøj, C. R., Austin, S. F., Thorup, A., Jeppesen, P., Mors, O., &
Nordentoft, M. (2015). Ten-year follow-up of the OPUS specialized early
intervention trial for patients with a first-episode of psychosis. *Schizophrenia
Bulletin*, *41*(3), 617–626. https://doi.org/10.1093/schbul/sbu155

Smith, T., Myers, R., Sederer, L., & Berezin, J. (2016). How value-based payment
arrangements should measure behavioral health. *Health Affairs Blog*.
Retrieved from: https://www.healthaffairs.org/do/10.1377/hblog20161129
.057660/full/

Smith, T. E, & Dixon, L. B. (2020). Early intervention in psychosis: From science to
services. In H. H. Goldman, R.G. Frank, & J. P. Morrissey (Eds.), *The Palgrave
Handbook of American Mental Health Policy* (pp. 297–330). Palgrave Macmillan.

Smith, T. E., Kurk, M., Sawhney, R., Bao, Y., Nossel, I., Cohen, D. E., & Dixon, L. B.
(2019). Estimated staff time effort, costs, and Medicaid revenues for coordinated
specialty care clinics serving clients with first-episode psychosis. *Psychiatric
Services*, *70*(5), 425–427.

Squires, D. A. (2012). Explaining high health care spending in the United States: An
international comparison of supply, utilization, prices, and quality. *Issue brief
(Commonwealth Fund)*, *10*, 1–14.

Srihari, V. H., Shah, J., & Keshavan, M. S. (2012). Is early intervention for psychosis
feasible and effective? *Psychiatric Clinics of North America*, *35*(3), 613–631.
https://doi.org/10.1016/j.psc.2012.06.004

Srihari, V. H., Tek, C., Kucukgoncu, S., Phutane, V. H., Breitborde, N. J., Pollard, J.,
... & Woods, S. W. (2015). First-episode services for psychotic disorders in the
US public sector: A pragmatic randomized controlled trial. *Psychiatric Services*,
66(7), 705–712.

Tessler, R.C., & Goldman, H. H. (1982). *The Chronically Mentally Ill: Assessing
Community Support Programs*. Cambridge, MA: Ballinger/Harper & Row.

Thoegersen, M. H., Morthorst, B. R., & Nordentoft, M. (2019). Assertive community
treatment versus standard treatment for severely mentally ill patients in
Denmark: A quasi-experimental trial. *Nordic Journal of Psychiatry*, *73*(2),
149–158. https://doi.org/10.1080/08039488.2019.1576765

Turner, D. T., van der Gaag, M., Karyotaki, E., & Cuijpers, P. (2014). Psychological
interventions for psychosis: A meta-analysis of comparative outcome studies. *The
American Journal of Psychiatry*, *171*(5), 523–538. https://doi.org/10.1176/appi
.ajp.2013.13081159

Uzenoff, S. R., Penn, D. L., Graham, K. A., Saade, S., Smith, B. B., & Perkins, D. O.
(2012). Evaluation of a multi-element treatment center for early psychosis in the
United States. *Social Psychiatry and Psychiatric Epidemiology*, *47*(10),
1607–1615.

Westfall, M. B., Kohler, C. G., Hurford, I., Abegunde, C., Agosti, D., Brinen, A., ...
Calkins, M. E. (2020). Pennsylvania coordinated specialty care programs for first-
episode psychosis: 6-and 12-month outcomes. *Early Intervention in Psychiatry*,
15(5), 1395–1408.

Wykes, T., Huddy, V., Cellard, C., McGurk, S. R., & Czobor, P. (2011). A meta-analysis of cognitive remediation for schizophrenia: Methodology and effect sizes. *American Journal of Psychiatry*, *168*(5), 472–485. https://doi.org/10.1176/appi .ajp.2010.10060855

Yung, A. R., McGorry, P. D., Francey, S. M., Nelson, B., Baker, K., Phillips, L. J., . . . Amminger, G. P. (2007). PACE: A specialised service for young people at risk of psychotic disorders. *The Medical Journal of Australia*, *187*(7 Suppl), 43–46. https://doi.org/yun10343_fm [pii]

Part III

The Future

7   A Way Forward

Enhancing Training in Psychosocial Interventions
for Serious Mental Illness

Shirley M. Glynn and Mary A. Jansen

According to the 2018 National Survey on Drug Use and Health, approximately 11.4 million adults in the USA had experienced serious mental illness (SMI) in the prior year, with about 7.3 million (64.1%) having received mental health services (Substance Abuse and Mental Health Services Administration [SAMHSA, 2019]). Notably, about one third of adults with SMI reported not having received mental health services. The lack of treatment and undertreatment of individuals living with an SMI is well-documented (Mojtabai et al., 2009; Young et al., 2016) and has resulted in increases in homelessness, suicide, premature mortality, and heightened arrest and detention rates.

A key issue in discussions of enhancing treatment for those living with SMI is *"Where are the providers who can competently help them?"* At a basic level, workforce data indicate an aging population of psychologists (American Psychological Association, 2016) and psychiatrists (Olfson, 2016), whose retirements are likely negatively impacting on access to mental health care. Equally important, the past 35 years has witnessed dramatic developments in our knowledge about the lives and care of individuals with SMI, including (1) our increasing understanding that naturalistic prognosis may be better in schizophrenia than first envisioned (Harding et al., 1987a,b), (2) the availability of more effective SMI treatments (Bighelli et al., 2018), and (3) the growth and adoption of the recovery movement (Leonhardt et al., 2017). Unfortunately, these advancements have been slow to influence typical care in the field (Horvitz-Lennon et al., 2009, 2014), in part because of difficulties in establishing a cadre of mental health providers trained in the newer, more effective treatments. Training in psychology has been particularly critiqued as not including sufficient attention to SMI (Mueser et al., 2013; Roe et al., 2006). Nevertheless, these three factors – hope about the prognosis of SMI, the availability of more effective interventions, and changing attitudes conducive to supporting the dignity and autonomy of services users – are critical aspects of advancements in our knowledge and support for better SMI outcomes. To provide competent treatment, mental health providers must have expertise in all three domains. These factors, and the need to update mental health provider training models, and especially those for psychologists, to incorporate them, are examined in this chapter.

Long-Term Course of SMI

Data on improved outcomes in SMI come from two sources, longitudinal naturalistic studies and professionally-led intervention trials. With regard to naturalistic studies on the course of serious mental illnesses, for much of the last century, the concept of recovery from schizophrenia spectrum disorders was foreign to most mental health providers, although the prognosis of affective illnesses was considered better (see Hafner, 2004 for a historical review). Long-term naturalistic data contradict these beliefs. First, contrary to long held and pervasive beliefs about the deteriorating course of schizophrenia spectrum disorders, several meta-analyses and summaries of well-conducted studies have been published and all continue to document that many individuals diagnosed with these disorders can, and do, recover from the effects of their illness across their lifetimes (Warner, 2010), and indeed that perhaps 50–75% have the potential to achieve long-term remission and reasonable functional recovery (Harding et al., 1987; President's New Freedom Commission on Mental Health, 2003; Zipursky et al., 2012). With regard to bipolar illness, the original tenet that disease outcomes were better than schizophrenia does not appear to be supported by the data. While the cyclical nature of the disease fosters periods of both good and poor functioning (Judd et al., 2002), long-term outcomes are quite variable and, as with schizophrenia, many individuals continue to live with significant residual functional deficits (Gitlin & Miklowitz, 2017). A significant challenge in bipolar disorder is lack of treatment engagement, which is common and appears to have a particularly deleterious course on outcomes (Jawad et al., 2018).

Improving Outcomes Through Effective Interventions

While the data on the naturalist course of schizophrenia indicate long-term outcomes may be better than first thought, many individuals living with SMI exhibit significant functional deficits and can benefit from pharmacological and psychosocial treatment. Fortunately, there are now a wide array of successful psychosocial interventions to address broad-ranging difficulties associated with SMIs; note that these are generally initially tested and then more widely provided to individuals also receiving pharmacological interventions. Several meta-analysis and single study reports are available documenting the efficacy of psychosocial treatments for positive (Bighelli et al., 2018) and negative symptoms (Fusar-Poli et al., 2015) in schizophrenia spectrum disorders. Other studies find benefit for problems that are common across SMI diagnoses, such as social skills deficits (Kurtz & Mueser, 2008), un- or underemployment (Modini et al., 2016), internalized stigma (Tsang et al., 2016), and family education and communication deficits (McFarlane, 2016; Miklowitz & Chung, 2016).

The evidence base supporting use of clinically-oriented psychosocial rehabilitation services for people with serious mental health disorders has developed considerably over the past two decades and is now quite robust. Many of these specialized services have been shown in multiple randomized clinical trials to be highly effective and are considered to be evidence-based practices (EBPs) for this population. Provision of EBPs and promising practices have been shown to improve the functional capability of individuals with SMI/SED and improve outcomes across a broad spectrum of domains when compared with standard care (Patterson & Leeuwenkamp, 2008). Yet, despite these advances, EBPs and other specialized services are not routinely available in most mental health treatment settings (President's New Freedom Commission on Mental Health, 2003; Stirman et al., 2010).

Within SMI, research on psychosocial interventions has been most robust in the study of schizophrenia spectrum disorders, although there is increasing emphasis on SMI affective illnesses, such as bipolar disorder. The 2009 Schizophrenia Patient Outcomes Research Team (PORT) study remains the most rigorous and undisputed summary of efficacious interventions for schizophrenia spectrum disorders to date (Kreyenbuhl, Buchanan, Dickerson & Dixon, 2010). The PORT study identified eight evidence-based practices (EBPs) and four promising practices that are effective in schizophrenia spectrum disorders. These include:

- Assertive community treatment
- Supported employment
- Family psychoeducation
- Cognitive behavioral therapy (CBT) and CBT for psychosis (CBTp)
- Token economy
- Skills training
- Psychosocial interventions for alcohol and substance use disorders
- Psychosocial interventions for weight management
- Medication/illness management
- Cognitive remediation
- Psychological treatments for recent onset schizophrenia
- Peer support and peer-delivered services

Many best practice guidelines for bipolar disorder have a primary emphasis on pharmacological treatment (see for example, American Psychiatric Association, 2002; National Institute for Health and Care Excellence [NICE], 2014). Research on psychosocial treatment in bipolar illness has lagged, in part because interventions can impact differentially on manic or depressive symptoms, which complicates investigations. In their recent comprehensive summary and network meta-analysis of psychosocial treatments adjunctive to medication in bipolar illness, Miklowitz et al. (2020) found that psychoeducation with guided practice of illness management skills in a family or group format was associated with reducing symptom recurrences versus the same strategies used in an individual format. Cognitive behavioral therapy was associated with stabilizing depressive symptoms compared with treatment as usual; the data were less compelling on family or conjoint therapy and interpersonal therapy.

Ironically, many of the EBPs that we now know are useful to assist those with SMI or a serious emotional disturbance (SED) were designed, developed and empirically validated by psychologists, but the profession has not embraced this work as readily as might be expected (Mueser et al., 2013). This is a long-standing problem. In the early 1990s, an NIMH sponsored National Forum convened leaders from several disciplines to make recommendations about how to synthesize and transfer new knowledge to those in training (National Institute of Mental Health, 1990). The forum was led by an eminent psychologist (Harriett Lefley) and included leaders in four key disciplines (psychiatry, psychology, social work, nursing) plus experts in psychosocial rehabilitation and family members. One of the psychology leaders told the group that there were few faculty or clinical supervisors with the needed expertise, a lack of relevant coursework, and few mentors and role models (Hargrove, 1990). These concerns were echoed by Johnson (1990), who added: "work with the seriously mentally ill has not been highly regarded by psychologists, and opportunities for training to work with this population are seriously deficient" (p. 64). In each decade since the 1990s, it has been progressively more emphasized that specialized training is needed to provide adequate treatment for those with SMI/SED (Carr et al., 2014; Corrigan et al., 2001; Gill & Murphy, 2013; Hargrove, 1990; Mueser et al., 2013).

The Recovery Movement

While improving objective outcomes is important, there has also been a growing emphasis on enhancing personally valued outcomes as the field of SMI treatment has matured. This transition reflects an evolving definition of SMI recovery, which moves away from a traditional medical model conceptualization of reduction or elimination of pathology (Davidson, 2016) to a more person-centered one (SAMHSA, 2010).

The SAMHSA National Consensus Statement on Mental Health Recovery (2004) presented an early definition of recovery as ". . .a journey of healing and transformation enabling a person with a mental health problem to live a meaningful life in a community of his or her choice while striving to achieve his or her full potential." Ten fundamental components of recovery were provided – self-direction, individualized and person-centered, empowerment, holistic, nonlinear, strengths-based, peer support, respect, responsibility, and hope. More recently, SAMHSA (2012) has updated is definition of recovery to be "A process of change through which individuals improve their health and wellness, live a self-directed life, and strive to reach their full potential."

In this decade, virtually every mental health professional and advocacy organization in the United States has endorsed the recovery model of mental health care. The adoption of this new concept of recovery has been a primary mission of SAMHSA. Similarly, leadership from the Department of Veterans Affairs (Cohen et al., 2012) and community mental health facilities (Carr & Miller, 2017; Frost et al., 2017) have written eloquently about the system transformation required to infuse recovery orientations into their mental health services.

While the recovery approach has generated great interest, problems have also been noted. Some have critiqued the efforts to promote the recovery model as moving resources away from those who are most impacted by SMI (Satel, 2014). Others have argued that the movement has been co-opted by mental health professionals, who have not incorporated its often user-driven social justice roots (Hunt & Resnick, 2015). Perhaps most importantly, it is unclear if this movement is actually impacting on the care provided to individuals living with an SMI. Mabe and colleagues (2014, p. 347) observe that "Relatively neglected have been initiatives to educate physicians and doctorally-trained psychologists in the concepts and practices of recovery-oriented care." This observation about failures in psychologist training in recovery-oriented attitudes and practices echoes the work of Roe et al. (2006) and Mueser et al. (2013).

Growing Recognition of the Mental Health Provider Training Problem

There has been increasing concern among leaders in many mental health disciplines that existing training paradigms do not yield clinicians who can meet the needs of those living with SMIs, because they do not include sufficient instruction on evidence-based interventions specific or adaptable to SMI work and/or foster sufficient exposure to the recovery paradigm (Mueser et al., 2013; Olfson, 2016). For example, although Stewart et al. (1993) described a postdoctoral training program for SMI almost 30 years ago, a survey of the current websites of American Psychological Association (APA) accredited doctoral and postdoctoral programs reveals they rarely reference SMIs as a focus of study, and among those that do, the topics covered and the discussion of those topics center on highly traditional models of diagnosis and treatment according to traditional methods. Very few include any mention of the newer evidence-based interventions or the increasingly accepted recovery paradigm. A 2010 survey of training directors of the Council of University Directors of Clinical Psychology (CUDCP) training programs found that more than half of the training directors believed the factor that most discouraged training in this area is that psychologists prefer "clients with 'insight and motivation for treatment'" (Reddy et al., 2010, p. 259), further reinforcing the stereotypical beliefs about people with SMI – beliefs that are inevitably passed on to trainees and likely deter many from working with this population. Similarly, Kimhy et al. (2013) surveyed training directors in US clinical psychology doctoral programs to characterize the penetration of cognitive behavioral therapy for psychosis (CBTp) training and to assess their familiarity with basic CBTp facts. Respondents displayed limited knowledge of CBTp effectiveness, with only 40% of psychology training directors believing that CBTp is efficacious and only 30% of psychology training directors being aware that the CBTp evidence base is based on meta-analyses. These results are particularly disheartening, as CBTp is grounded in recovery concepts, such as personal goal setting and a simultaneous emphasis on reduction of symptom distress and functional improvement.

It is important to note that other mental health disciplines are also acknowledging deficiencies in training in working with individuals with serious mental illness. For example, Rapp and colleagues prepared a comprehensive survey of social work practices and training in support of the recovery movement in 2011 (https://www.cswe.org/getattachment/Centers-Initiatives/Institutional-Research/Recovery-to-Practice-Initiative/RecoverytoPractice-FINALpublishedreport.pdf.aspx). While they found the basic tenets and social work activities were consistent with the recovery movement, they identified a variety of training needs (e.g., integrating class work and field placements, development of a recovery curriculum) to support a full infusion of recovery principles into the discipline. Rubin et al. (2012) published a review of the information social workers should know in intervening with individuals diagnosed with an SMI and argued for competency-based training and evaluation for social workers in this domain. With regard to physicians, the Psychiatry Milestones project (2015) (https://www.acgme.org/Portals/0/PDFs/Milestones/PsychiatryMilestones.pdf) provides a framework for assessing the development of the resident physician in key dimensions, including the elements of physician competency in a specialty or subspecialty. The Milestones project includes items to assess how well residents can describe, refer to, and work effectively in a recovery-based program; there are also published studies showing the development of more recovery-based skills in psychiatric residents undergoing training in an innovative community program which embraced state-of-the-art treatment and recovery principles (Randall et al., 2011). There is also growing interest in the greater integration of evidence-based SMI treatment and the recovery approach in mental health nursing, with both thought pieces (Cleary et al., 2017) and studies on strategies to assess recovery knowledge in trainees (Happell et al., 2015) being published.

Exemplars of Innovative Local Provider Training Efforts

Nascent efforts have been directed at filling the gap between science and standard practice in the treatment of SMI through more systematic local training efforts. Beidas and Kendall (2010, p. 20) proposed that, with regard to specialized didactic and experiential training, "To achieve client change, it is necessary for therapists to reach proficiency levels in knowledge, adherence, competence, and skill. This perspective speaks to the importance of training therapists to criteria prior to implementing treatments," and that ongoing mentorship and support are needed. Consistent with this line of thinking, there are now published reports of specialized courses such as the Recovery Education in the Academy Program (REAP) program at the University of Illinois at Chicago (Razzano et al., 2010) and the Project Georgia Recovery-based Educational Approach to Treatment (GREAT) in the Department of Psychiatry and Health Behavior at the Augusta University (Mabe et al., 2014). These are initiatives to help academic mental health departments embrace the recovery orientation in their training of mental health providers. Both of these programs offer psychiatric residents, as well as other mental health trainees, intensive exposure to the recovery approach and newer training models. The work is didactic and experiential; as a key component, they include discussions with individuals with lived experience of an SMI as an essential component of their trainings.

The Department of Veterans Affairs (VA) has assumed a leadership role in promoting the implementation of the recovery orientation in mental health care through several initiatives, including creating a multi-site year-long Interprofessional Fellowship in Psychosocial Rehabilitation & Recovery Oriented Services. Fellows come from a range of disciplines, including nursing, social work, psychiatry, psychology, vocational rehabilitation, occupational therapy, and chaplaincy/clinical pastoral education. Kymalainen et al. (2010) assessed perceived program recovery attitudes rated by staff and veteran stakeholders from year 1 to year 4 of the fellowship program at a large Massachusetts VA, and found significant increases over time.

With regard to psychology, Chu et al. (2012a) reviewed the literature and then sought expert consensus on foundational and functional competencies necessary for effective work in public sector psychology. They identified

14 public sector psychology foundational competencies which constitute the basic knowledge, skills, and attitudes needed for work in the public sector. They include: (a) assessment/treatment of serious mental illness, (b) assessment/ treatment of substance use disorders/dual diagnosis, (c) clinical supervision and consultation, (d) community-based research, (e) consumer collaboration, (f) cultural competence in clinical work, (g) evidence-based practice (EBP) import-ation, (h) grant writing, (i) integration of traditional psychology with community clinical care, (j) needs assessment and program evaluation, (k) organizational consultation, (l) organizational management, (m) public policy/advocacy, and (n) strategies to decrease mental healthcare disparities. Key functional role com-petencies identified include the following: (a) administrator (program manager, director, or other), (b) clinician (direct service), (c) consultant or trainer, (d) policy advocate, (e) researcher (including program evaluator and grant writer), and (f) supervisor. Chu et al. (2012b) then proposed a doctoral training model for public sector psychology (encompassing work with SMI), which included development of the competencies listed above as well as helping trainees learn to create collaborative partnerships between academic, community, and county/state/ federal entities using group case–method learning beyond the classroom.

Although many individuals living with an SMI are treated in the public sector, they are also increasingly seeking services in integrated health care settings (Bartels et al., 2018) and, for those with financial resources, from private sector providers. To meet the emerging and rapidly changing needs within the health care environment, specialized training needs to be broadly available. Some have even called for the mental health field to consider treatment of people with SMI/SED a unique discipline. "Since the 1980s, it has been asserted in the scholarly literature that education in psychiatric/ psychosocial rehabilitation theory and techniques is a necessary component of academic preparation for practitioners providing services to people with serious mental illness (SMI) and, in fact, may be considered an academic discipline in itself" (Gill & Murphy, 2013, p. 260).

The goal of psychiatric/psychosocial rehabilitation (PSR) is to help people with SMI recover and attain their full functional capability. Improved func-tioning, life satisfaction, and the individual's participation in environments of choice are the desired outcomes; symptom improvement may also occur but is not the primary focus of PSR. The majority of services provided are interven-tions designed specifically for those with SMI, empirically tested, and shown to improve outcomes for persons with SMI. These interventions and tech-niques are known as PSR and are designed to improve the capabilities and competencies of persons with SMI so they can attain their full potential.

PSR can be provided by any of the mental health disciplines, by peers, and support staff and/or community workers. Provision of PSR services rests on a platform of principles that are essential for successful outcomes. In addition to the core values of empathy, trust, and genuineness, PSR services must be guided by the following:

(1) Recognition that recovery and return to a satisfying and productive life are possible;
(2) Provision of interventions that are grounded in research and achieve results;
(3) Involvement of those with SMI and their families is key and ensuring they are full partners with the service delivery system to determine the services they will receive.

Consistent with the thinking of Chu et al. (2012b) described above, Stacy et al. (2018) reported on the positive outcomes of a PSR / SMI Psychology residency at a large, Northeastern Veterans Affairs Medical Center. Program data of residents' self-ratings at the beginning and end of the training year suggest that the postdoctoral training program contributed to significantly increased self-confidence as entry-level psychologists and also as PSR practitioners. Of note, a majority of residents from the program went on to SMI/ PSR-related jobs immediately post-residency.

The National Recovery to Practice Initiative

One large scale national effort to improve care for those living with SMIs merits mention – the interprofessional initiative supported by SAMHSA, entitled Recovery to Practice. For decades, SAMHSA has widely promoted recovery principles in its materials on mental health treatment in the United States and in May 2009, it began its *Recovery to Practice (RTP) Initiative*. The RTP Initiative is described more fully by del Vecchio (2015). It was designed to increase awareness, acceptance, and adoption of recovery-based practices in the delivery of mental health and addiction-related services and was grounded in SAMHSA's definition and fundamental components of recovery, outlined above. Six discipline groups (listed below) were funded to develop and disseminate recovery-based curricula, tailored to the needs of the professionals working in the specialty:

- American Psychiatric Association
- American Psychiatric Nurses Association
- American Psychological Association
- Council on Social Work Education
- NAADAC, the Association for Addiction Professionals
- National Association of Peer Specialists

Separate curricula were developed by each discipline via a thorough evidentiary review of current clinical education, a series of pilot trainings (including qualitative data collection and analyses for material refinement), and the creation of multimodal knowledge delivery systems. Both the recovery approach and evidence-based practices were highlighted. The curricula are available on the organizations' websites. These curricula are meant to be accessible and informative and can be used and reviewed by all levels of learners – students, trainees, or licensed professionals.

As part of this initiative, in 2010 the American Psychological Association received a grant from SAMHSA to develop a curriculum to train psychologists in the principles and practices of the recovery paradigm and psychosocial rehabilitation. That curriculum, entitled *Recovery to Practice Initiative Curriculum: Reframing Psychology for the Emerging Health Care Environment*, was completed and released by APA in 2014 (American Psychological Association & Jansen, 2014) and is available for free from APA at https://www.apa.org/pi/mfp/psychology/recovery-to-practice/all-curriculums .pdf. The 15-module course (see Table 7.1) includes both factual information based on the latest scientific and professional literature as well as guidance for trainers on how to augment this resource with practice activities and the inclusion of individuals with lived experience as trainers. The curriculum can be used as part of a postdoctoral specialty training program in SMI Psychology, and a review of the topics highlights some of the distinctive elements of practice in this field (e.g., the importance of advocacy for community inclusion for this population; the place of peer-delivered services, among others).

Promoting Specialization to Address the SMI Treatment Competency Problem in Psychology

Many mental health providers continue to be unprepared to provide the interventions that are most helpful to people with these illnesses (i.e., those interventions that can help people live successful lives in the community) (Olfson, 2016; Reddy et al., 2010; Roe et al., 2006; Rollins & Bond, 2001). Many providers, including psychologists, are still trained to see SMIs as chronic deteriorating illnesses and then to arrive at a diagnosis and provide traditional mental health treatment, namely medications, psychotherapy, etc. (Mueser et al., 2013). While these may be of some assistance, they are not sufficient to help those with SMI to live successfully in the community. With regard to SMI training, there are a paucity of mentors in doctoral or postdoctoral training programs and there are few practicum, internship, and residency programs that have supervisors who themselves have been trained and or have sufficient experience in the newer intervention methods to provide the level of

Table 7.1. *Modules from Recovery to Practice initiative curriculum: reframing psychology for the emerging health care environment*

1. Introduction to Recovery-Based Psychological Practice
This module introduces the recovery model applied to behavioral health. Characteristics and fundamental components of recovery are defined.

2. Role of Psychologists and Healthcare Reform
This module provides a historical overview of the concept of recovery as applied to mental health and describes its evolution. An understanding of the role of psychologists and how healthcare reform is shaping the future of recovery is explored.

3. Assessment
This module discusses clinical assessment methodologies consistent with a recovery framework that are strengths-based and focused on the functional capabilities of the individual.

4. Partnership and Engagement
This module examines the importance of engaging people in the service delivery process and presents some of the impediments that keep people from becoming partners in this process. A discussion of how to successfully engage and involve individuals is presented.

5. Person-Centered Planning
This module provides an overview of person-centered planning in recovery-oriented care. At its core, person-centered planning is a collaborative and interdisciplinary approach to treatment in which individuals are empowered to find their own path to recovery.

6. Health Disparities
This module provides an overview of the causes of the premature death experienced by people with serious mental illnesses and includes a discussion of the intersection of race, ethnicity, gender and culture related to these causes.

7. Interventions I: Guiding Principles and Integrated Framework
This module is the first in a series of three intervention modules designed to be used together. Guiding principles that underlie the provision of all psychosocial rehabilitation services (PSR) are discussed, and an integrative framework is presented.

8. Interventions II: Evidence-Based Practices
This module is the second in a series of three intervention modules designed to be used together. The evidence-based practices developed, researched, and found to help people achieve their desired outcomes are presented.

9. Interventions III: Promising or Emerging Practices and Supporting Services
This module is the third in the series of intervention modules, and describes services that have shown promise of achieving specified outcomes. Supporting services that are widely acknowledged as essential services for helping people recover from the effects of serious mental illness are also highlighted.

10. Issues in Forensic Settings
This module is the first of two forensics modules designed to be used together. This first module highlights the many issues and impediments people with serious mental health disorders face in the justice system.

11. Interventions in Forensic Settings
This is the second in the series of two forensics modules designed to be used together. This module presents information about the interventions currently recommended to help people in the system avoid re-incarceration and achieve a stable and satisfying life in the community.

Table 7.1. *(cont.)*

12. Community Inclusion

This module presents an overview of the issues that serve to exclude people with mental health disorders from participation in their communities. These include stigma, discrimination, poverty, and vulnerability. The circular and detrimental impact of social isolation and exclusion on an individual's mental health are explored.

13. Peer-Delivered Services

This module focuses on the role of peers in helping individuals recover and achieve a satisfying and productive life in the community. Peer support as an integral component of the mental health service delivery system is presented.

14. Systems Transformation

Transforming a mental health system or an organization to one that is focused on helping people recover requires a fundamental paradigm shift from a system that is provider driven to one that is driven by the individuals who use the system and their families. This module presents key ingredients, challenges, successes and the role of psychologists in systems change.

15. Scientific Foundations

This module provides the empirical basis for recovery, and presents the pros and cons of using quantitative versus qualitative methods to study interventions for people with serious mental illnesses. An introduction to mixed methods research, which offers a solution to the problems of using either quantitative or qualitative methods, is presented.

supervision needed for trainees to become skilled in the provision of these services. Knowing how to implement the concepts and having the ability to appropriately use the proper interventions are skills that continue to be foreign to most psychologists (Mueser et al., 2013).

In order to work effectively with people with these diagnoses, psychologists must not only identify the symptoms of the disorder and be able to correctly diagnose each person, but they must also recognize and understand the unique aspects of these illnesses and the concerns faced by the individuals with these disorders, including additional challenges that may coexist or interact with the primary disorder. Factors such as co-occurring physical and or mental health conditions, gender identity/preference, socioeconomic status, homelessness, and stigma can affect the behaviors and needs of an individual and can affect the way others, including health and mental health professionals, respond to them. Not surprisingly, many psychologists feel inadequately prepared to treat individuals with SMI, are uncomfortable doing so, and prefer to work with individuals they feel prepared to help achieve success (Bernheim, 1990; Buck et al., 2014).

One key to addressing the competency problem among psychologists treating individuals living with SMI lies in reexamining our training processes.

Roberts (2006) described the tension between generalist and specialty training in psychology. Most undergraduate and health service graduate psychology programs, including internships, train clinicians as generalists. Several types of psychopathology are typically covered in these initial training experiences, and internships often involve rotations to provide exposure to several types of service users. While generalist training is very appropriate at the introductory training level, it does not engender the highly technical skills and facilitative attitudes needed to treat SMI adequately. The situation is further complicated by the fact that postdoctoral fellowships are optional in psychology, and relatively few psychologists seek board certification, so licensed professionals have limited encouragement to develop new skills. The prevalent generalist training model provides little opportunity to obtain the competencies needed for SMI work.

In contrast to health services psychology generally, specialist instruction and board certification have been a prominent feature of medical training for over 100 years. As the scientific knowledge base in psychology has expanded over the past 50+ years, however, there has been a small but increasing emphasis on codifying specialty training in several circumscribed fields of the discipline (child clinical, behavioral and cognitive, health, clinical, etc.) (Baker & Cox, 2014). Kaslow and colleagues (2012) highlighted many social and political forces that have fostered the specialization movement in psychology, including service users' preferences for specialists, academic medical centers and insurance companies favoring (and in some cases requiring) specialization and board certification for hiring or promotion, and a growing emphasis on quality improvement and accountability as a requirement for public reimbursement for services.

As the drive for specialization in psychology has grown, the process for psychology board certification has become more standardized; US health service psychologists seeking specialty training and board certification must undergo a planned and rigorous training process. Note that at this level, *academic training programs* are recognized as providing specialty training in APA through the Commission for the Recognition of Specialties and Proficiencies in Professional Psychology (CRSPPP); *individuals* are recognized as being competent in these specialties through the process of board certification by the American Board of Professional Psychology (ABPP). Specialty training in psychology is typically acquired at the postdoctoral level, but may occur at the doctoral level of training in selected instances. In psychology, CRSPPP is charged with facilitating the development, implementation and review of effective and coordinated policies and procedures to improve quality in specialty training and to facilitate the process of recognizing specialties in professional psychology.

Psychologists typically obtain a license to practice independently following receipt of the doctoral degree and, after practicing for some years, can apply for board certification through ABPP. Following board certification, psychologists must maintain their competence to practice (Cox & Grus, 2019). Early career psychologists can also apply for board certification and may have an advantage in achieving certification (Bordes et al., 2019), which may reflect the rapid growth of new knowledge across specialties (Neimeyer et al., 2014).

The Evolving Specialty Certification in SMI Psychology

The Groundwork to Obtain APA SMI Postdoctoral Training Program Specialty Recognition. To counter the dearth of training available for psychologists treating individuals living with an SMI, work to develop postdoctoral specialty training in SMI Psychology and to provide ABPP board certification for psychologists in the specialty began in 2010, led by members of APA's Division 18 (Psychologists in Public Service) and APA's Task Force on SMI/ SED. This effort came to fruition in 2019 and is briefly described immediately below. It was grounded in the knowledge that SMI (and SED in children and adolescents) are major public health concerns affecting large segments of the population, that there was little recognition of this among generalist clinical or counseling psychologists, and even less formal training in how to effectively treat persons with these conditions.

Beginning in 2004, with the joint support of APA Division 18 and the APA Task Force, symposia on SMI/SED were offered every year, and continue to this day, at the APA convention. Pre-conference workshops have frequently been offered as well; attendance at these events grew considerably over time reflecting the increasing number of psychologists interested in the area. In 2010, members of Division 18 and the APA Task Force recognized that SMI and SED met the criteria for an APA specialty in professional psychology and plans were initiated to develop the SMI Psychology specialty application for APA. Concurrently, several members of Division 18 began discussions to form a new section within the Division. After consultations with other relevant sections, and as a result of the growing recognition of the importance of SMI/SED among Division members, in 2012 Division 18 gave formal approval for the formation of its newest section: the Division 18 Section on SMI/SED.

Work on writing the specialty application began in earnest in 2012–2013. The SMI Psychology Specialty Council was formed in 2013 and the first submission of the application was made to CRSPPP in 2017. This submission resulted in a request for revisions and following completion of the revisions requested by CRSPPP, the final application was submitted to CRSPPP in December 2018. CRSPPP recommended approval of the SMI

Psychology specialty in April 2019 and it was formally approved by the APA Council of Representatives (CoR) in August 2019; see APA's Education Directorate Specialty webpage which lists the SMI Psychology Specialty: https://www.apa.org/ed/graduate/specialize/recognized. As soon as the specialty was formally recognized by APA, the Specialty Council petitioned the APA Council of Specialties in Professional Psychology (CoSPP) for membership. CoSPP approved the SMI Psychology specialty request for membership in November 2019 (see https://www.cospp.org/).

An Overview of the SMI Psychology Specialty Training Program. Recognition of a postdoctoral specialty in SMI/SED is intended to promote the goal of providing more relevant training for psychologists to meet the needs of those living with an SMI. With such specialized training, psychologists can provide the broad set of services shown to help individuals with serious mental illnesses recover and lead satisfying and productive lives. The specialized training is envisioned to include: assessment methods which assess functional capability rather than symptomatology; EBPs and promising practices designed specifically for this population; interventions modified and found to be effective with people in this population within the forensic mental health system; research methods adapted for populations such as this; and systems transformation methods specific to large mental health systems that serve this population, to name but a few.

The goal of the specialty training program is to ensure that residents attain competency in the skills to support SMI recovery, measured not only as a reduction in symptoms but also as improved functioning and life satisfaction, and participation in environments of one's choice. Many of the skills provided in specialty training are PSR interventions, although residents in this specialty may also provide traditional treatments such as psychotherapy, illness management, and supportive therapy. Embedded in this training model is an interprofessional approach based on a recovery model that empowers persons with SMI/SED to develop personalized goals and choose from a menu of treatment program opportunities, including inpatient and outpatient services that are designed to help each person achieve the goals he or she has determined to be personally relevant. The goal of services is to improve community functioning and quality of life for persons with SMI/SED. Ensuring an active partnership with consumers and community linkages is an essential element of this work.

Training for postdoctoral residents in this specialty occurs in several domains: primary and secondary placements, seminars, didactics, research, supervision, consultation, teaching, and administration. While the postdoctoral residency training requirements will vary at individual training programs, a core of required education and training experiences exists across all programs. These may be called by different names but the content is to be focused on learning how to use the specialized psychosocial rehabilitation assessments and interventions to help people with SMI/SED recover and attain their full functional capability – all within a recovery orientation.

Training is sufficiently broad to build on and enhance the foundation of knowledge, skills, and proficiencies that define professional health service psychology, and of sufficient depth to develop more focused competence and expertise in the specific area of SMI/SED. This is accomplished through involvement in focused didactics and clinical experiences on an SMI/SED team/unit and more general placements and didactics with postdoctoral psychology residents in other specialty areas where these exist at a given academic training site.

Each resident's training plan is individually created to meet the specific training needs of the resident and to develop competence in the range of mental health and psychosocial rehabilitation skills specifically designed for individuals with SMI/SED. Training activities include attention to advancing development of core skills such as: specialized assessments, treatment interventions developed and researched specifically for this population, consultation and interprofessional teamwork, research and scientific inquiry, supervision and teaching, ethics, program management and administration, and cross-cultural and diversity sensitivity. Residents are prepared to leave their residency ready to function successfully as independent scientist-practitioners and work effectively with persons with SMI/SED. Expertise in clinical decision making can be guided by the toolkit provided by Jansen (2018). Echoing the functional competencies outlined by Chu et al. (2012a) above, another goal of the residency is to train residents to function in leadership positions in settings for persons with SMI/SED. As a result, the resident is prepared to transition to practice with an interprofessional team, promoting client-centered, recovery-oriented care and interprofessional collaboration for specialized assessment and treatment of persons with SMI/SED.

Residents spend at least 20 hours per week in a supervised, primary placement setting working with persons who have SMI/SED. This and all placements must operate based on a recovery orientation and utilize psychosocial rehabilitation practices as primary interventions. As residents increase their skill, confidence, and levels of responsibility, they are provided with more complex cases, more independent clinical work, and the freedom to pursue their own training goals and take on additional cases if desired. Residents also typically work with pre-doctoral interns and practicum students (where these are present), and are involved with the hierarchical supervision of these interns and students along with their clinical responsibilities on their rotations. The intensity and level of these activities is determined in a collaborative nature between trainee, supervisors, and the Director of Training.

The Work Toward SMI Psychology Board Certification

Once trained as an SMI psychologist, the final level of professional recognition is ABPP certification. For the applicant, board certification involves submitting an application with verification of training and experience, approval of credentials, and an examination of relevant knowledge, which typically includes an oral examination and review of a practice example. These tasks can take several months.

The process of establishing ABPP board certification is not automatic for an APA specialty. As with establishing recognition of an APA training specialty, approval of ABPP board certification in a specialty has several steps – submitting an initial brief application describing the specialty area to ABPP, being approved and invited to submit a formal application to the ABPP Board, being approved and invited to develop a plan for implementing the board certification process, and final approval for individual specialty certification. The entire process can take 3–5 years.

In December 2019, the ABPP Board of Trustees (BoT) gave the SMI Psychology specialty permission to proceed with submission of the formal application for affiliation with ABPP. In December 2020, the BoT gave the specialty permission to develop criteria to be used by psychologists applying for board certification in SMI Psychology; it is anticipated that psychologists will be able to apply for ABPP board certification in the specialty in mid-2022.

Conclusion

Professional organizations overseeing the training and licensure of clinical psychologists in the United States, starting with the American Psychological Association as the most influential such organization, have begun to make a welcome public commitment to increasing the competence of the workforce treating individuals with SMI through the specialty process. Helping psychologists and other mental health providers attain competency in treating individuals living with an SMI is a moral imperative incumbent upon our professional responsibilities to society. Such required training is economically strategic in light of trends in health care policy suggesting a potentially expanded role for psychologists, as the funding of health care moves toward demanding greater accountability for the delivery of evidence-based services to persons with a serious mental illness. The specialty training described here is an asset to the profession of psychology, and may prove useful to other disciplines as they refine their efforts to meet the needs of individuals living with an SMI. Much has been accomplished, but there is also much more to do.

REFERENCES

American Psychiatric Association. (2002). *Practice Guideline for the Treatment of Patients with Bipolar Disorder* (2nd edition). Washington, DC: American Psychiatric Association Press.

American Psychological Association. (2016). *2015 Survey of Psychology Health Service Providers*. Washington, DC: American Psychological Association's Center for Workforce Studies. Retrieved from: https://www.apa.org/workforce/ publications/15-health-service-providers/report.pdf

American Psychological Association & Jansen, M. A. (2014). *Recovery to Practice Initiative Curriculum: Reframing Psychology for the Emerging Health Care Environment*. Washington, DC: American Psychological Association. Retrieved from https://www.apa.org/pi/mfp/psychology/recovery-to-practice/all-curriculums .pdf

Baker, J., & Cox, D. R. (2014). The history and importance of specialization in professional psychology. In W. B. Johnson & N. J. Kaslow (Eds.), *Oxford library of psychology. The Oxford handbook of education and training in professional psychology*. Oxford University Press. p. 120–132.

Bartels, S. J., DiMilia, P. R., Fortuna, K. L., & Naslund, J. A. (2018). Integrated care for older adults with serious mental illness and medical comorbidity: Evidence-based models and future research directions. *Psychiatric Clinics*, *41*(1), 153–164, https://doi.org/10.1016/j.psc.2017.10.012

Beidas, R. S. & Kendall, P. C. (2010). Training therapists in evidence-based practice: A critical review of studies from a systems-contextual perspective. *Clinical Psychology: Science and Practice*, *17*(1), 1–30. https://doi.org/10.1111/j.1468-2850.2009.01187.x

Bernheim, K. P. (1990). Additional comments to key issues in training in psychology for service to the seriously mentally ill. In H. P. Lefley (Ed.), *Clinical Training in Serious Mental Illness*. Washington, DC: National Institute of Mental Health, DHHS Pub No (ADM), p. 90–1679.

Bighelli, I., Salanti, G., Huhn, M., Schneider-Thoma, J., Krause, M., Reitmeir, C., . . . Leucht, S. (2018). Psychological interventions to reduce positive symptoms in schizophrenia: Systematic review and network meta-analysis. *World Psychiatry*, *17*(3), 316–329. https://doi.org/10.1002/wps.20577

Bordes Edgar, V., Holder, N., Cox, D. R., & Suris, A. (2019). Competence in psychology board certification: Unlike a good wine, it does not get better with age. *Training and Education in Professional Psychology, 13*(4), 264–269. https://doi.org/10.1037/tep0000246

Buck, B., Romeo, K. H., Olbert, C. M., & Penn, D. L. (2014). Self-reported comfort treating severe mental illnesses among pre-doctoral graduate students in clinical psychology. *Journal of Mental Health*, *23*(6), 297–302. https://doi.org/10.3109/ 09638237.2014.924048

Carr, E. R., Bhagwat, R., Miller, R., & Ponce, A. N. (2014). Training in mental health recovery and social justice in the public sector. *The Counseling Psychologist*, *42*(8), 1108–1135. https://doi.org/10.1177/0011000014555200

Carr, E. R., & Miller, R. (2017). Expanding our reach: Increasing the role of psychologists in public and community mental health. *Psychological Services, 14*(3), 352–360. https://doi.org/10.1037/ser0000094

Chu, J. P., Emmons, L., Wong, J., Goldblum, P., Reiser, R., Barrera, A. Z., & Byrd-Olmstead, J. (2012a). Public psychology: A competency model for professional psychologists in community mental health. *Professional Psychology: Research and Practice, 43*(1), 39–49. https://doi.org/10.1037/a0026319

Chu, J. P., Emmons, L., Wong, J., Goldblum, P., Reiser, R., Barrera, A. Z., & Byrd-Olmstead, J. (2012b). The public psychology doctoral training model: Training clinical psychologists in community mental health competencies and leadership. *Training and Education in Professional Psychology, 6*(2), 76–83. https://doi.org/10.1037/a0028834

Cleary, M., Lees, D., Molloy, L., Escott, P., & Sayers, J. (2017). Recovery-oriented care and leadership in mental health nursing. *Issues in Mental Health Nursing, 38*(5), 458–460. https://doi.org/10.1080/01612840.2017.1314738

Cohen, J. L., Abraham, K. M., Burk, J. P., & Stein, C. H. (2012). Emerging opportunities for psychologists: Joining consumers in the recovery-oriented care movement. *Professional Psychology: Research and Practice, 43*(1), 24–31. https://doi.org/10.1037/a0024394

Corrigan, P. W., Steiner, L., McCracken, S. G., Blaser, B., & Barr, M. (2001). Strategies for disseminating evidence-based practices to staff who treat people with serious mental illness. *Psychiatric Services, 52*(12), 1598–1606. https://doi.org/10.1176/appi.ps.52.12.1598

Cox, D. R., & Grus, C. L. (2019). From continuing education to continuing competence. *Professional Psychology: Research and Practice, 50*(2), 113–119. https://doi.org/10.1037/pro0000232

Davidson, L. (2016). The recovery movement: Implications for mental health care and enabling people to participate fully in life. *Health Affairs, 35*(6), 1091–1097. https://doi.org/10.1377/hlthaff.2016.0153

del Vecchio, P. (2015). Bringing recovery to practice: Improving provider competencies and promoting positive outcomes. *Psychiatric Services, 66*(7), 750–752. https://doi.org/10.1176/appi.ps.201400310

Frost, B. G., Tirupati, S., Johnston, S., Turrell, M., Lewin, T. J., Sly, K. A., & Conrad, A. M. (2017). An integrated recovery-oriented model (IRM) for mental health services: Evolution and challenges. *BMC Psychiatry, 17*(1), 22. https://doi.org/10.1186/s12888-016-1164-3

Fusar-Poli, P., Papanastasiou, E., Stahl, D., Rocchetti, M., Carpenter, W., Shergill, S., & McGuire, P. (2015). Treatments of negative symptoms in schizophrenia: Meta-analysis of 168 randomized placebo-controlled trials. *Schizophrenia Bulletin, 41*(4), 892–899. https://doi.org/10.1093/schbul/sbu170

Gill, K., & Murphy, A. (2013). Psychiatric/psychosocial rehabilitation (PSR) education: Academic and professional. *Current Psychiatry Reviews, 9*(3), 260–269. https://doi.org/10.2174/1573400511309030008

Gitlin, M. J., & Miklowitz, D. J. (2017). The difficult lives of individuals with bipolar disorder: A review of functional outcomes and their implications for treatment. *Journal of Affective Disorders, 209*, 147–154. https://doi.org/10.1016/j.jad.2016.11.021

Häfner, H. (2004). Schizophrenia: Still Kraepelin's dementia praecox? *Epidemiologia e Psichiatria Sociale, 13*(2), 99–112. https://doi.org/10.1017/s1121189x00003328

Happell, B., Byrne, L., & Platania-Phung, C. (2015). The Recovery Knowledge Inventory for measurement of nursing student views on recovery-oriented mental health services. *Issues in Mental Health Nursing, 36*(10), 799–808. https://doi.org/ 10.3109/01612840.2015.1049310

Harding, C. M., Brooks, G. W., Ashikaga, T., Strauss, J. S., & Breier, A. (1987a). The Vermont longitudinal study of persons with severe mental illness, I: Methodology, study, sample, and overall status 32 years later. *American Journal of Psychiatry, 144*(6), 718–726. https://doi.org/10.1176/ajp.144.6.718

Harding, C. M., Brooks, G. W., Ashikaga, T., Strauss, J. S., & Breier, A. (1987b). The Vermont longitudinal study of persons with severe mental illness, II: Long-term outcome of subjects who retrospectively met DSM-III criteria for schizophrenia. *American Journal of Psychiatry, 144*(6), 727–735. https://doi.org/10.1176/ajp.144 .6.727

Harding, C. M., Zubin, J., & Strauss, J. S. (1987). Chronicity in schizophrenia: Fact, partial fact, or artifact? *Psychiatric Services, 38*(5), 477–486. https://doi.org/10 .1176/ps.38.5.477

Hargrove, D. S. (1990). Key issues in training in psychology for service to the seriously mentally ill. In Lefley, H. P. (Ed.). *Clinical training in serious mental illness.* Washington, DC: National Institute of Mental Health, DHHS Pub No (ADM), p. 90–1679.

Horvitz-Lennon, M., Donohue, J. M., Domino, M. E., & Normand, S. L. T. (2009). Improving quality and diffusing best practices: The case of schizophrenia. *Health Affairs, 28*(3), 701–712. https://doi.org/10.1377/hlthaff.28.3.701

Horvitz-Lennon, M., Volya, R., Donohue, J. M., Lave, J. R., Stein, B. D., & Normand, S. L. (2014). Disparities in quality of care among publicly insured adults with schizophrenia in four large US states, 2002–2008. *Health Services Research, 49*(4): 1121–1144. https://doi.org/10.1111/1475-6773.12162

Hunt, M. G., & Resnick, S. G. (2015). Two birds, one stone: Unintended consequences and a potential solution for problems with recovery in mental health. *Psychiatric Services, 66*(11), 1235–1237. https://doi.org/10.1176/appi.ps.201400518

Jansen, M. A. (2018). Psychosocial services for individuals with serious mental illness/ severe emotional disturbance: Clinical practice guideline toolkit. *Psychiatry, 81*(1), 3–21. https://doi.org/10.1080/00332747.2018.1440116

Jawad, I., Watson, S., Haddad, P. M., Talbot, P. S., & McAllister-Williams, R. H. (2018). Medication nonadherence in bipolar disorder: A narrative review. *Therapeutic Advances in Psychopharmacology, 8*(12), 349–363.

Johnson, D. L. (1990). Response to key issues in training in psychology for service to the seriously mentally ill. In H. P. Lefley (Ed.). *Clinical training in serious mental illness.* Washington, DC: National Institute of Mental Health, DHHS Pub No (ADM), p. 90–1679.

Judd, L. L., Akiskal, H. S., Schettler, P. J., Endicott, J., Maser, J., Solomon, D. A., . . . Keller, M. B. (2002). The long-term natural history of the weekly symptomatic status of bipolar I disorder. *Archives of General Psychiatry, 59*(6), 530–537. https://doi.org/10.1001/archpsyc.59.6.530

Kaslow, N. J., Graves, C. C., & Smith, C. O. (2012). Specialization in psychology and health care reform. *Journal of Clinical Psychology in Medical Settings*, *19*(1), 12–21. https://doi.org/10.1007/s10880-011-9273-0

Kimhy, D., Tarrier, N., Essock, S., Malaspina, D., Cabannis, D., & Beck, A. T. (2013). Cognitive behavioral therapy for psychosis – Training practices and dissemination in the United States. *Psychosis*, *5*(3), 296–305. https://doi.org/10.1080/17522439 .2012.704932

Kreyenbuhl, J., Buchanan, R. W., Dickerson, F. B., & Dixon, L. B. (2010). The schizophrenia patient outcomes research team (PORT): Updated treatment recommendations 2009. *Schizophrenia Bulletin*, *36*(1), 94–103. https://doi.org/10 .1093/schbul/sbp130

Kurtz, M. M., & Mueser, K. T. (2008). A meta-analysis of controlled research on social skills training for schizophrenia. *Journal of Consulting and Clinical Psychology*, *76*(3), 491–504. https://doi.org/10.1037/0022-006x.76.3.491

Kymalainen, J. A., Henze, K. T., DeLuca, M., Mitton, T. A., Walton, H. M., Duffy, P., … & Pinsky, J. (2010). Are we there yet? The four-year impact of a VA fellowship program on the recovery orientation of rehabilitation programs. *Psychiatric Rehabilitation Journal*, *33*(4), 320–327. https://doi.org/10.2975/33.4 .2010.320.327

Leonhardt, B. L., Huling, K., Hamm, J. A., Roe, D., Hasson-Ohayon, I., McLeod, H. J., & Lysaker, P. H. (2017). Recovery and serious mental illness: A review of current clinical and research paradigms and future directions. *Expert Review of Neurotherapeutics*, *17*(11), 1117–1130. https://doi.org/10.1080/14737175.2017 .1378099

Mabe, A., Ahmed, A. O., Duncan, G. N., Fenley, G., & Buckley, P. F. (2014). Project GREAT: Immersing physicians and doctorally-trained psychologists in recovery-oriented care. *Professional Psychology: Research and Practice,* 45(5), 347–356. https://doi.org/10.1037/a0037705

McFarlane, W. R. (2016). Family interventions for schizophrenia and the psychoses: A review. *Family Process*, *55*(3), 460–482. https://doi.org/10.1111/famp.12235

Miklowitz, D. J., & Chung, B. (2016). Family-focused therapy for bipolar disorder: Reflections on 30 years of research. *Family Process*, *55*(3), 483–499. https://doi .org/10.1111/famp.12237

Miklowitz, D. J., Efthimiou, O., Furukawa, T. A., Scott, J., McLaren, R., Geddes, J. R., & Cipriani, A. (2021). Adjunctive psychotherapy for bipolar disorder: a systematic review and component network meta-analysis. *JAMA psychiatry*, *78*(2), 141–150.

Modini, M., Tan, L., Brinchmann, B., Wang, M.-J., Killackey, E., Glozier, N., Mykletun, A., & Harvey, S. B. (2016). Supported employment for people with severe mental illness: Systematic review and meta-analysis of the international evidence. *British Journal of Psychiatry*, *209*(1), 14–22. https://doi.org/10.1192/bjp .bp.115.165092

Mojtabai, R., Fochtmann, L., Chang, S.-W., Kotov, R., Craig, T. J., & Bromet, E. (2009). Unmet need for mental health care in schizophrenia: An overview of literature and new data from a first-admission study. *Schizophrenia Bulletin*, 35, 679–695. http://dx.doi.org/10.1093/schbul/ sbp045

Mueser, K. T., Silverstein, S. M., & Farkas, M. D. (2013). Should the training of clinical psychologists require competence in the treatment and rehabilitation of individuals with a serious mental illness? *Psychiatric Rehabilitation Journal, 36*(1), 54–59. https://doi.org/10.1037/h0094750

National Institute for Health and Care Excellence [NICE]. (2014). *Bipolar disorder: Assessment and management.* Available at https://www.nice.org.uk/guidance/cg185/resources/bipolar-disorder-assessment-and-management-35109814379461. Accessed 10/22/20.

National Institute of Mental Health. (1990). Clinical training in serious mental illness. (1990). Lefley, H. P. (Ed). DHHS Pub. No. (ADM) 90-1679. Washington, DC: Supt. of Docs., U.S. Govt. Printing Office. Available from http://babel.hathitrust.org/cgi/pt?id=mdp.39015050781247;view=1up;seq=3

Neimeyer, G. J., Taylor, J. M., Rozensky, R. H., & Cox, D. R. (2014). The diminishing durability of knowledge in professional psychology: A second look at specializations. *Professional Psychology: Research and Practice, 45*(2), 92–98. https://doi.org/10.1037/a0036176

Olfson, M. (2016). Building the mental health workforce capacity needed to treat adults with serious mental illnesses. *Health Affairs, 35*(6), 983–990. https://doi.org/10.1377/hlthaff.2015.1619

Patterson, T. L., & Leeuwenkamp, O. R. (2008). Adjunctive psychosocial therapies for the treatment of schizophrenia. *Schizophrenia Research, 100*, 108–119. https://doi.org/10.1016/j.schres.2007.12.468

President's New Freedom Commission on Mental Health. (2003). Achieving the promise: Transforming mental health care in America. Final report. DHHS Pub. No. SMA-03-3832. Rockville, MD: Author.

Randall, M., Romero-Gonzalez, M., Gonzalez, G., Klee, A., & Kirwin, P. (2011). Competency of psychiatric residents in the treatment of people with severe mental illness before and after a community psychiatry rotation. *Academic Psychiatry, 35* (1), 15–20. https://doi.org/10.1176/appi.ap.35.1.15

Razzano, L. A., Jonikas, J. A., Goelitz, M. A., Hamilton, M. M., Marvin, R., Jones-Martinez, N., . . . Cook, J. A. (2010). The recovery education in the academy program: Transforming academic curricula with the principles of recovery and self-determination. *Psychiatric Rehabilitation Journal, 34*(2), 130–136. https://doi.org/10.2975/34.2.2010.130.136

Reddy, F., Spaulding, W. D., Jansen, M. A., Menditto, A. A., & Pickett, S. (2010). Psychologists' roles and opportunities in rehabilitation and recovery for serious mental illness: A survey of council of university directors of clinical psychology (CUDCP) clinical psychology training and doctoral education. *Training and Education in Professional Psychology, 4*(4), 254–263. https://doi.org/10.1037/a0021457

Roberts, M. C. (2006). Essential tension: Specialization with broad and general training in psychology. *American Psychologist, 61*(8), 862–870. https://doi.org/10.1037/0003-066x.61.8.862

Roe, D., Yanos, P. T., & Lysaker, P. H. (2006). Overcoming barriers to increase the contribution of clinical psychologists to work with persons with severe mental illness. *Clinical Psychology: Science and Practice, 13*(4), 376–383. https://doi.org/10.1111/j.1468-2850.2006.00051.x

Rollins, A. L., & Bond, G. R. (2001). Psychology curriculum and psychiatric
    rehabilitation. *Psychiatric Rehabilitation Skills, 5*(3), 514–533. https://doi.org/10
    .1080/15487760108415450

Rubin, M., Menon, G. M., & Vanek, M. (2012). Relevance of competency-based
    education to work with individuals with serious mental illness. *Journal of Human
    Behavior in the Social Environment, 22*(2), 213–233. https://doi.org/10.1080/
    10911359.2012.647482

Satel, S. (2014). Delivering services to individuals with severe mental illness:
    SAMHSA falls short. *Psychiatric Services, 65*(9), 1160–1161. https://doi.org/10
    .1176/appi.ps.201400259

Stacy, M., Klee, A., & Jansen, M. (2018). Postdoctoral psychology training in
    preparation for specialization in serious mental illness. *Training and Education in
    Professional Psychology, 12*(2), 96–104. https://doi.org/10.1037/tep0000179

Stewart, J. A., Horn, D. L., Becker, J. M., & Kline, J. S. (1993). Postdoctoral training in
    severe mental illness: A model for trainee development. *Professional Psychology:
    Research and Practice, 24*(3), 286–292. https://doi.org/10.1037/0735-7028.24.3
    .286

Stirman, S. W., Bhar, S. S., Spokas, M., Brown, G. K., Creed, T. A., Perivoliotis, D.,
    . . . Beck, A. T. (2010). Training and consultation in evidence-based psychosocial
    treatments in public mental health settings: The access model. *Professional
    Psychology: Research and Practice, 41*(1), 48–56. https://doi.org/10.1037/
    a0018099

Substance Abuse and Mental Health Services Administration. (2004). SAMHSA's
    National Consensus Statement on Mental Health Recovery. Rockville, Md, US
    Department of Health and Human Services, Substance Abuse and Mental
    Health Services Administration. Retrieved from https://www.cibhs.org/sites/main/
    files/file-attachments/10_fundamental_components_of_recovery.pdf

Substance Abuse and Mental Health Services Administration. (2005). Transforming
    mental health care in America. Federal Action Agenda: First Steps. (DHHS
    Pub No. SMA-O5–0460). Rockville, MD: U. S. Department of Health and Human
    Services. Retrieved from http://cretscmhd.psych.ucla.edu/nola/Video/MHR/
    Governmentreports/TRANSFORMING%20MENTAL%20HEALTH%20CARE
    %20IN%20AMERICA.pdf

Substance Abuse and Mental Health Services Administration (SAMHSA) (June 11,
    2010). Mental health recovery: A journey of healing and transformation.
    https://www.mentalhealth.va.gov/featurearticle_may2010v2.asp

Substance Abuse and Mental Health Services Administration. (2012). SAMHSA's
    working definition of recovery updated. SAMHSA Blog. Retrieved from
    https://store.samhsa.gov/sites/default/files/d7/priv/pep12-recdef.pdf

Substance Abuse and Mental Health Services Administration. (2019). Key substance
    use and mental health indicators in the United States: Results from the
    2018 National Survey on Drug Use and Health (HHS Publication No.
    PEP19–5068, NSDUH Series H-54). Rockville, MD: Center for Behavioral Health
    Statistics and Quality, Substance Abuse and Mental Health Services
    Administration. Retrieved from https://www.samhsa.gov/data/sites/default/files/
    cbhsq-reports/NSDUHNationalFindingsReport2018/
    NSDUHNationalFindingsReport2018.pdf

Tsang, H. W., Ching, S. C., Tang, K. H., Lam, H. T., Law, P. Y., & Wan, C. N. (2016). Therapeutic intervention for internalized stigma of severe mental illness: A systematic review and meta-analysis. *Schizophrenia Research, 173*(1–2), 45–53. https://doi.org/10.1016/j.schres.2016.02.013

Vieta, E., Pacchiarotti, I., Valentí, M., Berk, M., Scott, J., & Colom, F. (2009). A critical update on psychological interventions for bipolar disorders. *Current Psychiatry Reports, 11*(6), 494–502. https://doi.org/10.1007/s11920–009–0075-0

Warner, R. (2010). Does the scientific evidence support the recovery model? *The Psychiatrist, 34*(1), 3–5. https://doi.org/10.1192/pb.bp.109.025643

Young, A. S., Cohen, A. N., & Miotto, K. A. (2016). Improving the quality of care for serious mental illness. *Quality Improvement in Behavioral Health*, 275–288. https://doi.org/10.1007/978-3-319-26209-3_18

Zipursky, R. B., Reilly, T. J., & Murray, R. M. (2012). The myth of schizophrenia as a progressive brain disease. *Schizophrenia Bulletin, 39*(6), 1363–1372. https://doi.org/10.1093/schbul/sbs135

8 From Deinstitutionalization to Deprescribing and Beyond

Rebecca Miller and Anthony Pavlo

The history of deinstitutionalization in mental health care tells various stories about the movement, from people spending long periods of time in hospitals that were often oppressive and coercive to community-based approaches where people could live outside of hospitals and receive the care they needed. The mixed result of this movement into the community, evident in cross-institutionalization to prisons and nursing homes, is relatively uncontested, albeit the remedies continue to be debated. A variety of solutions have been proposed, with some advocates supporting a return to psychiatric institutions via more hospital beds or an increase in restrictive outpatient commitment statutes (Jaffe, 2017; Torrey, 2010; *Treatment Advocacy Center*, 2021). Others focus on the lack of full funding for community supports (Harrington, 2019; Whitaker, 2001). Alongside this debate is the emphasis, or overemphasis, on the role of pharmaceutical developments in the deinstitutionalization movement. What is less often focused on are the intersections with the broader civil rights movement in the USA and globally, including the economic, social, and political dimensions of this drastic shift in models of care (Miller et al., 2011). In particular, the stories from people most affected – those living with mental health diagnoses and receiving care in these institutions, are often omitted.

In this chapter, we will use epistemic injustice (Scrutton, 2017) as it relates to social justice issues in mental health systems and examine how the voices of people receiving services are excluded. We then use this concept to describe future directions in the movement toward a rights-based perspective in care for people diagnosed with mental illness. This chapter will include scientific evidence, social and cultural trends, as well as economic influences as they relate to more radical trends in psychiatry, and how they coalesce in potential trajectories for the future of this movement. We then turn to possible ways of remedying this injustice with several suggestions for achieving this, including the growing focus on deprescribing (Gupta et al., 2019; Scott et al., 2012), the questioning of medical diagnoses, the movement to address structural inequities as they relate to mental health, and the increased focus on lived experience, in the context of the reemergence of "critical psychiatry" (Rose, 2018; Steingard, 2019).

Epistemic Justice and Injustice

The concept of epistemic injustice is helpful in understanding the various stories told about the history of deinstitutionalization and explains the lack of input from people whose lives are most affected by and might have the most to offer to reforms in psychiatry. Epistemic injustice refers to the "harm done to a person in her capacity as an epistemic subject (a knower, a reasoner, a questioner) by undermining her capacity to engage in epistemic practices such as giving knowledge to others (testifying) or making sense of one's experiences (interpreting)" (Crichton et al., 2017, p. 65). Epistemic injustice refers to denoting some perspectives as less valuable than others based on some characteristic of the person holding this perspective, effectively silencing some voices. Furthermore, epistemic injustices diminish one's agency, as the act of creating and sharing knowledge is one aspect of power, and through the means of discrediting one's stories, one's power is compromised, and they become delegitimized.

Psychiatry has a long history of excluding certain voices and privileging others by creating a way of understanding, most often referred to as the medical model, in which the people who can act as epistemic subjects are those without a mental health diagnosis. In other words, the medical model may legitimize only the voices of those without a diagnosis, delegitimizing voices of "patients." This lens operates to disenfranchise individuals by diminishing communication that disagrees with the dominant narrative. For example, those with a mental health diagnosis, especially a more serious mental health condition, are seen as irrational, lacking in reality testing, and suffering from faulty cognitions. By placing distress solely within the individual rather than in the social, political, and cultural realms, power is granted to the psychiatric system as the remedy for this distress, and the person's perspective is delegitimized. Communication that disagrees with the dominant narrative is interpreted as further evidence of pathology. Furthermore, the application of a particular model of understanding to personal experience in either a medical, disability, or civil rights perspective in inflexible ways contributes to epistemic injustice. The question of who is in control of creating knowledge, who is believed, and whose story is considered true is an essential question in psychiatry and provides an additional lens for viewing the questions of diagnosis and self-definition. Epistemic injustice can be used as a critical lens for several areas in psychiatry, including the use of the medical model framework and the overreliance on medication, the co-opting of peer support and recovery, and the misuse of diagnosis.

Patients in healthcare are particularly vulnerable to epistemic injustices (Carel & Kidd, 2014). Delegitimizing people based on their diagnosis creates a fundamental imbalance in treatment as it often results in reducing one's credibility because of their diagnosis. Crichton et al. (2017) describe a man who claimed to be related to a famous politician, a belief which physicians treated as grandiose delusion, but later was discovered to be true. A more common example is the labeling of patients as paranoid when they are dissatisfied or distrustful of their providers or of a particular treatment. This experience is reminiscent of the challenge of the *pseudopatients* in Rosenhan's (1973) study of people who were hospitalized through endorsing fake symptoms, and who were then unable to convince the staff that in fact they were not ill. Their credibility was delegitimized by their status as "mental patient," which led to a disbelief of their claims, and subsequent denial of their attempts to rightly be released from the hospital.

This delegitimizing of patients can magnify already existing power inequities and make true collaboration more challenging. In a qualitative study on barriers to participating in shared decision-making in psychiatry, Grim et al. (2019) found that participants often felt dismissed and edited their stories to comply with dominant narratives. Epistemic challenges often included feeling that concerns were not taken seriously, not having access to or knowledge of medical terminology, and the perception of their diagnosis discrediting their opinions. This seemed particularly true for those who had experienced past episodes of psychosis. These difficulties serve as reminders of the challenge of having true collaboration in partnerships between providers and people receiving services. We will use the concept of epistemic injustice to several areas in psychiatry, including medical model approaches, diagnosis and misdiagnosis.

Medical Model

The medical, or illness, model provides a way to include mental illness within the realm of medical care yet carries significant repercussions for our understanding of emotional distress. While the medical model includes the conceptualization of mental illness via a biopsychosocial model, this "three-legged stool" is often unbalanced, with biological explanations overemphasized and psychological and social aspects seen as secondary or treated in a cursory manner. The medical model also presumes that there is some identifiable entity (an illness or disease) that is something "real" that can be diagnosed like in most of medicine, with the hope that eventually we will locate the biological markers and develop targeted drugs or interventions – a dream that has gone largely unfulfilled.

In addition, when responding to questions in regard to diagnosis and use of medication, the delegitimizing of people's assessment and understanding of their experience is also relevant. The use of the term "lack of insight" to describe people's disagreement with a professional's assessment of their experience, and the use of the neurological condition *anosognosia* to describe this condition are both examples of epistemic injustice (Washington, 2018). Anosognosia, a neurological condition where one is unaware of one's medical condition as a symptom of that condition, was imported for use in psychiatry with some controversy. When a person questions if their diagnosis is accurate, that is then used as evidence of lacking insight into their condition. The idea itself is enshrined as a part of the diagnosis itself – so to question the diagnosis is to confirm the diagnosis, creating a Catch-22 of sometimes catastrophic proportions (Harris, 2020; Hunter, 2018). The medicalization of disagreement into a further symptom of illness stands out as a particularly challenging situation that can be perceived and experienced as invalidating at best, and at worst, grounds for removal of rights via involuntary hospitalization or medication.

Once a diagnosis is in place, people are often provided with a variety of clinical and rehabilitative services. Reflecting the imbalance in the biopsychosocial model, medication is often emphasized as the most important aspect of treatment. While a variety of options are available, people are often educated to believe that they will need to be on medications for the remainder of their lives. This is especially evident in the lack of support for prescribers, clinical staff, people receiving services and other involved parties to address the multitude of additional issues that arise when talking about decreasing or stopping psychiatric medications. Rather than viewing stopping one's medication as a sign of recovery, being "off your meds" is akin to a slur or insult of being seen as crazy (Urban Dictionary, 2021). This speaks most broadly to the difference in the symbolic meaning of stopping, for example, olanzapine (Zyprexa^{TM}, an "antipsychotic" medication) vis-à-vis stopping omeprazole (Prilosec^{TM}, an acid reflux medication). A moral judgment of the person arises in the case of psychiatric medications, along with a fear of violence or aggression, something that does not arise when one hears of someone stopping an antacid medication. This also plays into longstanding racial stereotypes and over diagnosing of Black men with schizophrenia around the conflation of dangerousness, race, and mental illness (Metzl, 2010).

Longstanding distrust and dismissal of patient complaints around negative effects of psychiatric medications contribute to epistemic injustice. Characterization of patients as "non-compliant" reflects the perspective of the practitioner and a denial of the experience of the person making the decision to take or not take the medications. The self-management movement in healthcare is a broader movement to incorporate patient self-monitoring to support better disease management, particularly in chronic conditions (Holman & Lorig, 2004). In mental health, this approach is represented in such interventions as Illness Management and Recovery (IMR, Mueser et al., 2002). These interventions can have unintended negative consequences. At its worst, the approach can be considered to potentially reinforce a deficit identity by focusing heavily on self-monitoring for symptoms. It can also reinforce the internalization of an illness narrative by encouraging the viewing of experiences in the context of a disease model.

This illness identity can also be reinforced by interventions like the Wellness Recovery Action Plan (Copeland, 1997), when self-monitoring becomes a kind of hypervigilance around symptom reemergence that can come from the provider or other family members. Even more challenging is the foreshortening of the person's own experiencing in life for fear of relapse (Scott & Wilson, 2010). Another example emerges in the reporting of withdrawal effects with selective serotonin reuptake inhibitor (SSRI) medications, a condition long reported by patients (Strata, 2021), but only recently more globally recognized by the field of psychiatry. One recent study found withdrawal symptoms when reported by patients were likely to be interpreted as further relapse, misdiagnosed as a medical condition, or just not believed (Guy et al., 2020). In these examples, the person is either encouraged to reframe their experience into a disease framework, or their concerns are actively disbelieved or dismissed.

The entrenched nature of the illness model is further reflected in the renaming of psychiatrists to being referred to as "prescribers." Historically trained in psychotherapy and medicine, their current role has often been curtailed and limited to psychiatric medications (Moran, 2009). The term prescriber can also be used as a generic term to represent this skill and practice beyond the specific discipline. At the same time, this moniker also reduces any of those professions regardless of the breadth of training to a pharmaceutical intervention, limiting their interactions with patients to clinical matters. This is reflected in the lucrative but brief 15–20 minute "med check" (Chen et al., 2018). Carlat (2010) outlines the toll these limited visits take on both the psychiatrist and the person being treated, with little time to discuss any substantive life experiences beyond addressing side effects and raising or lowering doses (Gabbard, 2009). As well, Carlat describes his own realization of the influence that pharmaceutical companies and insurance reimbursement policies have had on his practice, and on the field as a whole. While many psychiatrists cringe at a moniker that minimizes their role and training in a biopsychosocial model, it speaks to the dominant narrative in the USA and increasingly elsewhere, that to treat what is considered psychiatric "illness," one goes to a psychiatric doctor or APRN to receive medications. This is in line with the commonly accepted way of teaching about psychiatric formulation using the *perspectives* model (McHugh & Slavney, 1998), in which symptoms equate with underlying disease that should be treated with medication. Even in the face of unyielding and oppressive social conditions, the "bio" in the purported "biopsychosocial" model seems to eclipse any environmental contributors such as trauma, historical oppression, systemic racism or other factors. The influence of pharmaceutical companies and reimbursement structures on the practice of psychiatry contributes to the medicalization of distress and potentially fore-shortening the valuing of individual experiences by providers.

Diagnosis and Misdiagnosis

The emergence of the consumer/survivor/ex-patient movement during the late 1950s and early 1960s reflected the empowerment of people who had been incarcerated by the mental health system for many years. Included in these imprisonments were a large number of casualties of misdiagnosis due to racism, sexism, homophobia and transphobia, with people who were gender nonconforming and/or LGBTQ being hospitalized. Homosexuality continued to be a diagnosis in the *Diagnostic and Statistical Manual of Mental Disorders* (DSM) until 1980 (Kirk & Kutchins, 1994), and less overtly through DSM-IV until 2000 (i.e., ego-dystonic homosexuality, sexual disorder not otherwise specified), and gender identity disorder was eliminated in 2013. DSM-5, the most recent version, includes a "non-diagnosis" of "gender dysphoria," meant to capture the distress of an incongruence between experienced and assigned gender. Psychiatry has played an oppressive role for many generations of LGBTQ individuals.

Along with other minoritized and racialized individuals who did not con-form to expected societal roles, the civil rights movement led to the politiciza-tion and radicalization of these groups around advocating for equal treatment and an end to unjustified incarceration. The experience for women within the psychiatric system is significantly different than for men, with examples including systemic sexism, and the pathologizing of women's experiences through such diagnoses of hysteria and borderline personality disorder. The experience of institutionalization and deinstitutionalization for women experi-encing psychosis includes risk for sexual assault, fear of losing parental rights, and lack of support and dissuasion of their desire to be a parent (Carr et al., 2015). For example, women with serious mental illness are more likely than women without to attempt suicide following sexual assault, but are unlikely to disclose such violence to healthcare professionals (Khalifeh et al., 2015). Intersecting identities compound this oppression for Black women and other people of color, which included forced sterilization and removal of children for many (Kline, 2010).

With the adoption of more stringent criteria for being hospitalized, new pharmacological and psychological treatments, and the emergence of rehabili-tation models, psychiatry increasingly relied on a disability model. These developments drew from two different strands of political movements – that of disability rights and creating equal access for those who experience limita-tion via a "psychiatric disability," and that of a civil rights movement seeking to de-pathologize expressions of human distress and expanding the acceptable expressions of human experience (Read et al., 2013).

The dangers of epistemic injustice are starkly clear in experiences of medical misdiagnosis of people with psychiatric diagnoses when they present with emergent symptoms. The incidents of missed cardiac events, resulting in premature death, occurs much more for those with a mental health diagnosis than would be expected as compared with the population base rates. This is in part due to diagnostic overshadowing (Shefer et al., 2014), or one's psychiatric diagnosis overshadowing a true medical (not psychiatric) emergency, which has led to many medically ill people being wrongfully admitted to psychiatric units (Reeves et al., 2000). Discrimination has been well-documented vis-à-vis those with psychiatric diagnoses trying to receive medical care (Thornicroft et al., 2007), which may contribute to the 10–25 year disparity in life expectancy for those diagnosed with mental illness, and is recently being addressed through attempts to find ways to ease this disparity, particularly in emergency services (Shefer et al., 2015).

One criticism of the traditional treatment model includes placing societal problems on the individual and locating the source of the distress in that individual. This raises the question, "[h]ow often does therapy become a process of oppressed people learning to accept their oppressed position and keeping quiet about their sense of powerlessness?" (Proctor, 2006). This issue also is seen in racial disparities in diagnosis and the use of particular types of medications. The racial bias in schizophrenia diagnoses, where Black people are 2–3 times more likely to be diagnosed than Whites, is a longstanding finding (Olbert et al., 2018). Further, the use of long-acting injectable medications varies by race. Black patients were disproportionately predicted being prescribed injectable medications in 12 states according to state Medicaid data (Brown et al., 2014). This racial disparity has been shown in retrospective analyses of prescribing practices elsewhere (Aggarwal et al., 2012) and is not a new phenomenon (Covell et al., 2002), reflecting the racism inherent in our society that inevitably is recreated in our healthcare system.

Future Directions: The Pursuit of Epistemic Justice

What are possible remedies to epistemic injustices in the field and practice of psychiatry? This is not a simple pursuit, as many of the initiatives over the past 20 years working to move the psychiatric system toward being more recovery-oriented and person-centered have made some progress, but much more is needed to truly change the dynamic and center of power. The giving up of power is not an easy task as it involves more than granting a metaphoric "seat at the table," but instead must grant the control of the room, when the meeting happens, and who calls it to order. We have chosen a few areas to discuss in thinking through this shifting in power, including prescribing of medication, diagnosis, the theoretical framework, who provides care, and considerations of social conditions. Each of these areas involve the telling of stories and the shifting of power through that act.

Deprescribing

Deprescribing serves as a convenient moniker that most of all offers legitimacy to the common experience of people wanting to decrease or discontinue their use of psychiatric medications. Until quite recently, there has been little to no literature focused on decreasing medications in a collaborative way with a provider; instead, the literature has emerged around adherence, non-compliance, insight, and how to provide psychoeducation to patients to convey the importance of medications (Corrigan et al., 2015).

The process of *deprescribing*, defined as "tapering, stopping, discontinuing, or withdrawing drugs, with the goal of managing polypharmacy and improving outcomes" (Thompson & Farrell, 2013), is best conducted in a collaborative way (Miller & Pavlo, 2018). Deprescribing began as a focus in geriatric medicine with the realization of the complications developing from complex polypharmacy regimens and unintended negative consequences of such (Woodward, 2003). In other areas of medicine, deprescribing practice focuses more on the medical and pharmaceutical considerations along with an informed and/or shared decision-making process with the patient (Reeve et al., 2014). Within psychiatry, a focus on deprescribing psychotropic medications has emerged over the past five years, and certain additional considerations have been identified that are specific to the field of mental health (Gupta & Cahill, 2016).

Collaboration between prescribing provider and patient in psychiatric drug deprescribing is both necessary and challenging. Evidence from shared decision-making (SDM) research points to areas of tension. Barriers identified in a study looking at creating a psychiatric shared crisis plan included providers lacking trust in patients' ability to make decisions, ambivalence about sharing power, and the sense that SDM was already how they practiced (Farrelly et al., 2016). Communication difficulties, including not understanding clinical language and struggling to accurately describe their experience, were highlighted as barriers for patients participating in SDM in another qualitative study (Giacco et al., 2018). Furthermore, people being respected in the doctor-patient relationship is an important aspect of collaboration and SDM (Pavlo et al., 2019). While collaboration not only serves to maximize the likelihood of success and to ensure consistency with the philosophy of recovery-oriented care, challenges in ensuring true partnership continue, particularly highlighted by relational power differentials. Similarly, a person whose perspective is delegitimized (i.e., not an "epistemic subject") cannot "share" in decision-making.

Interest in deprescribing of psychiatric medications has increased exponentially in recent years. This has come from both the professional and prescriber perspective (Gupta & Cahill, 2016) and from the patient perspective (Delano, 2021; Hall et al., 2007; Strata, 2021) along with a newly founded organization, the International Institute for Psychiatric Drug Withdrawal (IIPDW, 2021), focused on withdrawing from psychiatric drugs with perspectives from an array of disciplines as well as people with lived experience. There has been particular emphasis on the deprescribing of SSRI-type medications most commonly used for depression. There is a growing online lay-literature and set of resources detailing protocols for tapering as well as support groups for managing withdrawal effects due to attempting to cease these medications (cf. Hengartner et al., 2020; Strata, 2021). SSRI and benzodiazepines are the two most commonly addressed by people interested in stopping or reducing the use of medications; antipsychotics and mood stabilizers present more challenges as they are more controversial to reduce. Increasingly withdrawal is being recognized as a real syndrome along with new resources, such as micro-dosing via tapering strips, which allow for the decreasing of SSRI doses in very small increments (Groot & van Os, 2018, 2020).

Deprescribing in psychiatry is unique in that it requires adjustments and alterations considering specific history and circumstances of people taking psychiatric meds. In particular for those diagnosed with serious mental illness, shared decision-making, decision support, empowerment, and education is important. For those people who have been coerced and convinced for many years to take psychiatric medication, the idea of suddenly being asked if they would like to decrease or stop these medications can be disconcerting and may leave the person making erroneous assumptions about the provider's intent. There may be serious pushback from their friends or family members, or from other providers, as the dominant narrative of the importance of taking medications for the remainder of one's life is called into question. The question of decreasing medications, which may have been asked by the person themselves many years ago, is being reversed when it is now being posed by the doctor.

Some of the considerations to address these concerns in approaching deprescribing include talking to the person ahead of time. Taking the time to discuss in detail their concerns and questions, particularly their fears about what it would be like to start reducing medications, is an important first step. One of the biggest fears is that of relapse and hospitalization. Medication regimens that are consistent with people's wishes and effective for them may be hard-won after many years of challenging difficulties and the stress of being hospitalized multiple times. The fear of going back to the hospital is often reinforced by service providers and family members as well, through for example, including "stay out of the hospital" as one of the treatment goals. Only one measure to these authors' knowledge assesses the fear of relapse, appropriately called the Fear of Relapse Scale (Gumley et al., 2015). Addressing this fear and discussing alternatives and plans ahead of time can greatly reduce anxiety around these anticipated negative outcomes, reassuring all involved.

Interestingly, a hospital unit recently established in Norway is the first medication-free unit. Decreed by legislation based on the demands of consumer groups, the unit provides psychological treatment but does not use any type of psychiatric medication in the care of people. Initial research highlights the appreciation of the choice of treatment when choosing psychiatric care (Oedegaard et al., 2020). This included improved reported relationships with therapists and greater motivation in treatment. This unit and the decision by the Norwegian government to require its development has been sharply criticized by some psychiatrists (Yeisen et al., 2019). The criticisms by psychiatrists highlighted the belief that the decision to open such a unit was unscientific and would potentially increase stigma around the taking of psychiatric medications. Also, those psychiatrists interviewed felt this decision represented the problem of the "minority" of opinions being in charge, possibly reflecting a reaction to epistemic justice being enforced.

The pursuit of deprescribing lends itself to a shift in the narrative that is often told by our culture and by the field of psychiatry, including the purported need to stay on medications and the concept of a chemical imbalance to be corrected by such. Normalizing tapering or eliminating medications shifts the power dynamic and can bring about an identity shift in the person as to how they envision themselves as an active participant and with choice over taking or not taking medications.

Recovery and Disability Rights Model

Policy, including the Americans with Disabilities Act (Americans with Disabilities Act, 1990) and the Olmstead vs. L.C. (1999), have led to increased support, access, and inclusion. These ideas have also led to reforms in psychiatry. However, when applied to the psychiatric world, certain assumptions underlie this approach including that a mental illness diagnosis is a medical condition, that a person is subsequently disabled if they cannot function in society as others might, and that a person can continue to function while still experiencing symptoms with appropriate assistance (such as supported education, supported employment, and other assistive services or devices).

Within this movement emerged a philosophical shift from a deficit-focused, symptom-based view of psychiatric illness to a strengths-based, hope promoting approach, most generally termed the "recovery model" (Anthony, 1993). The idea that "people can and do recover from mental illness" may fall within the medical or disability approach to psychological distress when the underlying assumption is that there *is*, in fact, an illness to be recovered from. This model gained national and international recognition, particularly in the USA in the early 2000s as the US federal government adopted it as the guiding vision for the mental health system (New Freedom Commission on Mental Health, 2003).

A human rights or civil rights approach to these experiences informs the more radical wing of psychiatry (or what might be termed anti-psychiatry) and may help in ameliorating the shift toward viewing recovery in a narrow, clinical sense. This approach sees traditional diagnosis as more a form of social control rather than the identification of an underlying condition or medical problem (Leifer, 1990; Szasz, 1960). Instead, the need is to expand the acceptance by broader society of the range of human behavior, and not to cast societal oppression as an individual problem. The experiences of trauma, racism and other forms of oppression weigh heavily into this approach with the importance of understanding people's experiences. Language describing what might be otherwise termed psychosis as "extreme states" and approaches such as Open Dialogue (Seikkula et al., 2006), and Hearing Voices groups (Styron et al., 2017) would be examples of such alternative approaches. These approaches include, for example, seeing the experience of hearing voices as part of a continuum of human experiences, where the experience may be distressing yet not necessarily something to treat or extinguish. Rather, the focus becomes more on accepting these experiences rather than denying them. Maintaining this focus on human rights, expanding the accepted range of human behavior, and focusing on approaches that support people in living a full life in the community is the ideal outcome of this approach.

Peer Support

Included in the recovery model is a focus on peer support, or people with "lived experience of mental illness" acting in roles to support others. While some more radical activists contested that true peer support could not operate within the traditional mental healthcare system (Mead, 2003), the role was widely adopted as an essential service in public and private non-profit systems of care. Peer support has been a growing and much touted new area in mental health services, with the idea of drawing upon lived experience of mental health and addictions as a key element of recovery-oriented care.

Since the early 1990s, the profession has grown along with the research base supporting its effectiveness (Davidson et al., 2012). Peer support has been integrated across large systems, especially the Veterans Health Administration

(VHA), as a way of connecting, engaging and supporting those who experience mental illness and/or substance use disorders (Chinman et al., 2014). Peer support has also been mandated in *Olmstead*-based legal settlements working to promote movement from institutions to community living. Relying on concepts of mutual support and with the use of self-disclosure, peer support provides an ally and source of hope to people receiving services in the mental healthcare system (Pistrang et al., 2008). The role modeling and resource guidance provided by peer support specialists can act as agents of remoralization and inspiration. Peer support also can provide a translation and bridging function between the person and provider, helping to build greater understanding and perspective-taking by both into account. By having been on both sides of the system, presumably a peer support specialist can help clarify misunderstandings and support trust building in the relationships.

Much of peer support, though, is paid for and provided within the context of mental health systems. A danger of this adoption within traditional mental health systems is that instead of being a "disruptive" presence, changing "business as usual," peers were often co-opted into the system (Adams, 2020). Work behaviors and dynamics change substantially when one is paid versus volunteer (e.g., Heyman & Ariely, 2004; Himmelstein et al., 2014). In hiring peers, it is difficult to balance "putting your money where your mouth is" by paying peers versus quieting disruptive voices through assimilation. There is some evidence that peers in a healthcare system may be more effective when paid (e.g., Barber et al., 2008; Singh et al., 2015) but there is intrinsic value to mutual support outside the system, which is often purposefully unpaid. Within the system, more work is needed to achieve equitable and impactful peer support roles.

Peer support in many places has become a source of underpaid case managers. They are often asked to be enforcers of psychiatric norms and tasked by clinical staff to "get that person to take their medications." Peer staff often feel obligated both to follow the directions of their coworkers and superiors, as well as wanting to help the person. Understanding the nature of the experience and allowing for different interpretations of that experience beyond the traditional medical or disability model often is not something taught, nor a principle espoused in many peer support roles in the traditional psychiatric system. The common experience of being the only person with acknowledged and disclosed mental illness on a team or in a workplace is a stressful position and can leave a person less likely to diverge from the existing culture (Bellamy et al., 2017; Jones et al., 2019). Instead, there may be a continuation of more clinical approaches just by virtue of cultural pressure and reluctance to be an outsider in the group. This may happen even if the person is not being actively pressured to do so, but instead as a natural human tendency to adhere to group norms.

Harnessing the power and promise of peer support as a true source of allyship is a work in progress. Peer support rooted in the civil rights movement and in mutual support ethos has the potential to be a force in moving toward greater inclusion and epistemic justice for people receiving services.

Diagnosis and De-Diagnosis

"De-diagnosing" or undiagnosing a mental illness is a concept rarely discussed but seems a somewhat natural reordering and recalibration of the past three decades of diagnostic expansion. Noted by Patfield (2011), the concept of de-diagnosing may serve as a counterpoint to deprescribing, a reaction to over-prescribing and polypharmacy. The uptick in diagnosing in psychiatry reflects broader cultural movements and is both impacted by and has influenced the need for deprescribing, and a similar approach may be taken with diagnosis (Frances, 2013; Whitaker, 2005). At the root of this issue, however, is whether a medical approach to understanding human distress is most appropriate. In its approach, the DSM views symptoms as manifestations of an underlying disorder much like the rest of medicine despite the authors' claims to be atheoretical (American Psychiatric Association, 1980). Rather than a theoretical framework, the diagnoses of the DSM become reified as illnesses, solidifying the illness identity. This approach continued to reinforce the idea that the source of distress resides within the person rather than within the broader social context.

This reification of the illness metaphor is of particular significance in the care of individuals diagnosed with a serious mental illness, particularly schizophrenia. People receiving a schizophrenia diagnosis are not only confronted with the severity of the diagnosis but also with pessimistic messages. For example, one is often confronted with the idea that one cannot truly recover from schizophrenia – a belief that often permeates care – despite strong evidence to the contrary (DeSisto et al., 1995; Harding et al., 1987a, 1987b; New Freedom Commission on Mental Health, 2003). For some, recovering from schizophrenia must suggest one never had it at all and had been incorrectly diagnosed. Furthermore, there is evidence that long-term antipsychotic use may hinder meaningful recovery and pose more dangers than benefits (Harrow & Jobe, 2013; Wunderink et al., 2007). While a diagnostic label often serves to alleviate the isolation, confusion, and shame in early aspects of treatment, it may not be useful for everyone over time, as it tends to reinforce an illness identity (Yanos et al., 2010).

Even with the ubiquity of the DSM in psychiatry, a variety of alternative diagnostic approaches have been proposed and guidelines for development of new diagnostic systems have been developed (Kamens et al., 2019). The approaches offer a variety of solutions, including relying on psychological formulation (Johnstone, 2018; Johnstone & Dallos, 2013), continued and ongoing collection of client data regarding outcome and the therapeutic alliance (Duncan & Reese, 2015; Duncan et al., 2018), and classifying mental health concerns rather than disorders (see Kamens et al., 2018, for a more thorough review). While different in terms of structure, content, and focus, each of these approaches actively try to reimagine how to identify, or diagnose, issues of focus for care, develop deliberately collaborative diagnostic practices, and provide dynamic diagnoses that can be change over time. Others have argued that diagnostic approaches should be judged by their ability to inspire collaboration, hope, and meaning (Pavlo et al., 2019).

Addressing Structural Inequities

Another emerging area for addressing epistemic injustice is the growing focus on addressing structural inequities and identifying their impact on mental health. Structural inequities include systemic racism, gender bias, socioeconomic inequities, food insecurity, and the interaction of each of these conditions with individual identity markers. The consideration of race and gender discrimination in particular highlights the need for the conceptualization of interpersonal and intrapsychic distress as happening both within the person and between the person and environment.

These structural factors, such as lack of access to healthy fresh food, or the enduring legacy of racism in the USA, can be underestimated in their impact by practitioners. For example, lower incidences of suicide are related to a higher minimum wage (Gertner et al., 2019). Another study found that giving money to people had a more significant impact on quality of life than psychotherapy over a one year period (Haushofer et al., 2020). These findings indicate the impact of economic inequities on quality of life and highlight further the question of psychiatric symptoms as an illness versus a response to social conditions.

Racial disparities are another significant area for focus, particularly in the diagnosis of psychotic illnesses. Protesting during the 1960s became confounded with race. Black men in particular had their protest pathologized and therefore were more likely to be diagnosed with schizophrenia (Metzl, 2010). This has continued and is evidenced by the higher rates of diagnosis of Black men with schizophrenia and higher rates of injectable medications prescribed to Black men (Lawson et al., 2015). In an ironic reversal of this trend, in an examination of media portrayals of mass shooters, results indicated that White men shooters were more commonly portrayed as sympathetic characters who experienced mental illness, while Black and Latino men were more often described as "perpetually violent threats to the public" (Duxbury et al., 2018). The narratives publicly perpetuated through the news media and through cultural stories contribute to the enduring negative portrayal of people of color.

New training programs and education for providers are working to address these deep and persistent problems. Curricula that involve people in recovery and people from the community to teach about structural inequities has been one approach to doing this (Bromage et al., 2018). Using experiential exercises to illuminate the perspective of the person with lived experience, such as storytelling and drawing on personal reflection is another way of approaching these disparities (Carr & Miller, in preparation). People with lived experience of mental illness serving as educators is another promising direction. For example, one psychiatrist worked with a peer support specialist in an "inverted" relationship – the peer served as his advisor and mentor, to help him better understand the work he was doing (Agrawal & Edwards, 2013). This same psychiatrist later built a program based on this experience to provide this education in a larger context with positive results showing increases in understanding of others' perspectives (Agrawal et al., 2020). Another example is of an orientation program for all new employees at a mental health center to provide stories and examples of what works well in care (Miller et al., unpublished manuscript). By highlighting the personal stories and experiences of people with these inequities and legitimizing their experience of oppression and systemic racism, we may begin to address these inequities as they manifest in healthcare.

In these ways, some have taken steps to be more inclusive of people with lived experiences in ways that integrate their unique knowledge into treatment delivery. By integrating those perspectives, these groups are simultaneously moving toward epistemic justice by addressing structural inequities directly. It is important to note that when groups include persons with the experience of the marginalized groups they aim to help (e.g., racial minorities, lived experience of psychosis), significant effort should be made to integrate these voices in a way that respects those unique perspectives and acknowledges and attempts to minimize any potential power differentials. For example, a person with lived experience of psychosis may have internalized the negative conceptualization of themselves, and thereby be more sensitive to power differentials when invited to be a member of a training team (Jones et al., 2019).

Final Thoughts

Where does this leave us when thinking about the future of mental health and treatment for people experiencing the most concerning of symptoms, those we term psychosis? For one, we need to find ways to center the voice of people with the lived experience in ways that are not just an afterthought. Or, what does this discussion say to us about the future of treatment and the situating of the experiences called psychosis? We must consider the voices of people with lived experience as a respected, valued, and essential source of knowledge. Despite recent efforts that are valuable, such as the increasing prevalence of advisory boards of people with lived experience in federally funded grants, these efforts need to be considered absolutely essential and as equally valued voices and experts, as opposed to add-ons or after thoughts, by incorporating them as foundational aspects of gathering knowledge. The levels of epistemic injustice occur not just at the individual, clinical level, such as the examples given earlier in the chapter, but also at the organizational and policy levels (e.g., funding decisions and systemic changes at a broad national level).

The rise of social media is one source of democratization and shifting the center of power by allowing for open platforms for more voices to be heard. Recent exchanges between psychiatrist and psychiatric survivors highlight this new and novel point of contact that is outside of the office and the traditional doctor-patient hierarchical relationship. Instead, with the doctor and (ex-) patient interacting as two equals (relative to followership) on a social media platform, a different type of conversation can potentially take place. This movement toward greater epistemic justice has been met with defensiveness and hostility by some, resulting in online harassment at times (Stea, 2020). At the same time, the professionals continue to have access to mainstream publication venues not necessarily available to the patient community (Stea et al., 2020).

In moving forward, the question becomes how to address these systemic problems and bring about social change while also ameliorating the individual effects of these systems on the individual. As Rose (2018) puts it, this would be, for psychiatrists, creating "a radical shift in their ways of working so they can address the social determinants of mental distress and not merely seek to manage the effects" (p.173). The recent experience of the global COVID-19 pandemic has highlighted the social inequities and racial disparities that contribute further to epistemic injustice. The multiple minoritized identities and racialized experience of those in the mental healthcare system is a reflection of the broader cultural quagmire currently facing many in the United States. How does the recent focus on social justice and antiracism tie into this? The events surrounding the death of George Floyd and the ensuing protests and renewed focus on issues of racism in the USA have led to a refocusing of the importance of looking at epistemic justice within our various systems of care. The recent apology issued by the American Psychiatric Association (2021) for psychiatry's involvement and perpetuation of systemic racism represents a movement toward reconciliation as the dominant narrative shift to acknowledge a history of oppression. Realizing that the perspective of the White majority is not universal and that the impacts of racism are broad has come as a shock to some. For others, this window of opportunity feels refreshing but potentially short-lived; finding ways to convert funding and focus into legitimate systems change is the task at hand. With the resurgence of a civil rights and social justice focus in many sectors of society, there is the opportunity to implement some of the substantive changes to shift power to those who have traditionally gone unheard.

REFERENCES

Adams, W. E. (2020). Unintended consequences of institutionalizing peer support work in mental healthcare. *Social Science & Medicine, 262,* 113249.

Aggarwal, N. K., Rosenheck, R. A., Woods, S. W., & Sernyak, M. J. (2012). Race and long-acting antipsychotic prescription at a community mental health center: A retrospective chart review. *The Journal of Clinical Psychiatry, 73*(4), 513–517. https://doi.org/10.4088/JCP.11m07161

Agrawal, S., & Edwards, M. (2013). Personal accounts: Upside down: The consumer as advisor to a psychiatrist. *Psychiatric Services, 64*(4), 301–302.

Agrawal, S., Kalocsai, C., Capponi, P., Kidd, S., Ringsted, C., Wiljer, D., & Soklaridis, S. (September 12, 2020). "It was great to break down the walls between patient and provider": Liminality in a co-produced advisory course for psychiatry residents. *Advances in Health Sciences Education.* https://doi.org/10.1007/s10459–020-09991-w.

American Psychiatric Association. (1980). *Diagnostic and statistical manual of mental disorders* (3rd ed.) APA and Washington, DC.

American Psychiatric Association (APA). (2021). *APA's apology to Black, Indigenous and People of Color for its support of structural racism in psychiatry.* American Psychiatric Association. Retrieved January 20 from https://www.psychiatry.org/newsroom/apa-apology-for-its-support-of-structural-racism-in-psychiatry.

Americans with Disabilities Act, Pub. L. No. 101-336, 42 § 12101 et seq. (1990).

Anthony, W. A. (1993). Recovery from mental illness: The guiding vision of the mental health service system in the 1990s. *Psychosocial Rehabilitation Journal, 16*(4), 11.

Barber, J. A., Rosenheck, R. A., Armstrong, M., & Resnick, S. G. (2008). Monitoring the dissemination of peer support in the VA healthcare system. *Community Mental Health Journal, 44*(6), 433–441.

Bellamy, C., Schmutte, T., & Davidson, L. (2017). An update on the growing evidence base for peer support. *Mental Health and Social Inclusion, 21* (3), 1–7.

Bromage, B., Encandela, J. A., Cranford, M., Diaz, E., Williamson, B., Spell, V. T., & Rohrbaugh, R. M. (2018). Understanding health disparities through the eyes of community members: A structural competency education intervention. *Academic Psychiatry, 43*(2), 244–247.

Brown, J. D., Barrett, A., Caffrey, E., Hourihan, K., & Ireys, H. T. (2014). State and demographic variation in use of depot antipsychotics by Medicaid beneficiaries with schizophrenia. *Psychiatric Services, 65*(1), 121–124. https://doi.org/10.1176/appi.ps.201300001

Carel, H., & Kidd, I. J. (2014). Epistemic injustice in healthcare: A philosophial analysis. *Medicine, Health Care and Philosophy, 17*(4), 529–540.

Carlat, D. (2010). *Unhinged: The trouble with psychiatry – A doctor's revelations about a profession in crisis.* Free Press: A Division of Simon & Schuster, Inc. New York, NY.

Carr, E., & Miller, R. (in preparation). *Experiential context training: Using an inpatient guided visualization to increase empathy.*

Carr, E. R., Green, B., & Ponce, A. N. (2015). Women and the experience of serious mental illness and sexual objectification: Multicultural feminist theoretical frameworks and therapy recommendations. *Women & Therapy, 38*(1–2), 53–76.

Chen, J. A., Kontos, N., & Wilson, S. N. (2018). What's in a med check? Unpacking the "psychopharmacology" encounter. *Harvard Review of Psychiatry, 26*(1), 27–35.

Chinman, M., George, P., Dougherty, R. H., Daniels, A. S., Ghose, S. S., Swift, A., & Delphin-Rittmon, M. E. (April 01, 2014). Peer support services for individuals with serious mental illnesses: Assessing the evidence. *Psychiatric Services, 65*(4), 429–441. https://doi.org/10.1176/appi.ps.201300244

Copeland, M. E. (1997). *Wellness recovery action plan.* Peachtree Press.

Corrigan, P. W., Kosyluk, K., & Kottsieper, P. (2015). The problem of adherence and the importance of self-determination. In P. Corrigan (Ed.), *Person-centered care for mental illness: The evolution of adherence and self-determination.* Washington DC. American Psychological Association.

Covell, N. H., Jackson, C. T., Evans, A. C., & Essock, S. M. (2002). Antipsychotic prescribing practices in Connecticut's public mental health system: Rates of changing medications and prescribing styles. *Schizophrenia Bulletin, 28*(1), 17–29. https://doi.org/10.1093/oxfordjournals.schbul.a006920

Crichton, P., Carel, H., & Kidd, I. J. (2017). Epistemic injustice in psychiatry. *BJPsych Bulletin, 41*(2), 65–70.

Davidson, L., Bellamy, C., Guy, K., & Miller, R. (2012). Peer support among persons with severe mental illnesses: A review of evidence and experience. *World Psychiatry, 11*(2), 123–128.

Delano, L. (2021). *The inner compass initiative.* Retrieved Janary 8 from www .theinnercompass.org

DeSisto, M. J., Harding, C. M., McCormick, R. V., Ashikaga, T., & Brooks, G. W. (1995). The Maine and Vermont three-decade studies of serious mental illness: I. Matched comparison of cross-sectional outcome. *British Journal of Psychiatry, 167*(3), 331–338.

Duncan, B. L., & Reese, R. J. (2015). The Partners for Change Outcome Management System (PCOMS) revisiting the client's frame of reference. *Psychotherapy: Theory, Research & Practice, 52*(4), 391.

Duncan, B. L., Sparks, J. A., & Timimi, S. (2018). Beyond critique: The partners for change outcome management system as an alternative paradigm to psychiatric diagnosis. *Journal of Humanistic Psychology, 58*(1), 7–29.

Duxbury, S. W., Frizzell, L. C., & Lindsay, S. L. (2018). Mental illness, the media, and the moral politics of mass violence: The role of race in mass shootings coverage. *Journal of Research in Crime and Delinquency, 55*(6), 766–797.

Farrelly, S., Lester, H., Rose, D., Birchwood, M., Marshall, M., Waheed, W., . . . Thornicroft, G. (2016). Barriers to shared decision making in mental health care: Qualitative study of the Joint Crisis Plan for psychosis. *Health Expectations, 19*(2), 448–458.

Frances, A. (2013). The crisis of confidence in psychiatric diagnosis. *Annals of Internal Medicine, 159*(3), 221–223.

Gabbard, G. O. (2009). Deconstructing the "med check." *Psychiatric Times, 26*(9), 48.

Gertner, A. K., Rotter, J. S., & Shafer, P. R. (2019). Association between state minimum wages and suicide rates in the US. *American Journal of Preventive Medicine, 56*(5), 648–654.

Giacco, D., Mavromara, L., Gamblen, J., Conneely, M., & Priebe, S. (2018). Shared decision-making with involuntary hospital patients: A qualitative study of barriers and facilitators. *BJPsych Open, 4*(3), 113–118.

Grim, K., Tistad, M., Schön, U.-K., & Rosenberg, D. (2019). The legitimacy of user knowledge in decision-making processes in mental health care: An analysis of epistemic injustice. *Journal of Psychosocial Rehabilitation and Mental Health, 6*(2), 157–173.

Groot, P. C., & van Os, J. (2018). Antidepressant tapering strips to help people come off medication more safely. *Psychosis, 10*(2), 142–145.

Groot, P. C., & van Os, J. (2020). Outcome of antidepressant drug discontinuation with tapering strips after 1–5 years. *Therapeutic Advances in Psychopharmacology, 10,* 1–8.

Gumley, A. I., MacBeth, A., Reilly, J. D., O'grady, M., White, R. G., McLeod, H., ... Power, K. G. (2015). Fear of recurrence: Results of a randomized trial of relapse detection in schizophrenia. *British Journal of Clinical Psychology, 54*(1), 49–62.

Gupta, S., & Cahill, J. D. (2016). A prescription for "deprescribing" in psychiatry. *Psychiatric Services, 14*(1), 4–11.

Gupta, S., Miller, R., & Cahill, J. (2019). *Deprescribing in Psychiatry.* Oxford University Press, New York.

Guy, A., Brown, M., Lewis, S., & Horowitz, M. (2020). The 'patient voice': Patients who experience antidepressant withdrawal symptoms are often dismissed, or misdiagnosed with relapse, or a new medical condition. *Therapeutic Advances in Psychopharmacology, 10,* 2045125320967183.

Hall, W., Bergman, C., McNamara, J., & Sorensen, J. (2007). *Harm reduction guide to coming off psychiatric drugs.* Icarus Project, New York.

Harding, C. M., Brooks, G. W., Ashikaga, T., Strauss, J. S., & Breier, A. (1987a). The Vermont longitudinal study of persons with severe mental illness, I: Methodology, study sample, and overall status 32 years later. *American Journal of Psychiatry, 144*(6), 718–726.

Harding, C. M., Brooks, G. W., Ashikaga, T., Strauss, J. S., & Breier, A. (1987b). The Vermont longitudinal study of persons with severe mental illness, II: Long-term outcome of subjects who retrospectively met DSM-III criteria for schizophrenia. *American Journal of Psychiatry, 144*(6), 727–735.

Harrington, A. (2019). *Mind fixers: Psychiatry's troubled Search for the biology of mental illness.* WW Norton & Company, New York.

Harris, L. (2020). The "Anosognosia" label is psychiatric gaslighting masquarading as science. *Rooted in Rights.*

Harrow, M., & Jobe, T. H. (2013). Does long-term treatment of schizophrenia with antipsychotic medications facilitate recovery? *Schizophrenia Bulletin, 39*(5), 962–965.

Haushofer, J., Mudida, R., & Shapiro, J. P. (2020). *The comparative impact of cash transfers and a psychotherapy program on psychological and economic well-being.* National Bureau of Economic Research in Cambridge, Mass. http://www.nber.org/papers/w28106

Hengartner, M. P., Schulthess, L., Sorensen, A., & Framer, A. (2020). Protracted withdrawal syndrome after stopping antidepressants: A descriptive quantitative analysis of consumer narratives from a large internet forum. *Therapeutic Advances in Psychopharmacology, 10*, 2045125320980573.

Heyman, J., & Ariely, D. (2004). Effort for payment: A tale of two markets. *Psychological Science, 15*(11), 787–793.

Himmelstein, D. U., Ariely, D., & Woolhandler, S. (2014). Pay-for-performance: Toxic to quality? Insights from behavioral economics. *International Journal of Health Services, 44*(2), 203–214.

Holman, H., & Lorig, K. (2004). Patient self-management: A key to effectiveness and efficiency in care of chronic disease. *Public Health Reports, 119*(3), 239–243.

Hunter, N. (2018). *Trauma and madness in mental health services.* Palgrave McMillan.

IIPDW. (2021). *International Institute for Psychiatric Drug Withdrawal.* www.iipdw.org

Jaffe, D. (2017). *Insane consequences: How the mental health industry fails the mentally ill.* Prometheus Books.

Johnstone, L. (2018). Psychological formulation as an alternative to psychiatric diagnosis. *Journal of Humanistic Psychology, 58*(1), 30–46.

Johnstone, L., & Dallos, R. (2013). *Formulation in psychology and psychotherapy: Making sense of people's problems.* Routledge.

Jones, N., Niu, G., Thomas, M., Riano, N. S., Hinshaw, S. P., & Mangurian, C. (2019). Peer specialists in community mental health: Ongoing challenges of inclusion. *Psychiatric Services, 70*(12), 1172–1175.

Kamens, S. R., Cosgrove, L., Peters, S. M., Jones, N., Flanagan, E., Longden, E., . . . Miller, R. (2019). Standards and guidelines for the development of diagnostic nomenclatures and alternatives in mental health research and practice. *Journal of Humanistic Psychology, 59*(3), 401–427.

Kamens, S. R., Flanagan, E. H., & Robbins, B. D. (2018). Introduction to the second special issue on diagnostic alternatives. *Journal of Humanistic Psychology, 58*(1), 3–6.

Khalifeh, H., Moran, P., Borschmann, R., Dean, K., Hart, C., Hogg, J., . . . Howard, L. (2015). Domestic and sexual violence against patients with severe mental illness. *Psychological Medicine, 45*(4), 875–886.

Kirk, S. A., & Kutchins, H. (1994). The myth of the reliability of DSM. *The Journal of Mind and Behavior*, 71–86.

Kline, W. (2010). Eugenics in the United States. In A. Bashford & P. Levine (Eds.), *The Oxford handbook of the history of eugenics.* Oxford Handbooks Online. https://www.oxfordhandbooks.com/view/10.1093/oxfordhb/9780195373141.001.0001/oxfordhb-9780195373141-e-31?print=pdf

Lawson, W., Johnston, S., Karson, C., Offord, S., Docherty, J., Eramo, A., . . . Nasrallah, H. A. (2015). Racial differences in antipsychotic use: Claims database analysis of Medicaid-insured patients with schizophrenia. *Annals of Clinical Psychiatry, 27*(4), 242–252.

Leifer, R. (1990). Introduction: The medical model as the ideology of the therapeutic state. *The Journal of Mind and Behavior*, 247–258.

McHugh, P. R., & Slavney, P. R. (1998). *The perspectives of psychiatry.* JHU Press.

Mead, S. (2003). Defining peer support. *Intentional peer support: An alternative approach.* http://www.intentionalpeersupport.org

Metzl, J. M. (2010). *The protest psychosis: How schizophrenia became a black disease*. Beacon Press.

Miller, R., Howe, D. M., Olsen, S., & Carr, E. R. (Unpublished manuscript). "We're people first": Peers as educators to new employees in behavioral health.

Miller, R., & Pavlo, A. J. (2018). Two experts, one goal: Collaborative deprescribing in psychiatry. *Current Psychiatry Reviews, 14*(1), 12–18.

Miller, R., Ponce, A. N., & Thompson, K. (2011). Deinstitutionalization and the community mental health movement, 1954–1976. In M. Rowe, M. S. Lawless, K. Thompson, & L. Davidson (Eds.), *Classics of community psychiatry* (pp. 9–20). Oxford University Press.

Moran, M. (2009). Psychiatrists lament decline of key treatment modality. *Psychiatric News, 44*(8).

Mueser, K. T., Corrigan, P., Hilton, D. W., Tanzman, B., Schaub, A., Gingerich, S., … Herz, M. I. (2002). Illness management and recovery: A review of the research. *Psychiatric Services, 53*(10), 1272–1284. https://doi.org/10.1176/appi.ps.53.10.1272

New Freedom Commission on Mental Health. (2003). *Achieving the promise: Transforming mental health care in America*.

Oedegaard, C. H., Davidson, L., Stige, B., Veseth, M., Blindheim, A., Garvik, L., … Engebretsen, I. M. S. (August 08, 2020). "It means so much for me to have a choice": A qualitative study providing first-person perspectives on medication-free treatment in mental health care. *BMC Psychiatry, 20*(1), 399. https://doi.org/10.1186/s12888–020-02770-2

Olbert, C. M., Nagendra, A., & Buck, B. (2018). Meta-analysis of Black vs. White racial disparity in schizophrenia diagnosis in the United States: Do structured assessments attenuate racial disparities? *Journal of Abnormal Psychology, 127*(1), 104–115. https://doi.org/10.1037/abn0000309

Olmstead v. L.C., 527 Supreme Court of the United States (1999).

Patfield, M. (2011). Undiagnosis: An important new role for psychiatry. *Australasian Psychiatry, 19*(2), 107–109. https://doi.org/10.3109/10398562.2010.539226

Pavlo, A. J., Flanagan, E. H., Leitner, L. M., & Davidson, L. (2019). Can there be a recovery-oriented diagnostic practice? *Journal of Humanistic Psychology, 59*(3), 319–338.

Pavlo, A. J., O'Connell, M., Olsen, S., Snyder, M. K., & Davidson, L. (2019). Missing ingredients in shared decision-making? *Psychiatric Quarterly, 90*(2), 333–338.

Pistrang, N., Barker, C., & Humphreys, K. (2008). Mutual help groups for mental health problems: A review of effectiveness studies. *American Journal of Community Psychology, 42*(1–2), 110–121.

Proctor, G. (2006). Therapy: Opium of the masses or help for those who least need it. In G. Proctor, M. Cooper, P. Sanders, & B. Malcolm (Eds.), *Politicizing the person-centred approach: An agenda for social change* (pp. 66–79). PCCS Books.

Read, J., Bentall, R., Mosher, L., & Dillon, J. (2013). *Models of madness: Psychological, social and biological approaches to psychosis*. Routledge.

Reeve, E., Shakib, S., Hendrix, I., Roberts, M. S., & Wiese, M. D. (2014). Review of deprescribing processes and development of an evidence-based, patient-centred deprescribing process. *British Journal of Clinical Pharmacology, 78*(4), 738–747.

Reeves, R. R., Pendarvis, E. J., & Kimble, R. (2000). Unrecognized medical emergencies admitted to psychiatric units. *The American Journal of Emergency Medicine, 18*(4), 390–393.

Rose, N. (2018). *Our psychiatric future.* John Wiley & Sons.

Rosenhan, D. L. (1973). On being sane in insane places [10.1126/science.179.4070.250]. *Science, 179*(4070), 250. http://science.sciencemag.org/content/179/4070/250.abstract

Scott, I. A., Gray, L. C., Martin, J. H., & Mitchell, C. A. (2012, June). Minimizing inappropriate medications in older populations: A 10-step conceptual framework. *American Journal of Medicine, 125*(6), 529–537.e524. https://doi.org/10.1016/j.amjmed.2011.09.021

Scott, A., & Wilson, L. (2010). Valued identities and deficit identities: Wellness Recovery Action Planning and self-management in mental health. *Nursing Inquiry, 18*(1), 40–49.

Scrutton, A. P. (2017). Epistemic injustice and mental illness. In *The Routledge Handbook of Epistemic Injustice* (pp. 347–355). Routledge.

Seikkula, J., Aaltonen, J., Alakare, B., Haarakangas, K., Keränen, J., & Lehtinen, K. (March 01, 2006). Five-year experience of first-episode nonaffective psychosis in open-dialogue approach: Treatment principles, follow-up outcomes, and two case studies. *Psychotherapy Research, 16*(2), 214–228. https://doi.org/10.1080/10503300500268490

Shefer, G., Cross, S., Howard, L. M., Murray, J., Thornicroft, G., & Henderson, C. (2015). Improving the diagnosis of physical illness in patients with mental illness who present in emergency departments: Consensus study. *Journal of Psychosomatic Research, 78*(4), 346–351.

Shefer, G., Henderson, C., Howard, L. M., Murray, J., & Thornicroft, G. (2014). Diagnostic overshadowing and other challenges involved in the diagnostic process of patients with mental illness who present in emergency departments with physical symptoms – A qualitative study. *PLoS One, 9*(11), e111682.

Singh, D., Negin, J., Otim, M., Orach, C. G., & Cumming, R. (2015). The effect of payment and incentives on motivation and focus of community health workers: Five case studies from low-and middle-income countries. *Human Resources for Health, 13*(1), 1–12.

Stea, J. (January 14, 2020). When promoting knowledge makes you a target. *Scientific American.* https://blogs.scientificamerican.com/observations/when-promoting-knowledge-makes-you-a-target/

Stea, J., Black, T., & Pierre, J. (2020). Op-ed: Why anti-psychiatry now fails and harms. *Medpage Today*, (1).

Steingard, S. (2019). *Critical psychiatry: Controversies and clinical implications.* Springer Nature. https://doi.org/https://doi.org/10.1007/978-3-030-02732-2

Strata, A. (2021). Retrieved January 8 from Forums – Surviving Antidepressants. www.survivingantidepressants.org.

Styron, T., Utter, L., & Davidson, L. (February 01, 2017). The hearing voices network: Initial lessons and future directions for mental health professionals and systems of care. *Psychiatric Quarterly*, 1–17. https://doi.org/10.1007/s11126–017-9491-1

Szasz, T. S. (1960). The myth of mental illness. *American Psychologist, 15*(2), 113.

Thompson, W., & Farrell, B. (2013). Deprescribing: What is it and what does the evidence tell us? *The Canadian Journal of Hospital Pharmacy, 66*(3), 201.

Thornicroft, G., Rose, D., & Kassam, A. (2007). Discrimination in health care against people with mental illness. *International Review of Psychiatry, 19*(2), 113–122.

Torrey, E. F. (June 01, 2010). Documenting the failure of deinstitutionalization. *Psychiatry, 73*(2), 122–124. https://doi.org/10.1521/psyc.2010.73.2.122

Treatment Advocacy Center. (2021). Retrieved January 9 from www .treatmentadvocacycenter.org

Urban Dictionary. (2021). *"Off your meds."* https://www.urbandictionary.com/define .php?term=Off%20Your%20Meds

Washington, N. (2018). Contextualism as a solution to paternalism in psychiatric practice. *Philosophy, Psychiatry, & Psychology, 25*(4), 235–243.

Whitaker, R. (2001). *Mad in America: Bad science, bad medicine, and the enduring mistreatment of the mentally ill.* Basic Books.

Whitaker, R. (2005). Anatomy of an epidemic: Psychiatric drugs and the astonishing rise of mental illness in America. *Ethical Human Psychology and Psychiatry, 7*(1), 23.

Woodward, M. C. (2003). Deprescribing: Achieving better health outcomes for older people through reducing medications. *Journal of Pharmacy Practice and Research, 33*, 323–328.

Wunderink, L., Nienhuis, F. J., Sytema, S., Slooff, C. J., Knegtering, R., & Wiersma, D. (2007). Guided discontinuation versus maintenance treatment in remitted first-episode psychosis: Relapse rates and functional outcome. *Journal of Clinical Psychiatry, 68*(5), 654–661.

Yanos, P. T., Roe, D., & Lysaker, P. H. (2010). The impact of illness identity on recovery from severe mental illness. *American Journal of Psychiatric Rehabilitation, 13*(2), 73–93.

Yeisen, R. A., Bjørnestad, J., Joa, I., Johannessen, J. O., & Opjordsmoen, S. (2019). Psychiatrists' reflections on a medication-free program for patients with psychosis. *Journal of Psychopharmacology, 33*(4), 459–465.

9   The Road Ahead

A Call to Action

Marci L. Gaither and Helen J. Wood

We Can Do Better

Access to effective psychosocial treatment for psychosis continues to be elusive in the United States. For years, the literal and figurative costs associated with the diagnosis of schizophrenia have been known, policies to promote improved national mental healthcare have been in place and recommendations for evidence-based treatments have existed. And yet, the implementation and uptake of such policies and recommendations within psychosis treatment have only been moderately successful. Why? We suggest that the importance of the *clinician* has been overlooked as a tool for change. Clinicians have not been adequately equipped to routinely access and avail themselves of the progress that has been made in research and treatment. To move from policy-level aspirations to provider-level actions, we need to better support and develop these "boots on the ground" as agents of change within the field of recovery for individuals living with psychosis.

Psychosis Treatment is a National Problem

According to the National Institute of Mental Health (NIMH), the lead federal agency for research on mental disorders, the diagnosis of schizophrenia and related psychosocial factors are a leading cause of disability worldwide (NIMH, 2018). The diagnosis is linked to a greater risk for shortened life span than that of the general population, due to a combination of comorbid medical conditions and a greater risk of dying by suicide. In addition, financial burden on society is greater due to multiple factors such as treatment costs (e.g., monies spent on acute inpatient admissions), greater legal involvement, lower job productivity and a potential overreliance on drug treatments. Bringing top-notch care to individuals living with psychosis makes sense through every lens one might view it. Investment in services tailored to people with psychosis makes fiscal sense at a policy level of care, with economic burden estimates exceeding $60 billion per year in the USA (Chong et al., 2016). From a facility perspective, these individuals tend to frequently use the most intensive, and expensive, levels of care. From a liability and safety perspective, adequate assessment and treatment of the intricate ways that psychosis interacts with other vulnerability factors makes good sense. And, of course, ethically it is the right thing to do: these individuals are as deserving as anyone else of high quality treatment. While they are some of the most warranted consumers of services, these people are often also among the most underserved. This continued underinvestment is simply unacceptable and perpetuates stigma on all fronts. Contrary to widely held belief, meaningful recovery is possible with empowerment and access to appropriate services and support.

Policies that Should Apply to Mental Health Treatment of Psychosis Have Had Modest Success

This challenge of inadequate access to evidence-based psychosocial treatment for those living with psychosis has been recognized and policies to address this need have been developed. For example, the President's Freedom New Commission on Mental Health, a sweeping project designed to evaluate the US mental healthcare system and make recommendations for improvement, proposed six broad aspirations: (1) Americans understand that mental health is essential to overall health, (2) mental health care is consumer and family driven, (3) disparities in mental health care are eliminated, (4) early mental health screening, assessment and referral to services are common practice, (5) excellent mental health care is delivered and research is accelerated, (6) technology is used to access mental health care and information (Hogan, 2003; see also Chapter 2).

We will use the six aspirations from the President's New Commission on Mental Health as an organizing framework to consider progress and existing resources for clinicians, continuing challenges, and suggestions in order to move the field forward. Though not exhaustive, we have chosen to address areas under each aspiration that are of particular relevance or interest to the mental health providers who are regularly working with individuals who live with psychosis. As two clinical psychologists working across a range of psychosis services, we hope that this chapter will activate clinicians to not just read the text but to choose to put their values into action using the information we provide.

Americans Understand that Mental Health is Essential to Overall Health

The stigmatization of mental health issues is a significant barrier to mental health care, particularly for people experiencing psychosis (see also Chapter 4). Schizophrenia, the diagnostic label most commonly linked to psychosis, is among the most stigmatized of mental health diagnoses, being wrongly associated with untreatability and violence (Passerello, Hazelwood, & Lawrie, 2019; Rossler, 2016). Such stigmatization contributes to a reluctance to seek help whether via mental health specialists or primary care professionals, by both individuals experiencing psychosis and their families. Fear of disclosing such a diagnosis, for example to employers or schools, presents a barrier to seeking appropriate accommodations and sustaining functioning. Additionally, this stigmatization is often internalized by individuals as self-stigma, contributing to negative views of self (Lucksted & Drapalski, 2015). Perniciously, it is also identifiable in clinicians themselves (Schulze, 2007), impacting their own belief in their clients' capacity for recovery. Stigma also affects decisions made by healthcare leaders, where low priority is given to upgrading psychosis service infrastructure or to cultivating the specialty expertise of clinicians.

Parity, meaning equal coverage for mental and physical healthcare, is federal law in the USA since the Mental Health Parity Act of 1996 and Patient Protection and Affordable Care Act of 2010 (Beronio, Glied, & Frank, 2014). Legislation has acknowledged that mental health is essential to overall health and well-being, but this perspective has not filtered into dominant American culture and is complicated by broad cultural differences in beliefs about mental health (Chen & Mak, 2008). At a service level, the President's New Commission on Mental Health (2004) invited us to make seeking mental health care comparable in approach to seeking physical health care. While individuals experiencing psychosis may also struggle to access adequate physical health support, this form of care is still less stigmatized than mental health care, particularly for ethnic minority groups (see section below: 'Disparities in mental health are eliminated'). Positively, there have been significant attempts to enhance access to mental health support through embedding it in physical health systems; primary care mental health integration is already evolving for more common mental health issues, such as anxiety and depression. Psychosis services would do well to follow this trend, and the example set by some first episode psychosis services, for example by clinicians offering appointments one day per week in several local primary care physical health services.

What can we do as individual clinicians to address the stigmatization of psychosis? At a psychosocial treatment level, we can target the impact of stigma as a specific intervention focus (Morrison et al., 2016) or as part of broader approaches, for example within the normalization promoted in the early stages of Cognitive Behavioral Therapy for psychosis (CBTp; Kingdon & Turkington, 2005). However, such approaches, combined with general awareness of mental health prejudice and misinformation, are not sufficient on their own. We need to move beyond this to being anti-stigma both in and beyond our clinical practice. We need to question the ethics of treating internalized stigma without also challenging the broader context that causes this in the first instance. Without doing so we risk pathologizing a societal issue. For some clinicians, actions might involve challenging and exploring evidence of stigma within their services, for others it could involve outreach and education to community groups or joining a national campaign, such as NAMI's (n.d.) StigmaFree pledge. Professionals who have teaching or supervision roles also have a crucial voice in shaping healthcare culture. There is substantial evidence that first-person narratives and experiential exercises can make a real impact on future healthcare professionals (Chew & Sim, 2020; Yamaguchi, Mino, & Uddin, 2011).

Mental Health Care is Consumer- and Family-Driven

Involving consumers and their families is critical to improving psychosocial treatments for those experiencing psychosis. These individuals are frequently overlooked in regard to their capacity to act as experts and contribute to the development of psychosocial treatment plans. This omission is for a variety of reasons, including stigma, as discussed above, and the intersection of race and socioeconomic factors, as explored below. Consumers have also been eclipsed by the predominant emphasis on a disease model, under such labels as schizoaffective disorder or schizophrenia, being seen as people to whom treatment is delivered, as opposed to individuals capable of driving their recovery and offering knowledge (Johnstone et al., 2018).

Research shapes the development of psychosocial treatments, yet the voices of service users have been marginalized in this context (Geekie, 2004). We need to see consumers as experts on their own recovery, capable of informing research questions and partnering with both clinicians and academics to enhance quality of care. The USA lags behind countries, like the UK and Australia, in involving service users in research (Jones & Shattell, 2016). Encouragingly, there are some examples of research methods being used that enable this relationship-building. Participatory research is an approach aimed at direct partnering with relevant communities, simultaneously acknowledging social injustice and power differentials (Desai et al., 2019; Wilkinson-Lee et al., 2018). This approach requires investigators to observe distress through the lens of community members, for example through different cultural perspectives. It provides a way of facilitating engagement and ownership of psychosis-related mental health research by marginalized communities experiencing mental health disparities (including determining factors such as racism and poverty) with the aim of improving outcomes and ownership of them (Davidson, Stayner, Lambert, Smith, & Sledge, 1997; Okazaki, Kassem, & Tut, 2014; Wilkinson-Lee et al., 2018).

We need to expand the involvement of service user collaboration in service design. Participatory research, and comparable approaches, give us a way of involving community members, including consumers and their families, in improving services and translating research into practice (Desai et al., 2019). Experience-based co-design (EBCD) is a model used primarily in physical health settings, with growing use in mental health contexts (The Point of Care Foundation, n.d.). EBCD facilitates collaboration between consumers, families, and staff (including management-level) (Larkin, Boden, & Newton, 2015). Examples of its use in the UK and Ireland include improving inpatient care for people experiencing first episode psychosis and improving physical activity for people accessing mental health rehabilitation and recovery services (Larkin et al., 2015; Matthews et al., 2017). Advantages of this approach are the way in which it situates service users at the center of service improvement, fosters more equal status between groups where there is typically a power imbalance, and leads to change in both operational process and relational aspects of care, as well as increased acceptability of services to consumers and staff (Larkin et al., 2015).

The majority of clinicians, however, do not work in research or academic medical centers. Approaches such as EBCD may seem daunting or simply not viable resource-wise. In this case, what can we do to ensure mental health care is consumer-driven? First, we can ensure we collaborate with consumers in treatment planning and that our outcomes are client-oriented. Providers must be careful not to overfocus on the goal of symptom reduction, as frequently targeted in healthcare and psychosocial treatment research trials (see also Chapter 4 in this book). Improvements in functioning and an increased sense of agency may be both more meaningful to people and more realistic as a treatment focus. The Questionnaire for the Process of Recovery, developed from consumers' accounts of recovery, is one way to monitor such progress that is being used internationally, with outcomes associated with psychological well-being, quality of life and empowerment (Kanehara et al., 2017; Neil et al., 2009). Secondly, providers should consider when peer-driven support is relevant, including referring people beyond our services, for example to Hearing Voices groups (Hearing Voices USA, 2020). Finally, we believe that making space for dialogue with consumers and families is vital. Here in Pittsburgh, Allegheny County's Collaborative for Recovery Dialogue hosts participatory dialogues, forums for conversation between service users, stakeholders, and practitioners with the aim of improving services and deepening respect and understanding about each other's experiences and roles (Allegheny County Coalition for Recovery, n.d.; United States Department of Health and Human Services, 2000).

Disparities in Mental Health Care are Eliminated

In the broader mental health context, membership in a racial/ethnic minority community has been linked to a number of mental health disparities, such as lower access to and utilization of care, less satisfaction with care and higher attrition rates. Recent evidence suggests that these themes are mirrored in individuals who have also been diagnosed with a serious mental illness (Maura & Weisman de Mamani, 2017a). Evidence suggests that racial/ethnic and other discriminated-against groups are more often diagnosed with schizophrenia-spectrum disorders, but also have less access to quality psychosocial treatments and case management after discharge from a psychiatric admission (Maura & Weisman de Mamani, 2017a). Notably, an individual's cultural context may impact services at many junctures, from assessment and diagnosis (e.g., paranoia versus institutional racism) to current distress level (e.g., recent increase in violence against people of color) to treatment interventions (e.g., cognitive and experiential frameworks within which clients understand their world).

As clinicians we need to attend to intersectionality, the experience of marginalization and disempowerment in relation to psychosis. We should consider ways in which these areas have impacted the development of psychosocial support, as well as mistrust of services delivering it. The psychosocial treatments we use are frequently products of research contexts where past and present experiences of socioeconomic power imbalances and abuses, including racism, have been neglected, including ways in which they restrict dialogue and trust between researchers, clinicians and potential service users and their communities (Desai et al., 2019). Mote and Fulford (2020), in a call to action for addressing bias in research as it applies to Black Americans living with SMI, suggest that if "we do not study the effects of racialized experiences on our research questions, we unintentionally suggest that social constructs like race are not worthy of such scrutiny...we may perpetuate the notion that has long plagued human behavioral research that White participants from Western cultures are representative of all human experiences" (p. 2).

From training contexts, to treatment team meetings and in our own clinical supervision we can be attending to our biases and how they enter into the therapeutic relationship. We should also reflect on the potential limitations of our assessment and treatment approaches. In our services, we need to be flexible in our application of evidence-based practice. Maura & Weisman de Mamani (2017b) have suggested that culturally adapted therapy approaches should regularly explore how constructs such as collectivism or interdependence and spirituality or religion may play a role in service users' lives. Building clinicians' cultural humility and related skills also builds critical skills in collaborative case conceptualization and planning (Warner, 2015; Yamada & Brekke, 2008). We recommend Maura and Kopelovich's (2019) guide to using CBT with racial/ethnic minority groups and Weisman de Mamani and colleagues' (2021) *Culturally Informed Therapy for Schizophrenia* as excellent starting points.

Early Mental Health Screening, Assessment, and Referral to Services are Common Practice

Lack of treatment within the months, and sometimes years, after symptom onset has been demonstrated to have numerous deleterious effects on symptom reduction, response to treatment and functioning; therefore, reducing the duration of untreated psychosis (DUP) is pivotal (Hardy, Neindam & Loewy, n.d.). To do that, we need to help people within the larger system to better understand the signs and symptoms of emerging psychosis and appropriate referrals. Both individuals within the healthcare system and those in the community can play a role in supporting individuals to early access to treatment. Teachers and cultural or religious leaders may be an underutilized source of timely access of support, as well as reducing stigma, with the benefit of enhancing recovery outcomes (Maura & Weisman de Mamani, 2017a; Meyer et al., 2020).

This may also include outreach by behavioral health providers to their colleagues in more general medicine areas, such as primary care providers (PCPs) and the emergency department (ED). Ethnic/minority groups may be especially likely to seek treatment via this path, as it is less stigmatizing; unfortunately, primary care providers are less likely to adequately diagnose and treat mental health concerns (Maura & Weisman de Mamani, 2017a). There is a need for tools to support PCPs and ED providers to better identify individuals needing assistance, thus reducing the potentially critical duration of untreated psychosis (Kennedy, Johnson, Cheng, & Woodberry, 2020). Frontline clinicians can share psychoeducation and screening information as part of in-services for colleagues within their institutions.

Approaching this challenge from another direction might include us providing outreach to community stakeholders, collaboration with school system staff and local police or building connections with clergy and other community partners. One example of this type of collaboration is the Crisis Intervention Team program for police, which "improves communication, identifies mental health resources for those in crisis and ensures officer and community safety" (National Alliance for Mental Illness, n.d.). Our local CIT is an example of a context in which peer support specialists share their experiences of psychosis with police (K. Parham, personal communication, June 18, 2020). CIT has been linked to improved understanding of psychosis and correspondingly decreased stigmatization (Compton et al., 2006). In some police forces it has been linked to successful diversion into treatment and away from the jail system (Rogers, McNiel, & Binder, 2019). This is an especially important issue for individuals of color diagnosed with SMI, as they are more likely to enter treatment via the legal system than their White counterparts

(Maura & Weisman de Mamani, 2017a). Mental health psychosis-related educational training cannot stand alone. We also need to support officers to reflect more on the intersections of race with perceptions of "unpredictability" and "dangerousness" (Compton et al., 2011, p. 743). Clinicians who are interested in early intervention can reflect on which organizations or individuals in their community they could reach out to for collaboration. Readers are also referred to American Psychological Association (APA)'s Division 18, *Psychologists in Public Service*, which includes sections focused on SMI and Police and Public Safety, among others (https://www.apadivisions.org/division-18/).

Ideally, once individuals have been referred into mental health treatment, they may be further engaged with coordinated specialty care (CSC) services for follow-up regarding first episode psychosis. CSC involves a multidisciplinary team approach to recovery-oriented services for people with first episode psychosis (FEP). Services geared toward early psychosis experiences may be more frequent and have a greater focus on education and employment and family involvement than treatment programs more typical of later course psychosis (for example, see Chapters 5 and 6 in this book). Clinicians wanting to further explore FEP work can easily access examples of such treatment manuals for free and begin to explore ways to adjust their practice with this population accordingly.

Excellent Mental Health Care is Delivered and Research is Accelerated

How do we define excellence and how can mental health professionals implement it? Some of the largest contributors to the provision of psychosocial treatments for psychosis thus far are the Substance Abuse and Mental Health Services Administration (SAMHSA), NIMH, APA, the Council for Serious Mental Illness (SMI) Psychology and the Veterans Health Administration (VHA). Both NIMH and SAMHSA fall under the auspices of the United States Department of Health and Human Services, with NIMH focused on research and SAMHSA dedicated to improving access to information about mental health treatment and research. APA identifies itself as "the leading scientific and professional organization representing psychology in the United States" with a mission to "promote the advancement, communication and application of psychological science" (APA, 2020). The Council for SMI Psychology (2020) "encourages all those interested in working with the SMI/SED population to remain current and up-to-date with the latest research, practice developments and the continuing education offerings." The VHA is the clinical arm of the United States Department of Veterans

Affairs and the largest organized system of healthcare in the United States (McHugh & Barlow, 2010). We briefly summarize below some of the efforts by these and other organizations to support gold standard services and recovery for everyone, as well as the remaining challenges. We follow this with discussion of actions mental health professionals can take to further these goals.

SAMHSA broadly defines recovery as "a process of change through which individuals improve their health and wellness, live a self-directed life and strive to reach their full potential" (2020). How do we know how to best help address these dimensions of recovery? The most recent Schizophrenia Patient Outcomes Research Team (PORT) project promoted eight psychosocial interventions based on the weight of the psychotherapy efficacy evidence: assertive community treatment, supported employment, skills training, cognitive behavioral therapy, token economy interventions, family-based services, psychosocial interventions for alcohol and substance use disorders, psychosocial interventions or weight management and smoking cessation. Continuous development and transmission of the latest evidence and practices for psychosocial treatments with individuals with schizophrenia-spectrum disorders is paramount to serving this population in the manner deserved. The good news is that there are decades' worth of evidence-based practices for the treatment of psychosis (see Chapters 2–4) and we can utilize those gains for meaningful life change within a recovery framework.

However, there remains a significant gap between the development of effective psychosocial treatments and the availability of training in these practices, their implementation within non-research clinics, and access for service users (Briand & Menear, 2014). In order for service users to have ready access to evidence-based interventions, there must be adequate numbers of clinicians competent to provide them. Therefore, clinicians need access to systematic, high quality training in interventions proven to be effective. Roadblocks include insufficient instructors and supervisors familiar with and competent in such modalities, lack of high quality didactics with sufficient hours dedicated to this learning and supervised access to clients seeking empirically-based treatments (EBPs) for psychosis. Within the mental health field, providers must have readily accessible opportunities for education regarding best practices and there must be an infrastructure in place to allow interested practitioners the means to delve into evidence-based practice and gold standard treatment certifications.

Such an infrastructure could include access for students to quality educational programs, access for providers/trainees to continuing clinical education (e.g., webinars, conferences), and access for providers/supervisors/trainees to specialty competencies. There must be mechanisms in place to disseminate the knowledge and achieve certifications that are well-known and easily available.

If they are not in place, or are actively prohibited, then the system is preventing providers from practicing at the top of their license and, by extension, blocking patient access to that level of care. We want the benefits of EBPs for the most effective care but ideally using formulation-based, flexible care rather than a basic "cookbook" approach (Cook, Schwartz, & Kaslow, 2017). As Karlin & Cross (2013) have noted, successful dissemination and implementation is a complex process including "policy, provider, local systems, patient and accountability levels" (p. 1) and that "the intensive consultation component of the training programs is essential" (p. 10).

Mechanisms for Change

Student Education

Graduate studies present an ideal opportunity to provide accurate information regarding the treatment options and prognosis for recovery in individuals with serious mental health conditions. Yet most training programs are not up-to-date on the evidence base for psychosocial rehabilitation and recovery (PSR). For example, Kimhy et al. (2013) found that most psychology training directors remain unfamiliar with the evidence base supporting cognitive behavioral therapy for psychosis (CBTp) as an effective means to decrease both positive and negative symptoms and improve social and vocational outcomes and its inclusion in both the American Psychiatric Association and Schizophrenia PORT recommendations. Similarly, Reddy et al. (2010) found that most clinical psychology trainees in scientist-practitioner model doctoral programs do not have access to PSR training and experience. Efforts have been made to fill this gap. In 2014, the results of SAMHSA's 5-year project, the Recovery to Practice Initiative, which was "designed to hasten awareness, acceptance and adaptation of recovery-based practices" (NAACDAC, n.d.) became available. As one of the organizations tasked with developing the initiative, the American Psychological Association sought to "develop an online resource on recovery principles and practices. . .and develop recovery-focused trainings for mental health professionals" (APA, 2011). The result is the APA Recovery to Practice Curriculum, a comprehensive syllabus of 15 modules emphasizing the psychosocial rehabilitation principles ideally suited for training mental health professionals with an interest in treating individuals with serious mental illness at the graduate, predoctoral and post-doctoral levels (APA, 2014, "Recovery curriculum"). Available free of charge, this curriculum offers an empirically-based standard of education in recovery (APA & Jansen, 2014, see also Chapter 7 in this book).

After completion of graduate school, advanced training with close supervision of clinicians' on-the-job training is needed, through internships and postdoctoral fellowships. Internships have not typically been able to offer significant focus with a psychosis population, although some programs do offer psychosis-specific rotations or pieces of SMI training. However, shifts have been occurring. Starting in 2002, VHA began a gradual rollout of the Interprofessional Fellowship Program in Psychosocial Rehabilitation and Recovery Services (PSR), which provides targeted training with veterans with serious mental illness and also adds an "education dissemination project" to further increase others' knowledge of issues important to individuals living with serious mental health conditions (United States Department of Veterans Affairs, 2019). In 2019, the Specialty Council for SMI Psychology succeeded in petitioning APA to recognize a SMI Psychology postdoctoral specialty, which included submissions of curriculum, training guidelines and a competency evaluation instrument (see Chapter 7 in this book). Stakeholders from all the relevant disciplines are encouraged to support the development of this sort of specialty SMI training in their fields.

Workforce Development

While some progress has been made, all too often providers are still unaware of effective interventions or are overwhelmed by how to go about trying to educate themselves about the options. One great prospect for providers is developing and/or participating in centralized resource hubs (i.e., listservs, sharepoints, websites) as efficient means of communicating opportunities for learning (i.e., webinars, workshops). Once aware of training and other developmental opportunities, providers are often met with lack of departmental support (just read a book) or other facility barriers, such as a lack of protected time for such education, a lack of funding for relevant trainings or rigidity from their facilities in terms of allowing recorded sessions to be reviewed by specialist supervisors. If clinicians are expected to identify and participate in specialty training on their own time, with their own funds and without the benefit of their own clients, it's no wonder uptake is stalled. Providers need support from their organizations in the form of educational funding and time for training, as well as logistical support for allowing session content, with client permission, to be reviewed for fidelity to the treatment model.

International communities of practice and dialogue with colleagues and consumers throughout the world will allow us to build upon their wisdom when addressing our needs at home. In addition to promoting high-fidelity training and treatment implementation, CBTpNet is one such organization that seeks to provide opportunities for fellowship among providers in the United States and Canada as a means to continually stay abreast of the latest challenges and advances and to leverage and share clinical experience (Riggs, Kopelovich, & Gottleib, 2019). The International Society for Psychological and Social Approaches to Psychosis (ISPS) is a valuable international organization across professional and personal levels, with scope for multiple voices, and increasingly representing a variety of theoretical frameworks at its conferences (ISPS, 2020).

Specialty Competencies

Providers interested in achieving specialty competencies need to have a means to do so. For example, the VHA allows staff to apply for training in various evidence-based practices. If selected, the organization subsidizes the training costs for the multi-day didactics followed by extended periods (e.g., six months) of consultation for competence and fidelity to the model. Other mechanisms for achieving high standards of education, training and competency in psychosocial treatments of psychosis have begun to develop as well. Providers can turn to these resources as caches of information regarding specialty training. Although it is not an official accrediting body, the North American Cognitive Behavioral Therapy for Psychosis Network (North American CBTpNet, n.d.) was established in 2018 as a vehicle to drive forward efforts to thoughtfully and comprehensively operationalize excellent training in CBTp. This effort has identified benchmarks in three areas: full CBTp competency, CBTp-informed care competency and CBTp competency in training, consultation and supervision, lending itself to a wide array of provider disciplines. Several members of this collective are also part of direct training efforts through medical schools (e.g., Stanford Medicine Department of Psychiatry and Behavioral Medicine, n.d.), independent practices (e.g., NYC CBTp, 2015) or training centers such as the Beck Institute, which recently launched the Center for Recovery Oriented Cognitive Therapy, billed as a strengths-based extension of CBTp (Beck Institute, 2019).

The Council for SMI Psychology is currently paving the way for psychologists to become board certified in SMI Psychology by the American Board of Professional Psychology (ABPP) (Specialty Council for SMI Psychology, 2020; Chapter 7 in this book). This is important for several related reasons. First, it serves as a way to allow seasoned psychologists to formally demonstrate their competence, where no means was previously available. Second, it provides a systematic way for senior psychologists to operate at the top of their licenses. Third, supervisors must be able to take advantage of those opportunities in order to provide rigorous and comprehensive training to the clinicians of tomorrow. Once available, SMI psychologists should pursue this capstone of professional training.

Accelerated Research

Continuous feedback loops between research findings and clinical application are important to translational research endeavors. One recent effort to conduct important research with a dissemination component built in was the Recovery After Initial Schizophrenia Episode (RAISE) project which focused on treatment in the USA for individuals experiencing their first episode of psychosis. It led to the creation of the NAVIGATE program which was tasked with providing recovery-focused care specifically within the challenges of the multi-payer US healthcare system (Mueser et al., 2015). This approach is interdisciplinary, includes medication, family, individual, vocational/educational and case management components, and offers their detailed free open-access manuals. Clinicians in leadership positions who want to advance the treatment of FEP in their facilities could look into starting such a program (see Chapter 5, this book).

Clinical work and research should be two sides of the same coin, where clinical concerns drive research questions and research results are fed back into clinical practice. Meaningful collaboration among clinicians and researchers is also an area for improvement. Too often, the two groups are working in separate silos rather than in tandem. Clinical care should inform research, not just receive it. Clinicians should not be seen just as a recruitment vehicle, yet clinical staff are often unable to access newer treatments in a timely fashion unless part of a research group. Could researchers converse with clinicians about what topics they are interested in knowing more about, based on in vivo clinical experiences, and be presented with a summary of the latest literature? Could employers provide protected time for clinicians to be consumers of the research? Could there be regular forums where clinicians present challenges they are coming up against in the provision of therapy and collaborate with researchers in ways to evaluate them empirically? Could it become standard for research groups to put out clinical briefs summarizing their progress and findings along the way in quick, easily digestible and directly relevant format?

Technology is Used to Access Mental Health Care and Information

The COVID-19 pandemic has thrown the already emerging importance of telehealth into stark relief. Greenbaum (2020) noted that "more than 90% of the US population was under stay-at-home orders this spring" (p. 48), forcing a dramatic conversion to telehealth in its wake. Existing teletherapy research suggests that for a wide range of presenting problems, video sessions match the effectiveness of face-to-face sessions, with higher retention rates; comparative studies are lacking between face-to-face and telephone sessions (Greenbaum, 2020). Similarly, preliminary data supports the feasibility, acceptability, attendance and adherence in videoconferencing with individuals diagnosed with schizophrenia-spectrum disorders, which were preferred to audio-only interactions (Santesteban-Echarri, Piskulic, Nyman, & Addington, 2020).

Clinicians can draw on the existing evidence base to ensure people experiencing psychosis can gain new treatments and enhanced access to care made possible by technological developments. Pre-pandemic technological advances in psychosocial support include: the use of smartphone apps as a potential precursor to therapy (Greenwood et al., 2018) and a CBT-based digital intervention for early psychosis (Bucci et al., 2018). During the pandemic telesupport has necessarily expanded, including consumers and families accessing peer-based support online via the Hearing Voices Network (Hearing Voices USA, 2020), and group teletherapy being shown as acceptable for people experiencing first episode psychosis (Wood et al., 2020). Online and phone-based support promises much in regard to increasing access to primary and supplemental services not only during but beyond a global pandemic (Lawes-Wickwar, McBain, & Mulligan, 2018; Santestaban-Echarri, Piskulic, Nyman, & Addington, 2020). Telehealth offers advantages in terms of social distancing measures, but also for individuals facing childcare, transportation and time challenges. Technology's role in psychosocial services for psychosis is here to stay and we need to find ways to maximize its availability, which will include addressing practical issues and provider and consumer perceptions.

Amidst the promise of telehealth, mental health professionals are well-positioned to attend to accessibility, related to technology ownership, skill and social circumstances to avoid perpetuating a "digital divide" in mental health (Ennis, Rose, Denis, Pandit, & Wykes, 2012, p. 395). Non-specific phone ownership among people with psychosis (80%) is close to that of the general population (90%) (Firth et al., 2016). However, only 49% people with psychosis in the UK, USA or Canada have smartphones, compared to 63% in the general population, limiting video conferencing capability (Firth et al., 2016). Although it is now possible to get a smartphone via the federal Lifeline assistance phone program for low income households, in our experience many people lack access to Wi-Fi, or still have cellphones without video capability (Assurance Wireless, 2020). We must also consider disparity in access to digital technology for those who are older, economically disadvantaged, and members of minority racial/ethnic groups (Daker-White & Rogers, 2013; Ennis et al., 2012; Firth et al., 2016). Even once access is secured, there may be a greater need for coaching consumers regarding the basics of internet use with smartphones, tablets or computers, and for help identifying workarounds, such as Wi-Fi hotspots, and incorporating instructional video segments (Bell, Lim & Thomas, 2020). Torous and colleagues have amassed a body of work on these topics, including free manuals to help teach digital health literacy (Hoffman et al., 2020).

Sometimes teletherapy training cautions against teletherapy with people with psychosis. This recommendation may reflect the wisdom of offering multidisciplinary support to people experiencing psychosis, compared to practicing as a solo practitioner. However, this belief may actually belie a number of false assumptions regarding the appropriateness of a teletherapy based merely on diagnostic group membership, without consideration of data and individual differences. For example, there may be a judgment that people experiencing suspiciousness or social wariness will automatically not want to engage via remote means. Or there may be an underlying assumption that individuals with serious mental health conditions are too incapacitated or too high risk to be considered for anything other than face-to-face interventions. Such an attitude threatens to perpetuate marginalization, including limits to telehealth (Santesteban-Echarri et al., 2020; Talley et al., 2021).

Instead, we can encourage clinicians to offer their clients the option and, if interested, support them in accessing and testing out teletherapy. This may also require ancillary departments, such as telehealth setup, to spend more time problem-solving and practicing getting these individuals online successfully. While difficulties with anxiety or unusual beliefs may impact willingness to use technology, as with any person, they are too readily pathologized in individuals experiencing psychosis, framed predominantly as paranoia versus relatively common concerns about information technology and security. Clinicians should be willing to offer the option and actively try to support clients' attempts to use the internet-based interventions. Of note, sometimes it is as much the clinician's lack of confidence with the modality as the client's!

In addition to actually providing the mental health services via technology, we can also harness technology to access and share information about psychosocial treatments in psychosis; several excellent examples already exist. In 2018, the American Psychiatric Association and SAMHSA partnered to develop the Clinical Support System for Serious Mental Illness, or SMI Adviser, which more broadly defines SMI to include individuals living with severe non-psychotic illness as well. SMI Adviser is a web-based resource geared toward a wide range of helping professionals, including psychologists, psychiatrists, nurses and social workers, as well as service users and family members. They provide live and on demand webinars, bite-size answers to common questions with links to additional information, service locators, and consultation (APA, 2020).

In 2019, SAMHSA began a 5-year project, the Mental Health Technology Transfer Center (MHTTC) network (n.d., "Technology transfer model"; see: https://mhttcnetwork.org/), whose goal is to "seek to accelerate the ability of the mental health field to use evidence-based practices that will improve the lives of people with or at risk for developing mental health disorders." The MHTTC network is comprised of eight regional and two national centers focused on SMI. They offer a variety of resources such as online and in-person trainings, conferences, calls, practice briefs and newsletters, all aimed at getting useful information quickly into the hands of clinical providers.

Finally, we can use technology to build virtual communities of practice to support individual providers in their daily work. Given the low number of providers trained in psychosocial interventions within the USA, it's likely that many of these individuals lack a local source of colleagues with whom to engage. This may be particularly true for our colleagues working in rural areas. Behavioral health clinicians working in all types of settings (e.g., VA, community mental health, university-affiliated) and with all phases of severe mental health issues can join networks whereby they may share lessons learned, build upon one another's successes and collaborate collectively to move the field forward. This also presents an opportunity for reflection upon the various intricate ways that culture and counseling intersect. Communities of practice for providers whose jobs are primarily or solely focused on conducting therapy have been especially lacking. This cohort is especially important as they can provide a rich source of nuanced feedback and problem-solving for one another by leveraging their clinical experience in service of clients. In addition, such a community can act as a buffer against burnout and a font to replenish and energize clinicians who have a passion for working in a subfield that poses a number of unique challenges (Morse et al., 2012).

Efforts to harness the power of technology, in the form of direct services, transfer of information, education and training and building communities have begun. Going forward, we need to make training in the provision of telehealth services standard, further research the acceptability, adherence and efficacy of those services and create spaces where individual providers are plugged into communities that are supporting their continued education, training and daily work providing excellent services for individuals living with psychosis.

We Can Do Better

It is an exciting time for psychosocial interventions in psychosis treatment and their contribution to recovery work in our community. On the road ahead we must embrace the opportunities noted above from a number of directions, but an important driver is the individual clinician. To move from policy-level aspirations, through cultural and organizational frameworks, to the provider-client level of implementation of services is no easy feat. It will demand a good measure of creativity and flexibility, as psychosis training, education and treatment have often been undervalued and underfunded (Grazier, Mowbray, & Holter, 2005), perhaps reflecting the stigma generated toward the population itself.

Nonetheless, individual providers can be great agents of change on a daily basis through small, consistent action. However, the work is hard, and we need a community to help activate and sustain us. Now is the time to take a step in the right direction on this lifelong journey and join in fellowship to help improve awareness, communication, education and training, policy and advocacy. Below is a menu of ideas for easily actionable items, cutting across all six of the aforementioned aspirations, to get you started:

- Join a local, state or national organization, such as APA Division 18's Serious Mental Illness Section (https://www.apadivisions.org/division-18/sections/mental-illness) or the ABCT Psychosis and Schizophrenia-Spectrum Special Interest Group (https://schizpsychosis.org) and consider participating in leadership
- Sign up for a newsletter (https://sardaa.org/about-sardaa/newsletter)
- Join a listserv
- Read an article or book (e.g., *Cultural Adaptation of CBT for Serious Mental Illness*)
- Bookmark/subscribe to a website (http://www.psychtrainingsmi.com/index.htm)
- Check out a manual (http://navigateconsultants.org)
- Subscribe to a consumer voice podcast (e.g., Coffee and Psychosis)
- Subscribe to a YouTube channel (https://www.livingwellwithschizophrenia.org/videos)
- Sign up for a webinar (https://smiadviser.org/)
- Check if your facility offers educational funds
- Pursue psychosis-specific continuing education (https://mhttcnetwork.org/)
- Attend a conference, such as the Association for Behavioral and Cognitive Therapies (https://www.abct.org/Conventions/?m=mConvention&fa=dConvention) and incorporate your learning into one case or group
- Get individual supervision and/or get certified
- Retweet or share posts from reliable sources on social media (e.g., https://www.facebook.com/div18smised)
- Participate in fundraising efforts
- Join a hospital peer advisory board
- Join ISPS-US: http://www.isps.org/
- Join a NAMI family support group: https://www.nami.org/Support-Education/Support-Groups/NAMI-Family-Support-Group
- Explore mental health opportunities at a county level, for example recovery groups, advisory groups
- Look up seminars/conferences run by local academic institutions
- Read books on family and consumer perspectives
- Read a history of psychosocial treatments
- Join a mental health advocacy community organization
- Join a discussion group, (e.g., https://www.nami.org/About-Mental-Illness/Mental-Health-Conditions/Schizophrenia/Discuss)

- Implement collaborative approaches to service improvement: https://www
  .pointofcarefoundation.org.uk/resource/experience-based-co-design-ebcd-
  toolkit/
- Explore the International Hearing Voices Network and find a group meeting
  near you: https://www.intervoiceonline.org
- Learn about your local Crisis Intervention Team (e.g., https://www.nami
  .org/Advocacy/Crisis-Intervention/Crisis-Intervention-Team-(CIT)-
  Programs)
- Learn about running an Ending Self Stigma group (e.g., https://www.mirecc
  .va.gov/visn5/training/ess/ESS.asp)

REFERENCES

Allegheny County Coalition for Recovery. (n.d.) Collaborative for recovery dialogue. Retrieved from http://coalitionforrecovery.org/committees/consumer-provider-collaborative/

American Psychological Association. (2011). Overview of the recovery to practice initiative. Retrieved from https://www.apa.org/pi/mfp/psychology/recovery-to-practice/index

American Psychological Association. (2014, October). Recovery curriculum. Retrieved from https://www.apadivisions.org/division-18/sections/mental-illness/recovery-curriculum

American Psychological Association & Jansen, M. A. (2014). *Reframing Psychology for the Emerging Health Care Environment: Recovery Curriculum for People with Serious Mental Illnesses and Behavioral Health Disorders*. Washington, DC: American Psychological Association.

Assurance Wireless. (2020). Assurance wireless. Retrieved from https://www.assurancewireless.com

Beck Institute. (2019). The home of cognitive behavioral therapy. Retrieved from https://beckinstitute.org/

Bell, I. H., Lim, M. H., & Thomas, N. (2020). The therapeutic use of digital technologies in psychosis. In J. C. Badcock & G. Paulik (Eds.), *A clinical introduction to psychosis* (pp. 637–662). Academic Press: An Imprint of Elsevier. London.

Beronio, K., Glied, S., & Frank, R. (2014). How the Affordable Care Act and Mental Health Parity and Addiction Equity Act greatly expand coverage of behavioral health care. *The Journal of Behavioral Health Services & Research, 41*(4), 410–428.

Briand, C., & Menear, M. (2014). Implementing a continuum of evidence-based psychosocial interventions for people with severe mental illness: Part 2 – Review of critical implementation issues. *Canadian Journal of Psychiatry, 59*(4), 187–195.

Bucci, S., Barrowclough, C., Ainsworth, J., Machin, M., Morris, R., Berry, K., ... Haddock, G. (2018). Actissist: Proof-of-concept trial of a theory-driven digital intervention for psychosis. *Schizophrenia Bulletin, 44*(5), 1070–1080.

Chen, S. X., & Mak, W. W. (2008). Seeking professional help: Etiology beliefs about mental illness across cultures. *Journal of Counseling Psychology, 55*(4), 442.

Chew, Q. H., & Sim, K. (2020). Psychiatry teaching amongst medical undergraduates: Stories that matter and mediators of better learning outcome. *Postgraduate Medicine, 132*, 590–594.

Chong, H. Y., Teoh, S. L., Wu, D. B., Kotirum, S., Chiou, C. F., & Chaiyakunapruk, N. (2016). Global economic burden of schizophrenia: A systematic review. *Neuropsychiatric Disease and Treatment, 12*, 357–373. https://doi.org/10.2147/NDT.S96649

Compton, M. T., Demir Neubert, B. N., Broussard, B., McGriff, J. A., Morgan, R., & Oliva, J. R. (2011). Use of force preferences and perceived effectiveness of actions among Crisis Intervention Team (CIT) police officers and non-CIT officers in an escalating psychiatric crisis involving a subject with schizophrenia. *Schizophrenia Bulletin, 37*(4), 737–745. https://doi.org/10.1093/schbul/sbp146.

Compton, M. T., Esterberg, M. L., McGee, R., Kotwicki, R. J., & Oliva, J. R. (2006). Brief reports: Crisis intervention team training: Changes in knowledge, attitudes, and stigma related to schizophrenia. *Psychiatric Services, 57*(8), 1199–1202. https://doi.org/10.1176/ps.2006.57.8.1199

Cook, S. C., Schwartz, A. C., & Kaslow, N. J. (2017). Evidence-based psychotherapy: Advantages and challenges. *Neurotherapeutics, 14*, 537–545. DOI:10.1007/s13311-017-0549-4

Council for Serious Mental Illness (SMI) Psychology. (January 2020). Introduction. Retrieved from http://psychtrainingsmi.com/index.htm

Daker-White, G., & Rogers, A. (2013). What is the potential for social networks and support to enhance future telehealth interventions for people with a diagnosis of schizophrenia: A critical interpretive synthesis. *BMC Psychiatry, 13*, 279. https://doi.org/10.1186/1471-244X-13-279

Davidson, L., Stayner, D. A., Lambert, S., Smith, P., & Sledge, W. H. (1997). Phenomenological and participatory research on schizophrenia: Recovering the person in theory and practice. *Journal of Social Issues, 53*(4), 767–784. https://doi.org/10.1111/0022-4537.00048

Desai, M. U., Bellamy, C., Guy, K., Costa, M., O'Connell, M. J., & Davidson, L. (2019). If you want to know about the book, ask the author: Enhancing community engagement through participatory research in clinical mental health settings. *Behavioral Medicine, 45*(2), 177–187.

Ennis, L., Rose, D., Denis, M., Pandit, N., & Wykes, T. (2012). Can't surf, won't surf: the digital divide in mental health. *Journal of Mental Health, 21*(4), 395–403.

Firth, J., Cotter, J., Torous, J., Bucci, S., Firth, J. A., & Yung, A. R. (2016). Mobile phone ownership and endorsement of "mHealth" among people with psychosis: A meta-analysis of cross-sectional studies. *Schizophrenia Bulletin, 42*(2), 448–455.

Grazier, K. L., Mowbray, C. T., & Holter, M. C. (2005). Rationing psychosocial treatments in the United States. *International Journal of Law and Psychiatry, 28*, 545–560.

Geekie, J. (2004). Listening to the voices we hear: Clients' understandings of psychotic experiences. In J. Read, L. R. Mosher, & R. Bentall, R. (Eds). (2004). *Models of madness: Psychological, social and biological approaches to schizophrenia* (pp. 178–190). Hove, UK: Routledge.

Greenbaum, Z. (July/August 2020). How well is telepsychology working? *Monitor on Psychology, 51*(5), 46.

Greenwood, K., Alford, K., O'Leary, I., Peters, E., Hardy, A., Cavanagh, K., . . . Garety, P. (2018). The U&I study: Study protocol for a feasibility randomised controlled trial of a pre-cognitive behavioural therapy digital 'informed choice' intervention to improve attitudes towards uptake and implementation of CBT for psychosis. *Trials, 19*(1), 644. https://doi.org/10.1186/s13063–018-3023-7

Hardy, K. V., Neindam, T. A., & Loewy, R. (n.d.). *Measuring the duration of untreated psychosis within first episode psychosis coordinated specialty care.* Retrieved from https://www.nasmhpd.org/content/information-providers

Hearing Voices Network USA. (2020). Hearing Voices Network USA: Voices, visions and other unusual or extreme experiences. Retrieved from: https://www .hearingvoicesusa.org

Hoffman, L., Wisniewski, H., Hays, R., Henson, P., Vaidyam, A., Hendel, V., . . . Torous, J. (2020). Digital Opportunities for Outcomes in Recovery Services (DOORS): A pragmatic hands-on group approach toward increasing digital health and smartphone competencies, autonomy, relatedness, and alliance for those with serious mental illness. *Journal of Psychiatric Practice, 26*(2), 80–88. https://doi.org/10.1097/PRA.0000000000000450

Hogan, M. F. (2003). The President's New Freedom Commission: Recommendations to transform mental health care in America. *Psychiatric Services, 54*(11), 1467–1474.

ISPS. (2020) International Society for Psychological and Social approaches to psychosis (ISPS). Retrieved from http://www.isps.org

Johnstone, L., Boyle, M., Cromby, J., Dillon, J., Harper, D., Kinderman, P., Longden, E., Pilgrim, D., & Read, J. (2018). *The Power Threat Meaning Framework: Towards the Identification of Patterns in Emotional Distress, Unusual Experiences and Troubled or Troubling Behaviour, as an Alternative to Functional Psychiatric Diagnosis.* Leicester: British Psychological Society. Retrieved from https://www.bps.org.uk/sites/bps.org.uk/files/Policy%20-%20Files/PTM%20Main.pdf

Jones, N., & Shattell, M. (2016). Taking stock of the challenges and tensions involved in peer leadership in participatory research about psychosis and a call to do better. *Issues in Mental Health Nursing, 37*(6), 440–442. https://doi.org/10.3109/01612840.2015.1124955

Kanehara, A., Kotake, R., Miyamoto, Y., Kumakura, Y., Morita, K., Ishiura, T., . . . Kasai, K. (2017). The Japanese version of the questionnaire about the process of recovery: Development and validity and reliability testing. *BMC Psychiatry, 17*(1), 360. https://doi.org/10.1186/s12888-017-1520-y

Karlin, B. E., & Cross, G. (September 2, 2013). From the laboratory to the therapy room: National dissemination and implementation of evidence-based psychotherapies in the U.S. Department of Veterans Affairs Health Care System. *American Psychologist,* DOI:10.1037/a0033888.

Kennedy, L., Johnson, K. A., Cheng, J., & Woodberry, K. A. (2020). A public health perspective on screening for psychosis within general practice clinics. *Frontiers in Psychiatry, 10*, 1025. https://doi.org/10.3389/fpsyt.2019.01025

Kimhy, D., Tarrier, N., Essock, S., Malaspina, D., Cabannis, D., & Beck, A. T. (2013). Cognitive behavioral therapy for psychosis – Training practices and dissemination in the United States. *Psychosis*, *5*(3), 10.1080/17522439.2012.704932. https://doi.org/10.1080/17522439.2012.704932

Kingdon, D. G., & Turkington, D. (2005). *Cognitive therapy of schizophrenia: Guides to evidence-based practice*. New York: Guilford.

Larkin, M., Boden, Z. V., & Newton, E. (2015). On the brink of genuinely collaborative care: Experience-based co-design in mental health. *Qualitative Health Research*, *25*(11), 1463–1476. https://doi.org/10.1177/1049732315576494

Lawes-Wickwar, S., McBain, H., & Mulligan, K. (2018). Application and effectiveness of telehealth to support severe mental illness management: Systematic review. *JMIR Mental Health*, *5*(4), e62. https://doi.org/10.2196/mental.8816.

Lucksted, A., & Drapalski, A. L. (2015). Self-stigma regarding mental illness: Definition, impact, and relationship to societal stigma [Editorial]. *Psychiatric Rehabilitation Journal*, *38*(2), 99–102. https://doi.org/10.1037/prj0000152

Matthews, E., Cowman, M., & Denieffe, S. (2017). Using experience-based co-design for the development of physical activity provision in rehabilitation and recovery mental health care. *Journal of Psychiatric and Mental Health Nursing*, *24*(7), 545–552. https://doi.org/10.1111/jpm.12401

Maura, J., & Kopelovich, S. (2019). *Cultural considerations in applying cognitive behavioral therapy to racial/ethnic minority groups with serious mental illness*. Mental Health Technology Transfer Center Network. Retrieved from: https://mhttcnetwork.org/centers/northwest-mhttc/product/practice-brief-cultural-considerations-applying-cognitive.

Maura, J., & Weisman de Mamani, A. (2017a). Mental health disparities, treatment engagement, and attrition amazon racial/ethnic minorities with severe mental illness: A review. *Journal of Clinical Psychology in Medical Settings*, *24*, 187–210. DOI:10.1007/s10880-017-9510-2

Maura, J., & Weisman de Mamani, A. (2017b). Culturally adapted psychosocial interventions for schizophrenia: A review. *Cognitive and Behavioral Practice*, *24*, 445–458.

McHugh, R. K., & Barlow, D. H. (2010). The dissemination and implementation of evidence-based psychological treatments: A review of current efforts. *American Psychologist*, *65*(2), 73–84.

Mental Health Technology Transfer Center. (n.d.). Technology transfer model. Retrieved from https://mhttcnetwork.org/centers/mhttc-network-coordinating-office/technology-transfer-\model.

Meyer, M. S., Rosenthal, A., Bolden, K. A., Loewy, R. L., Savill, M., Shim, R., . . . Niendam, T. A. (2020). Psychosis screening in schools: Considerations and implementation strategies. *Early Intervention in Psychiatry*, *14*(1), 130–136. https://doi.org/10.1111/eip.12858.

Morrison, A. P., Burke, E., Murphy, E., Pyle, M., Bowe, S., Varese, F., . . . Wood, L. J. (2016). Cognitive therapy for internalised stigma in people experiencing psychosis: A pilot randomised controlled trial. *Psychiatry Research*, *240*, 96–102. https://doi.org/10.1016/j.psychres.2016.04.024

Morse, G., Salyers, M. P., Rollins, A. L., Monroe-DeVita, M., & Pfahler, C. (2012). Burnout in mental health services: A review of the problem and its remediation.

Administration and Policy in Mental Health and Mental Health Services Research, *39*(5), 341–352.

Mote, J., & Fulford, D. (2020). Now is the time to support Black individuals in the US living with serious mental illness: A call to action. *The Journal of the American Medical Association Psychiatry*. DOI:10.1001/jamapsychiatry.2020.2656

Mueser, K. T., Penn, D. L., Addington, J., Brunette, M. F., Gingerich, S., Glynn, S. M., . . . Kane, J. M. (2015). The NAVIGATE program for first-episode psychosis: Rationale, overview, and description of psychosocial components. *Psychiatric Services*, *66*(7), 680–690. https://doi.org/10.1176/appi.ps.201400413.

National Alliance on Mental Illness. (n.d.). Crisis Intervention team (CIT) Programs. Retrieved from https://www.nami.org/Advocacy/Crisis-Intervention/Crisis-Intervention-Team-(CIT)-Program.

National Alliance on Mental Illness. (n.d.). StigmaFree Pledge. Retrieved from: https://www.nami.org/Get-Involved/Pledge-to-Be-StigmaFree.

National Association of Alcoholism and Drug Abuse Counselors (NAACDAC). (n.d.). Recovery to practice initiative. Retrieved from https://www.naadac.org/recovery-to-practice-initiative

National Institute of Mental Health. (2018). Schizophrenia. Retrieved from https://www.nimh.nih.gov/health/statistics/schizophrenia.shtml

Neil, S. T., Kilbride, M., Pitt, L., Nothard, S., Welford, M., Sellwood, W., & Morrison, A. P. (2009). The questionnaire about the process of recovery (QPR): A measurement tool developed in collaboration with service users. *Psychosis*, *1*(2), 145–155.

North America CBT for Psychosis Network. (n.d.). CBTp competence standards. Retrieved from https://www.nacbtp.org/cbtp-competence-standards

NYC CBTp. (2015). Online courses. Retrieved from https://www.nyccbtp.com/online-courses.html

Okazaki, S., Kassem, A. M., & Tu, M.-C. (2014). Addressing Asian American mental health disparities: Putting community-based research principles to work. *Asian American Journal of Psychology, 5*(1), 4–12. https://doi.org/10.1037/a0032675

Passerello, G. L., Hazelwood, J. E., & Lawrie, S. (2019). Using Twitter to assess attitudes to schizophrenia and psychosis. *BJPsych Bulletin*, *43*(4), 158–166. https://doi.org/10.1192/bjb.2018.115

Riggs, S., Kopelovich, S. & Gottlieb, J. (December 2019). CBT for Psychosis. In Schumpf, J. (Ed.) *Advances in Cognitive Therapy Newsletter.* Academy of Cognitive & Behavioral Therapies and the International Association of Cognitive Psychotherapy

Rogers, M. S., McNiel, D. E., & Binder, R. L. (2019). Effectiveness of police crisis intervention training programs. *Journal of the American Academy of Psychiatry and the Law*, https://doi.org/10.29158/JAAPL.003863-19

Rössler, W. (2016). The stigma of mental disorders: A millennia-long history of social exclusion and prejudices. *EMBO Reports*, *17*(9), 1250–1253. https://doi.org/10.15252/embr.201643041

Santesteban-Echarri, O., Piskulic, D., Nyman, R. K., & Addington, J. M. (2020). Telehealth interventions for schizophrenia spectrum disorders and clinical high-risk for psychosis individuals: A scoping review. *Journal of Telemedicine and Telecare, 26*(1–2), 14–20. DOI:10.1177/1357633X18794100

228   Marci L. Gaither and Helen J. Wood

Schulze, B. (2007). Stigma and mental health professionals: A review of the evidence on an intricate relationship. *International Review of Psychiatry, 19*(2), 137–155. DOI:10.1080/09540260701278929

Shean, G. D. (2013). Empirically based psychosocial therapies for schizophrenia: The disconnection between science and practice. *Schizophrenia Research and Treatment.* https://doi.org/10.1155/2013/792769

Specialty Council for Serious Mental Illness (SMI) Psychology. (updated January 2020). Psychology training in assessment and treatment for persons with serious mental illness. Retrieved from http://www.psychtrainingsmi.com/aboutus.htm

Stanford Medicine Department of Psychiatry & Behavioral Sciences. (n.d.). Education: Cognitive behavioral therapy for psychosis training. Retrieved from https://med.stanford.edu/psychiatry/education/training/cbtp.html

Substance Abuse Mental Health Services Administration. (2012). SAMHSA's working definition of recovery [Brochure]. Retrieved from https://store.samhsa.gov/product/SAMHSA-s-Working-Definition-of-Recovery/PEP12-RECDEF

Substance Abuse Mental Health Services Administration (April 23, 2020). Recovery and recovery support. United States Department of Health and Human Services. Retrieved from https://www.samhsa.gov/find-help/recovery

Talley, R. M., Brunette, M. F., Adler, D. A., Dixon, L. B., Berlant, J., Erlich, M. D., ... & Siris, S. G. (2021). Telehealth and the community SMI population: Reflections on the disrupter experience of COVID-19. *The Journal of Nervous and Mental Disease, 209*(1), 49–53.

The Point of Care Foundation (n.d). EBCD: Experience based co-design toolkit. Retrieved from https://www.pointofcarefoundation.org.uk/resource/experience-based-co-design-ebcd-toolkit/

United States Department of Health and Human Services. (2000). *Participatory dialogues: A guide to organising interactive discussions on mental health issues among consumers, providers, and family members.* Retrieved from: https://www.theweb.ngo/history/Docs/SAMHSADialogue.pdf.

United States Department of Veterans Affairs. (last updated October 10, 2019). Interprofessional fellowship in psychosocial rehabilitation & recovery oriented services. Office of Academic Affiliations. Retrieved from: https://www.va.gov/oaa/fellowships/psychosocial-rehab.asp.

Warner, C. B. (2015). The role of clinical supervision in moving cultural awareness to cultural competence through case conceptualization. *World Journal of Psychotherapy, 1*(8), 33–39.

Weisman de Mamani, A., McLaughlin, M., Altamirano, O., Lopez, D., & Ahmad, S. S. (2021). *Culturally informed therapy for schizophrenia. Treatments that work series.* New York: Oxford University Press.

Wilkinson-Lee, A. M., Armenta, A. M., Leybas Nuño, V., Moore-Monroy, M., Hopkins, A., & Garcia, F. A. R. (2018). Engaging promotora-led community-based participatory research: An introduction to a crossover design focusing on reproductive and mental health needs of a Latina community. *Journal of Latina/o Psychology, 6*(4), 291–303. https://doi.org/10.1037/lat0000119

Wood, H. J., Gannon, J. M., Chengappa, K., & Sarpal, D. K. (2020). Group teletherapy for first-episode psychosis: Piloting its integration with coordinated specialty care during the COVID-19 pandemic. *Psychology and Psychotherapy*, 10.1111/papt.12310. Advance online publication.

Yamada, A. M., & Brekke, J. S. (2008). Addressing mental health disparities through clinical competence not just cultural competence: The need for assessment of sociocultural issues in the delivery of evidence-based psychosocial rehabilitation services. *Clinical Psychology Review*, *28*(8), 1386–1399.

Yamaguchi, S., Mino, Y., & Uddin, S. (2011). Strategies and future attempts to reduce stigmatization and increase awareness of mental health problems among young people: A narrative review of educational interventions. *Psychiatry and Clinical Neurosciences*, *65*(5), 405–415.

10   Recovering US Mental Healthcare
Systems, Culture, and Change

Meaghan A. Stacy and Charlie A. Davidson

The preceding chapters include recollections, history, evidence, and recommendations from experts in the field of psychosis and serious mental illness (SMI), all highlighting the importance of optimism, respect, inclusion, autonomy, and effective psychosocial interventions. This book raises questions and provides answers that are gleaned from research, history, clinical success stories within the USA, and lessons learned from other countries, to demonstrate that evidence-based psychosocial interventions for schizophrenia and psychotic spectrum disorders have been a proven concept that can be applied and disseminated more broadly in the USA.

This concluding chapter cannot do our co-authors justice, and is offered as a relatively simple summary, seen through the lens of the co-editors, two early career psychologists who hope to: internalize and disseminate the knowledge of our mentors and predecessors; motivate readers and our colleagues to engage in advocacy, specialized training, and provision of services for psychosis; promote a more evidence-based, psychosocially-oriented system of care for those with psychosis; and generate culture change toward a more inclusive society for people with psychosis and all mental illnesses. The concepts in this book closely align with current social movements, especially in the USA, at a time of political and social transition in which hope for change and equity, calls for challenging biases, and advocacy are featured prominently. It is in the context of this opportunity that we write this chapter, identifying key themes from this compilation and linking them to best practices for cultural change. We hope we can engage all audiences who are positioned to champion such change: students, individuals with mental illness, family members, healthcare workers, clinicians, administrators, and policymakers.

Decades of evidence have supported the fact that recovery for people with SMI is possible, and the goal of psychosocial rehabilitation (PSR), in its many definitions and forms, is to help facilitate that. It is now recognized that many of the challenges experienced by those with SMI are the result of larger, external forces such as institutionalization, systemic oppression, and limited opportunities and resources. Addressing these disadvantages at the individual and systems levels can aid consumers in meeting their social, occupational, and other self-defined goals. It is with this in mind that larger efforts such as the Clubhouse Model, legislation (e.g., The Community Mental Health Act of 1963), and the Coordinated Specialty Care (CSC) programs came to fruition. The successes highlighted in this book include: the adaptation of PSR strategies to CSC for people with first episodes of psychosis and federal legislation to support its implementation; new work applying evidence even earlier in the trajectory of psychosis and SMI to determine how to prevent or mitigate sequelae of psychosis by identifying and working with people at risk for these diagnoses; implementation of PSR principles in the Veterans Health Administration; the development of specialized training and the potential for future board certification for SMI Psychologists; and the development of key roles for people with lived experience as peer support specialists and essential players in research and practice.

Despite these efforts and gains, the needed community resources for those with psychosis and SMI have not been widely implemented. What has been implemented lacks accountability and fidelity assessment that would ensure quality care, funding is not sufficient, and peer specialists have been unevenly adopted into clinical settings. In short, sustainable implementation of these successes has not been demonstrated. The result of this has been the cyclical creation of good programs and policies based on science and hope, their subsequent dismantling or waning quality, the re-emergence of previous problems, and the reinvention of the wheel. Ultimately, many individuals with psychosis and SMI lack access to evidence-based care, housing, employment, and valued social roles in their desired community. Promises remain largely unfulfilled and, in some instances, good intentions have gone wrong. For example, while there is a strong evidence base for psychosocial treatments and recovery, the result has not been improved mental healthcare systems, but rather a shift of the locus of the same models of care from inpatient units to community mental health centers (at times with mandated treatment) and prisons. Further, programs implemented without careful application of evidence-based models tend to become palliative at best and often harmful. Some of the best research evidence supports operant behavioral approaches in intensive services (e.g., token economies), when used with fidelity and in a recovery-oriented program. When such behavioral approaches are applied inconsistently or not according to best practices, they can become manipulative, punitive, and harmful. These issues must be addressed in order to further advance and implement evidence-based care and establish a meaningful place in society for people with psychosis and SMI.

The Connection Between Mental Health Care and the Larger Social Climate

Perhaps the most apparent theme in this book is that mental health care in the USA is strongly tied to sociopolitical context. Throughout the past several decades mental health advocacy has intersected with broader civil rights movements. Those with psychosis and SMI have similar experiences to other non-dominant groups and the ways in which their civil and human rights are treated with indignity, delegitimized, or disempowered in our society and systems (e.g., Metzl, 2010). The core principles of recovery-oriented care were in line with the movement for ensuring civil rights for people with disabilities, and larger civil rights movements contributed to the development of the consumer movement and even anti-psychiatry movements. These various forces have gradually increased consumer participation in the development and evaluation of new treatments.

This book has highlighted how the complex social, economic, and political dimensions of our culture and society can cause drastic shifts in the models of care provided for those with SMI and psychosis. We have also learned how political priorities drive funding toward or away from mental health prevention and treatment, that there is a lack of, and perhaps even a disincentive to, conduct long-term planning, and there is minimal support for the sustainment of mental healthcare infrastructure and resources. For example, there are CSC services that must be subsidized through federal grants, state funding, or other means, but these are often lacking or short-term. We must get federal and local agencies to value the evidence-based psychosocial treatment of psychosis, prioritize it, and strategically plan for its provision over time, regardless of political changes.

As Chapter 6 notes, this begs the question of who should determine what services are provided to Americans with SMI and psychosis? Is it the government and its often politically motivated funding priorities? Is it science, evidence, and research telling us what is most effective for whom? Or is it consumers and their treatment preferences? The current state of the USA has demonstrated an underlying mistrust of science (e.g., debates about climate change, COVID-19 transmission and vaccination) that likely must be addressed before science is the primary driver of mental healthcare policy. It is also unlikely that the consumer will drive healthcare changes, given the aforementioned stigma and negative beliefs about people with SMI and psychosis having enough insight to make good treatment decisions. Those with SMI have very little capital with which to participate in consumer-driven market changes. This leaves us with the government, politics, insurers, and lobbyists driving policy and funding, with change and turnover that can be rapid. For example, between January 20 and 21, 2021 a number of Executive Orders were revoked and overturned by President Biden. For better or worse, this can rapidly flip the focus of education, training, and/or healthcare, leaving those with limited stake and voice (as those with SMI and psychosis often are) as potential collateral damage. As we advocate for changing the fact that US politics often drive mental healthcare, we must accept that for now it is a reality. While we work to change this, we must empower those with SMI and psychosis to lead such movements and we must act as allies, provide them with platforms, and amplify their voices to dismantle the power differentials that exist.

We are living in a time when many people are advocating for their own and others' rights, questioning powerful individuals and systems, and challenging the existing narratives of dominant groups (e.g., #MeToo, Black Lives Matter). This self-advocacy and championing for equality is now more normalized, and may no longer be viewed as a lack of insight or further evidence of psychosis, distorted reality, and/or aggression. Instead it is an epistemic subject questioning the status quo and the inequality they are facing. It is a prime opportunity to capitalize on and reaffirm their place as experts. The increasing fervor for equity and addressing disadvantages for certain groups in the USA, that have been brought into focus by recent racial injustice and the COVID-19 pandemic, can propel us forward. Capitalizing on this period of US history where allies from all backgrounds are working together to foster racial, gender, and other forms of equity, mental health advocates can promote the fair, respectful, and high quality treatment of all historically disenfranchised and oppressed groups, including those with SMI and psychosis. We can do better, and with scientific, social, and political movements well-aligned, there is hope that we will.

The Need to Combat Stigma and Change Beliefs and Attitudes

The preceding chapters have clearly demonstrated that implementation of evidence-based psychosocial programs for those with psychosis and SMI are impeded by a number of factors. These include: a lack of providers interested in SMI; a de-emphasis on recovery and SMI in healthcare education programs; minimal training opportunities for established clinicians; poor funding for mental health programs; and limited community resources, to name a few. What link might there be connecting these barriers preventing the development of a high quality, evidence-based mental healthcare system for people with SMI and psychosis? The least common denominator is likely the underlying negative and stigmatizing beliefs about SMI, psychosis, and the prospect of recovery. The assumptions that people with SMI lack insight into their illnesses, have minimal motivation for treatment, cannot obtain meaningful social roles (e.g., spouse, parent, employee), and require life-long medication, all perpetuate myths and stereotypes across settings and generations. These attitudes are so ingrained in US society and culture and reinforced by media portrayals they are even internalized among those living with these diagnoses.

Given that these falsehoods and biases likely serve as the underpinning common to many of barriers listed by our co-authors, challenging them is essential. As we have pointed out, training may be beneficial in changing attitudes and beliefs. By increasing awareness about myths and assumptions about SMI, the possibility of recovery, and the effectiveness of treatment, we can begin laying the foundation for larger scale changes. Such training opportunities can include simulations and personal reflection for clinicians and staff, storytelling by a person with lived experience, or a lecture led by an individual diagnosed with SMI and psychosis.

Inclusion is particularly pertinent to addressing stigma. Providing society, clinicians, and family members opportunities to interact with people with SMI and psychosis can be a powerful tool for dismantling stigma. This could involve the inclusion of consumers in their own treatment, peer specialists on clinical teams, or people with lived experience in research and teaching. Such inclusion provides opportunities to interact with individuals with SMI in multiple settings and roles, to appreciate individual differences, and to see individuals with SMI at various stages of recovery. This type of inclusion can also empower those with SMI and psychosis, help them challenge their own internalized and self-stigma, and begin to identify potential communities and organizations where they may want to connect. The inclusion of a stigmatized group of individuals can address deep and persistent stigma that still impedes the attainment of the goals set by the President's Freedom Commission over twenty years ago. Progress in inclusion is visible in some major policies and programs. The internet has made it easier for people to share and find recovery stories, and peer specialists are integrated in many clinical, research, and training programs. However, their potential is often hindered by hierarchies and power differentials in traditional medical models, where the "patient" is often allocated the weakest voice and the least power. Goals of inclusion and autonomy require empowerment. In our healthcare system, the default mode is a patriarchal hierarchy. We must not only listen and include people with SMI and psychosis, we must also amplify and prioritize their voices.

The Need for Training

Research and evidence demonstrating that people with psychosis and SMI can recover, and that psychosocial treatments are effective, are useless unless they are shared with those who can apply this information. In this case, those stakeholders include not only clinicians and policy makers, but also the general population. Through this awareness we can begin to challenge assumptions about psychosis and SMI. The previous chapters repeatedly point out that scientific advancements have had limited impact on the field, highlight dissemination and implementation challenges, and craft the argument that support in this area is necessary to maximize impact. For example, the penetration rate of Supported Employment is approximately 2% (Davidson, 2016). This is despite decades of evidence demonstrating its effectiveness for individuals with SMI, and its inclusion in The Schizophrenia Patient Outcomes Research Team (PORT) psychosocial treatment recommendations (Dixon et al., 2010) and the National Institute for Health and Care Excellence (NICE) Clinical Guideline "Psychosis and Schizophrenia in Adults: Prevention and Management" (NICE, 2014).

The barriers to implementation of evidence-based psychosocial interventions are broad, multi-faceted problems deeply ingrained in our healthcare system and society. Addressing these problems will require a multi-pronged and targeted approach. Each system, site, and clinic has unique barriers that need to be addressed individually. However, a common barrier is the lack of trained providers. For consumers to have accessible evidence-based care, there must be adequate numbers of clinicians competent to provide it. The quality of treatment in the USA not only varies by consumer location and financial status, but also differs based on the skills and competence of the specific therapist. Unfortunately, there is a limited corps of clinicians who are trained in effective treatments for SMI. There is an even smaller number who have expertise in these effective interventions, remain optimistic about the prognosis of SMI, and hold beliefs that promote the dignity and autonomy of consumers.

Training, educational resources, and ongoing consultation and supervision are necessary to build a cadre of providers who can care for those with SMI and psychosis; they are also prerequisites for establishing high fidelity and high quality care. These types of efforts will increase the awareness of providers about recovery, and the existence of evidence-based services for individuals with SMI and psychosis, beyond medication. Educational efforts can be further enhanced through the creation of communities of practice. Creating a network for clinicians who work in PSR can spread information and attitude change, provide a resource for asking questions, and also create a centralized location to identify providers who specialize in SMI. This may help to answer the question "where are the providers who can competently work with individuals with psychosis and SMI?"

Providing high quality training and consultation to expand and enhance the workforce is essential. However, it is a simple, and at times incorrect, solution to complex problems, and there are significant barriers. Resistance, organizational culture, funding, insufficient instructors and supervisors, protected time, and institutional support will be just a few of the hurdles to the "simple" answer of "provide training and consultation." Later in this chapter we address how organizations change, when during that process training is appropriate, and how change management models can be applied to overcome barriers to improving mental healthcare systems.

The Need for Breaking Down Silos

Readers perhaps noticed the word "provider" in this and previous chapters to describe the individuals who work with people with psychosis and SMI. This seemingly reflects an unstated, but essential, need in the field: the need for the integration of mental health care disciplines. Historically, each discipline has provided its own unique service (e.g., prescribers prescribe, psychologists provide therapy) and the medical culture is often hierarchical, with physicians at the top. However, as healthcare systems have grown larger, consumers' problems have become more complex, and the biopsychosocial model of illness has gained prominence, there has been an increased focus on team-based care. As noted in Chapter 2, milieu-based social learning programs require flexibility in professional hierarchies and staff roles, which medical models cannot offer. Chapters 5 and 6 highlight the importance of each discipline in NAVIGATE, and CSC programs in general, and underscore the team-based nature of the work. Dismantling the patriarchal structure and emphasizing the provision of more multi-disciplinary care has the potential to de-emphasize the seemingly central role of medication and create an opportunity for an enhanced focus on the psychosocial aspects of care.

This is not to say that all "providers" should be stripped of their discipline and perform the same tasks with no differentiation. On the contrary, a collaborative environment where clinicians, peer specialists, and consumers are all recognized for the expertise they bring to the table is essential. The goal is that (A) one discipline and its offerings are not emphasized over another and (B) that no single discipline "owns" the psychosocial aspects of treatment of psychosis and SMI. Indeed, this is the mission of the Recovery to Practice Initiative described in Chapter 7: to encourage all disciplines to capitalize on their profession's respective assets to further the psychosocial care for psychosis and SMI. This will hopefully foster an environment where ALL providers – nurses, physicians, social workers, psychologists, pharmacists, peer specialists, among others – see the use of evidence-based psychosocial interventions as being within their purview and therefore begin to seek training and consultation.

As silos are broken down between disciplines and schools of thought, the consumer cannot be forgotten. The power differential between provider and consumer must be diminished. The consumer brings with them their own expertise as an epistemic subject (Chapter 8) that should be capitalized on as part of the treatment team, both as peer specialists and consumers. Peer specialists share a lived experience with consumers, and other providers should benefit from this form of expertise. Sadly, too often peer specialists either become tasked with busy work or become pseudo-clinicians, rather than peers. Further, peer specialists are often the only member of their profession on a team, which can result in tokenism. The mere presence of a peer specialist on a team is insufficient to claim a team is recovery-oriented and that peer support has been incorporated into the team. Peer specialists must be recognized for their expertise, called upon for their contribution, and respected as equal members of the care team. Barriers and power differentials between providers and consumers must also be dismantled as part of this effort. Consumers should be involved in their own treatment as an essential part of the treatment team and invited to actively participate in their treatment planning. They can offer significant insight into their own past, strengths, experiences, and preferences that can make treatment successful. How could a treatment team respect dignity and autonomy if a consumer is not part of the team deciding his or her treatment? The first author (MS) once worked with a consumer who said, "I told my psychiatrist he needed to tweak this and that with my meds, and he jokingly asked me if I knew so much, what did I need him for? I told him, 'a second opinion.' He agreed to try the changes out and I feel better." This type of relationship, where the psychiatrist is open to input and the consumer feels empowered to provide feedback, is one that has the potential to demonstrate respect, foster autonomy and responsibility, and be person-centered. Omission of people with mental illness from treatment and policy conversations serves no one; it disenfranchises and questions the legitimacy of those individuals while simultaneously suppressing advancements in the field because of their omission. This continues to carry forward the paternalistic, disability-focused narrative that inhibits the implementation of evidence-based care and cross-discipline training of clinicians. A system that ignores a person is unlikely to help that person.

Beyond the mental health context, Chapters 6 and 9 highlight the need to remove barriers and silos so providers and recovery programs can work with a multitude of partners and organizations, including primary care providers, schools, prisons, and other individuals and agencies involved in the lives of people with psychosis and SMI. This will require open communication and flow of information, beliefs, and practices between various stakeholders. This will further improve providers', stakeholders', and society's knowledge and attitudes regarding psychosis-related symptoms. Cross-fertilization and partnership between professions, consumers, and organizations may also disseminate information and awareness through communities of practice and listservs with similar values and interests, leading to a community of advocates attempting to improve mental health care for those with psychosis. As awareness and the size of the group grows, we may see increasing numbers of clinicians across generations who will embrace hope for those with SMI, champion for change, and seek out training in evidence-based treatment. Fostering a sense of community, a shared sense of purpose, and supportive spaces to prevent burnout during advocacy offer the potential to reach critical mass.

The Need to Learn from Others

Another key theme that emerged in the preceding chapters is the need to learn from others, including those who came before us, as well as our contemporaries in the USA and other countries. Mental health systems are continuously built, dismantled, and rebuilt in the USA. Often things change unexpectedly and with insufficient time provided for new programs to be successfully implemented or for their impact to be evaluated. As a result, administrators and clinicians often "wait out" policy changes in anticipation of another paradigm shift, which is most certainly right around the corner. Other times, the same treatment components and/or ideas are repackaged in a different way and presented as new, resulting in wasted effort, frustration, and confusion. This process also likely contributes to the common statement that it takes approximately 17 years for research to translate into clinical practice (e.g., Green et al., 2009; Trochim, 2010; Westfall, Mold, & Fagnan, 2007). To avoid this, we must ensure that we learn from the past to build on successes and failures, and learn from others to avoid recreating the wheel every decade or so. Chapter 2 repeatedly highlights this for us. We have known since the 1930s that there are social determinants to mental health (Faris & Dunham, 1939), and yet the fundamental attribution error (i.e., minimizing situational causes for an individual's behavior or problems while relying on explanations involving something within the individual), is alive and well with regard to psychosis and SMI. Since 1948 there has been an emphasis on the scientist-practitioner model of psychology, and yet, there is a significant gap between research and practice, and at times we fail to apply pre-existing science to our current research, clinical work, or policy. Another example from Chapter 2 is that we have known about the involvement of cognitive impairment in schizophrenia since at least the mid-twentieth century yet it took 40 years for this knowledge to influence treatment. We must be able to identify successes that have occurred in the past and ensure that they are carried forward in order to provide the best psychosocial services possible.

PSR is the best supported model for addressing the many barriers to recovery in psychosis and SMI. PSR is not new; it is the latest evolution of over 50 years of valuable research and programs. During the last half-century, this research and experience has created progress in healthcare and policy many times and in many ways. However, progress and good ideas (like deinstitutionalization, behavioral treatment models, rights to treatment in the community, etc.) have not been implemented in earnest or sustainably, resulting in cycles of progress and regression. We must learn from what has worked as well as how well-intentioned good ideas failed to make real long-term changes for people with psychosis and SMI.

One example of building on the successes of the past is the NAVIGATE program. This CSC model is built on the accumulated knowledge and experience from years of PSR research, and filled a critical gap in the US mental healthcare system by learning from the experiences of past research in the USA and other countries. Future researchers would be wise to learn from this program. It has incorporated multiple evidence-based interventions, shared decision-making, and a strengths-based approach. It focused on real-world implementation and sustainability. Regarding sustainment, the NAVIGATE program can teach us that flexibility is essential to maintain competence and relevance with current evidence. NAVIGATE's ability to pivot quickly in the face of new science allowed them to add intervention elements that were aligned with the most current evidence. Nimble programs and organizations can be challenging to create, and even more difficult to maintain, especially after the start-up phase; once bureaucracy, hierarchy, and rigid structures settle in, organizations may become less agile and able to keep up with the times and science. However, it is essential that programs continue to grow and learn from others as time passes, or they will become antiquated.

Another means by which providers and training programs may learn from others is from observing other disciplines. Mental health professions can learn from psychology's more recent efforts to establish a specialty area of SMI psychology. This has provided both a way the discipline can demonstrate its commitment to changing the mental healthcare system for those with SMI, and a means by which the field can remain up to date with the research. Having entities within The Council for Serious Mental Illness (SMI) Psychology (http://www.psychtrainingsmi.com/aboutus.htm) that focus on maintaining awareness of cutting edge research (Research Committee) and education (Education and Training Committee), enable the Council to propose high accreditation and board certification standards that ensure training programs and individual psychologists are getting high quality training and maintaining strong competence in the most effective psychosocial treatments. While other disciplines have identified gaps in their training and emphasis on SMI, psychosis, and recovery, none to our knowledge has taken the next step to create a subspecialty in this area. Social work, psychiatry, nursing, pharmacy, and other fields can learn from the process that psychology has undertaken and join them in demonstrating the need for specialized education and training in SMI and psychosis. With more professional groups advocating for recovery-oriented, evidence-based psychosocial treatment for SMI and psychosis, there will be a greater sense of community and shared vision, and it will be more difficult for policymakers, administrators, and others who make healthcare and policy decisions to ignore.

Beyond the lessons learned from large-scale projects in the USA there is also much to be learned from other countries. Several of our co-authors (Chapter 6) highlight the mental healthcare system in Denmark (for comparisons between US and other systems see Williams et al., 2020), and rightly point out that even with the same scientific foundation, clinical practice recommendations, and types of services being created, the consumer's reality is extremely different in the two countries. Perhaps the most apparent difference is the financial burden placed upon consumers and their families. Denmark has socialized medicine, and so consumers there can receive healthcare without navigating complex insurance issues or accruing large bills, as occurs in the USA. The financial costs of psychosocial healthcare in the USA are often additionally burdensome given the need for insurance, ability to pay co-pays and/or fees for services, and costs for transportation to appointments. The logistical barriers in the USA are striking when reviewing the US consumer's experience; depending on their geographic location they may or may not be within the catchment area of a funded, high quality rehabilitation program, or may be many miles from a reputable source of care. What we can learn from Denmark is that when healthcare is viewed as a right, policies and funding are guided by science and expertise, and programs are built with accountability and flexibility, we can use the existing research and experience to better support people with psychosis and SMI and continue to improve as research, practice, and society change. We can also learn from our Danish counterparts the importance of designing for implementation; by requiring the inclusion of plans for dissemination in research proposals, Denmark ensures the widespread uptake of effective interventions. In our current sociopolitical and healthcare climate, our history suggests that we will repeat the building up and tearing down of services without discarding the skeletons of systems that were harmful rather than helpful, and without the possibility of building on what we have learned. The ability to receive evidence-based psychosocial (and other) care without significant financial or logistical barriers is not likely in the near future for the USA, but we can learn from Danish services in that they have specifically allocated time and funding for clinical services, fidelity (a prerequisite for high quality clinical services), and quality improvement, with plans and infrastructure for sustainment.

Norway is another country with a form of universal health coverage, known as the National Insurance Scheme (e.g., Ringard et al., 2013). The goal is for the national government, with the involvement of regional health authorities and municipalities, to provide healthcare that is equally accessed by individuals of all socioeconomic statuses and geographic locations. It is in this context that a model of medication-free mental health hospitalization emerged. We are eager to see research studies on short- and long-term consumer outcomes, and to determine what the USA can glean from Norway's experience. Countries around the world are testing different models to implement the evidence base on supporting recovery from psychosis and SMI, and within the USA, some programs, systems, counties, and states have been somewhat successful with implementation and sustainment. We have the chance to learn from this wealth of information and experience, in our own history and compared across the world, or we can continue repeating our mistakes.

Organizational Change and the US Mental Healthcare System

The major steps that the authors of this book are suggesting (i.e., investing in training, encouraging clinicians to provide care for those with SMI, learning from others, breaking down silos, changing attitudes, combating stigma, inclusion of people with SMI, fostering a social climate conducive to an improved mental healthcare system) all require large, overarching, sweeping changes at organizational and societal levels. However, what is notable in reading these chapters is that, at least in the US mental healthcare system, top-down processes rarely effect long-standing change. Efforts like Coordinated Specialty Care were overdue, large-scale, formalized efforts to redress the harms caused by failed deinstitutionalization efforts; however, even these efforts did not have the intended widespread impacts.

What most of these efforts are overlooking is the individual level of change. All large systems, whether a clinic, a hospital, or a country are comprised of individuals. For large-scale changes to be successful, individuals within those systems must be motivated to engage in the change process. It is for this reason perhaps that we see that grassroots movements, connecting with other civil rights groups, and gathering an increasing group of advocates have been somewhat successful. These efforts largely involve engaging people individually or in small groups, rather than focusing on the organization as the unit of analysis. It is perhaps for this reason that Karlin and Cross (2013) noted the importance of including multiple levels (e.g., patient, provider, policy, systems levels) in successful dissemination and implementation. Just as we have learned that civil commitment processes and outpatient commitment laws have not consistently enhanced treatment availability or provided other benefits, it is unlikely that national legislation will be enough to drive the long-standing change for which this book advocates. This leaves us with the question of: how does culture change?

Organizational change theory and change management can be applied to our efforts to drive systems change and promote a society where individuals with SMI can easily access high quality treatment and be included in all aspects of their communities. Change management is a systematic approach to implementing and sustaining change within a system that specifically emphasizes the "people side" of change (Hiatt & Creasey, 2003). Change management minimizes the common negative impacts of human factors on systems change by generating buy-in, utilizing strong and consistent communication plans, assuming there will be resistance, and planning for sustainment from the beginning. While there are certainly overlaps and parallels with the field of implementation science, including understanding the context in which individuals will be implementing a change and developing plans that specifically incorporate facilitating factors and barriers (e.g., Damschroder et al., 2009; Wiltsey Stirman & Beidas, 2020), our goals go beyond implementing evidence-based practices. Yes, the diffusion of innovative psychosocial interventions for SMI is a key component of our ideal future state, but we also must focus on changing attitudes, combating stigma, and shifting organizational culture more broadly.

We have learned from the extant organizational change literature that successful cultural change requires strong leadership and executive sponsorship. Government, professional, and healthcare organizations and their leaders must embrace, endorse, and embody the change they are attempting to implement; passive engagement or providing lip service is not enough. However, just as top-down policies and procedures will be insufficient, engagement solely at the top of the hierarchy will be ineffective. Cultural changes necessitate involvement of all levels of a given system. As such, any initiative must involve well-respected formal (e.g., department chiefs, training directors, team leaders, politicians) and informal leaders (e.g., clinicians, trainees, medical support assistants, students, training faculty) throughout the system, not only those at the top. Influential people at every level should be given responsibility for the development and implementation of change efforts, so that communication and change permeate the organization through multiple networks, rather than relying on a trickle-down process. These influential people must clearly communicate, demonstrate, and reward the behaviors and attitudes that are essential to the new mental healthcare system we envision. One model of change management, called ADKAR (Hiatt, 2006), is particularly applicable to this scenario given its focus on individual change and the use of best practices. This model also parallels the stages of change and motivational interviewing (e.g., DiClemente & Velasquez, 2002; Miller & Rollnick, 2004; Prochaska & Norcross, 2001), making it particularly relevant and relatable to mental health providers. An acronym standing for *Awareness, Desire, Knowledge, Ability, and Reinforcement*, this model details the five stages individuals must go through to generate and maintain organizational change.

The ADKAR model suggests that for a system to change, the individuals within it must first develop an *Awareness* for why change is necessary and why the current state is problematic. This is an essential building block prior to attempting to make any changes, and closely parallels the clinical relationship in which a consumer must first identify a problem prior to a provider attempting to offer an intervention. Too often, change efforts jump directly to training as a panacea for all problems. Early on in change efforts, pre-work must deliberately target specific audiences to foster an interest or awareness so later on any training will have its intended impact.

Communications often address this need. Newsletters, emails, and fact sheets can be disseminated that include facts and evidence against myths. Advocates should use platforms of all kinds (e.g., social media, talks, presentations, discussions in meetings) to their advantage in this effort. It is for this reason that we sought to publish this book; we had a platform to advocate for improved psychosocial services for people with psychosis and SMI, and we took it as a small step toward driving awareness. In communicating about culture change, all communications must present a consistent message: the current mental healthcare system is flawed, people with SMI can and do recover, and psychosocial treatments are effective. Communications must highlight important reasons for change, and should include multiple justifications in order to resonate with as many individuals as possible. This message can be further carried through introductory level trainings about SMI, stigma, and recovery, as well as undergraduate and graduate mental health–related courses. Marketing materials for public and private mental health services, which target the public, clients, and families, should convey similar messages of hope, evidence-based care, and inclusion. Publications, such as journal articles, newspaper pieces, editorials, or even this book, can further the mission by engaging professional audiences.

Chapter 5 highlights an additional component that is a strong generator of awareness: readiness assessments. Conducting these types of evaluations as an initial step of a large, system-wide change provides insight into the current state of the organization and prepares the organization for change. Through a readiness assessment, systems can identify facilitators and barriers to change, such as: current infrastructure and technology; available resources; decision-making processes; motivation; leadership support; shared beliefs and attitudes; ability to adapt; past history with change efforts; and how the organizational mission and vision tie into its goal for improvement. This process can also raise awareness about how the current state is problematic, what needs to change, and what strengths can be leveraged to advance the change.

This *Awareness* must then generate a *Desire* to engage in the change; to do this change, efforts must capitalize on executive sponsorship, leadership engagement, and managing resistance to change. To motivate leaders, staff, and other people to improve the mental healthcare system, it is important to communicate the benefits of the proposed changes (e.g., access to evidence-based treatment for SMI and psychosis, help people recover, more rewarding day-to-day work, clinicians get advanced training, helping historically disadvantaged groups). These messages must be individually tailored to highlight the benefits to that specific person, and create tension between their values and the mental healthcare system's current state. For example, communications can highlight the discrepancy between the values of inclusivity and equity versus perpetuating the disenfranchisement of a group of people. These materials must also emphasize the risks of what could happen if the mental healthcare system does NOT change. The risks of not changing could include spending taxpayers' dollars on ineffective or possibly inhumane treatment, perpetuating stigma and myths, keeping clinicians untrained, continuing the shift of mental healthcare to the criminal justice system, having to "put out fires" of crises and risks as clients fall through the cracks rather than working on incremental positive change, clients having little reason to engage with providers in the absence of visible hope and recovery, etc. One of the most difficult barriers to generating *Desire* is resistance to change, which can manifest in many ways, ranging from tardiness at meetings to outright sabotage. Resistance will inevitably occur and must be preemptively addressed by preparing for anticipated negative responses (e.g., "This is just how we've always offered services;" "People with SMI don't get better;" "We don't have money or time.").

Knowing why a change is necessary (*Awareness*) and knowing that you want to participate in the change (*Desire*) is different than knowing what and how to change (*Knowledge*). It is at this point in the process where training can have an effective impact. Too early, and training is seen as irrelevant or mandated; too late, and motivation and interest for the training have waned. Many of the chapters in this book highlight the need and advocate for additional or specialized training, and they are correct; however, training must be done at an ideal time in the change process when *Awareness* and *Desire* have already been cultivated and remain active. When individuals have reached a shared understanding that the current system is untenable and want to be part of the improvement process, more technical, skills-based training can be provided. Several chapters in this volume have provided models or resources for self-training, and also highlight the role that professional organizations can play in identifying or providing trainings (e.g., SMI Adviser, Council for SMI Psychology). High quality trainings generally involve active, experiential learning, usually spread out over several sessions to provide opportunities for application of skills, with ongoing consultation and long-term follow-up to avoid drift and problem solve issues as they arise. Train-the-trainer models also support maintenance and fidelity, while also exponentially increasing the number of experts within a given system.

After completion of training, providers need additional supervision, consultation, and practice opportunities to develop an individual's *Ability* to implement the change. Supervision and consultation can take place in a myriad of ways, including individual and group clinical consultation, or implementation consultation for a specific team or organization. It can take place in person or virtually, and can involve the discussion of cases, evaluation of documentation, review of recorded sessions, or fidelity assessments. As programs are implemented and providers begin to practice evidence-based psychosocial treatments for SMI and psychosis, we should be establishing communities of practice and centers of excellence. These will provide professional homes for those providers who may be the sole SMI and psychosis "specialist" in a clinic or team. Challenging cases and implementation barriers can be discussed and collaborative problem-solving or lessons learned can be offered by others within the community of practice. This will not only foster individuals' and systems' abilities to implement changes, it will serve as a means by which to reinforce such improvements.

Reinforcement is needed to promote and draw attention to the benefits of desired behaviors, with the ultimate goal of increasing them within individuals and systems. Reinforcement can be incorporated into each of the preceding steps to maintain forward momentum and resist the gravity that pulls us back into old, stigmatizing thoughts and practice. In this scenario the target behaviors are those promoting PSR and evidence-based psychosocial care for those with SMI. These include participating in training, receiving board certifications or other specialty designations, demonstrating willingness to provide care for those with SMI and psychosis, presenting de-stigmatizing attitudes, integrating science and practice in the treatment of SMI and psychosis, de-prescribing, or collaborating with other disciplines and organizations.

As leaders and colleagues see others demonstrating these target behaviors, they must visibly reinforce them. This can be provided via individual feedback and praise, but systems may consider offering financial or other public incentives for providers and teams offering evidence-based care for those with SMI and psychosis. This could be in the form of publicized quality improvement projects, program monitoring, reports, or status updates via email or department meetings. The effects of simple gestures should not be underestimated. For example, simple displays, like posters tracking outcomes that are important to consumers and providers, can be valuable. Simple, visible, and regularly updated displays provide small but important and continuous reinforcement, and can encourage ongoing engagement and awareness while emphasizing the shared goals of consumers and providers. By clearly and visibly demonstrating which teams or clinics are succeeding, however that is defined, and the benefits that have been reaped from the changes, it will encourage the successful parties to maintain their gains and motivate others to increase their efforts.

On a larger scale, healthcare systems can be reinforced via additional funding or reimbursement for services. As the funding of healthcare demands a shift toward greater accountability and the provision of evidence-based services, healthcare systems will be incentivized to offer treatments in line with this goal. Similarly, as Chapter 6 points out, Supported Employment and peer support services are often not covered by Medicaid or insurance companies, despite being evidence-based interventions that promote recovery for those with SMI and psychosis. If we are to expect systems to offer these types of programs, reimbursement is an obvious form of reinforcement.

Conclusion

As we have described, the envisioning and revisioning of mental health services is a process often linked to political policy and social climate, but also one that is generally comprised of ill-planned changes with insufficient attention paid to the human factors impacting the process. These massive system realignments or the immediate assumption that "staff training" will fix a problem have had no real success and likely harm the experiences and lives of people with SMI and psychosis. We must hold ourselves accountable not to follow this pattern, and instead incorporate evidence-based practices for change management: an evidence-based implementation of evidence-based treatment.

To make our country more humane and equitable for people with SMI and psychosis we must "recover" our mental healthcare system. The lessons learned in the preceding chapters highlight that the practices essential to supporting recovery for any individual parallel those needed to support change and "recovery" of healthcare systems. The slow, foundational work to prepare people for change is essential and takes time; this can be frustrating for those eager to progress toward their ideal future state, as an individual or an organization. However, developing awareness that the current state is problematic and creating a tension for change is the essential first step to driving change in individuals who comprise organizations. The lessons learned also speak to the importance of engaging and training providers. This is essential because while the preparatory work will highlight the need for action and motivate the audience to participate in such action, it does not necessarily guarantee that people will know what or how to foster change or implement evidence-based practices. Several chapters highlight the benefits of building upon the unique strengths of each system during implementation of evidence-based practices, paralleling the importance of strengths-based care offered to individuals receiving PSR. Fitting the changes to the existing infrastructure and resources while also maintaining an ideal vision for the future is a challenge, and requires simultaneously capitalizing on existing resources and building capability within the system. This can be a challenging dialectic to hold; we have limitations AND an ideal future state we can achieve. Yet, it is similar to the dialectic we posed in the introduction; SMI and psychosis are serious AND people with SMI and psychosis can recover. By building on preexisting strengths we can avoid, as Chapter 1 puts it, throwing the baby out with the bathwater, and prepare the system for future changes and challenges.

REFERENCES

Damschroder, L. J., Aron, D. C., Keith, R. E., Kirsh, S. R., Alexander, J. A., & Lowery, J. C. (2009). Fostering implementation of health services research findings into practice: A consolidated framework for advancing implementation science. *Implementation Science, 4*(1), 1–15.

Davidson, L. (2016). The recovery movement: Implications for mental health care and enabling people to participate fully in life. *Health Affairs, 35*, 1091–1097.

DiClemente, C. C., & Velasquez, M. M. (2002). Motivational interviewing and the stages of change. *Motivational interviewing: Preparing People for Change, 2,* 201–216.

Dixon, L. B., Dickerson, F., Bellack, A. S., Bennett, M., Dickinson, D., Goldberg, R. W., ... & Kreyenbuhl, J. (2010). The 2009 schizophrenia PORT psychosocial treatment recommendations and summary statements. *Schizophrenia Bulletin, 36*(1), 48–70.

Faris, R. E. L., & Dunham, H. W. (1939). *Mental disorders in urban areas: An ecological study of schizophrenia and other psychoses.* University Chicago Press.

Glasgow, R. E. (2006). RE-AIMing research for application: Ways to improve evidence for family medicine. *The Journal of the American Board of Family Medicine, 19*(1), 11–19.

Green L., Ottoson, J., García, C., & Hiatt, R. (2009). Diffusion theory and knowledge dissemination, utilization, and integration in public health. *Annual Review of Public Health, 30,* 151–74

Hiatt, J. (2006). *ADKAR: A Model For Change in Business, Government, and Our Community.* Prosci, Inc.

Hiatt, J., & Creasey, T. J. (2003). *Change Management: The People Side of Change.* Prosci, Inc.

Karlin, B. E., & Cross, G. (2014). Enhancing access, fidelity, and outcomes in the national dissemination of evidence-based psychotherapies. *American Psychologist, 69*(7), 709–711. https://doi.org/10.1037/a0037384

Metzl, J. M. (2010). *The protest psychosis: How schizophrenia became a black disease.* Beacon Press.

Miller, W. R., & Rollnick, S. (2004). Talking oneself into change: Motivational interviewing, stages of change, and therapeutic process. *Journal of Cognitive Psychotherapy, 18*(4), 299–308.

National Institute for Health and Care Excellence (NICE). (2014). *Psychosis and schizophrenia in adults: Prevention and management.* NICE. https://www.nice.org.uk/guidance/cg178/chapter/1-Recommendations#subsequent-acute-episodes-of-psychosis-or-schizophrenia-and-referral-in-crisis-2

Prochaska, J. O., & Norcross, J. C. (2001). Stages of change. *Psychotherapy: Theory, Research, Practice, Training, 38*(4), 443.

Ringard, Å., Sagan, A., Sperre Saunes, I., Lindahl, A. K., & World Health Organization. (2013). Norway: Health system review. Retrieved from: https://apps .who.int/iris/bitstream/handle/10665/330299/HiT-15-8-2013-eng.pdf

Trochim, W. (2010). Translation won't happen without dissemination and implementation: Some measurement and evaluation issues. 3rd Annual Conference on the Science of Dissemination and Implementation. Bethesda, MD.

Westfall, J., Mold, J., & Fagnan, L. (2007). Practice-based research: "Blue Highways" on the NIH roadmap. *JAMA, 297,* 403–406.

Williams, R. D., Shah, A., Tikkanen, R., Schneider, E. C., & Doty, M. M. (2020). Do Americans face greater mental health and economic consequences from COVID-19? Comparing the US with other high-income countries. *Commonwealth Fund. Retrieved September, 15,* 2020.

Wiltsey Stirman, S., & Beidas, R. S. (2020). Expanding the reach of psychological science through implementation science: Introduction to the special issue. *American Psychologist, 75*(8), 1033–1037. http://dx.doi.org/10.1037/amp0000774a

Index

CPSIA information can be obtained
at www.ICGtesting.com
Printed in the USA
LVHW080954260222
712093LV00014B/609